Penguin Education

Economic Justice

Edited by Edmund S. Phelps

Penguin Modern Economics Readings

Economic Justice

Selected Readings

Edmund S. Phelps

Penguin Education

Penguin Education
A Division of Penguin Books Ltd,
Harmondsworth, Middlesex, England
Penguin Books Inc, 7110 Ambassador Road,
Baltimore, Md 21207, USA
Penguin Books Australia Ltd,
Ringwood, Victoria, Australia

First published 1973
This selection copyright © Edmund S. Phelps, 1973
Introduction and notes copyright © Edmund S. Phelps, 1973
Copyright acknowledgement for items in this volume
will be found on p. 471

Printed in the United States of America by
Kingsport Press, Inc., Kingsport, Tennessee
Set in Monotype Times

Contents

Introduction

Most government decisions raise, in most minds, what has been called the problem of social choice. Few are the red-letter days in which a government has the opportunity to innovate a social policy that will please everyone. The consuming political questions – like whether to increase taxes on upper incomes or whether to reduce tariff protection – all pose the ethical issues of how best to resolve conflicting individual interests which are the hallmark of the problem. It is sometimes called the problem of deriving a collective preference from a set of individual preferences; sometimes the problem of agreeing upon a social welfare function; sometimes the problem of arriving at a satisfactory conception of distributive justice. These are the various names given to the social choice problem by the several disciplines that touch on it, among them moral philosophy, decision theory, mathematical politics, group psychology and economics.

Economics is involved with the social choice problem in at least three ways. Being the science of choice (or one such science, anyway), economic theory has contributed to the formulation and analysis of social-choice models. By its efforts to depict or characterize the feasible set of social states that is the object of social choice, economics has pared down somewhat the range of value judgements left open for consideration; rightly or not, the dismal science killed off strict egalitarianism. In these ways economists have been producers of social choice theory.

Economists also stand, somewhat impatiently, on the demand side – both the economists present at the battlefront where social decisions are being made, and those academic economists who, with their scribblings on public policy, risk having an effect on social action a decade hence. There is the view that the economist in, or close to, the public sector ought to serve as a value-free vendor of information sought by government decision-makers, like a management consultant to a legal business. This hardly seems possible, whether or not desirable. The economist's selection of an analytical model with which to answer questions put to him by government officials is partially shaped by ethical beliefs within his profession, by his own ethical preferences, and possibly, unconsciously perhaps, by his expectation of his employer's ethical preferences. Moreover, the economist in or out of government, *qua* person, can hardly be expected to speak only when spoken to; he will no doubt continue to throw the weight of his expertise on behalf of this or that public policy, knowing that any position expressed usually depends on a not-unanimously-accepted ethical preference (and wishing that the appeal of this preference were clearer to others, perhaps even clearer to himself). Accordingly, this volume is aimed at the audience whose interests and background are primarily in economics, though it may serve as a convenient source-book for readers coming to the social choice problem from other backgrounds.

1. The informal survey by Vickrey (1953, Reading 1) gives an idea of the range of questions that are involved in the problem of social choice. For example, when one speaks of the preferences of the individuals in some society, whose preferences are meant and what kind of preferences are we to have in mind? Some propositions in ethical theory are neutral as to the class of persons that is to comprise the society. Yet the appeal of many value judgements or ethical postulates may sometimes depend on the definition of the society to which they refer. Are the preferences of pre-teens to count as much as living adults? Are the future preferences of hypothetical individuals, not yet born, to count? Bentham (1789) argued that the utilities of animals should be on all fours with that of the human animal.

It is presumably the rational preferences of individuals, their real interests somehow determined, to which social choice theory should attend, not the expressed or revealed preferences of the insane. But whether preferences that are short-sighted or destructive or guilt-ridden or that merely show normal regard for the well-being of others are the 'preferences' that we have to deal with (on one level or another) are important matters to be sorted out.

There is also the question of what the individual preferences are about, what the differences between individuals are over. In principle, the infant theory of social choice is broad enough to cover everything that individuals have preferences over. Jones may possess the social values of a hawk and want more government expenditures and subsidies of certain kinds while Smith, a dove, may want less of these. Jones might oppose Smith's drinking, while Smith is pained by Jones's style. Wherever the things that Jones wants more or less of, that give him more utility, clash with the things that Smith wants more or less of, that give him utility, there is the social-choice problem of resolving the interpersonal difference in preferences. But many philosophers would disallow the taking into account of a person's 'nosey', prudish, or paternalist preferences regarding another person's behaviour.

The political economists have traditionally concentrated upon, though not restricted their attention to, a simple case of the conflict of individual interests. Jones and Smith each want more real disposable income in order to increase his own purchases of goods that raise his own utility, but, given the technology of the moment, those government actions which could increase Jones's real spendable income must – in the interesting and unavoidable cases – reduce Smith's disposable income. Each person wants 'more' – less tax and more transfer payment – but not everyone can have more without someone having less. The classic case of the social choice problem is thus the distribution of income and wealth – or considering that individuals give up some income for preferred things (such as leisure), the distribution of utility between the poor and the rich, the privileged and the disadvantaged in earning power.

2. The 'new welfare economics' represented a retreat from, or an advance over, utilitarianism with its special and controversial ethical features. It is, from one point of view, an inquiry into the nature of the public-policy recommendations that can be drawn when only rather weak postulates are made concerning the ethical deservingness of the individuals in the society. One of the questions studied on this basis was the following: under what conditions could the economist-observer who limits himself to certain weak ethical postulates say that a change in the economic environment – due, say, to some fortuitous technological change or to some discretionary institutional change – constitutes an improvement in social welfare, either actual or potential?

The new welfare economics begins with Pareto and reaches

maturity with Bergson (1938), Samuelson (1948, 1950) and Graaff (1957). What has united the new welfare economists has been their willingness to subscribe to the Pareto Principle or Paretian value judgement:

Social state A is better than social state B if one or more individuals in the society prefer A to B and all other individuals are indifferent.

A variant of this that puts even milder demands on our ethical intuition is the Weak Pareto Principle:

State A is better than state B if all individuals in the society prefer A to B.

The tenor of the Pareto Principle is frequently expressed by saying that it makes the preferences of the individuals in the society 'count'. They are to count over somebody's higher-order morality that might demand society choose what each one of its members would prefer it to reject.

Various criticisms have often been made of the Paretian value judgement, though their effect has usually been a reinterpretation of the principle and its terms rather than a flat rejection of it. It has been said, for example, that the Paretian criterion falls to the ground if individual 2, a have-not, envies, and hence suffers a diminished sense of well-being as a result of, any gain experienced by the better-off individual 1. But such external effects in utility functions are allowed for in the Pareto principle if we interpret individual 2's preference for state A (good for 1) over state B (not so good for 1) as already taking account of his knowledge of the envied individual 1's preference for A. Yet there are harder criticisms. Another objection is that if nothing were sacred against Paretian hedonism, it might license a powerful society to inflict serious damage against human beings elsewhere or in the future whom it never heard of, never imagined or cared about. One may, therefore, wish to restrict the domain of choice over which Paretianism is given sway. Further, some sensitive ethical observers might recoil from the view that if 90-pound half-starved Mujib makes a mutually beneficial agreement with 300-pound Harry to carry him on his shoulders all day then, no one else in the society caring, there has been a Paretian improvement in social welfare. Analogously, an ethical observer of egalitarian bent might oppose a social innovation that would help the poor but enrich the top class much more, even if the poor and the rich did not mind.[1]

The function of the Pareto criterion is to restrict social choices to those states which are called Pareto-optimal or Pareto-efficient. A state is said to be Pareto-optimal if it is not possible, given the technology, to move to another state that would make one or more individuals in the society better off and no one worse off – that is, another state that one or more individuals would prefer and the others at least be indifferent to. In terms of utility functions, every Pareto-optimal state can be translated into a point on a Utility Possibility Curve, the term used by Samuelson (1950), or what is called by Graaff (1957) the Welfare Frontier. This curve indicates the maximum amount of utility that it is possible technologically for a given individual to have given the utility levels of the other individuals.[2]

Except in a world of perfect information, however, it is institutionally not feasible to attain most (really, all) points on the possibility curve if, as must be assumed, the government compensations or transfer payments and taxes which redistribute purchasing power among individuals create certain 'distortionary' disincentives to work and save in the appropriate amounts and directions. Ultimate interest therefore attaches to what Samuelson dubbed the Utility Feasibility Curve. This curve depicts the maximum amount of utility which it is institutionally feasible for an individual to have, given the utility levels of the other individuals. We may then want to say that the northeast points on this feasibility curve are Pareto-optimal in practice – in the sense that the social states to which they correspond are Pareto-inferior only to other states which, while hypothetically within technological possibilities, are not institutionally feasible to reach.[3]

1. For a discussion of the potential conflicts between Paretianism and liberalism, see Sen (1970b).

2. The curve may be represented by $u_1 = P(u_2, u_3,..., u_n)$. Any point on the northeast 'frontier' of this curve is Pareto-optimal. On such a frontier, if you would increase the utility of Mr North you must decrease the utility available to Mr East. At any Pareto-optimal point, the partial derivatives P_i are all non-positive ($i = 2,..., n$).

3. Again, only the points on the frontier to the northeast are Pareto-optimal (in the institutional sense).

Suppose the Pareto criterion is adopted as one of the principles that should govern ideal social choice. This means that a social state or resource allocation (with its distribution of income, utilities and what not) that is not Pareto-optimal should not be chosen; according to the criterion, such a state is worse than any of those states that are Pareto-better than it. This does not carry us very far, though, when there is a multiplicity of Pareto-optimal states. It is clear that the Pareto criterion is not generally a sufficient condition for social choice. We need further ethical criteria in order to identify the 'best' or 'just' point (resource allocation or distribution of utilities) from among the Pareto-optimal points on the feasible utility frontier.

Moreover, in the absence of the needed additional criteria for social choice, the Pareto optimality of a social state constitutes little or nothing in the way of a recommendation for choosing it. It is true that (in the normal case) a Pareto-optimal state is Pareto-better than some Pareto-inoptimal states, but it is not Pareto-better than all Pareto-inoptimal states. If society finds itself choosing between a Pareto-inoptimal point and some Pareto-optimal point that is not Pareto-better than the former state, the Pareto-optimality of the latter is of no particular relevance to that choice.

In the 1930s it came to be argued, notably by Robbins (1935), that the economist as scientist can endorse only those changes in public policy, in taxes and expenditures and so on, that produce a Pareto improvement, that make some individuals better off and make no one worse off. At the same time there continued to be a widespread endorsement of certain traditional liberal economic policies on the ground of their efficiency or Pareto-optimality. Harrod (1936) pointed out, however, that the repeal of the protectionist Corn Laws could hardly be based solely on the Pareto principle, for surely some individuals were made worse off by the repeal. Many economists no doubt considered their social function to be that of loyally pushing out the Utility Feasibility Curve. Yet, as Harrod emphasized, such outward shifts would not generally produce an actual Pareto-improvement, i.e. an actual benefit to some and no worsening for anyone. Economics needed a justification for Corn Law repeal going beyond Pareto.

In response, Kaldor (1939) and Hicks (1939) proposed a strengthening of the economist's value judgement over the insufficient

Pareto Principle. They argued for the principle of 'potential compensation'. Kaldor proposed, in effect, that the new social state, say R, that is actually produced by a certain policy change – easier money or lower tariffs – be considered an improvement in 'real income' over the old state, Q, if, under that new policy, there would be possible a set of redistributive income transfers that could produce *some* social state, R', that would be Pareto-superior to the old state Q – even if the actual R is not itself Pareto-superior to Q. Essentially, R is revealed to be politically preferred to R' – R was chosen over the equally feasible R', or would have been under the policy change – and R' is certainly better than Q, being Pareto-superior to the latter, so R must be better than Q. Kaldor, however, gave no reason for imputing ethical acceptability to the way the political system under the new system would dole out the gains and losses. In any case, such appeal as Kaldor's compensation criterion might have had was quickly weakened when Scitovsky (1941) demonstrated the logical possibility of a contradiction under the criterion, R being both better and worse than Q. Without the adoption of the new policy, there might exist a set of tax and transfer redistributions that could produce some state Q' that is Pareto-superior to R. So if Q is preferred to Q' and Q' is Pareto-better than R, then Q must be better than R. Ail this is possible in economic theory and apparently there exists no political theory to rule it out. It is bizarre, however, that the government would choose R rather than R' under the new policy if it rejected the even better Q' under the old policy. If politics were rational, it would choose a state like either Q' (sticking with the old policy) or a state like R' (adopting the new policy), thus averting the worst dangers of each policy.[4]

Scitovsky proposed the double Kaldorian test: There is under the new policy, some R'' Pareto-superior to the actual Q' under the old policy yet R' is chosen in preference to R'' *and* there is under the old

4. With reference to that case, the Kaldor criterion would then fail to designate R' as better than Q' and fail to declare Q' better than R'. The somewhat symmetrical criterion proposed by Hicks, however, would endorse Q' over R' because the gainers from the move to R' could not under the new policy compensate the losers and still be left some gain. But by the same logic, those who would lose from a move from Q' cannot compensate others for relinquishing R' so that R' is endorsed over Q' – another Scitovskian contradiction.

policy no Q'' Pareto-superior to R' to which Q' is preferred. It is easy to embrace this double test when it works in the right way, but its inadequacies emerge when it goes awry. Suppose that the new policy, while enabling the Pareto-better R'', so raised the cost of helping the poor that it caused the political decision-making process (however democratic) to 'substitute' much greater utility to the non-poor for greater utility for the poor, thus selecting R' over R''. An ethical observer might well feel that the political system has been mis-structured in such a way that it ends up choosing R' over R'' when, under more ethically revealing ground rules, R'' would really be judged better.

The possibility of the Scitovskian contradiction is due to the possibility that the Utility Feasibility Curve corresponding to the new policy crosses – or twists any number of times around – the old Utility Feasibility Curve and that the actual points chosen under each policy are on different sides of some intersection of these curves. The Scitovsky double test would ensure that one of these curves lies outside the other in the neighbourhoods of both actual points. Samuelson (1950, Reading 2) wishes to say that the new policy would be of unambiguous potential benefit if and only if the new Utility Feasibility Curve lies everywhere outside the old one – so that, whatever the political response, everyone could be left better off. But such a uniform shift of the Utility Feasibility Curve need not produce an actual Pareto improvement in everyone's lot any more than a Scitovsky-type shift (as Samuelson does not deny). Thus an economist needs a political theory of response to shifts in utility feasibilities *and* an ethical theory to appraise such responses if he is to be able to judge the desirability of such shifts.

3. The other enterprise of modern welfare economics has been quite different from that of searching (in vain) for criteria that would permit judgements or recommendations as between two states. It has been the description of certain formal efficiency conditions that must hold if the economy is to attain Pareto optimality. On that great day that society agrees on an ethical criterion for picking out the morally best of the Pareto-optimal points on the Utility Feasibility Curve, economics will be ready to add this criterion to these efficiency conditions.

This theoretical welfare analysis is like the analysis that an economist might give a small farmer: Whatever the price of wheat and the price of corn that the market faces you with, to maximize your profit you must produce an amount of wheat such that its marginal production cost is equal to its price, and similarly for corn, etc. The validity of these formal conditions (expressed with suitable generality) is independent of the exact numerical value of these prices. In the same way, modern welfare economics has sought to spell out certain formal necessary conditions which have validity whatever the exact ethical weight given to an increase in individual 1's utility, the exact ethical weight given to an increase in individual 2's utility and so on. The result is such formal conditions as equality between the ratio of the marginal products of labour and land (respectively) in wheat production of corn and each other good produced.

The tool that came to be used increasingly widely for this purpose is Bergson's 1938 invention of the (Bergson) social welfare function, $W(U_1, U_2, U_3, ..., U_n)$. Here the Us are ordinal utility indicators having the property that a man's utility goes up if he moves from one state to another that he prefers. Bergson's W function is likewise purely ordinal; if the U functions are rescaled, the W is rescaled accordingly so that social states or resource allocations producing equal social welfare before the rescaling will produce equal social welfare after rescaling.[5]

The essential feature of the Bergson function is that it is individualistic. Each of the n individuals enjoys positive marginal ethical deservingness; that is, the derivatives W_i are all positive (no matter what the pattern of Us). By finding the conditions for a maximum of this function subject to the various economic constraints, one obtains the conditions for Pareto optimality; if W is at a maximum, no social state is being passed by that would be Pareto-superior. One also obtains the conditions that a point on the Paretian utility frontier be 'Bergson optimal'. These formal optimality conditions are as valid for one particular, exact W function with its ethical weights as for another specification of the W function. This type of modern Pareto-

5. On the other hand, it is not denied that the ethical observer who wishes to specify a set of 'weights' to attach to the U's (these weights need not be constants and will not generally be constants) may perhaps have cardinal-type musings about the intensity-of-joy added to an individual from adding more goods to his shopping basket.

Bergson welfare analysis is well expounded by Graaff (1957, Reading 3) and by Bator (1957).

'Every generation or so,' Gilbert Ryle is reported to have remarked, 'philosophical progress is set back by the appearance of a genius' (Craft, 1972). Welfare economics was sent into confusion in the 1950s when Arrow produced his celebrated general impossibility theorem (1950, 1963, 1967; Reading 4). Arrow proved that if it was desired to have, for *each* logically possible configuration of individual preferences over the feasible social states, a social ordering of these social states that satisfied two obviously appealing logical properties – collective rationality (or transitivity) and independence from irrelevant alternatives – then we would have to violate either of two ethically appealing properties – the weak Pareto principle and 'non-dictatorship'. Arrow's proof recalls the 'voting paradox' of Condorcet (1785) where 1 prefers A to B and B to C; 2 prefers B to C and C to A; and 3 prefers C to A and A to B. Then there is a majority available to vote A over B, another majority to vote B over C but another majority to vote C over A and so on in indefinite 'cycling'.

Now it is clear that if one were to specify the weights in the Bergsonian W function one would obtain from it a ranking of social states according to their social welfares, that is, a social ordering of the social states. Arrow seems therefore to have proved that such an exact social welfare function cannot *generally* be constructed without violating those ethical properties.

It is possible for the economist to be so demoralized over Arrow's impossibility theorem that he no longer finds Pareto optimality interesting. It is only the ethically best point among the Pareto optimal states that is assuredly better ethically than every Pareto-inferior state. If there can be no satisfactory social welfare function that will ever identify that ethically best point then why not settle for Pareto *non*-optimality with the feeling that it may well be ethically as good as whatever point would be chosen by society from a menu of Pareto-optimal states?

It is also possible that the Bergsonian welfare economist will say: Arrow has raised a fascinating conundrum for political and maybe moral philosophy, but I remain free to use the unspecified Bergson W which tells us only that the weights are all positive in my mathematical inquiry into the formal necessary conditions for Pareto optimality. There presumably exists some set of satisfactory ethical principles for social choice, and presumably they will call for the selection of a Pareto-optimal social state. When we learn those principles and learn which of Arrow's other three postulates they violate, so much the worse for that untenable postulate. Little (1951, Reading 5) and Samuelson (1967), to name two, seem not to be shaken by the Arrow result.

The objections raised against Arrow's theorem are not objections to its formal validity. They are objections to the desirability or relevance of the ethical requirements and informational restrictions he imposes. Thus they are quarrels over the significance of the theorem for ethical theory, in particular for the concept of the social welfare function. For example, Samuelson and Little find scant appeal in Arrow's requirement that if one person changes his preferences to rank A over B instead of vice versa then A should certainly not be damaged thereby in its social ranking (that is, if A was socially preferred before, it is socially preferred after). This involves what Arrow calls the independence-of-irrelevant-alternatives property of the social welfare function. Arrow himself, in his 1967 paper, expresses some wavering over the desirability of this property. Another frequently heard criticism is that only persons' rankings of social states are utilized in the construction of a social ranking, not the 'intensity' with which each individual prefers one state to another. This is the matter of whether preferences are to be supposed representable only by an ordinal utility function or instead by a cardinal utility function.[6] It appears to have been proved by Sen (1970a), however, that the representability of the individual preferences in terms of cardinal utility does not suffice to dispel Arrow's impossibility-result.

Even the non-dictatorship postulate seems to be not generally acceptable when considered in the context of Arrow's other axioms and definitions, a point made tellingly by Little. Arrow's very definition of a social welfare function excludes us from making use of our information or beliefs about which persons live happy or at

6. A cardinal utility function is said by economists to be a function that is unique except for unit (or scaling) and zero point (or origin). Such a function is said to be determined 'up to a linear transformation' (or affine transformation, as mathematicians use these terms).

any rate rewarding lives and which persons live unhappy or un-rewarding lives in each feasible social state. A person who prefers A to B to C receives no more weight in the social choice among these states than another person with different preferences even if everyone would agree that all of these states leave the first person miserable compared to the second. There is thus no room in the Arrowian welfare function for favouring the weak over the top dogs. The man with acute appendicitis on a Mediterranean yacht is not allowed by Arrow to 'dictate' its course. To this criticism Arrow might reply that his theorem does not exclude the possibility that the people in society have feelings about other people's well-being or beliefs about human rights, in which case their preference orderings of the various feasible social states are to be understood as reflecting these altruistic feelings or beliefs, and consequently the impossibility theorem is about the impossibility generally of resolving interpersonal differ-ences in ethical opinion. Or possibly one might reply that the con-flicting ideals of two persons of unequal social advantage should have the same weight in the social decision provided that the conflict is not plainly self-seeking but is, rather, 'impartial' and 'philo-sophical'. In any case, it seems clear that Arrow's result does not close the door to ethical inquiry. If anything, it invites reopening the door. It cools the hopes that one-man/one-vote procedures (how-ever sophisticated) can provide nonarbitrary resolutions of current conflicts in individual values, and thus tends to pin the hopes for more satisfactory social choice on ironing out differences in those values. The next section of readings samples from some of the leading efforts of philosophers to construct a conception of distributive justice that would command wide acceptance.

4. Much of moral philosophy is concerned with the nature of the restraints that ought to be placed on the choices left to individuals. The selection of these restraints might be said to be a matter of people's ethical preferences. While these ethical preferences among alternative sets of restraints must take account of individuals' egoistic preferences or personal tastes, they must go beyond the latter.

This idealist tradition perhaps has its beginnings in the Greek Sophists with their notion of a social contract (see Guthrie, 1970).

In Rousseau (1763) we have the idea of a before-the-fact state of nature, a hypothetical anarchistic position, from which the individuals will agree to those governmental arrangements which are Pareto-improvements over anarchy. People's rights against the king are based on the argument that in a state of nature people would not have contracted into such arrangements.

In the same tradition is Kant (1797, Reading 6). Writing against Hobbes's views on voluntarism, Kant holds that the figurative 'original contract' which is distinct from those actually existing on paper, confers people with certain inalienable rights that they themselves cannot contract out of, and that cannot be overriden by the head of state, however wise and benevolent, acting on some 'principle of happiness'. It is unjust to set aside anyone's natural rights for the convenience of some others no matter how great.

With regard to the distribution of welfare, the state has the obligation to provide some sort of barely adequate maintenance of the poor. A person's preservation and protection by his society is one of his natural rights because the individuals who might be imagined the signatories to the original contract would surely have been unanimous in desiring assurance of survival as well as the assurance of other liberties.

Von Hayek, in his book *The Consititution of Liberty* (1960), contrasts (unfavourably) the contractarian view of the 'design theorists' – in large part the rationalists of the French Enlightenment – with the evolutionist approach developed by the Scottish philosophers, Hume, Smith and Ferguson. 'The rules of morality', writes Hume, 'are not the conclusions of our reason'; yet as if by some invisible hand, a free society enjoys the cumulative growth of institutions and laws that triumph over inferior ones, and which are at least superior to any which could have been constructed by rationalist design.

In Bentham and the subsequent classical utilitarians, reason is to rule over morality rather than be the mere servant of passion. Viner's essay (1949, Reading 7) describes Bentham's differences from Hume and Smith and, in turn, Mill's differences with Bentham. Both utilitarians use their notion of a 'moral arithmetic' to justify a wide range of government activities in the economy, including redistributive activities.

The notion of natural rights is not present in classical utilitarianism. The utilitarians would reject a person's claim to some alleged desert if it would produce 'more happiness on the whole' to do so. The poor therefore have no natural right to support (however minimal) from the state independently of the principle of social utility. Yet utilitarianism provided its own justification for government aid to the poor, and more aid than Kant's mere preservation.

As the distinctions between average and marginal utility developed, utilitarians came to consider that their doctrine led to equalitarian distribution of individual utilities – at any rate, would lead so if the frictional losses (as it were) from transferring individual utilities were abstracted from. Sidgwick (1893, Reading 8) argued that the utilitarian case for income equality is bolstered by consideration of the disutility from having a low *relative* income. Yet even with such 'external effects' being admitted into individual utility functions, it is theoretically possible, and likely in fact, that the sum of utilities – and indeed every other Pareto-type Bergson W function of those utilities – would be considerably smaller at complete equality (and near-complete equality) than under redistributive programmes allowing significantly more incentive for differentials in retained disposable income and utility. Also maximizing happiness 'on the whole' will not generally maximize the happiness of those with relatively low incomes – it will leave their utility less than it could be.

In the natural-rights view, just as the left shoe is useless for an individual without his having the right shoe, the enjoyment by some individuals of their natural deserts is no social gain unless the others are accorded their rights as well. Certain social and economic benefits are viewed as perfect complements, in the language of economics, so that social benefit is increased by an increase in certain individual benefits only when all individuals receive such benefits. In the classical utilitarian view, the individual utilities associable with economic benefits are perfect substitutes. In that scheme, a loss of one individual's utility – somehow cardinally measurable and made commensurate with other individuals' utilities – is no loss of social welfare if just offset by increments in other individuals' utilities of the same aggregate magnitude. No doubt the entire notion of social welfare as *some* function of individual utilities appears from some viewpoints as severely limited, perhaps absurdly so. A host of values – saintliness, heroics, artistic perfection – are not *in* (they are above or below) the abstract concept of a social welfare function. Nevertheless, the utilitarian position is plagued even at its own philosophical level by the question: Why the *sum* of utilities? Why not the product of the utilities, or something between or beyond that?

There have been some experiments with introducing certain axiomatic restrictions on the Bergsonian W function in order to see what kind of mathematical form they cause it to have. One property that it surely seems desirable to impose on the social welfare function is Sidgwick's concept of *equity*. If, under a certain circumstance, an action increasing one individual's utility and decreasing another's would be good, then the same action must be good if the roles of the two individuals are reversed. This leads to the symmetry or impartiality or 'impersonality' of the derived social welfare function. If the social welfare function is a sum of individual utilities, it is a simple sum, not a sum giving unequal weights. There are other appealing restrictions on the social welfare function. Fleming (1952, Reading 9) proposed the postulate that the trade-offs between individual 2's utility and individual 3's utility which are consistent with the same overall social welfare magnitude be supposed to be independent of the quantity of individual 1's utility. This sort of *independence* property makes the social welfare function describable in terms of a sum of *like functions* of individual utilities; this might be called modified utilitarianism. A special case is pure utilitarianism in which these functions are constants so that social welfare is the sum of individual utilities.

Despite such tough sledding for classical utilitarianism, it was given a revival in the 1950s in the form of contractarian neo-utilitarianism. Harsanyi (1955, Reading 10) and Vickrey (1961, Reading 11) envisioned an individual who ranks hypothetical versions of some society that are identical technologically but which differ in their social policies such as income redistribution. The individual is conceived as assigning equal probability of being in the position of, and having the preferences of, each of the n individuals in each hypothetical case. To each case there corresponds a von Neumann–Morgenstern expected utility indicator, and the individual then ranks in terms of desirability these alternative versions of the society according to the respective expected utility. Social welfare in the eyes of this individual is greatest under the social policies that give greatest expected utility. Thus, for this individual, social optimal policy calls for maximizing average or expected utility.

In so far as there is something objective about such an evaluation, all individual observers making such calculations might well exhibit the same 'ethical' rankings of the different social versions and all would agree as to which version is optimal. Yet these ethical preferences of different evaluators need not be identical, as Pattanaik (1968, Reading 12) has observed. When a Harsanyi–Vickrey observer identifies the social arrangement having highest expected utility for him, he is averaging the *utility for him* of the payoff or 'utility' of each dramatis personae, and the former utility increases with the payoff at a rate that diminishes more sharply the more risk averse he is; differing degrees of risk aversion by the observer-evaluators could generate different rankings of the social arrangements. We are back then to the Arrow problem of obtaining a social ranking from divergent individual rankings. Another objection to neo-utilitarianism, one possibly related to the foregoing point, is the criticism made by Diamond (1967) of the applicability of the 'sure-thing' principle (probabilistic independence axiom) to the problem of social choice. In lifeboat situations where it is 'women first', is it any consolation to a man that he had the same chance to be a woman as each of the women had before their assignment to roles in the society? What about blacks having to sit in the back of the bus?

The leading modern-day alternative to utilitarianism, new and classical, is provided by Rawls (1967, Reading 13; 1968). Rawls argues for a conception of justice according to which the 'primary' goods – liberty, income, other bases of self-respect – are to be distributed equally except where their unequal distribution is to the benefit of the least advantaged members of society. With reference to income distribution, the conception involves choosing the social structure (with its redistributions and so on) so as to maximize the economic benefits of the people receiving least benefit; the criterion stops well short of absolute income equality but goes much farther than utilitarianism (pure or modified) with its willingness to trade off reductions in low utilities for sufficient gains in larger utilities.

Whether or not this conception is ultimately judged satisfactory – certainly it has a very strong intuitive appeal – Rawls argues that the principles of justice (the general concept) for structuring society should be conceived in contractarian fashion: they are to be the object of an initial agreement that free and rational persons concerned to further their own interests would accept in a hypothetical original position that is fair in the sense that no one knows what place and wants in the society he will have. Rawls maintains that rational egoists, concerned with their self-respect, would agree, in such hypothetical situations, to select the 'maximin' or favour-the-bottom conception of distributive justice.

But whether this Kantian fairness is either necessary or sufficient for Rawls's maximin conception of justice are questions on which there is not yet wide agreement.

The foregoing sampler on justice does not, of course, exhaust the surviving heritage of ideas on this subject. Such twentieth-century egalitarians as R. H. Tawney and G. B. Shaw deserve at least honourable mention. It could be argued, if not by them then by us, that even so 'radical' a criterion as Rawls's maximin standard would call for a meritocracy of such colossal 'productive' inequalities as to deaden the spirit of most people and embarrass the rest. In this connection, the work of Runciman on relative deprivation should also be cited – though that author ultimately agrees that Rawlsian justice may be employed to decide whether a claim of deprivation is justified or the result of fate that cannot be redressed (Runciman, 1966).

There is also the Randian perspective. In Rand's short essay (1964, Reading 14), it is argued that the fortunate have no obligation to support the unfortunate whether or not the fortunate may be said to deserve their good fortune. If there are empty seats on a bus already sufficiently financed by paying customers, the poor are welcome as free riders, but they have no claim beyond that. The fortunate retain the opportunity to aid the poor as they desire, unilaterally as charity givers certainly and perhaps (this is not clear) cooperatively by voting one's neighbours' incomes as tax payments for that purpose.

The compulsive cataloguer will also make note of those conceptions of social welfare that are holistic – a term in which the *w* is not only silent but, I gather, invisible. In the class of such doctrines, one might want to examine the idea of perfectionism as developed by Nietschze and expounded more recently by DeJouvenal.

Last, but by no means least, there are Marx and the Marxists. The Marxists have usually been understood to assert that labour is entitled, as a kind of right, to the full product of its toil; the injustice of capitalism, in which capital may be privately owned and the owners may take a share of the product, is axiomatic rather than a result deduced from more 'basic' ethical postulates. It would be simply irrelevant to this position for anyone to contend that as an empirical matter the workers gain on balance from the marvels in resource allocation that impersonal markets and capitalist greed combine to produce; one would rather live in a just society however poor than in a society of riches made garish by injustice.

Marx himself did not criticize capitalism for being unjust. He did not specify a particular set of ethical principles, such as utilitarianism, in terms of which to make that claim. Presumably he believed that his condemnation of capitalism was robust enough as not to depend upon foreseeable vicissitudes in morality, was not so delicate as to need a special ethical theory.[7] For Marx's sketch of the way socialism ought to function in the here-and-now of resource scarcity, one may consult his essay, 'Critique of the Gotha Programme', in which he explains that goods are not generally to be free, wage rates not generally to be equal, the social dividend to the workers must be restricted to promote growth, etc.

Many contemporary Marxists appear to believe that it is idle to consider the various conceptions of distributive justice in a capitalist society because the consent to justice by the ruling class would mean consent to their own disestablishment and those who cry out at the 'injustices' of the system are usually appeased by marginal reforms that distract from the larger task of overturning the system. But these Marxist criticisms are off the mark when it comes to the standards of distributive justice surveyed in this volume. For these criteria of justice are meant to be fundamental and not to take a back seat to happenstance institutions prevailing at the moment.

7. As Wood (1972) says in his instructive paper, there is nothing problematic about saying that disguised exploitation, unnecessary servitude, economic instability and declining productivity (features that Marx argued capitalism possessed) are features of a productive system that constitute good reasons for condemning it. All the disputes with Marx have been over his economics and sociology rather than his ethical presuppositions.

Utilitarianism, for example, is not to be interpreted as sub-utilitarianism in which the sum of utilities is maximized subject to constraints on the preservation of private-property rights, and so on. The institutions themselves are among the variables which are to be set so as to realize the distributive justice which the criterion describes. The contention that realizing distributive justice entails the radical overhaul of basic institutions in many societies, far from turning the subject into an uninteresting one, makes the study of justice a good deal more exciting and colourful than it would be otherwise. This suggestion is not belied in the next section where the institution of property-ownership happens not to be in question. It is merely the case that the easiest and shortest steps are taken first.

5. In their applications to *some* economic models, the various conceptions of social welfare just surveyed are distinctions without a difference. In dividing a *fixed* pie, they would all call for equal slices (though some utilitarians would assign a larger slice, and some Rawlsians a smaller slice, to a gourmand). But this is not the case in sufficiently realistic economic models. It may be illuminating to see how the distinct distribution criteria of utilitarianism and maximin lead to different implications for government expenditure and taxation policies when these criteria are imbedded into a quasi-realistic economic model.

It could be that many of the foregoing ethical theorists would have little more than idle curiosity about such an enterprise. Would Rawls, on being told that his maximin justice will be very especially expensive for the rich or for the middle classes, say 'well, then, let's drop it'? Yet such inquiries can be revealing and important. We may find that the basic value judgement of a philosopher may conflict with another of his value judgements or with an appealing value judgement of some other philosopher.

In the several decades preceding 1940, say, tax theorists gave attention to myriad criteria of fair taxation, including equal sacrifice, proportional sacrifice, and ability to pay. The utilitarian economists Edgeworth (1897, Reading 15) and Pigou (1932) were clear, however, that the logic of their ethical position called for the principle of minimum (aggregate) sacrifice or *equimarginal* sacrifice so that aggregate utility after payment of the taxes would be left as large as possible. If lump-sum taxes were imagined to transfer utility among individuals without having substitution effects *and* income effects upon incentives to earn income, the utilitarian principle of least sacrifice would entail equalization of all individuals' utility levels. If, as they were ready to assume, there would be frictional costs in transferring utilities from one individual to another, as by the method of income taxes, the result of this tax principle would not be full equality of individual utilities. Edgeworth (1897) wrote, 'The principle of least sacrifice in trumpet tones proclaims that the rate of taxation ought to be progressive, except so far as this distributional presumption is cut into by the productional and other utilitarian conditions'. This was a big 'except'.

It should be noted that their work came under attack for its reliance on individual utility functions that were alleged to be cardinally measurable (and poorly-behaved if they were measurable). Lerner (1944) demonstrated that in a case – essentially the fixed-pie case – where utilities could be transferred without costs through lump sum taxation, maximization of the expected value of total utility would still call for equalization of income even though persons' utility functions were uncertain to the planner. This result would not survive in the face of incentive costs in making income transfers.

The implications of utilitarianism in the context of certain economic models are greatly sharpened by such modern-day analyses as those by Mirrlees (1971), Sheshinski (1972, Reading 17), and Atkinson (1972, Reading 16). In the latter two readings, it is shown that the very poorest members of society, those most disadvantaged in earning power, will receive a negative income tax bill if the government is conceived as selecting that linear tax on before-tax-and-transfer earnings which maximizes the Benthamite sum of utilities. In this respect, then, utilitarianism does not come out too badly in our intuitive moral evaluations. (Yet it is not clear that there would be any room for transfer payments to the poor (negative taxes) if huge amounts of tax revenue were required to finance a perfectly utilitarian programme of government-sponsored health care and public-television entertainments, *unless* the marginal utility of the first penny of income is infinite.)

The use of Rawls's maximin criterion does not affect the conclusion that a negative income tax system is indicated. The wrinkle that results from the Rawls criterion is simply that, given government expenditures and the budgetary surplus, the negative tax awarded to persons with zero earnings is to be as large as possible. Rawls's work is not a theory of support for the poor but a theory of maximum support. The question of interest here is the nature of the tax system that will provide this maximum support. For example, if one adopts a model of the Sheshinski or Mirrlees type, would maximum support for the poor be obtained through a linear tax on earnings, progressive marginal tax rates or regressive marginal tax rates? Phelps (1973, Reading 18) finds, to his surprise, that the answer tends to be the last one.

Of equal interest are the implications (in various economic models) of utilitarianism and its rivals for the distribution of public expenditures between the fortunate and the unfortunate. Arrow (1971, Reading 19) shows that, under certain assumptions, the maximization of Benthamite sum of utilities, or of any additive Fleming-type welfare function, calls for more resources to be spent on the mentally retarded, say, than on the mentally normal, though not so much more that the former have as much utility as the latter. Further analysis, and some differing conclusions, is contained in a forthcoming paper by Green and Sheshinski.

The non-economist may be struck that the economics of redistribution seems to be discussed entirely in terms of money transfers (and taxes) and public expenditures usually of the collective-goods type. He may wonder about food, housing, clothing, medicines, drugs – the whole list of goods that prosperous individuals are usually counted on to buy for themselves at their discretion under market mixed-capitalism and market socialism. The economist's case for primary reliance upon income transfers, rather than a system that offers individual goods free or at reduced cost, is based upon the Paretian character of the social-welfare criteria we normally consider. Accordingly, we want the resources of given market value which are to be transferred to increase the recipients' utility as much as possible. Tobin (1970, Reading 20) discusses the presumption that this is achieved if the transfer is made in money. Other writers have examined redistributive pricing without that presumption, including Graaff (1957) and Feldstein (1972). The issue is receiving close examination in present-day mathematical economics, though clearly not all aspects of the issue are matters of technical economics.

References

ARROW, K. J. (1950), 'A difficulty in the concept of social welfare', *J. polit. Econ.*, June.

ARROW, K. J. (1963), *Social Choice and Individual Values*, 1st edn 1951, Wiley.

ARROW, K. J. (1967), 'Values and collective decision-making', in P. Laslett and W. G. Runciman (eds.), *Philosophy, Politics and Society*, Blackwell; reprinted in this volume, Reading 4.

ARROW, K. J. (1971), 'The utilitarian approach to equality in public expenditure', *Q. J. Econ.*, August; reprinted in this volume, Reading 19.

ATKINSON, A. B. (1972), 'How progressive should income tax be?', in J. M. Parkin (ed.), *Essays on Modern Economics*, 1973, Longman; reprinted in this volume, Reading 16.

BATOR, F. M. (1957), 'The simple analytics of welfare maximization', *American Economic Review*, vol. 47, pp. 22–59.

BENTHAM, J. (1789), *Principles of Morals and Legislation*, 1823 edn, Doubleday, 1961.

BERGSON, A. (1938), 'A reformulation of certain aspects of welfare economics', *Q. J. Econ.*, vol. 52, pp. 310–34; reprinted in A. Bergson, *Essays in Normative Economics*, Harvard University Press, 1966.

CONDORCET, MARQUIS DE (1785), 'Essais sur l'application de l'analyse à la probabilité des décisions rendues à la pluralité des voix', Paris.

DIAMOND, P. A. (1967), 'Cardinal welfare, individualistic ethics and interpersonal comparisons of utility: a comment', *J. polit. Econ.*, October.

EDGEWORTH, F. Y. (1897), 'The pure theory on taxation', *econ. J.*, December, reprinted in F. Y. Edgeworth, *Papers Relating to Political Economy*, vol. 2, Macmillan, 1925; reprinted in this volume, Reading 15.

FELDSTEIN, M. S. (1972), 'Equity and efficiency in public pricing', *Q. J. Econ.*, May.

FLEMING, M. (1952), 'A cardinal concept of welfare', *Q. J. Econ.*, vol. 66; reprinted in this volume, Reading 9.

GRAAFF, J. DE V. (1957), *Theoretical Welfare Economics*, Cambridge University Press.

GUTHRIE, W. K. (1969), *History of Greek Philosophy*, Cambridge University Press.

HARROD, R. F. (1936), 'Another fundamental objection to laissez-faire', *econ. J.*, March.

HARSANYI, J. C. (1955), 'Cardinal welfare, individualistic ethics and interpersonal comparisons of utility', *J. polit. Econ.*, August; reprinted in this volume, Reading 10.

HICKS, J. R. (1939), 'The foundations of welfare economics', *econ. J.*, December.

KALDOR, N. (1939), 'Welfare propositions and interpersonal comparisons of utility' *econ. J.*, September.

KANT, I. (1797), *Grundlegung zur Metaphysik der Sitten*, trans. by T. K. Abbott, *Fundamental Principles of the Metaphysics of Ethics*, 3rd edn 1907, Longman.

KANT, I. (1970), *Kant's Political Writings*, H. Reiss (ed.), Cambridge University Press; excerpts reprinted in this volume, Reading 6.

LERNER, A. P. (1944), *The Economics of Control*, Macmillan.

LITTLE, I. M. D. (1951), 'Social choice and individual values', *J. polit. Econ.*, October; reprinted in this volume, Reading 5.

MIRRLEES, J. A. (1971), 'An exploration in the theory of optimal income taxation', *Rev. econ. Stud.*, April.

PATTANAIK, P. K. (1968), 'Risk, impersonality and the social welfare function',
J. polit. Econ., December; reprinted in this volume, Reading 12.

PHELPS, E. S. (1973), 'Taxation of wage income for economic justice', *Q. J. Econ.*,
vol. 87, August.

PIGOU, A. C. (1932), *The Economics of Welfare*, Macmillan.

RAND, A. (1964), 'Government financing in a free society', in A. Rand, *The Virtue of
Selfishness*, The New American Library; reprinted in this volume, Reading 14.

RAWLS, J. (1967), 'Distributive justice', reprinted in P. Laslett and W. G. Runciman
(eds.), *Philosophy, Politics and Society*, Blackwell; reprinted in this volume,
Reading 13.

ROBBINS, L. (1935), *An Essay on the Nature and Significance of Economic Science*,
Macmillan.

ROUSSEAU, J.-J. (1763), *The Social Contract*, trans. by M. Cranston, Penguin, 1968.

RUNCIMAN, W. G. (1966), *Relative Deprivation and Social Justice*, Routledge &
Kegan Paul.

SAMUELSON, P. A. (1948), *Foundations of Welfare Economics*, Harvard University
Press.

SAMUELSON, P. A. (1950), 'The evaluation of real national income', *Oxford econ.
Pap.*, January; reprinted in this volume, Reading 2.

SAMUELSON, P. A. (1967), *Arrow's Mathematical Politics*, in S. Hook, (ed.) Human
Values and Economic Policy, New York, University Press, 1967.

SCITOVSKY, T. (1941), 'A note on welfare propositions in economics', *Rev. econ.
Stud.*, November.

SEN, A. K. (1970a), *Collective Choice and Social Welfare*, Holden-Day.

SEN, A. K. (1970b), 'The impossible Paretian Liberal', *J. polit. Econ.*, June.

SEN, A. K. (1970c), 'Interpersonal aggregation and partial comparability',
Econometrica, May.

SHESHINSKI, E. (1972), 'The optimal linear income tax', *Rev. econ. Stud.*,
October.

SIDGWICK, H. (1893), *The Method of Ethics*, Macmillan, 5th edn, Dover, 1966;
excerpts reprinted in this volume, Reading 8.

TOBIN, J. (1970), 'On limiting the domain of inequality', *J. Law Econ.*,
October; reprinted in this volume, Reading 20.

VICKREY, W. S. (1961), 'Risk, utility and social policy', *Soc. Res.*, Summer; reprinted
in this volume, Reading 11.

VINER, J. (1949), 'Bentham and J. S. Mill', *Amer. econ. Rev.*, March; reprinted in
this volume. Reading 7.

VON HAYEK, F. (1960), *The Constitution of Liberty*, University of Chicago Press.

WOOD, A. W. (1972), 'The Marxian Critique of Justice', *Philosophy and Public
Affairs*, Spring.

Part One
Ethical Questions in Social Choice

Vickrey's paper is an admirable discussion of the borders where economics ends and ethics begins. Published in 1953, at a time when welfare economics was entering a period of long quiescence, this paper shows how little the basic questions have changed.
One of its achievements is to trace out, entirely in words, the utility feasibility frontier in terms of successive experimental increases in inequality.

1 W. S. Vickrey

An Exchange of Questions between Economics and Philosophy

W. S. Vickrey, 'The Goals of Economic Life' in A. D. Ward (ed.), *Goals of Economic Life*, Harper, 1953.

The ethical content of economics

Economic theory, in its purest and most abstract form, can be treated as a system of logic, having no more immediate ethical content than a proposition in Euclidean geometry. And even with applied economics, it is possible to approach the study with the detachment of an entomologist observing an anthill. Yet no scientific investigation, however abstract or detached, can entirely escape the probability of having ethical consequences, remote though this possibility may at first appear. Roemer's observations of the eclipses of the moons of Jupiter, remote as they may have seemed at the time from human affairs, eventually proved to be not without relevance to the development of the atom bomb. No investigator in any field can entirely escape the possibility that his results may come to have ethical implications.

But while Roemer can hardly be held accountable for Hiroshima, somewhere down the line of the pursuit of knowledge there comes a time where the results cease to be purely abstract information and begin to have ethical implications. In economics this point is reached much sooner than in many other disciplines. Economics, as a social science, deals with human beings directly, rather than with inanimate objects or even the lower organisms whose development can be considered of relatively negligible intrinsic significance. Economics studied in complete abstraction from all human values would be an insubstantial discipline, for economics is pivotally concerned with values. And even though an economist restricts himself to the values of the market place as distinguished from the more fundamental ethical values of the philosopher, these values of the market place usually reflect these more fundamental values, in spite of frequent cases where the market values stand conspicuously at odds with ethical values.

Thus while it is possible for an economist to maintain an Olympian aloofness and declare that he is merely studying the techniques of adapting limited means to multiple ends, without in the least concerning himself with the source or justification of these ends, such economics is likely to prove limited and sterile. Whether he consciously admits it or not, the economist who goes far towards using his discipline as a means for recommendations, or who even steps beyond the stage of building abstract logical structures in a vacuum, must develop some scheme of ultimate values as a criterion for his judgements.

To be sure, an economist, like any other specialist, can abdicate his responsibility as a citizen and moral being, and offer his talents to the highest bidder, letting his employer determine the goals towards which his abilities will be applied. Or, engaging directly in business, he may act with an eye single to his own selfish interests. In economics as in other disciplines, in spite of much effort in a higher direction, far too much emphasis is still placed on training for material success in a 'devil-take-the-hindmost' world. In this case ethical considerations become irrelevant, except as one would need to consider as data the customs, mores, and prejudices of the world in which one is to operate. But to the extent that his discipline is more closely associated with values, the economist who thus fails in moral responsibility is even more culpable than the engineer or chemist who works on in indifference as to whether his product is to be a vehicle or a juggernaut, a therapeutic drug or a harmful adulterant.

Values in normative economics

Thus no morally responsible economist can get far, and no one who wants to make policy recommendations concerning economic matters can get anywhere, without at least implicitly calling upon some set of ultimate values. For some limited fields of economic decision, the values necessary may seem to be so clear and universally acceptable as hardly to need explicit expression; it is usually assumed that nearly everyone would agree that it is better for individuals to be well fed and clothed than to be hungry and naked (though even here a few masochists and ascetics may be heard objecting). But the interesting economic decisions, involving such matters as the distribution of income, methods or organization of economic activity, or the freedom of the individual, do involve matters of ethical values for which there is no obvious and unanimously accepted scale or ranking.

Latent and implicit values

But it is only recently that economists have begun to probe into the systems of values that underlie their discussions, and indeed in many cases the judgements are implicit, rather than explicitly stated.

When they have been specific about the ultimate goals that they are using, economists have been prone to specify their values in such a way that they lend themselves to economic treatment, with a tendency to ignore or subordinate those values that are less susceptible to quantification and analysis. This is justifiable only if the values so emphasized are treated as approximations and it is kept firmly in mind that conclusions are to be later modified so as to give effect to a more complete set of values. Unfortunately, it is easy to forget this supplemental process and to elevate the proxy values set up, because of their tractability to the level of ultimate values valid in their own right.

Individualistic values

The most striking example of this tendency is found in the individualistic approach of most modern Western economists. Here we find that the satisfaction of the desires and preferences of individuals comes close to being considered a final value. In the more extreme form of this approach, the world is represented by a model in which each individual exists in an isolated cell connected with the rest of the community only through the exchange of goods and services. The welfare of the individual, or his state of satisfaction with his circumstances, is supposed to depend solely on the kinds and quantities of goods and services that he provides for the rest of the community, and the kinds and quantities of goods and services that he receives in exchange. On the basis of such a model, perfect competition finds justification as the system that most nearly meets these desires and preferences.

But even the economist himself, when he gives it his attention, finds that such a formulation of final values is faulty. In the first place it is inadequate, in that even on its own presuppositions such a formulation of values is incapable of providing criteria that will yield answers to questions that involve a redistribution of income. Economics cannot supply from within itself a generally applicable and acceptable rule for comparing the merits of the degree of satisfaction achieved by different individuals. Thus, when asked to advise on a choice between two policies that involve different distributions of income, an economist as economist must be mute for lack of the appropriate value basis. If a judgement is tendered, it must be based either on an inadequate foundation of ultimate values, or on more or less unrecognized values which are held by the economist as an individual, and concerning which the economist can claim no greater knowledge than any layman.

The distribution of income

One of the first requests that the economist makes of ethics, then, is for a criterion for the making of interpersonal comparisons, or for judging choices of policy that involve the distribution of income. This is not a simple demand, and it may be one impossible to fill completely. The problem cannot be reduced to a mere matter of determining the best pattern of distribution of a given total aggregate 'income' among a number of individuals, for the manner of distribution may and probably will seriously affect the total amount to be distributed. The economist may be able to determine or at least to have an expert opinion concerning the relation between aggregate income produced and the degree of inequality permitted in the society that produces it. At one extreme, complete equality may be held to produce a low aggregate output, whether from lack of incentives or for other reasons. At the other extreme, there is presumably some degree of inequality that would give the maximum total product. Perhaps few egalitarians would be so extreme as to insist on equality regardless of the degree to which this would reduce the total product to be shared, and perhaps few rugged individualists would insist on the maximum total product (assuming this can be defined!), regardless of how unequal the corresponding distribution. This is an ethical problem on which individuals have differed widely in their answers, and perhaps no universally acceptable answer is possible. But the economist hardly knows even how to go about finding an answer, or how to start to appraise the merits of alternative answers.

Equality versus productivity

Of course, if it were possible to assert that complete equality could be achieved without impairing output, as through developing new incentives outside those of the market place or through developing altruism or social responsibility, then the issue would not arise. But the question here is not what the facts may be concerning the relationship between inequality and output, but rather, assuming that a conflict exists between these two objectives, how to determine the proper balance between them.

To be more concrete, if we have ten high-output farmers A and ten low-output farmers B, and if we allow each farmer to keep all he produces, each A may produce 300 tons per year and each B only 100. If we decide to give each an equal share in the total produce, then each may receive 200, but only if the removal of the direct incentive does not affect the effort of each farmer. This indeed may happen if social motivation is strong. But if a 'dole' psychology is created, production may fall off sharply, so that the A farms yield only 100 tons and the B farms only 50, each farmer gets only 75, and everyone is worse off than before.

But of course it is not necessary to go so far. We may allow each farmer to retain half of his own product, and put the rest in a pool to be shared equally. This leaves some incentive to effort, and we may suppose the A farms to produce then 200 tons and the B farms 80; they keep 100 and 40 respectively; the balance is shared out 70 to each farmer, so that the A farmers get 170, the B farmers 110. As compared to the individualistic case, the A farmers get 130 less, the B farmers 10 more. The ethical question is then whether the 10 more that the Bs get should be considered to outweigh the 130 less that the As get, by reason of the fact that the Bs are poorer. To be quite comprehensive, allowance should be made for the greater leisure enjoyed by both the As and the Bs under the redistribution plan than under the individualistic plan, but the essence of the ethical question remains unchanged.

It may not always be true that a redistribution reduces the total product. If each A under individualistic conditions produced only 300 tons because that was all he had much use for, but could without much additional effort produce 340, and if each B continued to produce 80, then the process of redistribution might actually induce each A to produce the 340 in order to retain 170 plus his share in the pool, which would now be 105, leaving him with 275 and each B with 145. Such extreme cases may not be entirely unrealistic; it is often asserted that heavy taxation of large inheritances may make productive workers out of heirs who might otherwise have been content with unproductive leisure. And to the extent that such cases arise, the ethical argument is virtually all on one side.

Ethical auras of income sources

In many cases one is tempted, in making an ethical judgement, to look to the nature of the source of the discrepancy in income. That is, some sources of higher income are conceived of as having a greater merit than others, and redistribution of such income as being less desirable. Thus if the superior output of the A farms was due primarily to the fact that the As had inherited superior farm lands, some might urge that redistribution of the product should be carried farther than if the differential were due to the superior skill of the As, or to greater effort on their part. 'Earned' differentials are often considered to be entitled to a higher respect on ethical grounds than inherited or accidental differentials.

However, here seems to be a point where an attempt is often made to substitute a spurious ethical notion as a basis for a judgement in place of a perfectly adequate economic criterion. On ethical grounds it is hard to see why an individual who has inherited a high I Q or a green thumb is more entitled to preserve for himself, as a matter of moral right, a larger share of the product of that capability than the person who has inherited a particularly fertile piece of land.

Economically, the two cases are different in that it is ordinarily possible to transfer some of the land of the As to the Bs, while it is not possible to transfer skills in this way. If the land is thus transferable, it may be possible to redistribute the land between the As and the B's, with an effect quite different from that of redistributing the product. The economist views inequalities in inherited wealth as different from inequalities in inherited or native ability only because transfers of either the wealth itself or its product differ, as to ease or as to consequences, from transfers of the product of ability. If, for reasons of technology or tradition or other overriding considerations, it were impossible to transfer land from one farmer to another, then the economist would have no reason to treat differentials derived from property any differently from differentials arising from ability. It is thus the transferability of the unequally distributed factor that should govern how it or the products attributed to it are to be treated, and not any spurious ethical aura that may become attached to the factor in one way or another. Ethical notions misapplied in this way can be seriously misleading.

The necessity for setting up some sort of basis for placing an ethical value on equality cannot be avoided merely by postulating some method or organization, or some all-pervading conversion to a more social motivation, that would maintain output without the aid of the incentives that become possible only when inequality is admitted. Even if everyone should become willing to work just as hard for the benefit of the community as a whole as for himself, complete equality would not solve the problem of the distribution of income. Inequality may be essential for maximum output for technological reasons wholly aside from any matter of incentives. Out of a community composed of equally endowed and equally worthy individuals, it could conceivably become necessary to select a small number for strategically important posts; and perquisites or other differentials, such as shorter hours, better food, more comforable working conditions, might have to be provided to enable the incumbents to work effectively; wholly aside from the provision of incentives, complete equality would then be impossible. Or, at least, if complete equality were insisted on, it could only be at the expense of a lower total output, regardless of how willing the members of the community might be to put forth their whole effort without individual reward; nor would it always be possible to equalize matters by a rotation of the strategic posts, or by an adjustment in the distribution of other goods, without some sacrifice in total out-put.

Here it is possible, at one extreme, to put so high a value on equality as a social aim as to maintain equality even when the allotment of added income to the strategic few would 'pay for itself' in added output. The individualist, finding all his values in each distinct individual, would doubtless reject such a 'dog-in-the-manger' type of social choice. Nevertheless, when equality as a social value is reinforced by, or perhaps rather used as a stalking-horse for, administrative convenience, we do get examples of this general nature. For example, in times of a shortage in a public water supply we may find that an edict against sprinkling of lawns or washing of automobiles is invoked even against those with their own ample private water supply, though in these circumstances enforcement may be rather perfunctory.

But in general we would expect the problem to resolve itself into a compromise between the objectives of output and equality, with the balance not going all the way to maximum output regardless of distribution on the one hand, nor to the point of unconditionally minimizing inequality, or perhaps maximizing the minimum share, on the other.

Equality, tastes, and resources

Yet even here the problem ultimately becomes more complicated than merely reconciling the conflicting aims of maximizing the quantity of some homogeneous output and providing for the equal distribution of this similarly homogeneous output. Neither production nor consumption is homogeneous, and to specify that equality should also mean a regimented uniformity would be repugnant to almost everyone. In a population containing vegetarians as well as carnivores, it is not at all obvious how one should measure the degree of equality or inequality between the two groups. An economist would tend to do it in terms of relative quantity of resources used, assuming that these also would be reduced to a common denominator. But this means necessarily that equality is relative to resources, and that for example an outbreak of some cattle pest would cause a redefinition of the relative states of the two groups.

All of which merely indicates that if an attempt is made to define values in terms of needs, there must be set up some kind of criterion for arriving at some kind of relative value judgements concerning meeting the needs of vegetarians as compared with those of meat eaters, or, for that matter, of smokers as against nonsmokers, or drinkers against abstainers. If we cannot do this, then we are driven back to defining distribution in terms of resources, according to which rule one might have the paradoxical result that equality might mean that meat eaters starve while vegetarians are surfeited, or vice versa.

Fortunately, perhaps, most decisions do not require so precise a formulation of values as would be required to resolve the various conundrums that might be propounded. But the conundrums are still useful in bringing into sharper focus some of the essential issues involved.

Where individual preferences fail as criteria

Thus even the most individualistic economist is compelled to go beyond the mere preferences of each individual in society if he is to make any but the most restricted recommendations as to policy, either individual or social. But even where decisions are to be made that do not involve interpersonal comparisons, the neat reliance on the preferences of the individual concerned as the ultimate test of values fails at many points. When these failures occur, new criteria will have to be found. There is, moreover, a need for determining when individual preferences can be properly overridden by other considerations.

Incompetence

There are fairly well-recognized special instances where by common agreement it is considered proper to disregard individual preferences, even when only the one person is directly concerned, and to impose choices from without. A child's preference for hopscotch over arithmetic, the suicide's preference for self-destruction, and the addict's preference for drugs are almost universally dishonoured in most concepts of the good society. While these instances are recognized, it is not clear on just what basis these instances are excluded from the values to be determined by individual preference, nor how far it may be justifiable in principle to set aside such individual preferences in other less clear cases.

Changes in taste

Another and more pervasive difficulty with the individualistic valuation scheme, one that the economist requires help to deal with, arises when individual preferences shift, become inconsistent, or, because of inadequate information, are untrustworthy. For some types of shift we can perhaps assume that we are justified in appealing from Peter drunk to Peter sober, or from John ignorant to John informed. But in some cases it is of the essence of the service sought that the purchaser is not the best judge of how much he needs or wants; for example, medical or legal advice. And on what basis, if any, can we say that the preferences of the person who has just been converted to vegetarianism, or to an aversion to nakedness, are to be considered more valid than his former preferences? In an earlier, less rapidly changing era, such questions were less likely to arise. In smaller, more homogeneous communities, individual tastes and patterns tended more to cluster more closely about rather widely accepted norms. But in a rapidly changing environment, with a wide variety of specialized patterns of preference in existence at one time, the implications of changes in tastes are of much greater importance.

Propaganda

Not only do we have the problem of reconciling conflicting preference patterns that arise spontaneously in succession in individuals, but far more seriously we have the problem of evaluating activity specifically designed to change preferences. Such activity ranges all the way from fraudulent misrepresentation, at one extreme, to informative advertising, education, propaganda, and missionary enterprise. To misleading advertising one can perhaps give short shrift, almost by definition, although any practical measure for the curtailment of such activity raises, in borderline cases, serious questions of how to distinguish between fraud and mere over-enthusiasm.

Concerning informative advertising and related activities, the economist wants help in determining how much they are really worth. If one could think of advertising as merely informing individuals how they can better satisfy a given fixed set of preferences, then perhaps it would be possible to compare the cost of the advertising with the cost of obtaining a comparable degree of satisfaction with a larger aggregate of goods chosen with less discrimination. But advertising almost inevitably does more than this and produces changes in the fundamental preferences of the individual himself. Even though this were interpreted as merely bringing nearer to the surface some latent preferences considered to be inherently present in the background, it would still mean that a measurement of the value of such advertising with the accepted tools of the economist would be virtually impossible, even conceptually.

Informative advertising shades over imperceptibly into propaganda, education, and missionary activity in the broad sense. What is the place, in the broad scale of values, of activity designed to change the opinions, preferences, and ideals of individuals? We can hardly rest content to leave the decisions, as to how much effort is to be devoted to various kinds of educational and propaganda effort, to be determined by the financial support of those who are interested, either commercially or emotionally. This would imply that the ability of an idea or a program to command financial support would be the prime measure of the importance attached to its propagation. Such a proposition seems morally indefensible as an absolute standard, and defensible as a practical standard only in the absence of alternatives. But no alternative seems available, unless it is to lump this with other social values to be determined in part or in whole by methods outside the sphere of economics.

Satisfaction and wantlessness

Another difficulty in appraising informational and educative activity lies in the fact that values may lie in the relationship of individuals to their environment and not merely in the degree to which the environment suits the individuals. We may have one group of individuals who are satisfied with their condition because they know of nothing better; others may be better off than the first group but nevertheless dissatisfied because they know of better circumstances that for one reason or another they are unable to attain for themselves; a third category may be fully aware of other possibilities but reconciled in one way or another to their present condition. Is the second condition ethically better or worse than the first? Assuming that the third condition of knowledge and reconciliation is better than the first condition of ignorance, is it possible to achieve it without passing through the second, and if not, is it worth while to make the passage?

Here we meet a dichotomy between the popular materialistic philosophy characteristic of much Western thinking and the more contemplative philosophy of the East. Economists of both cultures may formulate the goal of economics as one of bringing about a closer agreement between human wants and their satisfaction. But the Western economist takes wants as given (at least in a latent sense) and conceives of economic activity as providing more and more goods to satisfy these given wants. On the other hand, the Eastern economist is prone to consider also the possibility that wants and resources may perhaps be equally well reconciled by restraining wants to those which can in fact be satisfied. The pragmatic result of the Western philosophy is a dynamic urged to material progress, while the Eastern philosophy tends more to traditionalism and stagnation; but this is not necessarily in itself a sufficient basis for judging the ethical merits of the two approaches.

Ends and means

Nor can we confine our attention solely to the avowed or apparent goals, and the degree to which they are approached, without regard for the means. Often enough, if we examine the matter closely, we find that the means are as important as the goal, and indeed may form a part of the goal. Many things that are thought of as ultimate aims derive their value in large measure from the fact that their attainment is evidence of obstacles overcóme, and the removal of the obstacle often removes the value of the goal. If the satisfaction derived from the game of golf, for example, could be completely described in terms of the degree of success obtained in driving a ball into eighteen holes in succession, one would be driven to conclude that the golf-course architect who insists on installing traps is an antisocial character (a judgement possibly concurred in at times by frustrated golfers!).

The meaningfulness of processes

Such instances taken by themselves might be classed as trivial, were it not that they merely point up more dramatically an important and pervasive aspect of economic activity too often overlooked. In nearly all economic activity, satisfaction derives from the process of overcoming the obstacles as well as from reaching the goal. To some extent, to be sure, the economist can include the direct satisfactions of work in his pattern by merely treating them as another by-product. But to do this the economist has to ignore or gloss over the fact that such satisfactions are greatly influenced if not almost wholly conditioned by the social environment. Plowing a field behind a team may be exhilarating if done in a pioneer environment in which this represents the best technique available; it becomes drudgery if in the adjoining field there is a man with a tractor performing ten times the work with less effort. Or the satisfaction derived from the work may derive from the worker's realization of his role in a larger scheme, and may vary greatly according to whether the job is unique or merely one of a large mass. There is the classical story of the gang of labourers who were ordered (during the days when 'made work' was prevalent) to dig a series of trenches, then to fill them up again and dig in another place. The workers grew disgruntled and finally quit in disgust at what looked like fruitless work, but resumed cheerfully when it was explained to them that they were looking for a buried pipeline whose location had been lost.

Social values

Finally the individualistic economist must recognize that some values are social in their very nature. Over and above individual satisfactions that may be provided for collectively, such as postal service, and over and above the dependence of individual satisfactions on the environment in which they arise, are satisfactions inherent in the social structure itself, in the degree of equality, opportunity, freedom, range of choice, not only of a given individual but of individuals in general. There is satisfaction derived from being a part of something larger than oneself, from realizing that others likewise have their roles, from all the intangibles that go to make up a culture. And even though the economist cannot directly work these values into his nice theoretical framework, they nevertheless affect the values attaching to the more tangible economic goods and services, and the way in which the more purely economic objectives are achieved will greatly affect the values in the social structure.

Indeed, some economists have gone so far as to focus their attention on their conception of these social values, almost to the exclusion of the individualistic values. However, their writings have usually been outside the normal range of economics, tending to deal in vague social generalities rather than in the details of the day-to-day economic process. Such comments or recommendations as they have had to make concerning specific economic measures and activities have often not been too closely connected with their expressed ultimate values. In some cases the ultimate values are almost exclusively concerned with a remote future to which the present is to be completely subordinated. An extreme form of this is Marxism, in which almost any present means is acceptable if it can be claimed to promote progress towards the ultimate stateless communistic utopia.

Another type of approach is to consider the entire economic and social system as an organism in which the whole is supposed to have a motivation, purpose, and ultimate goal that transcend the purposes of any of the separate parts. All individuals become expendable where this would serve this organic purpose, as completely as a white corpuscle or a fingernail paring is expendable where the health or well-being of a human being is concerned. However, such a concept, at least in its pure form, is so repugnant to the traditions of freer countries as never to have gained much hold; and even where such a concept has served a temporary purpose as one of the apologiae of tyranny, the role has been an apologetic one rather than one of guidance.

Yet there is a sense in which some transcendent value must attach to the society as a whole. This becomes apparent when the economist is asked to determine what policy should be pursued with regard to the heritage to be passed on to future generations. To what extent should the present generation stint itself or exert itself to provide a greater heritage of resources for future generations? This is a topic concerning which little is said directly by economists. Yet their underlying attitudes toward this question distinctly colour a great deal of their thinking. On the other hand, many conflicts of opinion in this field turn out to be founded on misapprehensions which it should be the duty of economists to clear up.

The *laissez-faire* economist tacitly proposes that this problem should be solved by accepting that provision which individuals make for their heirs as the proper one. It is not always recognized however, that in addition to property passed on by gift and bequest, there must always be a substantial creation and transmission of the aggregate wealth of a society wholly aside from what we usually think of as inheritance. Even though every individual consumed all his wealth during his years of retirement, the process of saving during his productive years, holding wealth for awhile and dissaving during retirement, would, through the overlapping of generations, constitute him a member of a sort of relay team by which wealth is passed on and even accumulated over the centuries.

But this individualistic answer seems hardly enough even to determine a specific overall policy, let alone to command acceptance as the right criterion. Inheritance is greatly affected by the laws of mortmain, which are even more clearly a social artifact and have even less title to claim the status of natural law than have, say, the system of free exchange and other elements of property rights. The degree to which society will respect and even enforce adherence to the wishes of the deceased concerning the disposition of their property involves primarily ethical values, but also has profound influence upon the economic system as a whole.

But increasingly the social heritage is being influenced by collective decisions, many if not most of which are taken without conscious reflection of their effect upon the relative interests of the present and the future. The choice, for example, of whether to curb inflation by a proper combination of low interest rates and a relatively large government surplus, or instead to achieve the same end by higher interest rates and a smaller surplus, is a choice that should be made not merely in terms of current effectiveness but also in terms of the effect on the social heritage. Election of the low-interest-rate alternative, whether it is recognized or not, will tend to increase the social heritage, other things being equal, and will impose a correspondingly higher degree of stinting upon the current generation. Similar considerations are in order when the problem is one of preventing or reducing unemployment. And of course decisions are always being made concerning the expenditure of public funds that have profound influences on the social heritage. Public funds may be spent in ways that benefit primarily current generations, or in ways that benefit future generations, even though such distinctions are not ordinarily reflected in public account books.

Conservation

The most obvious and specific clash of the interests of the present and of the future, and the one that attracts the most attention, is in the area of conservation. Yet to the economist it often appears that the manner in which such issues are presented involves a misconception of the issue. We often hear about the wastage of such natural resources as timber, oil, gas, land, and the like, the implication being that the present generation is selfishly squandering these resources and leaving nothing for the future. It may be true that these resources are being wastefully used, but in many cases this waste arises not from an excessive preference for present gain over possible future benefits, but rather from a specific malfunctioning of our laws concerning rights in certain types of property. The fact that the effects will be felt only in the future seems to polarize attitudes toward the wasteful activity. Some tend to ignore the waste because it is not immediately apparent, while others seem to lay special emphasis upon it because of a special importance attached to the future, even to the point of belittling the actual consideration that the interests of the future receive at the hands of even the least socially minded exploiters.

To the extent that the form of property rights is responsible, ethics, tradition, and economics may come into apparent conflict, but it should be possible to resolve that conflict if the issue is properly understood. At this point it can probably be said that economists have on the whole failed to expound adequately the economic principles involved.

Competitive seizure

For example, one of the most flagrant examples of wasteful exploitation of natural resources occurs in the development of an oil pool, where the oil lying beneath an area has been held to belong to whoever can first pump it out of the ground. Traditional concepts of property rights failed to provide for this case: the treatment in the early years of oil exploitation was derived conceptually from the law concerning the capture of wild game. Important differences were, however, overlooked: one who overhunts his own property is by no means sure that his stock will be replenished by migration from his neighbour's land. The man who pumps out an oil well may be fairly confident that the oil will flow from under his neighbour's land to his. And game replenishes itself to a certain extent while oil pools once exhausted do not grow again.

Thus the traditionalistic attempt to solve this situation by analogy to precedent has produced disastrous results that had to be modified, not too successfully, by *ad hoc* regulations. It is not certain what the philosopher attempting to provide a solution to such situations on an ethical basis would prescribe. Assertion by the community in the form of the state to paramount title to such underground wealth seems quite logical, but if this leads to lease under a royalty, it is not at all clear that present and future interests are likely to be properly weighed. Indeed, it would certainly be possible for such a royalty to be set so high as to impair the social heritage; more oil would be left for the future, but possibly the curtailment of present consumption of oil would impair current productivity and result in less capital of other kinds being left for future generations.

A similar class of problems comes up where existing institutions concerning the use of a natural resource are such that private possession is secured by seizure or discovery from a common pool. The traditional staking of claims by prospectors is an example. A somewhat more difficult case is that of ocean fishing, in which there is not only the matter of preserving a natural resource, but of settling international conflicts. In a practical situation, it is not at all clear how one should decide how far the need of present-day Japanese for fish from the Aleutian area should be stinted to ensure a plentiful supply for future Americans.

Where important 'neighbourhood effects' exist, the problem can perhaps be treated more nearly in terms of economics: problems of soil erosion, flood control, waste disposal, and stream pollution, for example, are problems of bringing home to the responsible persons the injury they may cause to values that would not ordinarily appear to them in terms of profit or loss. The problem is not so much one of balancing present and future interests as it is of comparing values that are ordinarily not adequately represented in the market place.

Some values affected by 'conservation' are somewhat esoteric, and may be beyond the capacity of the economists' techniques of assessment: the extinction of the passenger pigeon, the preservation of the 'scenic spectacle' of Niagara, or of virgin wilderness. The relative place of material progress and sentimental nostalgia in our scale of values is a real problem, though its quantitative importance may not be great.

The possible effectiveness of private property

If, however, we strip the conservation issue of all of these side effects and look at the bare issue of consuming a specific resource now or saving it for later on, it becomes not so clear that private property is incapable of doing a reasonably adequate job of saving the kinds of resources most needed by future generations aside from the question of the aggregate volume. Thus, if a mineral deposit is reasonably well delimited and incapable of flowing away or being seduced or seized by interlopers, and if there is some expectation of a future shortage of this mineral such as would tend to drive its price up in the future, or if there are prospects of better and cheaper methods of extraction being developed, the economist can at least imagine the owner deferring its exploitation as long as such deferment will result in an increased ultimate recovery from the property by more than the return that could be earned on a comparable investment elsewhere. If the owner makes a reasonably accurate forecast, there will be no serious discrepancy between the choice made in his own interest and that which would be in accord with social welfare, provided the general rates of profit and interest adequately reflect the relative claims of present and future. And to the extent that they do not, the problem is a general one and is not peculiar to conservation of natural resources.

Of course, when we look at the way in which decisions are actually reached concerning the exploitation of natural resources, we find that most of the time attention is paid only to current costs and prices, or those of the relatively short future, and the possible circumstances of the remote future seem to get very little attention. Is this then to be taken to mean that the theoretical analysis of the economist is irrelevant to the real world, and that in fact decisions regarding exploitation of natural resources are in general made in a way inimical to social aims? Perhaps, but such a conclusion should be arrived at slowly. It may be that the lifetime of the individual, or even of the heirs to whose interest an individual owner would defer, is short compared with the period over which conservation would yield its returns; but this does not of itself imply that individualistic decisions are biased against the conservation of resources. Even though an investment might not yield its full return for centuries, an individual can, given an adequate market, recover for his own use the fruits of his careful custody by selling his property.

Even if in fact individuals seem to pay little attention to values that would be realized only in the distant future, it is still possible that there are socially valid justifications for this behaviour. If, for example, rates of interest are so high as to reduce values for the remote future to insignificance when discounted to the present, this is likely to be a general phenomenon not confined to the heritage of natural resources. If the threatened scarcity is so uncertain that it appears to be a bad risk for the individual to hold his resource off the market in the hope of a better price, it may also be a bad risk from the point of view of society. Shortages have a habit of appearing in other places than where they have been expected; new methods of extraction, substitute materials, and completely unforeseen developments have a habit of upsetting predictions. Before assuming that private interests necessarily make inadequate allowance for the future, one would have to inquire whether in fact the property owner's crystal ball, polished as it is by self-interest, is any cloudier than the one being used (possibly more casually) by the conservationist.

There remains, however, the possibility that future developments may rob the individual of the fruits of his abstention and foresight in a way that does not entirely destroy their value to society. The individual who postponed exploitation of his resource runs the risk of expropriation, onerous taxation, or private depredation. Political instability is thus inimical to conservation, or at least to conservation through the institution of private property. Excessive political stability on the other hand is inimical to progress and to many important values. At this point an extremely wide range of values conflict.

Population

Another topic on which economists and philosophers need closer collaboration is population. Economists are often prone to take population as one of the given variables. In spite of Malthus and diatribes against the 'dismal science', too little attention has often been paid to the effect of economic decisions on population. Moreover, once we turn from maximizing in some way the satisfaction or fulfilling the desires of an existing or at least an externally determined population, much of the economist's elaborate structure of welfare economics falls to the ground, or at least needs revalidating. For in spite of the fact that a surprising amount of economic writing ignores questions of population, a wide variety of economic measures have a substantial effect on population trends and distributions.

Transcendental standards

What are the goals of economic life, if we admit the possibility of differing population patterns and aggregates? Do we, at one extreme, allow other-worldly considerations to dominate, and consider the aim as the production of the maximum possible number of saved souls for eventual admission to Paradise? Such a goal might be interpreted as having for corollary objective the maximum possible population consistent with some minimum standard of living needed as an environment in which to practice salvation. Or should population be considered to be determined by an Act or Acts of God which it would be impious either to interfere with or try to influence? Or, if interference or influence is permitted, what types of interference or influence are morally admissible?

Or, if we return to a more materialistic level, one might at the other extreme set up as the objective such an adjustment of population as would provide the maximum real income per capita, or highest possible average standard of living. Even here, again we are confronted with the conflict between the present and the future. A population conducive to the highest average standard of living now or in the immediate future may not be at all the same as the population conducive to the highest standard of living in the more remote future. And should we look primarily at a moderately remote future, or at the distant future almost over the horizon of our powers of anticipation?

Or, taking a more organic point of view, should we aim more at the maximum possible development of 'culture', which would depend on and to some extent include the growth of technology and capital, as well as art, literature, and other more directly cultural phenomena, either currently or in the remote future? Conceivably this point of view would support measures tending in the direction of a larger total population with a greater concentration of resources in the hands of an elite, in order to promote the accumulation of capital and the diversion of resources to cultural pursuits.

Indeed the whole question of equality of distribution is bound up with both the question of heritage and the question of population. Unequally distributed incomes up to a point may lead to a greater social heritage than complete equality, and indeed one could argue cogently that this is what has happened in history. Now that a greater degree of social organization has been achieved and measures for maintaining or increasing the social heritage have developed that do not involve individual inheritance of concentrated wealth, inequality may not be so important a factor in determining the social heritage as it has been in the past; yet the redistributive techniques are still not perfected to the point where it is irrelevant.

Inequality and the Malthusian hump

On the other hand, the degree of inequality and the steps taken to mitigate it may affect the rate of population growth. Inequality may keep the bulk of the population near the subsistence level and limit its increase, while the elite attain a standard of living that fosters a low birth rate.

Here we may find two important sets of values in poignant conflict. Insistence on equality, even if not carried to the point of serious interference with incentives for production, may spread any improvement in total product so thin that it is merely absorbed by an increased population. It may be that the escape of much of Europe and the West from the Malthusian treadmill was made possible only by the persistence of a high degree of internal inequality, coupled with an even higher degree of international inequality through which the West was able to secure for itself almost the entire economic benefits of the Industrial Revolution and the opening up of new continents. It is possible that had there been greater internal equality, and had the benefits been spread more widely internationally, the spell of the 'dismal science' might never have been broken.

In terms of current problems, the economist is thus faced with a dilemma for the resolution of which the philosopher has thus far not provided the tools. In extending aid to 'underdeveloped' areas, whether under Point Four or any other program, how far should the allocation of assistance be based on current need, and how far on the prospects that in any particular instance the benefits of the assistance will not be swallowed up by the increase in population which it stimulates? Indeed, should one go further and single out some groups which are small enough so that with the resources available they can be raised rapidly over the Malthusian hump and brought to a standard of living at which they will no longer dissipate the added resources in proliferation, meanwhile leaving other no less needy or worthy groups to struggle along in squalor while waiting their turn? Should one actually condemn indiscriminate aid in the form of medical, public health, and sanitation services, on the ground that in spite of their striking immediate results they may in the long run defer the time at which the population can be raised to a stable and adequate standard of living?

Calculation versus impulse

Even if some sort of calculated compromise or balance can be produced along these lines, the results may still be subject to attack from another angle. Is, after all, calculated philanthropy entitled to as much esteem as the generous unpremeditated impulse? There is, after all, something less attractive, from some points of view, about an oversystematic, oversophisticated economic process than about a more human, less coldly calculating, and even erratic approach. The economist by nature tends to be much more of an 'economic man' than his neighbours; possibly the philosopher has something to add toward the correction of this bias, even if the economist has managed to stop short of complete obsession by an 'irrational passion for dispassionate rationality'.

Spurious ethics

But if the economist has some searching and fundamental questions concerning ultimate values to put to the philosopher, he is also prone to chafe considerably under many of the value judgements that have been urged upon him in the name of ethics.

'Just price'

Most prominent of these is the general attitude towards trade which can be summed up by the term 'just price'. In its original setting, the notion that each article had a 'just price' which truly represented its intrinsic value had as a corollary the notion that in trading articles at the just price neither party gained or lost, while any departure from this just price involved a gain to one party at the expense of the other. As long as circumstances changed slowly, this idea did much to prevent exploitation in potentially monopolistic situations. But it has persisted in a world where the rapidity of underlying changes makes the rigidity of the 'just price' notion unsuitable.

Insistence of economists that an exchange freely entered into involves some gain to both parties, else one would demur, has overcome a good deal of the attachment to this notion, but some of it seems to persist, carrying with it a spurious ethical sanction that often does much to interfere with the functioning of the price mechanism. Thus when a considerable period of normal supply and demand has established a certain price in the minds of buyers and sellers as being proper for a given commodity, there is often a great resistance to raising such a price in a period of scarcity. The issue is often confused by the fact that in many cases there are other perfectly adequate reasons for adhering to a customary price, such as difficulties of communication, effects of price change on the distribution of income, or the like, coupled with unsatisfactory performance of price change in stimulating supply or allocating use in the specific instance. But even where these other valid reasons do not operate, a policy of adherence to the established price is often followed with approval in spite of undesirable consequences, such as the waste through queues, grey markets, the intervention of speculators, and uneconomical allocation generally.

The 'just price' notion spreads its congealing influence even where no element of unexpected emergency exists. Many prices are, from the point of view of the economist, inadequately responsive to such peaks of demand as result from holidays, special events, seasonal factors, and the like. A premium is thus attached to making plans and reservations well in advance and a corresponding penalty attached to last-minute arrangements that unduly hinder the attainment of flexibility. The fairness of 'first come, first served' is at best only superficial; at worst it can be both arbitrary and wasteful. The price system has its faults, but the traditional antagonism between ethical values and the values of the market place should not be allowed to interfere with permitting the price system to function in those cases where it does function reasonably effectively.

Business 'ethics'

Another area in which a spurious ethical sanction is allowed to support practices of doubtful value is that of 'business ethics'. To a large extent, to be sure, the practices or restraints supported by business or professional men as 'ethical' are praiseworthy and in the public interest. But in many cases they constitute more nearly a sort of 'honour among thieves' representing an attempt to preserve the interests of a narrow group to the detriment of the public good. Perhaps nowhere else is this quite so prominent as in the 'fair trade practices' acts in effect in many states by which manufacturers are supported in attempts to eliminate price competition among the retailers handling their products. It is barely possible to argue for such provisions on the ground that they promote order in marketing, but this should be done on economic grounds alone, rather than pretending that the acts protect the more virtuous from the un-scrupulous competition of competitors. 'Free competitive enter-prise' must include price competition if it is to live up to what is claimed for it.

In a wider and more pervasive sense, the concept of ethics tends to be distorted by a kind of provincial bias in the practice of altruism. Many people find it easier to practice the golden rule towards persons in their own class or of their own culture, with whom it is easier to identify oneself and whose feelings and wants it is easier to imagine, than towards persons of greatly different status. Not only is it easier to put oneself in the other's place, but there is often a certain likeli-hood of deriving reciprocal benefits more or less indirectly. Thus, motorists may be more polite to other motorists than to pedestrians, and merchants more considerate of other merchants than of their customers. In many instances there may be much good and little harm in this, but it is something that must be watched lest it develop into an economic caste system, as some saw threatened at the time of the NRA. And even though no overwhelming damage is done, a subtle bias is introduced in the patterns of competition that should not be further consolidated by wrapping it in a mantle of 'ethics'.

Ethics, economics, and the individual

But while these searching questions are basic to any determination of public policy, they seem remote to the ordinary layman seeking to find out how he can uphold his ethical standards in the complexities of modern economic life. In a primitive economy, where the effects of a man's actions spread over only a limited area, ethical conduct and the practice of the golden rule had a clearer meaning to the individual. Such clarity did not lead to the millennium, however, and with the growing complexity of economic life, more and more of the decisions of the individual were wrenched from their moral moorings and left to the free play of self-interest. It is perhaps one of the essential miracles of our civilization that in this process the frequency with which morality and self-interest come into direct conflict has been kept as low as it has.

Economic motives as a relief of moral strain

From where we now stand, it seems clear that it is no longer possible, if it ever was, for an individual, in each decision he is called upon to make, to determine what is the correct choice, directly in terms of ultimate ethical values. Time for deliberation would be wanting, if nothing else. More important, for the average person there are limits, varying from one person to another, to the extent to which he can submerge his own interests in the interests of society as a whole. For some decisions, at least, a less demanding basis must be found, both in terms of sophistication and in terms of the powers of self-abnegation.

Fortunately our economic system has so developed that in a great number of cases the choice to be made on basic ethical grounds coincides with the choice that is made on the basis of self-interest, or at least so that the selfish choice is not materially incompatible with the achievement of the ultimate goals. In an appropriately organized economy, a choice between a new hat and a new pair of shoes, and indeed most choices among alternative types of consumption, can usually be left to individual self-interest without compromising any fundamental values.

This property of our economy has indeed been so remarkable that the temptation has been strong to assert that it works universally, and thus that everything can be left to the workings of the 'unseen hand'. In its extreme form, of course, this notion leads to the absurdity of denying that ethics has anything to contribute to the determination of proper choices. The obvious failures of the automatic workings of self-interest at a great number of crucial points are, however, sufficient to discredit any proposal that ethics should thus abdicate in favour of a complete *laissez faire*, even if it were possible to tolerate such a denial of all necessity for morality.

The domains of altruism and self-interest

In any actual world there will be, for the individual, cases in which he can give free rein to his personal predilections, and others in which it will be hoped that he will draw upon his moral resources and act in accordance with ultimate ethical values rather than indulge his own preferences. The initial problem, for the individual, will be one of learning how to distinguish readily between these two cases; the subsequent problem will be of finding out what decision to make where it has been determined that self-interest is not to be allowed free rein. One of the sins committed by the glorification of economic freedom has been precisely that it has tended to confuse individuals as to where the boundary between the two cases lies. And one of the great defects of our economic system is that its very complexity makes it difficult for the individual to see just when he is expected to look farther than his own self-interest, and that on those occasions when he is expected to do so the consequences of his acts have become so difficult to trace that in many cases the individual may still find it beyond his capacity to discover the ethical course of action.

Assisting the 'unseen hand'

One of the chief aims of public policy, therefore, should be to so organize the economic system as to make it easier for individuals to see in what respects they should attempt to look beyond their own interests, and easier for them to trace the consequences of their behaviour in such cases. One of the most important ways of doing this is to establish institutions which increase the extent to which self-interest is compatible with ultimate values. In effect, where the unaided unseen hand seems to fail, society should establish institutions that will help it out. By thus placing more of the individual's decisions in the noncritical self-interest area, even the most altruistically inclined individuals will be able to concentrate more attention on the socialization of their remaining decisions, and thus do a better job of approaching the satisfaction of the ultimate values.

The capacity for altruism

But further, it may be argued that in many people the capacity for altruistic behaviour is limited, and that the smaller the demands made upon this capacity the better will be the performance. To be sure, the opposite contention is also possible, that virtue grows by exercise, and that reducing the area in which altruism is to be exercised may stunt the development of this capacity. There may indeed be a point at which this would be true. But considering the world as it is, one can perhaps hazard the guess that we do not appear to have reached, nor does there appear to be any serious likelihood of our ever reaching, a situation in which there is a shortage of opportunities for the exercise of altruism. And if there is anything to Toynbee's thesis of progress being made through the challenge that strains but does not break, one may hazard the further guess that there will always be plenty of strain of this kind for individuals willing to take it on. Reducing the demands made on the resources of altruism seems more likely to reduce the casualties among those whose resources might be strained too far than to stunt the growth of the morally stronger.

Development of the moral society

This does bring us, however, to the searching question of how far our economic system is in its nature and philosophy conducive or otherwise to the moral development of mankind. At the extreme we have those who reject Western capitalism on the ground that no system relying so heavily on self-interest for its functioning can possibly bring out the best that man is capable of becoming. Possibly there is truth in this view. However, no large-scale high-productivity society has yet been successfully operated that has not relied to a large extent on self-interest as an organizing force. Perhaps a way may yet be found; and perhaps this way can be found only after having gone through the state we are now in.

As yet it is not possible to deny categorically that we may have bought material progress at too high a moral price. All that we can observe is that those who believe this strongly enough to attempt themselves to return to the primitive, small-scale, self-subsistent mode of life are but a minute minority. And, in any case, such a regression is out of the question for the world as a whole, short of an elimination of a large part of the present population. Our best hope is probably to make the self-interest-powered part of our economic system as smooth running as possible, so that more and more of our conscious effort can be directed toward the solution of those problems that cannot be resolved without explicit ethical considerations.

Part Two
Theoretical Welfare Economics

The two essays here give the flavour and much of the content of welfare economics of the Pareto–Bergson type. Samuelson's paper and the discussion he gave earlier in his *Foundations of Economic Analysis* is the basic work on what can and cannot be said from the point of view of welfare on matters of economic policy and history when no Bergson social welfare function, with its individualist Paretian property, is specified. The excerpt from Graaff's book, *Theoretical Welfare Economics*, provides an elegant exposition of many of the concepts in this type of analysis.

2 P. A. Samuelson

The Evaluation of Real National Income

P. A. Samuelson, 'The evaluation of real national income', *Oxford Economic Papers*, Clarendon Press, 1950.

Introduction

Improved measurement of national income has been one of the outstanding features of recent progress in economics. But the theoretical interpretation of such aggregate data has been sadly neglected, so that we hardly know how to define real income even in simple cases where statistical data are perfect and where problems of capital formation and government expenditure do not arise.

In 1940 Hicks made an important advance over the earlier work of Professor Pigou. This has given rise to recent discussions between Kuznets (1948), Hicks (1948), and Little (1949), but the last word on the subject will not be uttered for a long time. I have tried to treat the problem somewhat exhaustively in this paper, relating it to the modern theories of welfare economics of Pareto–Lerner–Bergson type. The result is not easy reading even to the author – but without such a careful survey I doubt that even the classical writings of Pigou can be adequately gauged.[1]

In Figure 1, the point A represents observed consumption data for a single consumer in equilibrium at the indicated price-slope line through A. All the other points are each to be regarded as alternative to A and have nothing to do with each other. The following statements are immediate consequences of the modern theory of a single consumer's behaviour and are based on $\sum pq$ data such as the national income statistician might be able to measure:

1. The principle references are to Hicks (1940, 1948); Kuznets (1948); Little (1949a and b); Pigou (1932, especially chapters 2, 3, 5 and 6); Samuelson (1948, chapter 8).

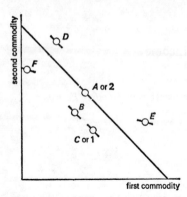

Figure 1

(a) We can immediately infer that B is on a lower indifference curve than A.

(b) Less directly, but with equal certainty, C reveals itself to be inferior to A.

(c) The point D reveals itself to be superior to A.

(d) The points E and A reveal nothing about their order in the consumer's taste-pattern.

(e) The point F is inconsistent with A. The consumer has changed his tastes, or he is not in equilibrium at the indicated points.

Problems of inference from group market data

Let us now regard Figure 1 as applying to market data for two or more individuals, so that each quantity q represents the total of two or more individuals' consumption, $q'+q''+...$, etc. The slope through A or any other point represents the market–price ratio of the first and second goods, the only commodities in our simplified world.

What can we now say about our points? Advances in the theory of welfare economics since 1940 – many of them growing out of Hicks's own researches – suggest that certain of the definitions and propositions then laid down need to be modified. I resurrect these matters only because most people who have seen the recent discussion between Kuznets, Hicks, and Little must find their heads swimming, and must be in considerable doubt as to what the proper status of this vital matter is.

First we may clear up one misunderstanding, in itself unimportant, but giving an initial clue that we cannot make any very sweeping inferences from aggregate price–quantity data. In 1940 it was held that a situation like that of A and F is quite impossible on the assumption that individuals preserve the same well-defined tastes and are in true equilibrium in competitive markets (Hicks, pp. 112–13). It was held that, for national totals,

$$\sum p_2 q_2 > \sum p_2 q_1 \quad \text{implies} \quad \sum p_1 q_1 < \sum p_2 q_2.$$

As stated earlier, for a single individual this would be a correct assertion; but it is definitely false for group data involving two or more individuals. Examples to show this can be given *ad lib*. No recourse need be made to the Kuznets case of necessaries and luxuries (understanding by the latter, goods which some individuals do not choose to buy at all) – but, of course, there is no reason why such examples should not also be used. Perhaps the very simplest example to illustrate the possibility of a contradiction would be one in which we keep the exact national totals of the point A, but re-allocate goods between the individuals so that they come into final equilibrium with a new and different price ratio. Then already we are on the borderline of a contradiction, and by making a slight change in the totals we can obviously get a strong outright contra-diction.

Already we are warned that $\sum p_2 q_2 > \sum p_2 q_1$ cannot imply that the second situation represents an 'increase in social real income' over that of the first – since this implication would leave us with the real possibility that each situation is better than the other!

This should also warn us against thinking that we can save such a definition by applying it only where there is no such outright contra-diction. For suppose that we consider a case which just escapes *revealing* itself to be contradictory; being so close to a nonsense situation, such a case can in no wise escape being subject to the same *fundamental* (as yet undiagnosed) difficulty, even though it may not be advertising the fact to us.

Inadmissibility of the 1940 definition of increased real income

This tells us already that either there is something inadequate about the 1940 definition of an 'increase in society's real income' or else there is something faulty about the logical proof that the index-number criterion $\sum p_2 q_2 > \sum p_2 q_1$ implies such a defined increase in real income.

The 1940 passage in question is so compact that one must be careful in interpreting it. In my judgement the root of the trouble lies more in the inadequacy of the definition enunciated than in the logic of the demonstration that the stated index-number criterion does imply an increase in defined real income. Although it has already been extensively requoted, the relevant 1940 passage is so brief that it can be given completely here.

... What does it signify if $\sum p_2 q_2 > \sum p_2 q_1$?

It should first of all be noticed that since this condition refers only to the total quantities acquired, it can tell us nothing about the distribution of wealth among the members of the group. There may be a drastic re-distribution of wealth among the members and the aggregates will remain exactly the same. Thus what the condition $\sum p_2 q_2 > \sum p_2 q_1$ tells us is that there is *some* distribution of the q_1s which would make every member of the group less well off than he actually is in the 2 situation. For if the corresponding inequality were to hold for every individual separately, it would hold for the group as a whole.

As compared with this particular distribution, every other distribution of the q_1s would make some people better off and some worse off. Consequently, if there is one distribution of the q_1s in which every member of the group is worse off than he actually is in the 2 situation, there can be no distribution in which everyone is better off, or even as well off. Thus if we start from any actual distribution of wealth in the 1 situation, what the condition $\sum p_2 q_2 > \sum p_2 q_1$ tells us is that it is impossible to reach, by re-distribution, a position in which everyone is as well off as he is in the 2 situation.

This would seem to be quite acceptable as a definition of increase in real social income. Let us say that the real income of society is higher in situation 2 than in situation 1, if it is impossible to make everyone as well off as he is in situation 2 by any redistribution of the actual quantities acquired in situation 1. If this definition is accepted, our criteria can be applied to it without change (Hicks, 1940, p. 111).

A diagram that we shall place major reliance on in the later discussion can be used to illustrate exactly what is involved in this definition of an 'increase in social real income'. On the axes in Figure 2 there is laid out the ordinal utility of each of two individuals:

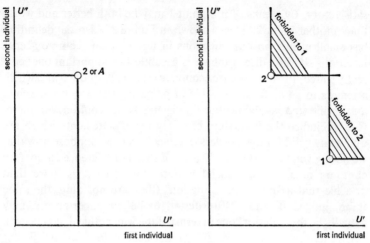

Figure 2   Figure 3

the exact scale of U'' or U' is of no consequence, only the north–south and east–west orderings being important. Corresponding to the point A or 2 in Figure 1, there will actually be some allocation of the total of goods between our individuals, and hence some determined level of well-being for each. Let the point labelled 2 in Figure 2 represent that actual level of ordinal well-being. Now consider the other situation that was labelled C or 1 in our earlier figure. Behind the scenes, unknown to us from the totals, there is again an actual allocation of the goods to the individuals and again a new point in Figure 2. If we knew where it was, we could write it in and label it 1. We do not know where this new point will fall: it may be south-west of point 2 so that all individuals are worse off, or south-east so that one individual is better off and the other worse off, and so forth.

Hicks's 1940 definition of an increase in real income from the point 1 to 2 consists of this: if we can be sure that neither point 1 nor any reallocation of its quantities among individuals lies north–east of point 2 (with both individuals better off in 1 than in 2), then point 2 is defined to represent an increase in real income over point 1.

How acceptable is this definition, leaving aside for the moment the question of whether the index-number criteria does permit us to place such a restriction on the admissible position of point 1? Upon reflection, we will all agree, I think, that such a definition is not very

P. A. Samuelson 69

satisfactory. By means of it a point 1 may be both better and worse than another point 2. This is shown in Figure 3. Also the definition has small claims on our affections in terms of our common-sense intuitions. Its last disadvantage is a subtle but important one: correctly stated, the new welfare economics is a body of doctrines which attempts to go as far as possible in preparing the way for the final a-scientific step involving ethical judgements; it should never, therefore, prejudice the final step, but only make statements which are uniformly valid for a wide class of ethical systems. Suppose now that we have given to us in Figure 2 a set of social indifference curves (the contours of a Bergson social welfare function). It is more than possible that a 'point' or 'situation' (they are not quite the same thing) judged by the 1940 criterion to be the superior one may actually be the 'inferior' one in terms of the wider ethical judgements.

Instinctively Hicks was reaching out, I believe, for a rather different definition than the one he actually enunciated. The simpler problem of comparing A and B in Figure 1 will bring this out and at the same time require no intricate index-number reasoning. As before, corresponding to the point A in Figure 1 there is in Figure 2 a point 2 representing the ordinal well-being of all individuals. Now with less of *all* goods available to society as shown by B, there will be a new point of individuals' well-being in Figure 2. Where will the new point lie with respect to the former point 2?

We would have to give the unsatisfactory answer 'anywhere' were it not for one important assumption. We have assumed that behind the scenes of A all individuals are in competitive equilibrium facing the same price ratio. This assures us that all marginal rates of substitution are equal and that there exists no reallocation of the goods of A between them which will permit them both to be better off. (In technical parlance the competitive solution lies somewhere on the *Edgeworth contract locus*.) *A fortiori*, for a point like B, which involves smaller totals for *every* commodity, there is *no* reallocation of goods that could possibly make all individuals better off than they were in A. Without introducing price or index numbers, we know therefore that the point B is forbidden to be north-east of the point A – and we know that B corresponds to a decrease in real income over A according to the old 1940 definition.

But that is not really saying much. It is possible that one individual may be worse off even though the other individual is better off. And we must still entertain the darkest suspicions of a possible contradiction. But this simple case turns out to have at least one surprising feature: if we try to reallocate goods in either of the two situations – always letting the individuals come ultimately into competitive equilibrium – it turns out that we shall *never* find a case where on the 1940 definition the situation B turns out to be 'better' (as well as 'worse') than A. I have not yet proved this in my discussion; but, accepting this fact as true, we find ourselves on the trail of a better way of defining an increase in real income – or more accurately, an increase in *potential* real income.

The crucially important 'utility-possibility function'

Let us consider all possible reallocations between individuals of the consumption totals corresponding to A or 2. For each way of allocating the goods there will be a given level of well-being for each and every individual – as can be indicated by a point on the $U'-U''$ diagram. The totality of all such possible points obviously cannot go indefinitely far in the north-east direction; equally obviously there is a frontier curve or envelope giving, for each amount of one person's utility, the maximum possible amount of the other person's utility. This frontier is the important 'utility-possibility function' corresponding to A.

The point 2 happens to lie on the frontier because at 2 all individuals are known to be in competitive equilibrium. Corresponding to the smaller totals of point B, there is also a utility-possibility function. We can now state the sense in which A or 2 is *potentially* better than B.

The total of all goods being greater in A than in B, the utility-possibility function of A is uniformly outside and beyond the utility-possibility function of B. (This is shown in Figure 4.) The reason for this statement is intuitively obvious and can be expressed in the language of a currently popular song: A can do everything B can do – (and) better.

This, then, is the sense in which we can, without introducing detailed ethical assumptions, define an 'increase in society's potential real income in going from point B to point A'. Such an increase means a uniform outward shift in society's utility-possibility function.

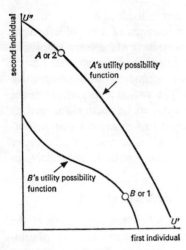

Figure 4

Let us now return to the index-number problem. Can we infer that *A* is superior to *C* in terms of our new definition of potential real income? If we can, then with minor modifications the 1940 analysis can be accepted. But, unfortunately for economic theory, we cannot make any such inference about potential superiority from the index-number analysis of aggregate price–quantity data.[2]

Any single counter-example will prove the falsity of the index-number criteria as applied to more than one individual. Perhaps the simplest such example would be one in which the first individual cares only for so-called necessaries. If less of total necessaries are available in *A*, then *A*'s utility-possibility curve must cut inside of *B*'s when we get in the region of the $U''-U'$ quadrant favouring the necessary-loving individual; and hence *A* cannot represent an unequivocal increase in potential real income. Simple as this example is, it is open to the objection that it seems to involve the case where the individuals consume nothing of some commodity. Actually this is an irrelevant feature of the example.

2. Simple logic tells us that this negative answer must be forthcoming in a comparison of *A* and *F* since each of two curves cannot both lie uniformly outside of each other; and already we have seen reason to believe that the *A* and *F* comparison does not differ materially from that of *A* and *C*.

But, in any case, greater insight into the nature of the problem can be had if we examine the steps in the reasoning linking up the index-number criterion and the 1940 definition of an increase in real income.

If we have between the points A and C, or 2 and 1,

$$\sum p_2(q_2' + q_2'' + \ldots) > \sum p_2(q_1^1 + q_1'' + \ldots),$$

then according to the 1940 argument we can find some redistribution of the quantities in C or 1, so that the new quantities of every good going to each individual, which we may call

$$q_3 + q_3'' + \ldots = q_1' + q_1'' + \ldots,$$

are such as to make the crucial index-number criteria hold for each and every individual; namely,

$$\sum p_2 q_2' > \sum p_2 q_3', \qquad \sum p_2 q_2'' > \sum p_2 q_3'', \ldots.$$

Hence there exists a new situation resulting from the reallocation of the q_1s which is worse for *every* individual than is situation 2.

A missing step in the 1940 logic must be filled in at this point. The fact that we can reallocate the q_1s to get a new point q_3 which makes both individuals worse off than they are in 2 is taken to mean that the utility-possibility curve of 1 must be south-west of the point 2. But nothing has been said to show that q_3 is a frontier point on the utility-possibility function of point 1. Fortunately, it can be easily proved that there does exist at least one (and actually an infinite number) reallocation of the q_1s that (a) lies on the utility-possibility function of 1, and (b) causes our index-number criteria to hold for each and every individual.[3]

3. Figure 5 shows all this. An Edgeworth–Bowley box has been drawn up with the dimensions of the quantities in the q_1 situation. From the south–west corner of the box we measure off the consumption of the first individual, U'. From the north–east corner we measure downward and to the left the consumption of the U'' individual. Any point in the box represents a possible allocation of the total q_1 quantities, with the point marked q_1 being the one actually observed.

On this same diagram we may also show the actual quantities consumed by the individuals in the q_2 situation. But now it takes two points in the box, as far apart from each other as C is from A. They are marked q_2' and q_2'' respectively, and the price-lines through their points are drawn in with the slopes of the p_2' situation.

As the picture stands q_1 does not satisfy the index-number criteria for the U'

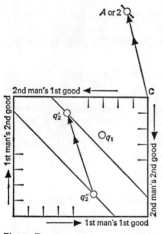

Figure 5

With the above provision, we may accept the 1940 demonstration that when aggregate data satisfy the index-number criterion, the 1940 definition of superiority is definitely realized.[4] But there is nothing in this demonstration that tells us whether the utility-possibility function of 2 lies above (or below) the point 1;[5] all we know is that 1's utility-possibility function lies somewhere southwest of the point 2.

Our final conclusions may be summarized briefly. The index-number criterion

---

individual since q_1 does *not* lie inside the crucial triangle of the point q'. Hicks's statement is that there is some reallocation which will move the point q_1 to a new point q_3 which lies between the two parallel lines. For any such point our index-number criteria are satisfied for both individuals. The missing step is to show that there exist points in this strip which are also on the Edgeworth contract curve. Since the contract curve must go from one corner of the box to the other and pass through all levels of U' and U'', it must obviously somewhere pass through the intervening strip between the parallel lines. This supplies the missing step. Readers of Kuznets should note that it is the totals of q_1, not of q_2, that are reallocated so as to lead to Hicks's conclusion.

4. This is apparently what Little means when he concludes that the 1940 definition is 'immune from Professor Kuznets's conditions' (1949, p. 13).

5. In any case, no one should think that the condition
$$\Sigma p_1 q_2 > \Sigma p_1 q_1$$
which is satisfied in C (but not in F) helps to rule out a contradiction.

$$\sum p_2(q_2' + q_2'' + \ldots) > \sum p_2(q_1' + q_1'' + \ldots)$$

tells us that the utility-possibility function of 2 does lie outside of that of 1 *in the neighbourhood* of the actual observed point 2 – but that is all it tells us. The curve may intersect and cross elsewhere – as shown in the later Figure 6.

The Hicks–Kaldor–Scitovsky version of new welfare economics

Having failed to relate the stronger definition of potential superiority to index-number criteria, we must reconsider whether, after all, the 1940 definition of superiority may not be tolerably acceptable. If we examine this definition, we find that it is in all essentials the same one as that earlier suggested by Kaldor (1939) and by Hicks in his earlier article (1939). It will be recalled that these two writers had ruled that situation X is better than situation Y if there exists a reallocation of the goods in X which makes everybody better off than he was in Y. Except that the 1940 definition applied to a *decrease* in well-being between 2 and 1, this is identical with the earlier 1939 definition.

Dissatisfaction early developed over the 1939 definition. In particular Scitovsky (1941 and 1942) came forward with the objection that it seemed to assume that there was something right (ethically) about the distribution of income in the *status quo ante* of the Y situation. To get around this he suggested (in effect) that a *double* test be applied.

To say that 'X is better than Y' we must be sure that (a) there exists a reallocation of the X goods that could make everybody better off than he actually was in Y; and (b) we must make sure there exists a reallocation of the goods in Y that could make everybody worse off than he actually was in X.

Or, in our terminology, the Scitovsky definition of superiority requires the utility-possibility curve of one situation to be beyond that of the other in the neighbourhood of *both* actual observed points.

In his criticism of the 1940 definition Kuznets can be generously interpreted to be trying (presumably independently) in effect to reiterate the Scitovsky double criterion. Kuznets says at one point that we must supplement the Hicks condition [that there must be a reallocation of the q_1s that makes everyone worse off than he actually was in the q_2 situation] by the further condition that '[it must not be] impossible to make *everyone* as well off as he is in situation 1 by any redistribution of the actual quantities acquired in situation 2' (1948, p. 4).

Kaldor has explicitly accepted the Scitovsky correction, and as far as I know so has Hicks. Therefore they would both presumably have no quarrel with this Kuznets reversibility condition.[6] But both Kuznets and Hicks do not seem to realize that the difficulty is basic and has nothing to do with the question of substitutability of necessaries or luxuries. On the Scitovsky-amended definition, the whole demonstration of superiority of one position over another by aggregate index-number criteria breaks down completely.[7]

Our whole theory of arriving at a measure of real income by aggregative price–quantity data has broken down. But the worst is still to come. The Scitovsky conditions are themselves very definitely unsatisfactory. It is not enough to double the 1939 conditions – we must increase them infinitely. Instead of a two-point test we need an infinitely large number of tests – that is to say, we must be sure that one of the utility-possibility functions *everywhere* lies outside the other. Without this test at an infinite number of points, no acceptable definition of an increase in potential real income can be devised at the non-ethical level of the new welfare economics.

Just as Scitovsky has criticized Kaldor and 'compensationists' for assuming the correctness of the *status quo ante*, so we must criticize him for assuming in some sense the correctness of the *status quo ante* and/or the *status quo post*.

Suppose, for example, we have *everybody actually* better off in situation 2 than in 1. Kaldor and Hicks will be satisfied to call 2 better than 1. So will Scitovsky. But the utility-possibility curves

6. Little has argued (*Economica*, 1949, pp. 12–16) that there is a confusion in Kuznets on the point of reversibility. Perhaps I am setting down what Kuznets should have meant rather than what he meant to say.

7. The best that we can say is the following. Imagine the change from point 2 to 1 to be a continuous one. So long as the two points are sufficiently (!) close together, then the condition $\Sigma p_2 q_2 > \Sigma p_2 q_1$ assures us that 2 is better than 1 in the Scitovsky sense. For changes of any size $\Sigma p_2 q_2 > \Sigma p_2 q_1$ tells us that 1 *cannot* be superior to 2 in Scitovsky or in my sense, and that is all it tells.

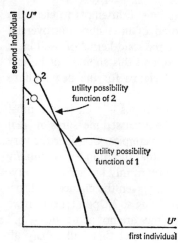

Figure 6

might very well cross as in Figure 6, so that according to many ethical welfare functions both Scitovsky and the others would be rendering false statements.

What Scitovsky should have done was to free all of his comparisons from any dependence upon either *actually observed U''–U'* situation. He should, instead, have made the comparison depend upon the totality of all *possible* positions in each situation. This would have led to the definition of potential real income earlier proposed, which seems to be the only satisfactory, self-consistent definition within the sphere of the 'new' (relatively *wert-frei*) welfare economics. Aggregate index numbers can tell us little about this except in a negative way. Even this definition is not – by itself – worth very much of anything for policy purposes, as will be shown.

Inadequacies for policy of the new welfare economics

We have seen that the new welfare economics is able to define an increase in potential real income which is unambiguous, consistent, and which will not turn out to contradict a wide class of ethical social welfare functions that must later be introduced into any problem. The new welfare economics does not go all the way in settling the problems of normative policy: taken by itself, and without supplementation, it goes virtually none of the way; but taken in conjunction with later ethical assumptions, it attempts to clear the way of all issues that can be disposed of in a non-controversial (relatively) ethical-free fashion. This is the solid kernel of usefulness in the new approach begun by Pareto, and this should not be lost sight of in the welter of exaggerated claims for the new welfare economics.

The inadequacy for actual policy decisions – even in the most idealized, simplified world – of all of the discussed measures of 'real income' can be illustrated by numerous examples. Consider the very best case where we can establish the fact that situation 2 is *potentially* better than 1 (in the sense of having a uniformly farther-out utility-possibility function). Would a good fairy given the chance to throw a switch from 1 to 2 be able to justify doing so? Upon reflection we must, I am afraid, answer *no*. Potentialities are not actualities – and unless she can give a justification of her act that will satisfy all reasonably defined social welfare functions, she cannot know whether or not to pull the switch.

A few negative remarks are possible: for any ethical system with the property that an increase in one individual's well-being is, others' being equal, a good thing[8] – for all such systems a final optimum position must necessarily be on 2 and not on 1. That we can certainly say. But without going into the realm of (modern, streamlined) 'old' welfare economics, we cannot say more or get conclusive advice on this problem of policy. The attempt to divide the problem into two parts so that one can say 'a change from 1 to 2 is *economically* desirable in the sense of objectively increasing production or wealth, whether or not the actual resulting situation will be ethically superior', only gets one into a semantic snarl and glosses over the intrinsic difficulties of the problem.

How much more severe are the policy limitations of some of the modern even weaker 'compensationist' definitions. Following them, the good fairy might do perpetual and irremediable harm. Suppose, for example, that our two *actually observed* points, 1 and 2, both lie above the intersection of the two schedules in Figure 6, but with the point 1 being south-east of point 2, so as to represent an increase in well-being of one individual and a decrease for the other. The Kaldor

8. i.e. for all social welfare propositions W, with the property $W = F(u', u'',...)$ and $\partial W/\partial u' > 0 < \partial W/\partial u'',....$

condition would be satisfied and so would the Scitovsky condition. Suppose that once the angel has thrown the switch, she can never again reverse it (e.g. capital sunk into a mine may be irrecoverable). Let her now follow the counsel of the compensationists and throw the switch from 1 to 2. According to any ethical view that considers individual U' to be of the elect (or relatively so) and U'' to be relatively undeserving of consideration, the good life lies in a rather easterly direction. For ever and ever 'society' is condemned to 'unhappiness' because of the premature decision based on the Kaldor–Hicks–Scitovsky rules.[9]

Production possibilities and group inferences

This completes the problem of making group inferences from simple index-number comparisons. At the non-philosophical level there are still two more grave difficulties to be faced. Up till now I have always spoken of the utility-possibility function of *point A*, not of situation A. But the totals of goods at A or 2 do not fall from heaven in fixed amounts. Obviously other total quantities might instead have been produced. Therefore, the true utility-possibility function corresponding to situation A is really wider and out farther than the one defined for point A. At best, if all markets are perfect and there are no external effects or government distortions, the utility-possibility function for point A may just touch that of situation A at the actual observed point, elsewhere being inside it. The wider schedule is the envelope of a family of schedules corresponding to each *possible* point of total consumption goods. (See Figure 8.)

Obviously it is the wider possibility function of a 'situation' rather than of a 'point' with which we should be concerned, and before we go throwing any switches or making policy decisions we must make sure how alternative production possibilities affect the problem. A few truths continue to remain self-evident, but, generally

9. If both individuals are better off in the observed 2 point than in the observed 1 point, how reasonable it seems to counsel that the switch be pulled. And if the only alternatives were these two situations, almost all old welfare economists might agree. But this need not be our choice of alternatives at all. Realistically, the choice may be between these two points and a third ethically superior point that lies on 1's locus. As a matter of tactics and *realpolitik*, one will sometimes want to follow such simple criteria *and* actually give compensation, or perhaps fail to compensate. But tactics aside, these rules are in principle incomplete.

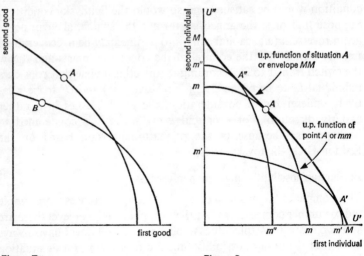

Figure 7   Figure 8

speaking, this new element makes the problem of definite inference even more difficult – an important but sad fact.

Let us consider an example. Up till now the one unshaken truth that remained was this: If more of every good is observed in point A than in point B, then A represents an increase in potential real national income over B. Even this is no longer necessarily valid! Suppose we draw up production-possibility curves showing how much of each good can be produced in total when the total of the other good is specified. Such a chart might look like Figure 6 except that now the two outputs rather than utilities are on the axes. In Figure 7 our observed point A lies north-east of the observed point B, and yet it is obvious that the production-possibility curves can still cross; and it is also obvious, upon reflection, that depending upon how much people like one good as compared to another, the *corresponding utility-possibility curve can most definitely cross* – making no unambiguous inference about an increase in potential real income possible.

So long as commodities are really economic rather than free goods, this much can be said: *If the production-possibility function of one situation lies uniformly outside that of a second situation, then the utility-possibility function of the one will also be outside that of the other*. In the limiting case where one or both individuals do not care at all for one of the goods, the schedules might just be touching at one or more points. Also it is to be understood that if the total of resources (land, labour, etc.) is not the same in the two situations, these resources are to be treated just like negative commodities, and it is in this sense that one production-possibility function must lie uniformly outside the other.

Hicks attempted in 1940 to explore the relationship between index-number criteria based on price–quantity data and productivity as measured by the position of the production-possibility function of society. His treatment was brief and much of it he had abandoned prior to Kuznets's 1948 criticisms. But even after the recent exchange of views I do not feel the subject is left in its proper state. To analyse the problem in its entirety would be too lengthy a task, but a number of observations are relevant to our discussion. In all that follows I shall assume that there are no excise taxes, so that the irrelevant distinction between income-at-factor-prices and income-at-market-prices can be disregarded.

Under this last assumption, would the same $\sum pq$ tests relevant to indicating a (1940-defined) increase in welfare also serve to indicate a shift in productivity? One is almost tempted to read such a belief into the following passage:

If competition were perfect, and if state activities were so designed as not to disturb the *optimum* organization of production, marginal utilities and prices and marginal costs would all be proportional, so that the same valuation which would give us the social income as a measure of economic welfare would also give us the social income as a measure of productivity (Hicks, 1940, p. 122).[10]

Kuznets objected to all this on the ground that production-possibility curves, unlike indifference curves, can intersect and can

10. Hicks goes on to say, parenthetically: 'It would not be very reliable as a measure of productivity, but it might usually satisfy the productivity tests for small displacements, over which the substitution curves might not differ very much from straight lines.' To make the only comparisons between different situations that are valid, this last linearity assumption can be shown to be un-necessary; but it foreshadows Hicks's later desire for an approximate represent-ation of the production-possibility function in the neighbourhood of an observed optimal point. A straight line gives, under the assumed conditions, an upper (rather than a conservative, lower) bound as to what is producible.

be of variable curvature. His instinct that something is rotten in Denmark may be a sound one, but the precise trouble had not really been isolated, nor a worse difficulty brought to light.

In the first place, there is no need for an individual's indifference curves always to be concave: he need only be assumed to be in equilibrium at the observed points. In the second place, it is untrue that collectively defined indifference curves (à la Scitovsky or otherwise) are forbidden to intersect and cross. Our earlier discussion of the points A and F may be referred to in this connection. Neither of these two reasons can serve to isolate the basic difficulties of making production inferences.[11]

In the production or firm field we have an institutional difficulty absent from the household markets: few families act like monopsonists, but many, if not most, firms sell in markets which are less than perfectly competitive. Let us waive this difficulty for the moment and assume that technological and market conditions are most suitable to perfect competition: namely, constant-returns-to-scale prevails and there is 'free entry'. In this case, any observed point of total output – such as A or 2 in Figure 1 – would represent a *maximum* of $\sum p_2 q$ subject to all the production possibilities of the situation. Geometrically the straight line running through A can never be inside the true production-possibility schedule.

Does this mean that the criterion $\sum p_2 q_2 > \sum p_2 q_1$ in Figure 1 assures us of *both* of the following: that 2 is better than 1 *in welfare*, and 2 is better *in a production-possibility sense* than 1? It must *not* be so interpreted. The production problem involves a certain *maximum* condition, the consumption case a related *minimum* condition. The

11. Kuznets has a third objection which has little or nothing to do with the problem here discussed. Working by analogy with the consumption problem, he makes the strange and unnecessary assumption that a perfect price system is in some sense maximizing 'producers' surpluses', and he raises the question whether specificity of some resources may not make it impossible for every producer to be as well off as previously. Both Hicks and I would consider producers and consumers to be the same units, who buy goods and also sell services; all such services can be treated as negative goods and all ordinal disutilities treated along with ordinal utilities. Firms (corporations) provide the place where producers work but themselves have no welfare feelings, although their owners' welfare is important. The problem at hand is what we can or cannot say about the production-possibility functions *of society* in two situations.

same index-number calculation can never serve as a crucial indicator for the two problems: if it is a reliable criterion for welfare, it tells us nothing about production; if it has unambiguous production implications, then welfare inferences are impossible.

There are essentially only four possible cases that have to be considered: a comparison of A and C in Figure 1, of A and D, of A and F, and the almost trivial case of A and B. In this last case, where the A situation has more of every good than the B, we know immediately that the production-possibility function of A lies outside that of B in the neighbourhood of both observed points, and we also know that A's utility-possibility function (defined narrowly for the points rather than broadly for the situations) lies everywhere outside of that of B. All this is obvious, so we can concentrate our attention on the three other possible comparisons. To keep the notation simple we can always give the point A the number 2 and give all other compared points the number 1. Our cases, then, are as follows:

	Concerning 1940 definition of welfare	*Concerning position of production-possibility function ($p.p.f.$)*
Case A (or 2) and C (or 1):		
$\Sigma p_2 q_2 > \Sigma p_2 q_1$ tells us	2 better than 1	nothing
$\Sigma p_1 q_2 > \Sigma p_1 q_1$ tells us	nothing	p.p.f. of 1 inside of p.p.f. of 2 near point 2
Case A (or 2) and D (or 1):		
$\Sigma p_2 q_2 < \Sigma p_2 q_1$ tells us	nothing	p.p.f. of 1 outside of p.p.f. of 2 near point 1
$\Sigma p_1 q_2 > \Sigma p_1 q_1$ tells us	nothing	p.p.f. of 2 outside of p.p.f. of 1 near point 2
Case A (or 2) and F (or 1):		
$\Sigma p_2 q_2 > \Sigma p_2 q_1$ tells us	2 better than 1	nothing
$\Sigma p_1 q_1 > \Sigma p_1 q_2$ tells us	1 better than 2	nothing

Under the present assumptions we can make inferences about the shifting of production-possibility functions that are no less strong than those about welfare. We can never hope to infer from index-number tests that one production-possibility curve has shifted *uniformly* with respect to another – but then we have earlier seen that we can never hope to make such welfare inferences either. It will be noted from the table that where light is thrown on productivity it is withheld from welfare, and vice versa. This might almost seem to offer comfort: we seem always to be able to say *something* about any situation. But, alas, this is an illusion.

The impossibility of unequivocal inferences

Even that which we have in the field of welfare indicators is to be taken away from us now that we have enlarged our alternatives to all the production possibilities of each situation rather than to the single observed points. *We shall never be able to infer a genuine change in potential real income as I have earlier defined the term* – no, not even in the simplest comparison of *A* which shows more of every good than the point *B*. (This was already shown in Figure 7.) Unsatisfactory as the 1940 definitions of welfare were, we are tempted to beat a hasty retreat back to them. But to no good purpose: even these fragile reeds are blown down by the new winds.

Specifically, the observation $\sum p_2 q_2 > \sum p_2 q_1$ no longer implies that the utility-possibility function of *situation* 1 lies inside that of *A* even in the neighbourhood of the point 2, or anywhere at all for that matter! The whole 1940 proof by Hicks – as supplemented in my earlier lengthy footnote concerning the box-diagram – breaks down completely. The demonstration fails, the argument no longer leads logically to the desired conclusion. By itself this does not show that there may not be found some different proof. However, the theorem can be proved to be false, so that no valid alternative proof exists.

A single example provides a decisive exception to the theorem (that we can infer a local shift in the utility-possibility function). The point *F* in Figure 1 has a utility-possibility curve which may be almost anywhere with respect to that of *A*, as far as anything we know. There is no reason why it could not always lie outside of *A*'s; there is also no reason why the point *F* should not lie on *C*'s production-possibility curve; there is also no reason why the utility-possibility function of the general situation *C* should not be close to or identical with the utility-possibility function of the point *F* (except possibly at the observed point *C* itself). It follows that we can easily imagine the utility-possibility function of the situation *C* to lie *above and beyond* the observed point *A* – which contradicts the Hicks-like theorem that situation *C*'s curve must lie somewhere south-west of the *A* point. This example shows that the Hicks's proof remains no longer valid when it ceases to be simply a question of reallocating a given fixed total in the 1 situation.

The interrelation between production and utility-possibility functions

Production possibilities as such have no normative connotations. We are interested in them for the light they throw on utility possibilities. This is why economists have wanted to include such wasteful output as war goods in their calculations of national product; presumably they serve as some kind of an index of the useful things that might be produced in better times. Our last hope to make welfare statements lies in spelling out the welfare implications of any recognizable shifts in production possibilities.

A uniform outward shift in the production-possibility function – such as can never be revealed by index-number comparisons – must certainly shift the utility-possibility schedule outward. The converse is not true. An outward shift in the utility-possibility function may have occurred as the result of a *twist* of the production-possibility curve. This is because people's tastes for different goods may be such that the points on the new production schedule that lie inward may be points that would never be observed in any optimal competitive market. An 'observable' point is one which, as the result of some allocation of initial resources or so-called 'distribution of income', would lead to one of the points on the utility-possibility frontier.

In the typical case where $\sum p_1 q_1 < \sum p_1 q_2$, so that we know that the production-possibility function of 2 is outside of that of 1 somewhere near the observed point 2, we should like to be able to say that 2's utility-possibility function lies outside that of 1 in the neighbourhood of the observed point 2. But we cannot. The utility-possibility functions of situation 2 and of point 2 both lie outside the utility-possibility function of the points which are known to lie south-west of the observed point 2 on the production-possibilities diagram. But all such points might turn out to be non-observable ones. Only if an observable point 2 is known to give more of all goods than an *observable* point of the situation 1 can we even infer that situation 2 is superior to 1 in the weak 1940 sense. Index-number data are never enough to provide us with knowledge of two such observable points except in the trivial case (like *A* and *B*) where one point is better in respect to every good, and where index-number calculations are unnecessary to establish the only fact that can be established: namely, the production-possibility function of A must lie outside that of B near the observed points and the same must be true about the related utility-possibility function.

Under the best conditions of the purest of competition very little indeed of welfare significance can ever be revealed by price–quantity data alone. Needless to say, with the actual statistical problems in a world of imperfect competition and decreasing costs, observed prices have even less significance as indicators of the shape of society's true production-possibility curve.

Political feasibility as a crucial condition in welfare economics

The last limitation on the applicability to policy of the new welfare economics concepts is in practice one of the most important of all. It hinges around the practical unattainability of the production-possibility and utility-possibility function earlier discussed. It is not simply that imperfections of competition are so widespread as to keep society from reaching its optimal production frontier; or that government interferences inevitably cause distortions; or that external diseconomies and economies can never be recognized and computed. All these are true enough.[12]

The essential point now to be stressed is that we could move people to different points on the utility-possibility function only *by an ideally perfect and unattainable system of absolutely lump-sum taxes or subsidies*. In point of fact, suppose that, in the simplest case, competitive *laissez-faire* puts us at one point on the utility-possibility function. Then we can only seek to change the distribution of income by a system of *feasible* legislation: e.g. progressive income tax,

12. They can be thought of as forces keeping us from reaching the true possibility frontier; or, if we are in a non-perfectionist mood and willing to compromise with evil, they may be thought of as defining a not-so-far-out but pragmatically obtainable frontier. If the latter interpretation is made, we must be careful to realize that the slopes of the defined frontiers need have little correspondence with market prices, marginal costs of production, etc. As I have earlier pointed out (1948, p. 221), the constraints under which society is conceived as working are arbitrary and must be given by non-economic assumptions. England's production possibilities would be different if the laws of physics could be disregarded or if we could assume that all workers would do their 'best', ...

rationing, etc. All such policies involve a distortion of marginal decisions, some involving great distortions but in every case some distortion. They move us then *inside* the utility-possibility curve. We can pick policies which strive to minimize the harmful effects of redistribution, but in practice we cannot reduce such effects to zero. A 'feasible utility function' can conceptually be drawn up which lies more or less far inside the utility-possibility function, depending upon how Utopian were our assumptions about legislation, public opinion, etc.

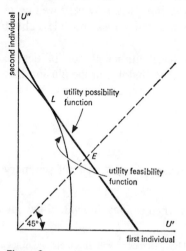

Figure 9

All this is shown in Figure 9. The point L represents the imputation resulting from a situation of relatively *laissez-faire*. It is made to lie on the heavy-line utility-possibility function – which it would only do in a very perfect competitive world.

Let us suppose that the tastes and abilities of the two individuals are identical so that we can use similar indicators of their ordinal preferences. But let them differ in their ownership of resources (say land) so that the income of U'' is much greater than that of U', as indicated by the position of L relative to the 45° line of 'equal income'. In a Utopia there might be some way of redistributing wealth or income that would move us along the outside curve from L to the point of complete equality, E, or even beyond. But in practice the only feasible path that Congress or Parliament could follow would be along the light-line utility-feasibility curve.[13]

Space does not permit me to work out the far-reaching implications of this point of view. It is enough to point out here that situation A may have a uniformly better production-possibility function than B, and also a uniformly better utility-possibility function. But a change from B to A might so alter the distribution of market-imputed income away from the 'worthy' and towards the 'unworthy' as to make it an undesirable move from many ethical viewpoints. The *utility-feasibility function* of A may very well cross that of B, so that no statement about potentialities, much less about actualities, can be validly made.

By all means let us pray that feasibilities and possibilities be brought closer and closer. But let us not indulge in the illusion that our prayers have been answered and that we can issue new-welfare-economics prescriptions accordingly.[14]

Final summary

This has been a long and closely reasoned essay. A brief summary may pull the threads together.

1. Certain $\sum pq$ calculations tell us when a single individual has improved himself.

13. A strong ethical equalitarian would have to reckon with this fact; and unless his social welfare functions had complete L-shaped corners along the 45° line, or even bent back *à la* Veblen and like the dog-in-the-manger, he would find his feasible optimum at some distance from equality of incomes. All this has a bearing, I believe, on the debate between Meade and Kahn as to whether rationing and food subsidies ought necessarily to be rejected by rational equalitarians in favour of greater reliance on income taxes or other more orthodox devices.

14. A few comments on the cited Little article (1949) are perhaps in order. There is much I agree with in this paper, and much I do not yet understand. His semantic jousts with the post-Kaldor school falls under the first heading; his analysis of the meaning of a *social or economic welfare function* under the second. The part of his paper that is most relevant to the present technical discussion is his proposed 'foundations' for a 'system' of welfare economics. In my present understanding of it – still admittedly vague – Little has stated a few theorems of one type. These are understandable in terms of the language of a welfare function, and are more in the nature of one arch or wing of a structure than its foundations.

2. The only consistent and ethics-free definition of an increase in potential real income of a group is that based upon a uniform shift of the utility-possibility function for the group. $\sum pq$ calculations based on aggregate data never permit us to make such inferences about uniform shifts.

3. The condition $\sum p_2 q_2 > \sum p_2 q_1$ does tell us that the utility-possibility function of the *point* 2 is outside the utility-possibility function of the *point* 1 somewhere near 2. It is not acceptable to define this as an increase in real income for a number of reasons, not the least being that we may end up with 2 defined to be both 'better' and 'worse' than 1.

4. Scitovsky and later Kuznets have suggested a partial strengthening of the earlier definitions of superiority so as to rule out certain revealed inconsistencies. But even these two-sided requirements are not stringent enough; when made infinite-sided, as they must be to avoid inconsistency or implicit ethics, they become equivalent to the definition based upon a uniform shift of the utility-possibility schedule. And even when this rigid definition is realized, we cannot properly prescribe complete policy prescriptions without bringing in ethics.

5. When we come to make inferences about two *situations*, each of which involves a whole *set* of production possibilities rather than about just the observed *points*, even the limited welfare inferences of point 3 break down completely. Under the most perfect conditions suitable for pure competition (where the production-possibility curve can never be concave) a few inferences concerning the local shifts of the production-possibility schedules are possible: e.g. $\sum p_2 q_2 < \sum p_2 q_1$ implies that 1's production-possibility function is outside 2's in the neighbourhood of the observed 2 point.

6. The inferred shifts of production-possibility functions are not enough to permit similar inferences about the utility-possibility functions. This is because that portion of a production-possibility curve which has clearly been revealed to be inside another or 'inferior' may (for all we know) consist entirely of 'unobservable points' that have no correspondence with the truly observable points along the related utility-possibility frontier.

7. The utility-possibility functions defined above are not really possible or available to society; they would be so only in a Utopian world of 'perfect' lump-sum taxes and other ideal conditions. Depending upon how optimistic our assumptions are, we must think of society as being contained within a *utility-feasibility function* which lies inside the *utility-possibility function*. At best these are close together in the neighbourhood of the 'points of relative *laissez-faire*'. Other things being equal, redistribution of income will usually involve 'costs', which have to be weighed against the ethically defined 'advantages' of such policies.

8. All this being true, we come to the paradoxical conclusion that a policy which seems to make possible greater production of all goods and a uniformly better utility-possibility function for society may result in so great (and ethically undesirable) a change in the imputation of different individuals' incomes, that we may have to judge such a policy 'bad'. Such a judgement sounds as if it necessarily involves ethics, but it may be reworded so as to be relatively free of value judgements by being given the following interpretation: A policy that shifts society's utility-possibility function uniformly outward may not at the same time shift the utility-feasibility function uniformly outward, instead causing it to twist inward in some places. One last warning is in order: to define what is feasible involves many arbitrary assumptions, some of them of an ethical nature.[15]

15. An appendix to this paper has been deleted here. [Ed].

References

HICKS, J. R. (1939), 'Foundations of welfare economics', *econ. J.*, vol. 49, pp. 696–712.

HICKS, J. R. (1940), 'The valuation of the social income', *Economica*, May, pp. 105–24.

HICKS, J. R. (1948), 'The valuation of the social income – a comment on Professor Kuznets' reflections', *Economica*, August, pp. 163–72.

KALDOR, N. (1939), 'Welfare propositions in economics', *econ. J.*, vol. 49, pp. 549–52.

KUZNETS, S. (1948), 'On the valuation of social income – reflections on Professor Hicks' article', *Economica*, February, pp. 1–16, and May, pp. 116–31.

LITTLE, I. M. D. (1949a), 'The valuation of the social income', *Economica*, February, pp. 11–26, and addendum, 'A note on the significance of index numbers'.

LITTLE, I. M. D. (1949b), 'The foundations of welfare economics', *Oxford econ. Papers*, June.

PIGOU, A. C. (1932), *Economics of Welfare*, part 1, 4th edn,Macmillan.

SAMUELSON, P. A. (1948), *Foundations of Economic Analysis*, Harvard University Press.

SCITOVSKY, T. (1941), 'A note on welfare propositions in economics', *Rev. econ. Stud.*, pp. 77–88.

SCITOVSKY, T. (1942), 'A reconsideration of the theory of tariffs', *Rev. econ. Stud.*, pp. 89–110.

3 J. de V. Graaff

Some Elements of Welfare Economics

J. de V. Graaff, excerpts from *Theoretical Welfare Economics*, Cambridge University Press, 1957.

The welfare frontier

Consider for geometrical simplicity a community of but two people, Alpha and Beta. Their utility indicators, u^a and u^β, we shall write a and β for short. No special significance attaches to the particular indexes selected; but, once adopted, they must be adhered to without change.

Let us fix β at some arbitrary level, say β_0, and make Alpha as well off as is possible under the circumstances. Just how great a value a will be able to attain will depend upon (1) the value β_0; (2) the supply of goods and services available to the community; and (3) the possibility of transforming goods and services of one kind into goods of another kind. This transformation can be performed in factories at home, or by trade with communities abroad – but we abstract from foreign trade for the present. The utility and social transformation functions therefore effectively summarize items (2) and (3). They determine a unique maximum value of a, say a_0, corresponding to β_0.

If we fix β at some other level, we shall obtain another level of a. Proceeding in this way, we can map out a locus in the $a\beta$ plane. We shall call it the community's *welfare frontier*. It has been independently introduced to welfare theory by Allais (1943) and by Samuelson (1947), who calls it the 'utility-possibility function'[1] – just as a production frontier is sometimes called a 'production-possibility function'. Let us set out its properties:

1. In my paper (1949–50), I used the term 'possibility locus'. I now think, however, that 'welfare frontier' is more appropriate.

1. In the general multi-person community of any size, the welfare frontier tells us the maximum level of well-being any one man can enjoy, given the levels enjoyed by the remaining members of the community. It represents society's *welfare potential*, just as the social production frontier represents its productive potential. Its significance hinges on the fact that, while no point outside it is attainable by society with the existing 'state of the arts', no point lying inside it can ever represent a maximum of social welfare in terms of any Pareto W. For to any interior point (like C in Figure 1a) there necessarily corresponds a better point (like R) on the frontier (labelled PP). It is 'better' in terms of any Pareto W, since both Alpha and Beta are better off.

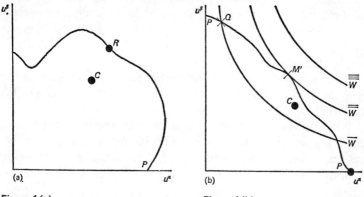

Figure 1 (a)   Figure 1 (b)

2. If, as in Figure 1b, we sketch in the contours of some Paretian functions, $W(u^a, u^\beta)$, we can find the point (or points) in which the highest level of social welfare is attained. This is the point M' in Figure 1b. In terms of the classical Cambridge W (which regards social welfare as the sum of the cardinal utilities of the members of the community), M' is the point at which the 'marginal utility of income' is the same for both Alpha and Beta.

3. The shape, curvature and position of the welfare frontier depend upon the particular indexes selected to represent individual levels of well-being – for convenience it has been drawn in the north-east quadrant in Figure 1b. But the *direction of slope* is invariant. It will

'normally' slope downwards: Alpha can be made better off only at Beta's expense. 'Occasionally', however, it may slope upwards. Three cases deserve especial notice:

(a) The first is where the social transformation function depends markedly upon the distribution of wealth. If workers are underfed, a redistribution of wealth in their favour may so increase efficiency that everybody benefits. In such cases the frontier will slope upwards. One might suppose, on crude empirical grounds, that this is likely only when there is *extreme* inequality in the distribution of wealth.

(b) External effects in consumption can bring about the same result. There is no need for them to be excessive. Consider first a two-person community. External economies in consumption may be so marked and asymmetrical that a transfer of goods from Alpha to Beta increases the welfare of each. In a genuine two-person community one would expect such situations to be unstable, Alpha simply making Beta a gift. In a larger community, however, stability might plausibly be assumed.

(c) In a larger community, moreover, external *dis*economies can give the frontier an upward slope. Demonstration of this can be left for a footnote.[2]

When the frontier slopes upwards over a certain range there is not perfect symmetry in its definition. This is clear from Figure 1a. We get one result when we choose to hold α constant, and maximize β; another when we reverse the procedure. The first will give β as a

2. Consider a community comprising Alpha, Beta and Gamma. Assume that Alpha's welfare is uninfluenced by the goods possessed by either Beta or Gamma, and that they in turn are uninfluenced by Alpha's possessions. But assume, too, that marked external diseconomies exist between Beta and Gamma. Then, if we are interested in the slope of the frontier in the $\alpha\beta$ plane, we must examine the rate at which β changes when α is diminished slightly by a transfer of goods from Alpha to Beta, when γ (Gamma's utility indicator) is kept constant. But the increase in Beta's possessions makes Gamma worse off, so to keep γ constant it is necessary to transfer some to Gamma. This, however, makes Beta worse off on two scores: firstly, because the goods are taken from him, and, secondly, because Gamma's increase. It is easy to construct examples along these lines in which the original small decrease in α causes β to decrease too, γ being kept constant – i.e. where the frontier slopes upwards in the $\alpha\beta$ plane. The marked external diseconomies we assumed to exist between Beta and Gamma can secure this result in spite of the fact that after the decrease in α they both possess (in physical terms) more wealth than before.

single-valued function of a; the second a as a single-valued function of β. The complete frontier is obtained by combining the two (i.e. by holding each constant in turn) to obtain what will in general be a multi-valued function of a, β, or both.

The importance of the direction of slope of the frontier is considerable, for (if we confine ourselves to Pareto W's) we can rule out those parts which slope upwards as positions of maximum welfare. When it slopes upwards we can make everybody better off. In a sense, therefore, we can speak of the (possibly discontinuous) downward-sloping section as the 'true' welfare frontier; and we can also speak of a sense in which the distribution of real income is 'not optimal' on upward-sloping sections of the frontier.

4. Any point on a downward-sloping portion of the frontier represents a Paretian *maximum d'utilité collective* – or, put in our own terminology, is a potential optimum in terms of a Pareto W. Barring excessive external effects in consumption, therefore, *all the familiar marginal equivalences of the general optimum must be satisfied* at any point on a downward-sloping section.

Moreover, although the reasoning is less straightforward, they must hold on upward-sloping sections too. This is most easily seen by glancing at the appendix. The length of a verbal demonstration seems to be out of proportion to the importance of the result. It happens that the same marginal conditions are entailed if (a) we fix the levels of well-being of all men but one, and make the remaining man as well off as possible, or (b) we look for positions in which it is impossible to make any one man better off without making at least one other worse off. The first procedure leads us to the 'complete' welfare frontier; the second to the 'true' one, which (though possibly discontinuous) slopes downwards everywhere.

5. To move on to the welfare frontier, therefore, it is necessary to secure the satisfaction of the marginal equivalences of the general optimum. How are movements *along* the frontier secured? Clearly, they are secured by redistributions of wealth which do not destroy the marginal equivalences. Such redistributions we shall call *lump sum*.

6. What happens to the collection of goods produced by society's transformation process as we move along the welfare frontier? Generally speaking, it will change. If we consider a different point, there will usually correspond a different collection of goods.

Let us start from a point like M', and fix the collection of goods. Let us redistribute these goods among the members of the community by lump-sum measures. What happens? A new welfare frontier (corresponding to the fixed collection of goods) is traced out. It cannot lie outside the 'proper' one, PP, as that represents the best we can do when we take into account the possibilities of transforming goods and services of one kind into goods of another (and preferred) kind. It must, therefore, lie wholly inside PP, touching it in M' (and perhaps elsewhere). If we shift our starting-point on PP from M' to some other point, and again fix the collection of goods, we can trace out another welfare frontier, also lying wholly within PP, by lump-sum redistributions. These *exchange–economy* welfare frontiers – as we shall call those traced out by lump-sum redistributions of various fixed collections of goods – are infinitely many. Their *outer limit* (or envelope) is the 'proper' frontier, or *production–economy* welfare frontier, drawn with reference to the production possibilities open to society, and not just for a given collection of goods.

Potential benefit[3]

A movement from a point like C inside the welfare frontier to one like Q on it does not necessarily represent an increase in welfare (Figure 1b). There is no reason why Q should not lie on a lower welfare contour than C. But we can (and shall) say that Q is *potentially* better than C, for there necessarily exists a point on the frontier (like R in Figure 1a) in which both Alpha and Beta are better off and to which a mere redistribution of wealth can lead us.

Similarly, if we confine ourselves to positions actually on the welfare-frontier – the more general situation is discussed in the next chapter – we can define the *potential desirability* of a change such as might result from technological 'progress' or some other movement of the social production function. There are two distinct possibilities: (1) on the one hand, the new welfare frontier may lie wholly inside, or wholly outside, the old one. Such a movement we shall refer to as a *shift*. It is illustrated by $P_1' P_1''$ in Figure 2, which lies wholly outside $P_0' P_0''$. Any position on the new frontier is clearly at least potentially superior to any position on the old one. Thus the technological

3. Cf. Samuelson (1947), pp. 250–2, to which I am heavily indebted.

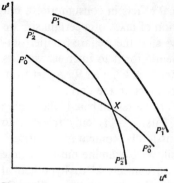

Figure 2

'progress' can be said to be at least potentially beneficial; (2) on the other hand, the new frontier may intersect the old one. This is represented by $P_2' P_2''$ in Figure 2, where the intersection is in X. We shall refer to it as a *twist*. All that can be said is that the situations on $P_2 X$ are at least potentially superior to those on $P_0'' X$; and that those on $P_0 X$ are at least potentially superior to those on $P_2 X$. We cannot say that the technological 'progress' is even potentially beneficial until we are given some criterion on the basis of which we can judge between situations on $P_2' X$ and those on $P_0'' X$ – some criterion for making interpersonal comparisons of well-being. In this simple case a very simple criterion – a very incompletely defined W – is sufficient: we only need to compare two broad and distinct distributions of welfare ($P_2' X$ and $P_0'' X$). In the general case, however, we should probably required a well-defined W to be able to discriminate: there is no reason why the frontiers should not intersect infinitely often. But, when we have a well-defined W, we can examine quite directly the desirability of any change – we need not rest content with statements about *potentialities*. It is important to note this point.

The essential indeterminacy which, in the absence of a well-defined W, arises whenever the frontier twists, seems at first sight to make the whole concept a rather clumsy one. To a certain extent this is true. It is not easy to find instances of unambiguous shifts in a welfare frontier. A uniform shift in the social production frontier will naturally translate itself into a similar movement of the welfare one (unless we have excessive external effects in consumption), but that is not very helpful. The imposition of taxes of a certain size on both imports and exports will always shift the welfare frontier outwards, and can never twist it sufficiently for it to intersect with its former position (see source of this Reading, Chapter 9). Apart from these examples, however, we are very much in the dark.

Moreover, there are several points to be remembered when using the concept of 'potential benefit'. Firstly, it is only relevant to Pareto Ws. Secondly, the whole discussion is 'comparative statical'. The change whose potential desirability we examine must not take place through time. We compare two conjectural or hypothetical situations at a given moment of time. Thirdly, we can really only apply the concept to changes which operate through production (or foreign trade) – it could yield no results if we were to discuss, for example, problems relating to the 'optimum population', for when the population changes, our standards of reference (individual tastes) change too. Finally, we must assume throughout that the time horizon and the terminal capital equipment are somehow given.

In the last section we discussed the 'potential desirability' of changes of two types. Firstly, those where we start from a position inside the welfare frontier, and move on to it, and secondly, those where we move from a position on one welfare frontier to a position on another. It is certain that only a few of the changes in which we are likely to be interested will fit into either of these categories. In general, we want to be able to say something about the potential desirability of changes which lead from a position inside one welfare frontier to a position inside another – or to another position inside the same frontier. We want to be able to compare sub-optimal situations.

The efficiency locus

Why do we want to be able to compare sub-optimal situations? Because it is, in the world about us, extraordinarily hard for a society to attain its welfare frontier. If external effects did not exist, if the production frontier were independent of the distribution of wealth, and if the relative curvature of the transformation and indifference curves were 'right', full competitive equilibrium might see it there – although there is no guarantee that it would unless we rule out the possibility of multiple equilibria. But, however favourable the circumstances and thoroughgoing the competition, full equilibrium is seldom attained. Moreover, the corrective taxes required whenever external effects do exist, or the relative curvature is 'wrong', are likely to be so exceedingly complicated that nothing better than the crudest approximations could be hoped for in practice. The same can be said of whatever corrective devices an enthusiast might succeed in inventing to allow for the dependence of the transformation functions on the distribution of wealth. In practice, therefore, it is probable that a society will find itself well within the frontier. Sub-optimal situations will usually be the only *feasible* ones.

Consider a point inside the welfare frontier whose co-ordinates represent the levels of well-being actually enjoyed by the various members of a community. A redistribution of wealth by lump-sum taxes and bounties (which are assumed to cost nothing to collect or distribute) will normally move society to another point within the frontier. The locus of all points traced out by redistributions of this kind we shall call the *efficiency locus*, because it depicts the allocative efficiency of an economy for various distributions of welfare.[4] Optimum allocative efficiency, for a particular distribution of welfare, is not attained unless the efficiency locus coincides with the welfare frontier in the point corresponding to that distribution.

It might be better to call the efficiency locus an 'actuality locus', since it always passes through the point where society actually is, and joins those to which it would actually be led by lump-sum redistributions. This would contrast suitably with the (usually unrealized) potentialities of the welfare frontier. But the idea of the allocative efficiency of an economy is an important one, and the term 'efficiency locus' serves to remind us of it.

It is perhaps most helpful to think of the relationship between the welfare frontier (or utility-possibility locus) and the efficiency locus in the following way. The welfare frontier shows the best we can do, given tastes and techniques, in an institutional vacuum. The efficiency locus shows the best we can do if we take the existing institutional set-up as a datum. It describes the result of

4. By a 'distribution of welfare' is meant no more than a 'point in utility-space' – or, thinking of a two-person community, a 'point in the $\alpha\beta$ plane'.

distributional changes (by lump-sum measures) within that frame-work. This must not be interpreted too literally, however, for it is at least conceivable that institutional changes (in a more ordinary sense of the term) will accompany the lump-sum redistributions which move us from one part of an efficiency locus to another. Industries, cartels, trade unions, forms of market organization – these and others will come and go as the redistributions shift the pattern of demand. Moreover, it is not altogether obvious that such institutional changes (again in an ordinary sense of the term) would be reversible. If a great redistribution causes social revolution, so that factories and forests are razed to the ground, a restoration of the original distribu-tion would not restore overnight the productive apparatus of society.

But the fact that movements along an efficiency locus may be irreversible is of little consequence. In any actual situation society will find itself in a particular position on the locus. Under certain circumstances it may be faced with a choice between remaining there and moving to another position on the locus. It is, generally speaking, a once-for-all change that is in question. Whether or not continuing to-and-fro movements can occur without changing the institutional set-up (and thus the locus itself) is largely irrelevant. The locus is defined by hypothetical lump-sum redistributions within the existing set-up at a given moment of time, not by a succession of redistributions through time. The observing economist is assumed to know the points to which they would lead. Any one of these points is attainable by making the appropriate redistribution; but they need not all be attainable in rapid succession.

The feasibility locus

These considerations have an important bearing on Professor Samuelson's view that lump-sum redistributions of wealth are im-practicable (1947, pp. 247–8). In any modern society redistributions are made by altering the existing tax-structure, by rationing or by some other means which *would* affect the marginal equivalences of the General Optimum – that is, by measures which are *not* lump-sum. Income-taxes, for instance, clearly destroy the marginal equivalences, often rather vividly. Assume that a man is working up to the point at which his marginal physical product in terms of some numéraire (we shall call it his 'wage') is just sufficient to compensate him for his extra effort. This is one of the familiar equivalences of the General Optimum. Now let a tax on income be imposed. He will work up to the point at which his 'wage' *net of tax* is just sufficient to compensate for the extra effort. The General Optimum is destroyed – the social rate of indifference between rendering more of the productive service and consuming more of the product is no longer equal to the technological social rate at which the service can be transformed into the product at the margin. To be truly lump-sum a tax must bear no relation whatsoever to a man's effort or earnings. Or, more strictly, no man must anticipate that the tax he is to pay will bear any relation to his effort or earnings. Once imposed, it may cause him to work and earn either more or less; the size of the tax may affect the amount of effort forthcoming, but it must not be affected by it.

It is clear that truly lump-sum measures are extraordinarily hard to devise. A poll-tax, of course, meets all the requirements; but it is not very helpful in securing desired redistributions unless we tax different men differently. But on what criteria should we discriminate between different men? Ethical ones? And what if a man cannot pay the tax? If we start taxing the poor less than the rich, we are simply reintroducing an income-tax. If we tax able men more than dunderheads, we open the door to all forms of falsification: we make stupidity seem profitable – and any able man can make himself seem stupid. Unless we really do have an omniscient observing economist to judge men's capabilities, or a slave-market where the prices they fetch reflect expert appraisals of their capacities, any taxing authority is bound to be guided by elementary visible criteria like age, marital status and – above all – ability to pay. We are back with an income-tax.

This, I think, states fairly the case against the practicability of lump-sum redistributions. With it one can only agree. But it is still possible to argue that once-for-all redistributions can be achieved by lump-sum measures. It is only when we think in terms of a continuing process that they appear quite hopeless. Quite often, however, it seems that we have to think in terms of a continuing process; and then the efficiency locus loses much of its relevance. Let us take an example.

Consider a change which moves the efficiency locus. It will lead from a point on the 'old' locus to a point on the 'new' one, and may result in a distribution of welfare of which we do not approve. Suitable lump-sum taxes and bounties can be imposed to 'correct' this unfavourable redistribution, penalizing those who have gained 'too much' and compensating those who have lost 'too heavily'. Such a correction is a clear-cut once-for-all measure. The efficiency locus is a useful tool for discussing the potential desirability of the original change. But if we consider a succession of such changes and a succession of corrective redistributions, the matter becomes more delicate. It is all too probable that the criteria on which the penalties and compensations (or taxes and bounties) are calculated will become known to the members of the community. If they discover these criteria – or come to think they have discovered them – they will suit their actions to them. If the losers by a change always seem to be compensated, and the gainers penalized (though not necessarily to the full extent of their loss or gain), it will be profitable to pretend that you have gained less, or lost more, than in fact you have. If the poor are compensated at the expense of the rich, it will be profitable to simulate a measure of poverty. But, falsification apart, the important thing is that incentives will be affected (see Pigou, 1932, part 4, chapters 9 and 10). There will result a locus different from that which would obtain in the absence of such anticipatory behaviour. In other words, the 'lump-sum' taxes and bounties will no longer be truly lump-sum. They will affect our marginal equivalences, much as income-taxes would. When we think in terms of a sequence of changes, each one of which is accompanied by a corrective redistribution, the efficiency locus may cease to be a useful concept.

Whether we think in terms of a once-for-all redistribution or a continuing process will therefore determine whether we judge the potential desirability of a change with reference to the efficiency locus or what Professor Samuelson calls the *feasibility locus* (Samuelson, 1950, pp. 18–19). The feasibility locus tells us how well off it is politically *feasible* to make any one man, given the levels of well-being enjoyed by the others. It does not necessarily take the existing institutional set-up as a datum, and movements along it are not secured by imposing lump-sum measures. We move along it by whatever means are for the moment regarded as feasible, changing the institutional set-up as we go.

Through any point on a feasibility locus there passes an efficiency locus indicating the results of hypothetical lump-sum redistributions in the institutional environment corresponding to that point. We know that if we move along the feasibility locus as a result of a change involving something more than a mere lump-sum redistribution, we move from a point on one efficiency locus to a point on another. That is to say, the efficiency locus itself moves. But we can never be certain whether we have moved to a different point on the old feasibility locus, or to a point on a new one. We cannot be certain whether the feasibility locus has moved too until we know whether the change in question has affected the notion of political feasibility entertained. This seems to make the feasibility locus rather an awkward tool.

Indeed, the whole concept of political feasibility is itself so flexible that there is not much point in retaining the feasibility locus as a tool of analysis. Its introduction does serve to emphasize that a long series of lump-sum redistributional changes may be impracticable; but, once that has been grasped, we can afford to dispense with it. There is, however, a slightly different context in which the idea of feasibility can be quite helpful. Let us turn to it.

Figure 3 illustrates the case – and, incidentally, also sums up the relationship between the three loci: utility-possibility (i.e. welfare frontier), efficiency, and feasibility. Society finds itself in C. Through that point both the efficiency locus, *EE*, and the feasibility locus,

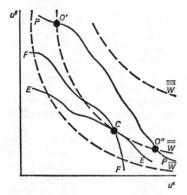

Figure 3

FF, must pass; but we can say little else about them except that they can never pass beyond the welfare frontier, or utility-possibility locus, *PP*. The *W* curves are social welfare contours. They indicate that welfare is higher in the 'sub-optimal' point *C* than in all points on the frontier, except those lying between *Q'* and *Q"*. Now if for some reason it is not feasible to attain the frontier between *Q'* and *Q"* – using 'feasible' in some broad and essentially arbitrary sense – we have a vague rationalization of the fact that society is at *C*, and not on the frontier. It is only vague, of course, because we have not ruled out the feasibility of approaching the frontier more closely than *C*; but that is easily remedied.

The rationing of common necessities in times of scarcity seems to provide a good example. Assume that, in the absence of rationing, society would be on its welfare frontier, but that the great scarcity of necessities entails a very 'unfavourable' distribution of welfare: the rich bid up the prices of the scarce goods to such an extent that the poor cannot buy enough to sustain life, even when they spend the whole of their incomes on them. A redistribution of wealth could lead to a more favourable position on the frontier. But it may have to be a somewhat far-reaching redistribution; and, especially if the extreme scarcity is thought to be a transient affair, it may not be regarded as practicable. Temporary rationing may be a better alternative, even if it does distort the allocative efficiency of the economy by destroying the marginal equivalences which characterize the frontier.[5]

5. Note that we started by assuming that society would be on the frontier in the absence of rationing. Baumol has correctly pointed out that such an assumption may obscure one of the most interesting aspects of many rationing schemes – viz. that they are introduced because external effects in consumption suddenly become very marked in times of scarcity. The appeal of an 'equal shares for all' slogan provides an obvious example. It might therefore be more realistic to argue that the imposition of rationing, far from destroying the marginal equivalences of the General Optimum, actually leads (when we take account of external effects) to a closer approach to the frontier (see Baumol, 1949, p. 166).

The methods devised by Rothbarth, Kaldor, Nicholson and the present writer for measuring the change in real income caused by the introduction of rationing all ignore external effects in consumption, and are valid only if their absence can be assumed. This limits their usefulness greatly. For a survey of the methods see Graaff (1947–8), pp. 91–5. When writing this paper I was unaware of the probable importance of Baumol's argument.

The word 'temporary' should be emphasized. Elsewhere (Graaff, 1948, pp. 35–50) I have argued that consumer rationing becomes less and less effective the longer it is kept in operation, unless it is buttressed by direct controls over the organization of production. (This is simply because rationing diverts expenditure to unrationed goods, and will, in the long run, tend to divert scarce factors of production to the industries producing them – and away from the industries where they are more urgently required.) The argument can be phrased in terms of the efficiency locus, or the point C in Figure 3, drifting inwards with the passage of time and the diversion of resources to the production of less wanted goods. Eventually C will drop below the welfare contour demarcating the section of the welfare frontier regarded as infeasible of attainment. Then the time for the removal of rationing has come. In general, of course, PP in Figure 3 need not be the true welfare frontier. It can be the efficiency locus corresponding to the institutional set-up obtaining when rationing is relaxed, in whole or in part.

Potential benefit

When, as in our discussion of rationing, we make explicit use of a particular welfare function, we can speak quite directly of the desirability of a change. But when we want our conclusions to have greater generality, we must speak more circumspectly. In the last chapter we defined the 'potential desirability' of a change in terms which are valid for all Pareto Ws – that is, without making any interpersonal comparisons of well-being. But our treatment was handicapped by the fact that we only had the welfare frontier at our disposal. It can only be applied to economies which are optimally organized. Now that we have a more general piece of apparatus in the efficiency locus (we shall not bother about the feasibility locus too), it is instructive to cover the ground once again.

Technological 'progress', or a change of some other kind, is likely to affect both the welfare frontier and the efficiency locus. It may shift one and twist[6] the other, or affect both in the same way. There are, in fact, nine different combinations to consider: any one

6. The reader will recall that 'twist' and 'shift' are not used synonymously with 'rotation' and 'translation'. The characteristic of a twist is simply the intersection of the old and new loci.

of the three different types of movement (inward shift, outward shift, twist) of the frontier can be associated with any one of the three different types of movement of the efficiency locus. For instance, an invention which shifts the frontier outwards may confer on the innovators monopoly power so great that the efficiency locus is given a twist, or even shifted inwards.

The question therefore arises: to which locus (or frontier) should we refer in judging the potential desirability of a particular change? The answer, I think, depends upon the context. If we regard the institutional framework inherited by society as malleable and subject to extensive alteration at will, the welfare frontier is attainable and therefore relevant. If, however, we are prepared (for the purposes in hand) to take the existing institutional set-up as a datum, and examine particular changes within the framework it provides, the efficiency locus becomes relevant. The same holds when we are not prepared to 'accept' (in an approbatory sense) the institutions which exist, if we feel that there is but little chance of altering them in a way which would lead towards the frontier.

In any event, a change will lead from a point on one efficiency locus to a point on another. Its potential desirability should normally be judged on that basis. Then we can consider the further question of altering institutions in a way which will improve the allocative efficiency of the economy so as to make the efficiency locus approach closer to the frontier. Such an improvement is always at least potentially beneficial. But it cannot be taken for granted. Its achievement is a matter quite distinct from the potential desirability of the original change. Thus an invention which shifts the efficiency locus inwards should normally be regarded as potentially harmful, even if it shifts the frontier outwards. But it may well be that the same invention *plus* a vigorous trust-busting campaign would shift the locus outwards. In that case the invention *plus* the trust-busting, as opposed to the invention alone, is to be judged at least potentially beneficial. This would be true even if the invention were to involve an inward shift of the frontier – although, in the latter eventuality, it might be thought that the trust-busting without the invention would be potentially even more beneficial. This would not necessarily be correct, however, as the success of a given trust-busting campaign might not be altogether independent of the invention.

It must not be inferred from the preceding argument that 'trust-busting' is in fact likely to cause an outward shift of the efficiency locus. It is, in the absence of an omniscient observing economist, almost impossible to say how trust-busting or anything else will affect it. For instance, in a world innocent of external effects and all the other embarrassing complications which require corrections even in a perfectly competitive economy, it cannot be said that the elimination of monopoly in a particular industry will shift the efficiency locus uniformly outwards. It cannot even be said that it will shift it outwards in the neighbourhood of the relevant point. It can be said that the elimination of monopoly *in all industries simultaneously* will perform this feat, but that is rather different – and not very helpful.

Is the efficiency locus then a tool worth introducing? It seems that it is. It provides us with a useful means for analysing the various 'compensation tests' which have been used by different writers in the last decade. The tests in their turn can be regarded as tackling part at least of the problem of determining movements in the locus.

Compensation tests

The compensation tests all spring from a desire to see what can be said about social welfare or 'real national income' (the difference may be important) without making interpersonal comparisons of well-being – or, in the case of one variant, without making *detailed* interpersonal comparisons. They have a common origin in Pareto's definition of an increase in social welfare – that at least one man must be better off and no one worse off – but they are extended to situations in which some people are made worse off. It is here that the possibility of compensation becomes relevant.

Let us consider a two-person community for simplicity – the method of reasoning is quite general. Let us assume that, where compensations are involved, they can be made by lump-sum measures, so that the efficiency locus is the tool to use. We shall, however, simply speak of 'the locus', so that the reader who is sceptical of their practicability can think in terms of a feasibility locus (if he can define 'feasibility' to his own satisfaction).[7] We

7. Thus Reder does not confine compensations to those attainable by lump-sum measures. He says that 'a compensating tax may be any kind of tax whatever' (Reder (1947), p. 16 n).

could, of course, use the welfare frontier instead of the locus; but then we should have to confine ourselves to optimally organized environments. Most of the compensation theorists seem to intend their tests to have greater generality.[8]

1. It is instructive to start with Pareto's definition, where no compensation is involved. An increase in social welfare is defined as a movement to the north-east (strictly: northwards, eastwards or in any intermediate direction) on either of the diagrams which follow, like that from Q_1 to Q_2 in Figure 4.

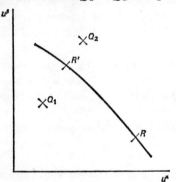

Figure 4

2. In 1939 Kaldor suggested what is in effect a simple extension of (1) as a definition of an increase in 'physical productivity' or 'aggregate real income'. If, in Figure 4, we move from Q_1 to R, and the locus through R passes north-east of Q_1 (i.e. 'outside' Q_1), the gainer by the change can profitably compensate the loser. This, it was suggested, enables us to say that 'real income' is greater in R than in Q_1.

3. In 1940 Hicks[9] used the reverse test for an increase in 'real social

8. The Hicks test described in (3) below was in effect proposed with reference to an exchange-economy welfare frontier (i.e. to redistributions of a fixed collection of goods). But from a production-economy viewpoint this is no more than an efficiency locus touching the true frontier in the point or points where the fixed collection of goods is an optimal collection.

9. In his *Studies in the Theory of Welfare Economics* (1947), Reder does not distinguish between the Kaldor test (which uses the *status quo ante* as the base) and the Hicks one (which uses the *status quo post*).

income'. If we move from Q_2 to R in Figure 4, we see that the locus through R passes inside Q_2. That is to say: the gainer by the change is unable to compensate the loser and remain a gainer. This, it was suggested, enables us to say that 'social income' was greater in Q_2 than in R; or that it would be increased by moving from R to Q_2. Note that this is not the same as the Kaldor test. For Q_2 to be 'better' than R on the basis of the Kaldor test it would be necessary for the locus through Q_2 to pass outside R. But we know nothing about the locus through Q_2. We are only told about the locus through R.

4. Scitovsky (1941–2, pp. 77–89; 1942, pp. 89–110) was not long in demonstrating that, if compensation is not actually paid, the original Kaldor test (and, by implication, the Hicks one too) can lead to a contradiction. Let us consider again Q_1 in Figure 4. The locus through R passes outside it, so R is 'better' than Q_1 on the Kaldor basis. But there is no reason why the locus through Q_1 should not pass outside R. If it does, we have, again on the Kaldor basis, Q_1 'better' than R. The two loci intersect and a contradiction emerges. Accordingly, Scitovsky argued that we need a *double* test. Before we can say that 'welfare' (the use of the term is Scitovsky's) increases when we move from Q_1 to R, we must know that the locus through R passes outside Q_1, *and* that the locus through Q_1 passes inside R. That is to say: the gainer by the change can profitably compensate the loser, or bribe him into accepting it; and the loser cannot profitably bribe the gainer into rejecting it.

5. In 1947 Samuelson[10] pointed out that even the Scitovsky test was unsatisfactory. What it does is to rule out the possibility of the loci intersecting (strictly: of their intersecting an odd number of times) between Q and R, but it does not rule out the possibility of their intersecting elsewhere (or of their intersecting an even number of times between Q and R). Figure 5 illustrates the matter. The Scitovsky 'double test' is satisfied for a movement from Q to R. The gainer can profitably bribe the loser into accepting the movement; and the loser cannot profitably bribe the gainer into rejecting it. Yet the loci intersect several times. We cannot claim that there has been

10. Samuelson (1947, p. 251), speaks in terms of the 'utility-possibility function', but there is no need to restrict his analysis to optimal environments.

an *actual* increase in welfare in the strict Paretian sense, for one man is made worse off by the movement. And we cannot say that there has been a *potential* increase, for that requires – as we have seen – a shift, rather than a complicated twist, of the locus. Whether the highest position of social welfare is attained on the locus through Q or on that through R will clearly depend on the shape of our W contours – that is, on the ethical judgements we care to make.

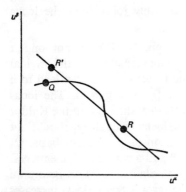

Figure 5

Note that this statement holds good even if we experience an *actual* increase in welfare, by moving from Q to R'. We still cannot say that the change which causes the movement is even potentially beneficial. For there is no reason why we should judge the situation depicted by the first locus with reference to the single point Q, and that depicted by the second locus with reference to the single point R'. To do so would be to attach undue weight to the distribution of wealth obtaining before and after the change – to the *status quo ante* and the *status quo post*.

Accordingly, the Samuelson criterion for 'an increase in potential real income' (Samuelson, 1950) is the same as the one we have used for 'potential benefit': an outward shift of the locus. It can be phrased in terms of the compensation tests in the following way. For every possible distribution of wealth, both before and after the change in question occurs, the Kaldor and the Hicks tests (and therefore the Scitovsky double one) must be satisfied.

6. Finally, Little (1949a and b, 1949–50) has suggested several variants of a rather different type of criterion – one which refers to an actual, not a potential, increase in real income or welfare (he uses the two terms synonymously). A typical variant is the following. Let us return to Figure 4. A movement from Q_2 to R satisfies the Hicks test, since the locus through R passes inside Q_2. There must, therefore, exist a point on the locus, say R', in which everybody is worse off than in Q_2. Now if we are prepared to make the broad ethical judgement that R' is 'no worse' than R (in the sense that $W(R') \geqslant W(R)$), it follows that welfare must be higher in Q_2 than in R.

Note that we require, in addition to the information that the Hicks test is satisfied, the definite value judgement that $W(R') \geqslant W(R)$. This is a rather curious requirement. Why should we have to judge between R' and R in order to be able to say whether or not Q_2 is better than R? Why can't we judge between Q_2 and R quite directly? It seems fair to remark that the introduction of an intermediate point R' serves no useful purpose whatsoever.[11]

Summary. The reader is no doubt impressed by the diversity of the six tests; and he will have observed that they refer to quite different concepts. The Pareto and Little tests refer to 'actual welfare'; the Samuelson one to 'potential welfare' in the sense we have used the term in this and the preceding chapter; the Kaldor and Hicks ones to 'real income'. Scitovsky says his refers to 'social welfare', but that is difficult to concede – it would be more correct to say that it refers to potential welfare, and that on the basis of the *status quo ante* and *status quo post* only. It is valid if, and only if, we are prepared to accept one or both of these questionable bases.

There is, moreover, a considerable difference in the meanings attached to 'real income' in the Kaldor and the Hicks tests. Hicks gives it a definite welfare connotation, which would be legitimate only if the compensation were actually paid. Then everybody would be better off and the Pareto test would tell us that 'actual welfare'

11. It may even be a hindrance. When, as in the third of his cited papers (1949b, p. 88 n.), Little applies his criterion to changes in the national income between one year and another, we actually experience both Q_2 and R. It may therefore be possible to judge between them. But we do not experience R' at all, and may not have much idea of what it would be like if experienced.

had increased. Kaldor uses 'real income' to mean the 'production of wealth', which he distinguishes from its 'distribution'. 'Welfare' depends on them both. An analysis of this attempted dichotomy is reserved for the next section. Here it is sufficient to note that, if the compensation were actually paid, the Kaldor test, like the Hicks one, would reduce to Pareot's – and would begin to refer to 'actual welfare' instead of 'production'.

When compensation is not actually paid, the Kaldor and the Hicks tests become rather difficult to interpret positively, but they do provide us with a piece of negative information for which we should be grateful. *If ' Q is better than R' in either the Kaldor or the Hicks sense, we know that R cannot be potentially better than Q in the full Samuelson sense – which is the only satisfactory one.*

There is an aspect of the Pareto and Little criteria which requires emphasis. They are merely intended to refer to two *points* in the diagrams – not to the *whole range* of positions on the two loci passing through the points. They refer to actual situations, not to hypothetical ones resulting from hypothetical redistributions of wealth. That is what is meant by saying that they refer to actual, rather than potential, welfare. If, for example, an invention increases actual welfare in this sense, it does not follow that its introduction is 'potentially beneficial'. Actual welfare might be increased still more by redistributing wealth in the absence of the invention.

References

ALLAIS, M. (1943), *À la Recherche d'une Discipline Économique*, vol. 1, printed for private circulation, Paris.

BAUMOL, W. J. (1949), 'Relaying the foundations', *Economica*, vol. 16, p. 166.

GRAAFF, J. DE V. (1947–8), 'Rothbarth's "virtual price system", and the Slutsky equation', *Rev. econ. Stud.*, vol. 15, no. 2.

GRAAFF, J. DE V. (1948), 'Towards an austerity theory of value', *South African J. Econ.*, vol. 16, no. 1.

GRAAFF, J. DE V. (1949–50), 'On optimum tariff structures', *Rev. econ. Stud.*, vol. 17, no. 1.

GRAAFF, J. DE V. (1968), *Theoretical Welfare Economics*, Cambridge University Press.

HICKS, J. R. (1940), 'The valuation of social income', *Economica*, vol. 7, pp. 105–24.

KALDOR, N. (1939), 'Welfare propositions and interpersonal comparisons of utility' *econ. J.*, vol. 49, pp. 549–52.

LITTLE, I. M. D. (1949a), 'The foundations of welfare economics', *Oxford econ. Papers*, vol. 1, new series, pp. 235–7.

LITTLE, I. M. D. (1949b), 'A note on the interpretation of index numbers', *Economica*, vol. 16, pp. 369-70.

LITTLE, I. M. D. (1949-50), 'Welfare and tariffs', *Rev. econ. Stud.*, vol. 16, no. 2, pp. 65-8.

PIGOU, A. C. (1932), *The Economics of Welfare*, 4th edn, London.

REDER, M. W. (1947), *Studies in the Theory of Welfare Economics*, New York.

SAMUELSON, P. A. (1947), *Foundations of Economic Analysis*, Harvard University Press.

SAMUELSON, P. A. (1950), 'Evaluation of real national income', *Oxford econ. Papers*, new series, vol. 2.

SCITOVSKY, T. (1941-2), 'A note on welfare propositions in economics', *Rev. econ. Stud.*, vol. 9, no. 1.

SCITOVSKY, T. (1942), 'A reconsideration of the theory of tariffs', *Rev. econ. Stud.*, vol. 9, no. 2.

Part Three
The Social Welfare Function

Arrow's 1967 paper is his best short exposition of the central idea in his shattering 1951 book, *Social Choice and Individual Values*. When the ink had scarcely dried on the early work, Little rose to the attack with a remarkably deep and penetrating critique of the significance of Arrow's theorem. Arrow's recent paper incorporates certain advances in the method of proof, and it hesitates a little over the 'austerity' of one or two of the conditions he imposes, but it shows no readiness to concede any of the main objections raised by Little.

4 K. J. Arrow

Values and Collective Decision-Making

K. J. Arrow, 'Values and collective decision-making', in P. Laslett and
W. G. Runciman (eds.), *Philosophy, Politics and Society*, Blackwell, 1967, vol. 3.

1 Values of a single individual

As an exercise in clarifying terminology, let us consider what can be
said about the values of an imaginary, completely isolated individual.
His personal skills and qualities and the physical world available to
him jointly delimit a range of *actions* possible to him. To be precise,
I shall so define the concept of action that alternative actions are
mutually exclusive. An action, then, means a complete description of
all the activities that an individual carries on, and two alternative
actions are any two descriptions which differ in any relevant way.
For example, an individual may describe his activities by indicating
the amount of time he spends on each of the alternative modalities of
performance available to him; thus, three hours at farming, three
hours at hunting, four hours of violin playing, etc. A change in any
one of these time allocations would represent a change in action.
This particular definition is truly a formal choice of language, and
does not by itself change the nature of the problem. It simply brings
out formally that the basic question of the individual is a choice of
actions.

(a) *Values, tastes, and hypothetical imperatives*

To an economist, and I suppose to most philosophers, a value system
would, in these terms, be simply the rule an individual uses to choose
which of the mutually exclusive actions he will undertake. If an individual is facing a given set of alternative actions, he will choose one,
and there seems to be little interesting to talk about. However, the
problem, at least to the economist, is put in slightly different form.
Consider an individual who does not yet know which actions will be

available and which will not. Let us term the set of available actions the *environment*. One might ask him what action he *would choose* if offered some particular environment. By repeating this question for many alternative environments we have obtained a description of his value system in the sense of a rule giving his hypothetical choice for many or all possible environments.[1]

One might want to reserve the term 'values' for a specially elevated or noble set of choices. Perhaps choices in general might be referred to as 'tastes'. We do not ordinarily think of the preference for additional bread over additional beer as being a value worthy of philosophic inquiry. I believe, though, that the distinction cannot be made logically, and certainly not in dealing with the single isolated individual. If there is any distinction between values and tastes it must lie in the realm of interpersonal relations.

(b) The assumptions of ordering

The description of a value system as a correlation between possible environments and the hypothetical choices to be made from them is not by itself a very informative procedure. Economists have been accustomed to adding considerable strength (empirical restrictiveness) by specifying that the value system shall have a particular structure – namely, being derivable from an *ordering*. To define this concept let us first consider environments consisting of just two alternative actions. For such two-member environments we can find the one chosen, in accordance with the individual's value system, and we will speak of it as having been *preferred* to the other action in the environment. We may have to admit that the individual is equally willing to choose neither of the two actions, in which case we speak of the two actions as being *indifferent*. The assumption of an ordering means that certain consistency assumptions are postulated about the relations of preference and indifference, and it is further assumed

1. For technical mathematical reasons one must admit that sometimes more than one action should be regarded as chosen in a given environment, by which is meant the individual does not care which of the chosen actions is in fact adopted in a particular set of circumstances. We must also allow for the fact that there may be no chosen action; for an example of the latter, consider an individual with a normal desire for money who can choose any amount of gold less than (but not equal to) one ounce.

that choices from any environment can be described in terms of the ordering, which relates to choices in two-member environments.

The first assumption is that of *connexity* (or connectedness, or completeness, or comparability). It is assumed that for each pair of alternatives, either one is preferred to the other or the two are indifferent. The second assumption is that of *transitivity*. Consider three alternatives, to be designated by x, y and z. Then if x is preferred to y, and y is preferred to z, we assume that x is preferred to z. We can and must also include in the definition cases where some of the choices are indifferent; for example, if x is indifferent to y, and y is indifferent to z, then x is indifferent to z.

For later use we introduce some symbolic notation to express these ordering relations. Specifically, we denote alternatives by $x, y,....$ Then xPy means 'x is preferred to y'; xIy means 'x is indifferent to y'; xRy means 'x is preferred or indifferent to y'.

If we start with the relation R (that is, only knowing for which ordered pairs of alternatives x, y the statement xRy holds), then we can define the relations P and I in terms of R: xIy is defined to be xRy and yRx; xPy is defined to be xRy and not yRx. The assumption of connectity can be stated: for all x and y, xRy or yRx. (Here, and below, 'or' does not exclude 'and'.) The assumption of transitivity can be stated: for all x, y and z, if zRy and yRz, then xRz.

Finally, and perhaps most important, it is assumed that the choice from any environment is determined by the ordering in the sense that if there is an alternative which is preferred to every other alternative in the environment, then it is the chosen element. This is an additional assumption not logically implied by the existence of an ordering itself.

In symbols, let S be any environment (set of alternatives), $C(S)$ the alternative (or alternatives) chosen from S. Then $C(S)$ is the set of alternatives x in S for which xRy for all y in S. It is easy to see that if x^1 and x^2 are both in $C(S)$ (both chosen alternatives in S), then x^1Ix^2.

Obviously, the assumption of ordering is by no means unreasonable. The notion of connexity carries the idea that choices have to be made whether we will or no. The idea of transitivity clearly corresponds to some strong feeling of the meaning of consistency in our choice. Economists have typically identified the concept of rationality with the notion of choices derivable from an ordering.

It may be worth while dwelling on the meaning of these two assumptions a little more, in view of their importance. It is not at all uncommon to find denials of the connexity assumption. Sufficiently remote alternatives are held to be incomparable. But I must say I do not find this line of argument at all convincing. If a choice has to be made, it has to be made. In most practical choice situations there is some *null* alternative, which will be chosen in the absence of what might be termed a positive decision. Thus, if there is dispute about the nature of new legislation, the pre-existing legislation remains in force. But this does not mean that no choice is made; it means rather that the system produces as its choice the null alternative. I think what those who emphasize incomparability have in mind is rather that if one is forced to make a choice between alternatives which are difficult to compare, then the choice is not apt to satisfy the assumption of transitivity.

The possibility of regarding inaction as an always available alternative is part of the broader question of whether social choices should be historically conditioned. It is here that the importance of transitivity becomes clear. Transitivity implies that the final choice made from any given environment is independent of the path by which it has been derived. From any environment there will be a given chosen alternative, and in the absence of a deadlock no place for the historically given alternatives to be chosen by default.

(c) Independence of irrelevant alternatives

Since the chosen element from any environment is completely defined by knowledge of the preferences as between it and any other alternative in the environment, it follows that the choice depends only on the ordering of the elements of that environment. In particular, the choice made does not depend on preferences as between alternatives which are not in fact available in the given environment, nor – and this is probably more important – on preferences as between elements in the environment and those not in the environment. It is never necessary to compare available alternatives with those which are not available at a given moment in order to arrive at a decision. It is this point which is being made when it is argued that only ordinal measures of utility or preference are relevant to decisions. Any cardinal measure, any attempt to give a numerical representation of utility, depends basically on comparisons involving alternative actions which are not, or at least may not be, available, given the environment prevailing at the moment.

(d) Omitted considerations

For the sake of economy of discussion we pass by many interesting issues. Most important, probably, is the relation between hypothetical choices and real ones. It is implied in the above discussion and below that a preference will in fact be translated into a choice if the opportunity ever comes. But the question may be raised how we can possibly know about hypothetical choices if they are not actually made. This is not merely a problem of finding out about somebody else's values; we may not know our own values until put to the crucial test.

Even the actual preferences may not be regarded as in some sense true values. An observer looking from the outside on our isolated individual may say that his decision was wrong either in the sense that there is some other standard of values to which it does not conform or in the sense that it was made on the grounds of insufficient information or improper calculation. The latter possibility is a real and important one, but I will simply state that I am abstracting from it in the course of the present discussion. The former interpretation I am rejecting here. For the single isolated individual there can be no other standard than his own values. He might indeed wish to change them under criticism, but this, I take it, means basically that he hasn't fully thought through or calculated the consequences of his actions and upon more consideration wishes to modify them.

2 Public values

(a) Interpersonal nature of social action

The fundamental fact which causes the need for discussing public values at all is that all significant actions involve joint participation of many individuals. Even the apparently simplest act of individual decision involves the participation of a whole society.

It is important to note that this observation tells us all non-trivial actions are essentially the property of society as a whole, not of individuals. It is quite customary to think of each individual as being able to undertake actions on his own (e.g., decisions of consumption, production, and exchange, moving from place to place, forming and dissolving families). Formally, a social action is then taken to be the resultant of all individual actions. In other words, any social action is thought of as being factored into a sequence of individual actions.

I certainly do not wish to deny that such factoring takes place, but I do wish to emphasize that the partition of a social action into individual components, and the corresponding assignment of individual responsibility, is *not* a datum. Rather, the particular factoring in any given context is itself the result of a social policy and therefore already the outcome of earlier and logically more primitive social values.

In economic transactions the point is clearest when we consider what we call property. Property is clearly a creation of society through its legal structure. The actions of buying and selling through offers of property are only at a superficial level the actions of an individual. They reflect a whole series of social institutions, and with different institutions different people would be having control over any given piece of property. Furthermore, the very notion of control over one's 'own' property, as is apparent upon the most casual inspection, itself acquires its meaning through the regulations of society.

These are no idle or excessively nice distinctions. When it comes to racial discrimination, notions of liability and responsibility for injury to others, or the whole concept of a corporation and its special and complex relations to the world as a whole, economic and social, we know that social values have altered considerably the terms on which property can be used in the market-place or transmitted to others. Needless to say, the taxation system constitutes one of the strongest examples in which the state, as one aspect of society, makes clear the relative nature of ownership. Nor, in this context, should it be forgotten that the claims of society, as modifying the concept of ownership, are by no means confined to the state. Our particular culture has tended to minimize non-coercive obligations relative to the predominant role they have played elsewhere, but they are far from absent even today. There is certainly a whole complex of obligations implied in the concept of a 'good neighbour'. The use of one's real property is limited by more than legal conditions. As everyone knows – sometimes painfully – there are obligations of generosity and organized giving appropriate to an individual's income status and social position. In short, we argue that the facts of social life show clearly that there is no universally acceptable division of actions with regard to property into mine and thine.

To be sure, there is another category of actions, those which involve the person himself as opposed to his property. We have a stronger feeling here that there is a natural meaning to speaking of one's own actions as opposed to others. Presumably there is a meaningful sense in which we say that *I* am writing this paper – not anyone else. But of course even here the action is full of social interconnections. I am here in a conference arranged by others, using words which are a common part of the culture, expressing ideas which draw upon a wide range of concepts of others, and which embody my education.

To be sure, I am using my own capacities at some point in this process. But how logically do we distinguish between the capacities which somehow define the person, and those which are the result of external actions of a society? I may see well because my vision is intrinsically good or because I have glasses. Is the vision more peculiarly *mine* in one case than in the other? One may concede that there is more of an intrinsic idea of property here in certain personal actions, but I think this whole matter needs deeper exploration than it has received thus far. In any case, there are obviously very strong social obligations on personal behaviour and the use of one's personal capacities, just as there are on the use of property.

To conclude, then, we must in a general theory take as our unit a social action, that is, an action involving a large proportion or the entire domain of society. At the most basic axiomatic level, individual actions play little role. The need for a system of public values then becomes evident; actions being collective or interpersonal in nature, so must the choice among them. A public or social value system is essentially a logical necessity.

The point is obvious enough in the contexts that we tend to regard as specifically political. The individuals in a country cannot have separate foreign policies or separate legal systems. Among economists the matter has been somewhat confused because economic analysis has supplied us with a model of factorization of social actions, that achieved through the price system. The system itself is certainly one of the most remarkable of social institutions and the analysis of its working is, in my judgement, one of the more significant intellectual achievements of mankind. But the factorization implied is a particular one made in a particular way. It is one that has turned out to be highly convenient, particularly from the point of view of economizing on the flow of information in the economic system. But at the fundamental level of discourse we are now engaged in we cannot regard the price system as a datum. On the contrary, it is to be thought of as one of the instrumentalities, possibly the major one, by which whatever social value system there may be is realized.

(b) Individual preferences for social actions

The individual plays a central role in social choice as the judge of alternative social actions according to his own standards. We presume that each individual has some way of ranking social actions according to his preferences for their consequences. These preferences constitute his value system. They are assumed to reflect already in full measure altruistic or egoistic motivations, as the case may be.

Following the discussion in Part 1, we assume that the values are expressed in the form of an ordering. Thus, in effect, individuals are taken to be rational in their attitudes toward social actions.

In symbols, we now let $x, y,...$, represent alternative social actions. Then the ith individual has an ordering among these actions which, as in 1b, can be represented by a relation, to be denoted by R_i: $xR_i y$ means 'x is preferred or indifferent to y in the view of individual i'. As before, we can define P_i (preference in the view of individual i) and I_i (indifference in the view of individual i) in terms of R_i: $xP_i y$ is defined to be $zR_i y$ and not $yR_i x$; $xI_i y$ is defined to be $xR_i y$ and $yR_i x$.

We are face to face with an extremely difficult point. A standard liberal point of view in political philosophy, which also has dominated formal welfare economics, asserts that an individual's preferences are or ought to be (a distinction not usually made clear) concerned only with the effects of social actions on him. But there is no logical way to distinguish a particular class of consequences which pertain to a given individual. If I feel that my satisfaction is reduced by somebody else's poverty (or, for that matter, by somebody else's wealth), then I am injured in precisely the same sense as if my purchasing power were reduced. To parallel the observations of the preceding section, I am in effect arguing here that just as we cannot factor social actions so as to make each component pertain to a given individual, so we cannot factor the consequences of social actions in any meaningful way into separable consequences to individual members of the society. That is, let me make it clear, we cannot do it as a matter of fact. The interdependence of mankind is after all not a novel ethical doctrine. The man who questioned whether he was his brother's keeper was, according to an ancient source, not highly approved of. The general conclusion here is not one that I find myself entirely comfortable with. I do share the general liberal view that every individual should have the opportunity to find his own way to personal development and satisfaction. The question of interference with the actions of others has been raised most acutely in recent years in legal rather than economic contexts, specifically in the English discussion on laws regulating deviant sexual behaviour. Homosexual behaviour between consenting adults is probably a classic example of an action affecting no one else, and therefore should be exempt from social control. Yet many find themselves shocked and outraged. They would strongly prefer, let us say, the situation to be different. Similarly, I may be disturbed that the Negro is discriminated against and judge accordingly social actions which lead to this result.

One could of course say that the general principle of restraint in judging the affairs of others is an empirical assumption that people in fact do not care about (or strictly have no preferences concerning) matters which would in the usual terminology be regarded as none of their business. But of course empirically we know that this is quite false. The very fact that restrictive legislation is passed or even proposed shows clearly that people are willing to sacrifice effort and time because of the satisfactions to be received from seeing others' patterns of life altered.

The only rational defence of what may be termed a liberal position, or perhaps more precisely a principle of limited social preference, is that it is itself a value judgement. In other words, an individual may have as part of his value structure precisely that he does not think it proper to influence consequences outside a limited realm. This is a perfectly coherent position, but I find it difficult to insist that this judgement is of such overriding importance that it outweighs all other considerations. Personally, my values are such that I am willing to go very far indeed in the direction of respect for the means by which others choose to derive their satisfactions.

At this stage I want to emphasize that value judgements in favour of limited social preference, just as other value judgements emphasizing social solidarity, must be counted as part of the value systems which individuals use in the judgement of alternative social actions.

3 Welfare judgements and the aggregation of preferences

The problem of social choice is the aggregation of the multiplicity of individual preference scales about alternative social actions.

(a) Welfare judgements and constitutions

Classical utilitarianism specifies that alternative social actions be judged in terms of their consequences for people. In the present terminology I take this to mean that they are to be judged in terms of the individual preference scales. This by itself does not supply a sufficient basis for action in view of the multiplicity and divergence of individual preference scales. It is therefore at least implicit in classical utilitarianism that there is a second level at which the individual judgements are themselves evaluated, and this point has been given explicit recognition in a classic paper of Bergson (1938). Let us call this second-order evaluation a *welfare judgement*; it is an evaluation of the consequences to all individuals based on their evaluations. If in each individual evaluation two social actions are indifferent, then the welfare judgement as between the two must also be one of indifference.

The process of formation of welfare judgements is logically equivalent to a social decision process or *constitution*. Specifically, a constitution is a rule which associates to each possible set of individual orderings a social choice function, i.e. a rule for selecting a preferred action out of every possible environment. That a welfare judgement is a constitution indeed follows immediately from the assumption that a welfare judgement can be formed given any set of individual preference systems for social actions. The classification of welfare judgements as constitutions is at this stage a tautology, but what makes it more than that is a specification of reasonable conditions to be imposed on constitutions, and it is here that any dispute must lie.

(b) Social decision processes and the notion of social welfare

While I have just argued that a welfare judgement is necessarily a constitution or process of social decision, the converse need not be true, at least not without further clarification of the meaning of 'welfare judgement'. A welfare judgement requires that some one person is judge; a rule for arriving at social decisions may be agreed upon for reasons of convenience and necessity without its outcomes being treated as evaluations by anyone in particular.[2] Indeed, I would go further and argue that the appropriate standpoint for analysing social decision processes is precisely that they not be welfare judgements of any particular individuals. This seems contrary to Bergson's point of view (1954). In my view, the location of welfare judgements in any individual, while logically possible, does not appear to be very interesting 'Social welfare' is related to social policy in any sensible interpretation; the welfare judgements of any single individual are unconnected with action and therefore sterile. In a more recent paper Bergson has recognized that there may be this alternative interpretation of the concept of social welfare; I quote the passage at length since it displays the issue so well:

I have been assuming that the concern of welfare economics is to counsel individual citizens generally. If a public official is counselled, it is on the same basis as any other citizen. In every instance reference is made to some ethical values which are appropriate for the counselling of the individual in question. In all this I believe I am only expressing the intent of welfare writings generally; or if this is not the intent, I think it should be. But some may be inclined nevertheless to a different conception, which allows still another interpretation of Arrow's theorem. *According to this view, the problem is to counsel not citizens generally but public officials.* [Emphasis added.] Furthermore, the values to be taken as data are not those which would guide the official if he were a private citizen. The official is envisaged

2. This point has been well stressed by Little (1952).

instead as more or less neutral ethically. His one aim in life is to implement the values of other citizens as given by some rule of collective decision-making (1954, pp. 37-8).

My interpretation of the social choice problem agrees fully with that given by Bergson beginning with the italicized statement, though, as can be seen, this is not the view that he himself endorses.

4 Some conditions for a social decision process and the impossibility theorem

The fundamental problem of public value formation, then, is the construction of constitutions. In general, of course, there is no difficulty in constructing a rule if one is content with arbitrary ones. The problem becomes meaningful if reasonable conditions are suggested, which every constitution should obey.[3]

(a) Some conditions on constitutions

I suggest here four conditions which seem very reasonable to impose on any constitution. More can undoubtedly be suggested but unfortunately, as we shall see in section b below, these four more than suffice.

Recall that a constitution is a rule which assigns to any set of individual preference orderings a rule for making society's choices among alternative social actions in any possible environment. Thus, for a given set of individual orderings the result of the process is a particular value system in the sense of part 1; that is, a rule for making selections out of all possible environments. The first condition may be termed that of:

Collective rationality: For any given set of orderings, the social choice function is derivable from an ordering.

In other words, the social choice system has the same structure as that which we have already assumed for individual value systems. The next condition is one that has been little disputed and is advanced by almost every writer in the economic literature:

Pareto principle: If alternative x is preferred to alternative y by every single individual according to his ordering, then the social ordering also ranks x above y.

3. The analysis that follows is based on my book (1963).

Notice that we can use the term 'social ordering' in view of the previous condition of *collective rationality*. The next condition is perhaps the most important as well as the most controversial. For my own part, I am less tempted to regard it as ultimately satisfactory than I formerly did, but it has strong pragmatic justification:

Independence of irrelevant alternatives: The social choice made from any environment depends only on the orderings of individuals with respect to the alternatives in that environment.

To take an extreme case, suppose that individuals are informed that there are a certain number of social actions available. They are not even aware that there are other conceivable social actions. They develop their own preference systems for the alternatives contained in this particular environment, and then the constitution generates a choice. Later they are told that in fact there were alternatives which were logically possible but were not in fact available. For example, a city is taking a poll of individual preferences on alternative methods of transportation (rapid transit, automobile, bus, etc.). Someone suggests that in evaluating these preferences they also ought to ask individual preferences for instantaneous transportation by dissolving the individual into molecules in a ray gun and reforming him elsewhere in the city as desired. There is no pretence that this method is in any way an available alternative. The assumption of *independence of irrelevant alternatives* is such that such preferences have no bearing on the choice to be made.

It is of course obvious that ordinary political decision-making methods satisfy this condition. When choosing among candidates for an elected office, all that is asked are the preferences among the actual candidates, not also preferences among other individuals who are not candidates and who are not available for office.

Finally, we enunciate probably the least controversial of all the conditions,

Non-dictatorship: There is no individual whose preferences are automatically society's preferences independent of the preferences of all other individuals.

There is a difference between the first two conditions and the last two which is worth noting. The assumptions of *collective rationality* and the *Pareto principle* are statements which apply to any fixed set of individual orderings. They do not involve comparisons between social orderings based on different sets of individual orderings. On the contrary, the condition of *independence of irrelevant alternatives* and of *non-dictatorship* are assertions about the responsiveness of the social ordering to variations in individual orderings.

(b) Impossibility theorem

The conditions of *collective rationality* and of the *independence of irrelevant alternatives* taken together imply that in a generalized sense all methods of social choice are of the type of voting. If we consider environments composed of two alternatives alone, then the condition of *independence of irrelevant alternatives* tells us that the choice is determined solely by the preferences of the members of the community as between those two alternatives, and no other preferences are involved. Define a set of individuals to be *decisive* for alternative x over alternative y if the constitution prescribes that x is chosen over y whenever all individuals in the set prefer x to y and all others prefer y to x. Then the rule for choosing from any two-member environment has the form of specifying which sets of individuals are decisive for x over y and which for y over x. The majority voting principle, for example, states simply that any set containing a majority of the voters is decisive for any alternative over any other.

Then, if the social value system is generated by a social ordering, all social preferences are determined by the choices made for two-member environments, and hence by pairwise votes (thus systems like plurality voting are excluded).

Now it has been known for a long time that the system of majority voting can give rise to paradoxical consequences. Consider the following example. There are three alternatives, x, y and z, among which choice is to be made. One-third of the voters prefer x to y and y to z, one-third prefer y to z and z to x and one-third prefer z to x and x to y. Then x will be preferred to y by a majority, y to z by a majority and z to x by a majority.[4]

4. This paradox seems to have been first observed by the Marquis de Condorcet (1785). That a rational voting scheme requires knowledge of all preferences among the candidates and not only the first choice was already argued even earlier by Borda (1781). For a modern analysis of Condorcet's work on voting, see Granger (1956) esp. pp. 94–129. For an English translation of Borda's work see de Grazia (1953). For a general history of the theory of social choice, see Black (1958), Part 2.

One might be tempted to suppose that the paradox of voting is an imperfection in the particular system of majority voting, and more ingenious methods could avoid it. But unfortunately this is not so. The following general theorem may be stated:

There can be no constitution simultaneously satisfying the conditions of collective rationality, the Pareto principle, the independence of irrelevant alternatives, and non-dictatorship.

The proof is given in the following section 3.

This conclusion is quite embarrassing, and it forces us to examine the conditions which have been stated as reasonable. It's hard to imagine anyone quarrelling either with the *Pareto principle* or the condition of *non-dictatorship*. The principle of *collective rationality* may indeed be questioned. One might be prepared to allow that the choice from a given environment be dependent on the history of previous choices made in earlier environments, but I think many would find that situation unsatisfactory. There remains, therefore, only the *independence of irrelevant alternatives*, which will be examined in greater detail in section 4 below.

(c) Proof of the impossibility theorem

We assume the existence of a social choice mechanism satisfying the conditions of *collective rationality*, the *Pareto principle*, the *independence of irrelevant alternatives*, and *non-dictatorship*, and show that the assumption leads to a contradiction. Since the condition of *collective rationality* requires that social choice be derivable from an ordering, we can speak of social preference and social indifference. In particular, as defined in the last section, a set of individuals V is *decisive* for x against y if x is socially preferred to y whenever all individuals in V prefer x to y and all others prefer y to x.[5]

The proof falls into two parts. It is first shown that if an individual is decisive for some pair of alternatives, then he is a dictator, contrary to the condition of *non-dictatorship*. Hence, no individual is decisive for any pair of alternatives, and the *impossibility theorem* itself then follows easily with the aid of the *Pareto principle*.

We first distinguish one individual, called 1, and introduce the following notations for statements about the constitution:

5. The following proof is quoted, with minor alterations, from Arrow (1963), pp. 98–100.

$x\bar{D}y$ means that x is socially preferred to y whenever individual 1 prefers x to y, regardless of the orderings of other individuals; xDy means that x is socially preferred to y if individual 1 prefers x to y and all other individuals prefer y to x.

1

If xDy, then $u\bar{D}v$ are for every ordered pair u, v from the three alternatives x, y, and z;

2

Notice that this notation is legitimate only because of the assumption of *independence of irrelevant alternatives*. Note too that the statement, $x\bar{D}y$, implies xDy and that xDy is the same as the assertion that 1 is a decisive set for x against y.

Suppose then that xDy holds for some x and y. We will first suppose that there are only three alternatives altogether. Let the third alternative be z. Suppose 1 orders the alternatives x, y, z in descending order, whereas all other individuals prefer y to both x and z, but may have any preferences as between the last two. Then 1 prefers x to y, whereas all others prefer y to x; from **2** this means that xPy. All individuals prefer y to z; by the *Pareto principle*, yPz. Then by transitivity, xPz; but then this holds whenever xP_1z, regardless of the orderings of other individuals as between x and z. In symbols,

xDy implies $x\bar{D}z$.

3

Again, suppose xDy, but now suppose that 1 orders the alternatives z, x, y, whereas all other individuals prefer both z and y to x. By a similar argument, xPy and zPx, so that zPy.

xDy implies $z\bar{D}y$.

4

Interchanging y and z in **4** yields

xDz implies $y\bar{D}z$.

5

Replacing x by y, y by z, and z by x in **3** gives

yDz implies $y\bar{D}x$.

6

Since $x\bar{D}z$ implies xDz, and $y\bar{D}z$ implies yDz, we can, by chaining the implications **3, 5** and **6**, deduce

xDy implies $y\bar{D}x$.

7

If we interchange x and y in **3, 4** and **7**, we arrive at

yDx implies $y\bar{D}z$,
yDx implies $z\bar{D}x$,
yDx implies $x\bar{D}y$,

and these can each be chained with the implication **7** to yield

xDy implies $y\bar{D}x$, $z\bar{D}x$, and $x\bar{D}y$.   **8**

Implications **3, 4, 7,** and **8** together can be summarized as saying

if xDy, then $u\bar{D}v$ are for every ordered pair u, v from the three alternatives x, y and z;   **9**

i.e., individual 1 is a dictator for the three alternatives.

We can extend this result to any number of alternatives by an argument due to Blau (1957, p. 310). Suppose aDb holds, and let x and y be any pair of alternatives. If x and y are the same as a and b, either in the same or in the reverse order, we add a third alternative c to a and b; then we can apply **9** to the triple a, b, c and deduce $x\bar{D}y$ by letting $u = x, v = y$. If exactly one of x and y is distinct from a and b, add it to a and b to form a triple to which again **9** is applicable. Finally, if both x and y are distinct from a and b, two steps are needed. First, add x to a and b, and deduce from **9** that $a\bar{D}x$ and therefore aDx. Then, again applying **9** to the triple a, x, y, we find that $x\bar{D}y$. Thus, aDb for some a and b implies that $x\bar{D}y$ for all x and y, i.e. individual 1 is a dictator. From the condition of *non-dictatorship* it can be concluded that

xDy cannot hold for any individual 1 and any pair x, y.   **10**

The remainder of the proof is now an appropriate adaptation of the paradox of voting. By the *Pareto principle*, there is at least one decisive set for any ordered pair x, y, namely, the set of all individuals. Among all sets of individuals which are decisive for some pairwise choice, pick one such that no other is smaller; by **10** it must contain at least two individuals. Let V be the chosen set, and let the ordered pair for which it is decisive be x, y. Divide V into two parts, V_1, which contains only a single individual, and V_2, which contains all the rest. Let V_3 be the set of individuals not in V.

Consider now the case where the preference order of V_1 is x, y, z, that of all members of V_2 is z, x, y and that of all members of V_3 is y, z, x. Since V is decisive for x against y, and all members of V prefer x to y while all others have the opposite preference xPy. On the other hand, it is impossible that society prefers z to y since that would require that V_2 be decisive on this issue; this is impossible since V_2 has fewer members than V, which, by construction, has as few members as a decisive set can have. Hence, yRz, and, since xPy, society must prefer x to z. But then the single member of V_1 would be decisive, and we have shown that to be impossible.

Thus the contradiction is established.

(d) The independence of irrelevant alternatives and interpersonal comparisons of intensity

Modern economic theory has insisted on the ordinal concept of utility; that is, only orderings can be observed, and therefore no measurement of utility independent of these orderings has any significance. In the field of consumer's demand theory the ordinalist position turned out to create no problems; cardinal utility had no explanatory power above and beyond ordinal. Leibniz's *principle of the identity of indiscernibles* demanded then the excision of cardinal utility from our thought patterns. Bergson's formulation of the social welfare function carried out the same principle in the analysis of social welfare. Social choices were to depend only on individual orderings; hence, welfare judgements were based only on inter-personally observable behaviour.

The condition of *independence of irrelevant alternatives* extends the requirement of observability one step farther. Given the set of alternatives available for society to choose among, it could be expected that ideally one could observe all preferences among the available alternatives, but there would be no way to observe preferences among alternatives not feasible for society.

I now feel, however, that the austerity imposed by this condition is stricter than desirable. In many situations we do have information on preferences for non-feasible alternatives. It can certainly be argued that when available this information should be used in social choice. Unfortunately, it is clear, as I have already suggested, that social decision processes which are independent of irrelevant alternatives have strong practical advantages, and it remains to be seen whether a satisfactory social decision procedure can really be based on other information.

The potential usefulness of irrelevant alternatives is that they may permit empirically meaningful interpersonal comparisons. The information which might enable us to assert that one individual prefers alternative x to alternative y more strongly than a second individual prefers y to x must be based on comparisons by the two individuals of the two alternatives, not only with respect to each other but also to other alternatives.

Let me conclude by suggesting one type of use of irrelevant alternatives, which may be termed 'extended sympathy'. We do seem prepared to make comparisons of the form: Action x is better (or worse) for me than action y is for you. This is probably in fact the standard way in which people make judgements about appropriate income distributions; if I am richer than you, I may find it easy to make the judgement that it is better for you to have the marginal dollar than for me.

How is this consistent with our general point of view that all value judgements are at least hypothetical choices among alternative actions? Interpersonal comparisons of the extended sympathy type can be put in operational form. The judgement takes the form: It is better (in my judgement) to be myself under action x than to be you under action y.

In this form the characteristics that define an individual are included in the comparison. In effect, these characteristics are put on a par with the items usually regarded as constituting an individual's wealth. The possession of tools is ordinarily regarded as part of the social state which is being evaluated; why not the possession of the skills to use those tools, and the intelligence which lies behind those skills? Individuals, in appraising each other's states of well-being, not only consider material possessions but also find themselves 'desiring this man's scope and that man's art'.[6] The principle of extended sympathy as a basis for interpersonal comparisons seems basic to many of the welfare judgements made in ordinary practice. It remains to be seen whether an adequate theory of social choice can be derived from this and other acceptable principles.

6. The moral implications of the position that many attributes of the individual are similar in nature to external possessions have been discussed by Walsh (1961).

References

ARROW, K. J. (1963), *Social Choice and Individual Values*, 2nd edn, Wiley.

BERGSON, A. (1938), 'A reformulation of certain aspects of welfare economics', *Q. J. Econ.*, vol. 52, pp. 310–34; reprinted in Bergson, 1966, pp. 1–49.

BERGSON, A. (1954), 'On the concept of social welfare', *Q. J. Econ.*, vol. 68, pp. 233–52; reprinted in Bergson, 1966, pp. 27–49.

BERGSON, A. (1966), *Essays in Normative Economics*, Harvard University Press.

BLACK, D. (1958), *The Theory of Committees and Elections*, Cambridge University Press.

BLAU, J. H. (1957), 'The existence of social welfare functions', *Econometrica*, vol. 25.

BORDA, J.-C. DE (1781), 'Mémoires sur les elections au scrutin', *Mémoires de l'Academie Royale des Sciences*, pp. 657–65.

CONDORCET, MARQUIS DE (1785), 'Essai sur l'application de l'analyse à la probabilité des décisions rendues à la pluralité des voix', Paris.

GRANGER, G.-G. (1956), *La Mathématique Sociale du Marquis de Condorcet*, Presses Universitaires de France.

GRAZIA, A. DE (1953), 'Mathematical derivation of an election system', *Isis*, vol. 44, pp. 42–51.

LITTLE, I. M. D. (1952), 'Social choice and individual values', *J. polit. Econ.*, vol. 60, pp. 422–32.

WALSH, V. C. (1961), *Scarcity and Evil*, Prentice-Hall.

5 I. M. D. Little

Social Choice and Individual Values

I. M. D. Little, 'Social choice and individual values', *Journal of Political Economy*, vol. 60, 1952, pp. 422–32.

The purpose of this article is to discuss the implications of Professor Arrow's conclusion that 'if we exclude the possibility of inter-personal comparisons of utility, then the only methods of passing from individual tastes to social preferences which will be satisfactory and which will be defined for a wide range of sets of individual orderings are either imposed or dictatorial (Arrow, 1963, p. 59).

Since Arrow's work may not be generally familiar, I will first give a brief summary of the central theorem.

1 The Arrow theorem

Imagine that there are n possibilities ($n > 2$) and m choosers ($m > 1$). Each chooser is deemed to have a self-consistent set of preferences ranging over all the possibilities and is assumed to choose or vote accordingly. Coalitions and bluffs are out of court; no one tries to be clever; everyone doggedly consults his own unswerving faith.

The problem is to find whether a self-consistent collective order of the possibilities, which obeys certain 'conditions of correspondence' with the individual orders, is conceivable. So that the problem will be reasonably difficult, it is stipulated that there are at least three possibilities such that no conceivable set of individual orders thereof is ruled out *a priori*.

The 'conditions of correspondence' laid down by Arrow can be formulated as follows:[1]

1. Arrow actually has five conditions, but his first condition is not comparable with the others in that it merely sets the requirements for the problem indicated above, i.e. that the collective ordering be a true self-consistent ordering and that individual orders should not be unduly restricted *a priori*.

1. If one possibility rises or remains still in the order of every individual, then, *ceteris paribus*, it must not fall in the collective order.

2. If the removal from, or insertion into, the set of possibilities of a certain possibility *x* results in no change in any individual order of the remaining possibilities, then it must cause no change in the collective order of those possibilities. This condition is named the 'independence of irrelevant alternatives'.

3. For all *x* and *y*, *x* must not rank above *y* in the collective order, regardless of the individual orders. This is called the condition of 'nonimposition'.

4. The collective order must not coincide with the order of any one chooser, regardless of the orders of the other choosers. This is called the condition of 'nondictatorship'.

Arrow has proved that no consistent collective order satisfying these conditions is conceivable. In his terminology no satisfactory social welfare function is possible. By 'satisfactory' is meant 'satisfying the arbitrary conditions above'. By 'social welfare function' is meant 'a process or rule which for each set of individual orderings for alternative social states (one ordering for each individual) states a corresponding social ordering of alternative social states' (Arrow, 1963, p. 23). In this definition the possibilities are interpreted as the different possible states of society. A 'social state' is defined thus: 'The most precise definition of a social state would be a complete description of the amount of each type of commodity in the hands of each individual, the amount of labour to be supplied by each individual, the amount of each productive resource invested in each kind of productive activity, and the amounts of various types of collective activity' (1963, p. 17). The process of proof need not detain us here (see pp. 51–9).

2 Relation of the Arrow theorem to 'welfare' economics

Let us suppose that each chooser orders different economic states strictly according to what he himself gets in each state. As is well known, this assumption enables one to isolate in principle an infinite number of 'Pareto-optimum' states, each of which is defined by the impossibility of selecting any alternative state which is higher on one man's order and lower on no one's.

Bergson suggested that this comparatively useless theoretical result could be improved on only if an 'economic welfare function' were postulated. What has this Bergson function to do with the Arrow function described above?

As I understand it, Bergson's welfare function was meant as a 'process or rule' which would indicate the best economic state as a function of a changing environment (i.e. changing sets of possibilities defined by different economic transformation functions), *the individuals' tastes being given*. It may at once be noticed that Arrow's condition 1 above is inapplicable if tastes are given. Consequently, if I have interpreted Bergson's meaning correctly, then Arrow's result has no bearing on the possibility or impossibility of such a function.[2]

Arrow has a different interpretation. Thus he writes: 'The ethical system is a rule which defines the social state chosen from a given environment *as a function of the tastes of all individuals*. If, for a given set of tastes, the environment varies we expect that the choices will be consistent in the sense that the choice function is derivable from a weak social ordering of all social states. Thus the Bergson social welfare function has the form of a rule assigning a social ordering to each possible set of individual orderings representing tastes' (1963, p. 72, italics mine).

I should agree that we must expect that, in principle, for a given set of tastes, as the environment varies, the choices will be consistent in the sense that they are derivable from a weak ordering. In other words, all logically possible social or economic states (not merely all scientifically possible ones) must be ordered. Then, as the scientific possibilities change, different states are selected as best. This is my idea of a Bergson function; or, if it is not what Bergson meant, it is what I think he should have meant. This conception has two important points of difference from Arrow's conception. First, tastes are given. If tastes change, we may expect a new ordering of all the

2. I am indebted both to the Rockefeller Foundation and to Samuelson for a conversation with the latter in which he pointed out this divergence between his concept of the Bergson function (as elaborated in 1947, chapter 8), and that of Arrow.

conceivable states; but we do not require that the difference between the new and the old ordering should bear any particular relation to the changes of taste which have occurred. We have, so to speak, a new world and a new order; and we do not demand correspondence between the change in the world and the change in the order.

The second important difference is that my interpretation of a Bergson function requires only that there should be an order. It does not require that it should be an order such that anyone would want to say of it that it represented the choices of society. To call an ordering a social ordering at all implies that one approves of the order, or of the mechanism (if any), through which it is determined by the individual choices or preferences. This is, of course, because 'social' is a persuasive word. In discussing the logic of welfare economics there is no need thus to involve oneself in political philosophy. Thus the so-called 'social welfare function', postulated by welfare economists, should on my view be regarded as a social ordering *only* in the sense that it orders states of society. Whether or not it is possible that such an ordering may be, in some further sense, a social ordering is a question we can, for the moment, leave on one side; we return to it later. The essential point here is that none of the advantage claimed for theoretical welfare economics, as a result of introducing such a function, depends in the least on the ordering of economic states being an ordering by society.[3] Instead of writing, with Bergson, $W = W(U_1,..., U_n)$, we can write $W_i = W_i(U_1,..., U_n)$ $(i = 1,..., n)$. There is no need, so far as pure theory is concerned, to introduce a further (social) welfare function of the form $W = W(W_1,..., W_n)$. We can deduce the whole effective corpus of welfare economics from, say, $W_{10} = W_{10}(U_1,..., U_n)$ – remembering only to put 'in the opinion of individual no. 10' after 'welfare' whenever we use the term.

Arrow wants to go much farther than this in two directions. He wants a 'process or rule' which will produce a social ordering as a function of the tastes themselves. As I have tried to indicate, neither of these requirements really has anything to do with what is commonly thought of as welfare economics. Traditionally, tastes are given; indeed, one might almost say that the given individuals are

3. It is, incidentally, clear from Samuelson's work (1947) that he would agree with me about this.

traditionally defined as the possessors of the given tastes and that no sense is attached to the notion of given individuals with changing tastes (certainly the individual's 'economic welfare' is not supposed to be comparable before and after a change of taste).

Quite apart from condition 1, Arrow's other conditions are defined in terms of changing tastes. Nevertheless, it is condition 1 which is crucial, because the other conditions have analogues if tastes are given. Condition 2 need merely be modified to read, 'The removal from or insertion into the set of possibilities of a certain possibility x must cause no change in the collective order of the remaining possibilities'. For, if the entry or exodus of a possibility *did* cause a change in the individual orders of the remainder, we should be faced with a new set of tastes which would require a new 'master'-order,[4] which, on my view, need not bear any relation to the old order. Condition 3, called 'nonimposition', can be modified to state simply that there must be some conceivable set of individual orders which precludes any given 'master'-order. In this form, 'non-imposition' is a traditional assumption of welfare economics equivalent to the postulate that if someone prefers x to y and no one y to x, then x is better than y. Condition 4 ('nondictatorship') must also, if tastes are given, be modified to the effect that the 'master'-order must not coincide with that of any one individual if this order is exactly reversed for all others.[5]

While we must conclude that Arrow's work has no relevance to the traditional theory of welfare economics, which culminates in the Bergson–Samuelson formulation, it remains, of course, true that his wider conception may have advantages of its own. Let us therefore examine his conditions on their own merits.

First, consider condition 1. Suppose that we have three individuals (defined independently of their tastes) and that the orders of three possible states are xyz for Mr A, zxy for Mr B and yzx for Mr C. Let the 'master'-order be zxy. Then, let there be a change of taste such that z rises or remains still in each order, letting the orders

4. I shall, where necessary, refer to a 'master'-order throughout the rest of this article, in order to try to avoid begging questions about the nature of the order.

5. This form of the 'nondictatorship' condition is, in any case, a consequence of the above conditions. See Arrow (1963, pp. 53–4).

become xzy for Mr A, zxy for Mr B and yzx for Mr C. Condition 1 requires that z remain top of the poll. But, looking at the matter from an Olympian point of view, one can ask, 'Why on Earth should it?' Could not, for instance, A's change of taste as between y and z justify a higher weighting of his first choice, so that xyz should become the 'master' order? There is, indeed, nothing in Arrow's theory which prevents us from supposing that the rise of z in the first order is due not to a change of taste on the part of an ostensibly defined Mr A but rather to the substitution of a new individual for Mr A. There is then even less reason why one should accept the view that z must remain top of the poll. I may want to attach a high weight to the new man's tastes.

Take now condition 2, called the 'independence of irrelevant alternatives'. Arrow himself gives an example which throws some doubt on this condition. He writes: 'Suppose that there are just two commodities, bread and wine. A distribution, deemed equitable by all, is arranged, with the wine-lovers getting more wine and less bread than the abstainers. Suppose now that all the wine is destroyed. Are the wine-lovers entitled, because of that fact, to more than an equal share of bread? The answer is, of course, a value judgement. My own feeling is that tastes for unattainable alternatives should have nothing to do with the decision among the attainable ones; desires in conflict with reality are not entitled to consideration, so that condition 3 . . . is a valid value judgement, to me at least' (Arrow, 1963, p. 73). It is, however, easy enough to argue the other way. Thus I can argue that if sacrifices must be made in an equalitarian society, then they should be equal sacrifices. But if the wine-lovers got only an equal share of bread, they would lose more heavily than the bread-lovers. What one would think in an actual case would depend so much on so many circumstances. At all events, I know that I should hate to commit myself *a priori* to Arrow's value judgement.

Condition 3 (nonimposition) needs no comment, since it has been discussed *ad nauseam* in the literature.

As put by Arrow, condition 4 ('nondictatorship') appears eminently acceptable. In his formulation, Tom is a dictator if, for all x and y and 'regardless' of the orderings of others, 'Tom prefers x to y' implies 'x is higher in the master-order'. What Arrow evidently has in mind is that if no change in the orders of others can upset the coincidence of Tom's and the master-order, then it would seem reasonable to call Tom a dictator. Here I should agree. But, when we discover that this condition, if combined with the others, produces the consequence that no more need be known to dub a man 'dictator' than that his ordering of any pair of alternatives has prevailed against the reverse ordering on the part of everyone else, we may well begin to feel uncomfortable.

Take an example. Let there be three men and two alternatives, x and y. Let the orders be xy for Tom and yx for both Dick and Harry. The conditions then preclude xy as the master-order. The two (economic) states may be such that in y Tom has one piece of manna, while Dick and Harry both have ninety-nine pieces; in x Tom has three pieces and Dick and Harry both have ninety-eight pieces. Might not then the master-ranking xy be desirable? Use of the word 'dictatorship' suggests that Tom's preference for x over y somehow causes society to choose x. But, in fact, the coincidence of Tom's and the master-order may be a result of his poverty and not of his power. The plausibility of the 'nondictatorship' condition may come partly from the ambiguity of the word 'imply'. In ordinary language it carries a suggestion of causation. But in logic 'p implies q' means no more than 'not both p and not q'. Thus poor Tom is deemed dictatorial merely because it happens to be the case that society agrees with him and not with the plutocrats. This may be an absurdly limited example (there being only three men and two alternatives), but, presumably, Arrow intended his conditions to be perfectly general. He does, it is true, find this sort of consequence paradoxical (for example, 1963, p. 55); but he draws no conclusion from the paradox. The conclusion, to my mind, is that it is foolish to accept or reject a set of ethical axioms one at a time. One must know the consequences before one can say whether one finds the set acceptable – which fact sets a limit to the usefulness of deductive techniques in ethics or in welfare economics.

It is evident that Arrow has introduced a most interesting logical framework for possible critiques of the behaviour of economic systems under conditions of changing tastes and changing income distribution. He fills out the framework with a set of value judgements which yield him entirely negative conclusions. The fact that I have argued that I can see no reason to accept, and some reasons not to accept, his conditions does not, of course, imply that I think that any generally acceptable set of value judgements, which would turn the logical framework into something useful, is likely or even possible. In fact, I think the opposite, as should become clear from what follows.

3 The general version of the Arrow social welfare function in its relation to ethics and political philosophy

In the preceding section it was supposed that each individual ordered states solely according to what he himself would get. Everything else which individuals thought significant could play its part only in determining the form of the function which would produce the 'master' ordering from these original orderings. But of course there is no need to suppose this. In general, Arrow assumes that the individuals take more into account than their own utility when compiling their original orders; more, indeed, than other people's utilities or welfare. In fact, quite generally, we may suppose that they arrange all states in order of what they regard as ultimate desirability, taking everything they know and feel to be significant into account. We shall call such an ordering a value ordering, although, of course, many of the discriminations made would not really be felt sufficiently strongly to be called value judgements. The problem, then, is to form a 'master' ordering; in Rousseau's language the problem is the well-known one of discovering the general will.

We must now make an important distinction which Arrow fails to draw. He calls his function both a social welfare function and a decision-making process. He believes that 'one of the great advantages of abstract postulational methods is the fact that the same system may be given different interpretations permitting a considerable saving of time'. Yes, but we must be careful not to give such a system a nonsensical interpretation, and it will be my contention that to interpret it as a social welfare function *is* to give a nonsensical interpretation.

Imagine the system as a machine which produces a card on which is written 'x is better than y', or vice versa, when all individual answers to the question 'Is x better than y?' have been fed into it. What significance are we to attach to the sentence on the card, i.e. to the resulting 'master' order? First, it is clear that the sentence, although it is a sentence employing ethical terms, is not a value *judgement*. Every value judgement must be *someone's* judgement of values. If there are n people filling in cards to be fed into the machine, then we have n value judgements, not $n+1$. The sentence which the machine produces expresses a ruling, or decision, which is different in kind from what is expressed by the sentences fed into it. The latter express value judgements; the former expresses a ruling between these judgements. Thus we can legitimately call the machine, or function, a decision-making process.

But what would it mean to call the machine a social welfare function? One would be asserting, in effect, that if the machine decided in favour of x rather than in favour of y, then x would produce more social welfare than y or simply be more desirable than y. This is clearly a value judgement, but it is, of course, a value judgement made by the person who calls the machine a social welfare function. Thus, in general, to call the machine a social welfare function is to assert that x is better than y whenever the machine writes the sentence 'x is better than y'. Now we may suppose that the individual who calls the machine a social welfare function is one of those who has fed his own value order into it. It is clear that this person must be contradicting himself unless the 'master' order coincides with his own value ordering. It follows that if the machine is to be called a social welfare function, then anyone who is called upon to accept or reject the principles on which it is built (i.e. the conditions of correspondence) must refuse to accept any principle which insures that the 'master' order will necessarily not coincide with his own. This is because the conditions of correspondence determine the 'master' order and because by calling the machine a social welfare function the person in question has accepted the 'master' order. (It should be noted that accepting or rejecting a value sentence entails agreement or disagreement with the corresponding value judgement.) In other words, it is inconsistent both to call the machine a social welfare function and to accept the condition of nondictatorship.

This may appear very surprising. First, it may be objected that, as in the case considered in the previous section, a rich man may, like Bernard Shaw, easily *prefer* a state which yields him more manna, but at the same time *disapprove* of it because he is an equalitarian and would therefore accept a rule which named as best a social state which yielded him less manna. This objection does not, however, apply in the case under consideration, because in this most general version it is presumed that the individual orders take the welfare of others into consideration. He would therefore *not* rank as higher the state which yielded him more manna.

It is true, of course, that, in the initial ordering, one thing which a person cannot take into consideration is other people's valuations, which he may very well regard as highly significant, if he is a tolerant sort of person. Even worse is the fact that valuations are expressed in value statements, whose whole purpose is to influence other people's value judgements and behaviour. It would consequently be surprising if an individual were entirely uninfluenced by the verdicts of others. Indeed, when a working agreement is reached, it is usually partly, if not wholly, the result of this kind of mutual influence. These are difficulties which Arrow does not seem to face. Nevertheless, they can, formally at least, be side-stepped. Thus we can suppose that we can have as much revoting, or rearrangement of individual orders, as the individuals want when they learn the opinions and verdicts of each other. Accordingly each order is, so to speak, a deadlock order. It is the individual order resulting when all persuasion has been used, and after an indefinite number of straw votes.[6]

Second, it will be objected that I may regard x as better than y but still be willing to submit to a ruling which proclaims y as society's choice. But it can easily be seen that this, though true, is no objection, for it interprets the machine as a decision-making process. I am not maintaining that there is anything inconsistent about accepting the nondictatorship condition when the machine is *thus* interpreted. The acceptability of the conditions of correspondence, given the decision-making-process interpretation, will be discussed in the next section.

6. This consideration alone would seem to limit the applicability of the Arrow theorem to a very small society. Moreover, it is quite reasonable to suppose that no such deadlock, or equilibrium, set of orders would ever result, especially in a large society. The dynamics of value formation may imply that values are, as a result of mutual influence, in a state of permanent flux.

Third, some people might not find convincing my statement that the sentences which the machine produces cannot themselves be regarded as value judgements. They may think that judgements do not necessarily require someone to judge. Though I believe it to be a nonsensical supposition, let us suppose, for the remainder of this section, that the machine *does* produce value judgements.

Now if I think x is better than y, and the machine announces that y is better than x, I have three choices. First I can say: 'I was wrong; y *is* better than x.' Thus Rousseau claims: 'When therefore the opinion that is contrary to my own prevails, this proves neither more nor less than that I was mistaken' (1763, p. 94). Rousseau's remark can be taken to mean merely that I was wrong in that my original vote was a guess at the general will which, *ex hypothesi*, is the majority decision. But Rousseau is nothing if not inconsistent, and the remark could be taken as an appeal to some mystical standard of right and wrong. But since few philosophers now believe that value judgements can be verified or falsified (i.e. be said to be true or false in any objective sense), and since the fact that they cannot be thus verified is the whole basis of Arrow's work, this choice can be dismissed. Second, I can say: 'I have changed my mind. I now wish to assert the same value judgement as the machine; y *is* better than x.' It is quite clear that we can dismiss this as a possibility for everyone; for if everyone always changed his values to be in conformity with the machine, no problem could arise. There would always be unanimous agreement in the end, however perverse the machine was. Third, I can say 'To hell with the machine; x is better than y, whatever it says.' If I always did this (and how could I do anything else, since, remember, we are supposing that all other people's values are already known; indeed I have taken into account everything I think significant!), then I should naturally have refused to accept the condition of nondictatorship. It is in the nature of value judgements that the only order which I can fully accept is one that coincides with my own, regardless of the orders of other people. In other words, no one can consistently accept the condition of 'nondictatorship'. At all events, it is sheer nonsense to say, 'A is better than B, but everyone else claims B is better than A; therefore, since I don't want to be a dictator, B is better than A'. Yet this is what acceptance of condition 4 would imply in this general case. Once again we are back at the conclusion that condition 4 makes nonsense of any interpretation of the Arrow system in ethical terms. In my opinion, this makes the title 'social welfare function' a dangerous misnomer.

Arrow presumably thinks differently, though it is difficult to be sure of this from his book. Thus, having shown that a 'social welfare function' satisfying his conditions is possible if individual orders happen to be of a certain form,[7] he proceeds to a brief discussion of some of the politico-ethical systems which various philosophers have vainly proposed and rightly says that they are based on some idea of an initial consensus of values; he then writes: 'The results . . . show that the condition of unanimity is mathematically unnecessary to the existence of a social welfare function, and we may well hope that there are still other conditions [i.e. conditions as to the form of the individual valuations] . . . under which the formation of a social welfare function will be possible' (1963, p. 83).

The very use of the phrase 'social welfare function' suggests that if such were possible, then somehow an objective moral code would have been erected. Political philosophers used to worry over the question 'Why ought I to obey the state (or society, or the general will)?' The pseudo-puzzle of how one can both be free and be subject to law is a variant of the pseudo-puzzle of how duty and self-interest can be reconciled. The philosophers tried to show that it was always really in one's own interest to abide by whatever the 'objective' code might be. Since, plainly, conflict must arise, at least in the absence of complete initial consensus, and since such consensus was obviously absent, they invented the doctrine of a metaphysical consensus. When people actually (i.e. really) disagreed about some matter affecting the common interest, they were really (i.e. metaphysically) agreeing. Rousseau, who was first responsible for this nonsense, found some difficulty in explaining how one found out what people were really metaphysically agreeing about when they disagreed; i.e. he found some difficulty in explaining the circumstances under which one could be sure that the general will had expressed itself. We may illustrate all this with a few quotations: 'The problem is to find a form of association which will defend and protect with the whole common force the person and goods of each associate, and in which each, while uniting himself with all, may still

7. So-called 'single-peaked' preferences. See Arrow (1963, chapter 7).

obey himself alone, and remain as free as before' (Rousseau, 1763, p. 14). 'Each of us puts his person and all his power in common under the supreme direction of the general will' (p. 15). 'Whoever refuses to obey the general will shall be compelled to do so by the whole body. This means nothing less than that he will be forced to be free' (p. 18). 'The general will is always right and tends to the public advantage' (p. 25).

It is but a very short step from here (a step which Hegel took) to maintain that acceptance of the social order (or obedience to the state) is really only self-obedience. Arrow's problem clearly has so much in common with Rousseau's that it seems worth while to point out again the insidious danger of this approach. Modern totalitarian philosophy may be not altogether unjustly fathered on Rousseau.

Ever since the objectivity of utilitarianism was called in question, economists have been searching for that old philosophers' stone, a scientific ethic. Recently many philosophers, those of the linguistic school, have given up the search, because they have realized that any attempt to define ethical terms is necessarily also an attempt to lay down a moral code; i.e. any supposed definition of an ethical word in nonethical terms is itself an ethical judgement. Thus, in view of the undoubted fact of disagreement about values, any assertion that such-and-such a given value statement is 'objectively true' is itself a value statement which persuasively twists words like 'objective' and 'true' in an attempt to get the given value statement accepted.

We can have an 'objective' ethic only when there is universal agreement. But when there is universal agreement ethics will have ceased to exist, since all moral judgements will have become futile and redundant. One does not tell people that they ought to do what they are doing or will do anyway. If everyone agreed, there would be no need to try to change other people's values and behaviour, which is the primary use of value statements. In Utopia, not only will the state have withered away, but also all morality; and naturally, since it is Utopia, not only all morality, but also welfare economics.

4 The general version of the Arrow social welfare function in relation to politics and decision-making

We indicated in section 3 that the so-called 'social welfare function' must be interpreted not (as the name might seem to imply) as a social welfare function but as a decision-making process. The question arises whether one can consistently accept Arrow's conditions, given this interpretation.

The importance of the distinction between a value order and a decision order, for our purposes, is as follows: In a given community, or committee, as many value orderings as there are individuals may coexist. On the other hand, as between two alternatives there can be only one effective decision. Thus we may all have our conflicting opinions as to whether we ought to go to war or not. But the decision to do so or not to do so is unique and binding for everyone. Where values are concerned, everyone must be a 'dictator' (i.e. the logic of value judgements is such that one cannot consistently *accept* any value ordering which differs from one's own); where decisions are in question, everyone cannot be a dictator, in Arrow's sense, unless there is unanimity.

Thus an individual will often be prepared to accept a decision which goes against him, because the same decision-making process (or 'procedure', for short) will be used for making many other decisions between other alternatives, some of which will go in his favour. This is, of course, true; but it is not an answer to the problem of why acceptance of Arrow's conditions does not imply inconsistency. I may be prepared, of course, to accept decisions which go against me because it is unwise to rebel against an established procedure with established sanctions. But this does not explain why, when I am free and still without my chains, I should accept certain *a priori* conditions to which any social contract must conform – *a priori* conditions which rule out all procedures which would ever decide in my favour against everyone else. To explain this, we require, I think, the hypothesis that, among the very limited number of procedures which would stand any chance of being established, none would make me dictatorial in Arrow's sense, together with the hypothesis that all such procedures would determine social states higher on my valuation than anarchy.

It may be suggested that the matter is much simpler than this and that I am making possible acceptance of the conditions depend too much on expediency and not enough on high moral purpose. Thus it may be said that, although one values x above y, one might prefer to accept a procedure which would yield y, if the only way to get x were to impose one's will on society.[8] This is true; but it is not a sufficient reason for accepting Arrow's condition of 'nondictatorship', which, barring the name, contains nothing about power or force. This is not, of course, Arrow's fault, given his technique. It springs from the fact that causal and power relations are not logical relations. Thus, since 'dictatorship', in the ordinary sense, involves the idea of causation, it cannot be adequately described in terms of implication. Even so, one must add that it is probably true that most people would attach intrinsic demerit to a procedure which ever allowed a minority of one to win.

To sum this up: One may say that expediency might, in most situations, counsel one to accept condition 4 as applied to procedure. It may also be widely acceptable on moral grounds. Indeed, conditions 3 and 4 might be said to contain the bare essentials of democratic procedures – but, perhaps, only the barest essentials, since there is nothing in them to prevent, say, a minority of two in a million from carrying the day.

We may now briefly consider conditions 1 and 2, taken in conjunction with the others. It would seem unlikely that anyone would want to attach intrinsic merit or demerit to them. Consequently, one may suppose that individuals would decide whether or not to accept them on the basis of whether, in conjunction with the remaining conditions, they would be likely to admit or exclude procedures more or less likely to lead to higher or lower states more or less often than alternative procedures. Thus the value of such conditions of correspondence would be derivative, though not derivative solely

8. It should be noted that to formulate this suggestion at all it is necessary to assume that the 'social states' contain only descriptions of the goods accruing to each individual. It presupposes that the procedures have intrinsic, and not merely derived, merit or demerit. In other words, since we are now dealing with decision-making processes or mechanisms, means may be valued apart from the ends attained by them. This distinction of 'ends' and 'means' could not, of course, arise when we were considering (or, rather, trying to consider) the function as a social welfare function. There cannot be procedures or mechanisms (means) for working out what is right or wrong. Means are, in the present context, means of arriving at a decision. It should be noted, however, that 'means' usually refers to social states which would necessarily precede some more distant social state aimed at. In this sense, the means are part of the ends in the present discussion: the individuals in willing the ends necessarily also will the means; they order the alternative future chains of social status.

from one's own present, or even expected future, ordering, but also from a consideration of probable changes in other orderings as well (e.g. if I disapproved of drunkenness very much and thought the taste for gin on the increase, I might not wish condition 1 to be satisfied for states involving alcohol). The chief difficulty with any such 'conditions of correspondence' is that, for both logical and factual reasons, it is exceedingly difficult to see what they involve one in. Nevertheless, Arrow's conditions undoubtedly have some prima facie plausibility, probably mainly for the reasons of expediency discussed above.

5 Conclusions

It was first concluded that Arrow's system is quite different from, and has little relevance to, traditional welfare economics. Second, it was found that it cannot without inconsistency be interpreted as a critique of social welfare functions. Last, we found that it, and no doubt similar deductive techniques, are in principle applicable to decision-making processes. Whether, in this sphere, Arrow's conditions of correspondence are sufficiently acceptable as minimum conditions for a satisfactory democratic decision-making procedure for it to be said that he has proved that consistent decisions cannot be reached via such procedures must be left an open question. Some people will no doubt think that such a proposition requires no proof. Others will think that the essence of democracy is something which must escape definition in terms of any functional relation between decisions and individual preferences.

References

ARROW, K. J. (1963), *Social Choice and Individual Values*, 2nd edn, Wiley.
ROUSSEAU, J.-J. (1763), *The Social Contract*, Penguin, 1968.
SAMUELSON, P. A. (1947), *Foundations of Economic Analysis*, Harvard University Press.

Part Four
Alternative Conceptions of Justice

This is the central part of the volume. It surveys some of the main positions taken on the concept of distributive justice over the past two hundred and fifty years. The contractarian doctrine of natural rights, with some discussion of rights to *minimal* economic support of each citizen, is represented by the excerpts from Kant. In this collection, Sidgwick carries the standard of classical utilitarianism. Modern-day neo-utilitarianism is expounded in the papers by Harsanyi and Vickrey. These are followed by an augmented version of the basic paper on the maximin criterion of justice by John Rawls. Under this theory of justice, each citizen has the right to the *maximal* economic support from the state. Utilitarianism hedges its bet, standing as a halfway house between Kant and Rawls. Finally the brief paper by Ayn Rand gives a glimpse of things from the Randian perspective.

6 I. Kant

Two Essays on Right

I. Kant, (a) in H. Reiss (ed.), *Kant's Political Writings*, Cambridge University Press, 1970, pp. 73–87; and (b) 'The metaphysics of morals', in *The Metaphysical Elements of Justice*, trans. by J. Ladd, Bobs-Merrill, 1965[1].

On the relationship of theory to practice in political right

Among all the contracts by which a large group of men unites to form a society (*pactum sociale*), the contract establishing a *civil constitution* (*pactum unionis civilis*) is of an exceptional nature. For while, so far as its execution is concerned, it has much in common with all others that are likewise directed towards a chosen end to be pursued by joint effort, it is essentially different from all others in the principle of its constitution (*constitutionis civilis*). In all social contracts, we find a union of many individuals for some common end which they all *share*. But a union as an end in itself which they all *ought to share* and which is thus an absolute and primary duty in all external relationships whatsoever among human beings (who cannot avoid mutually influencing one another), is only found in a society in so far as it constitutes a civil state, i.e. a commonwealth. And the end which is a duty in itself in such external relationships, and which is indeed the highest formal condition (*conditio sine qua non*) of all other external duties, is the *right* of men *under coercive public laws* by which each can be given what is due to him and secured against attack from any others. But the whole concept of an external right is derived entirely from the concept of *freedom* in the mutual external relationships of human beings, and has nothing to do with the end which all men have by nature (i.e. the aim of achieving happiness) or with the recognized means of attaining this end. And thus the latter end must on no account interfere as a determinant with the laws governing external right. *Right* is the restriction of each individual's

1. Kant seeks here to refute Hobbes's political theory, which found its classic expression in the *Leviathan* (1651). The actual argument is explicitly directed against Hobbes's *De Cive* (1642).

freedom so that it harmonizes with the freedom of everyone else (in so far as this is possible within the terms of a general law). And *public right* is the distinctive quality of the *external laws* which make this constant harmony possible. Since every restriction of freedom through the arbitrary will of another party is termed *coercion*, it follows that a civil constitution is a relationship among *free* men who are subject to coercive laws, while they retain their freedom within the general union with their fellows. Such is the requirement of pure reason, which legislates *a priori*, regardless of all empirical ends (which can all be summed up under the general heading of happiness). Men have different views on the empirical end of happiness and what it consists of, so that as far as happiness is concerned, their will cannot be brought under any common principle nor thus under any external law harmonizing with the freedom of everyone.

The civil state, regarded purely as a lawful state, is based on the following *a priori* principles:

1. The *freedom* of every member of society as a *human being*.
2. The *equality* of each with all the others as a *subject*.
3. The *independence* of each member of a commonwealth as a *citizen*.

These principles are not so much laws given by an already established state, as laws by which a state can alone be established in accordance with pure rational principles of external human right. Thus:

1. Man's *freedom* as a human being, as a principle for the constitution of a commonwealth, can be expressed in the following formula. No-one can compel me to be happy in accordance with his conception of the welfare of others, for each may seek his happiness in whatever way he sees fit, so long as he does not infringe upon the freedom of others to pursue a similar end which can be reconciled with the freedom of everyone else within a workable general law – i.e. he must accord to others the same right as he enjoys himself. A government might be established on the principle of benevolence towards the people, like that of a father towards his children. Under such a *paternal government* (*imperium paternale*), the subjects, as immature children who cannot distinguish what is truly useful or harmful to

themselves, would be obliged to behave purely passively and to rely upon the judgement of the head of state as to how they *ought* to be happy, and upon his kindness in willing their happiness at all. Such a government is the greatest conceivable *despotism*, i.e. a constitution which suspends the entire freedom of its subjects, who thenceforth have no rights whatsoever. The only conceivable government for men who are capable of possessing rights, even if the ruler is benevolent, is not a *paternal* but a *patriotic* government (*imperium non paternale, sed patrioticum*). A *patriotic* attitude is one where everyone in the state, not excepting its head, regards the commonwealth as a maternal womb, or the land as the paternal ground from which he himself sprang and which he must leave to his descendants as a treasured pledge. Each regards himself as authorized to protect the rights of the commonwealth by laws of the general will, but not to submit it to his personal use at his own absolute pleasure. This right of freedom belongs to each member of the commonwealth as a human being, in so far as each is a being capable of possessing rights.

2. Man's *equality* as a subject might be formulated as follows. Each member of the commonwealth has rights of coercion in relation to all the others, except in relation to the head of state. For he alone is not a member of the commonwealth, but its creator or preserver, and he alone is authorized to coerce others without being subject to any coercive law himself. But all who are subject to laws are the subjects of a state, and are thus subject to the right of coercion along with all other members of the commonwealth; the only exception is a single person (in either the physical or the moral sense of the word), the head of state, through whom alone the rightful coercion of all others can be exercised. For if he too could be coerced, he would not be the head of state, and the hierarchy of subordination would ascend infinitely. But if there were two persons exempt from coercion, neither would be subject to coercive laws, and neither could do to the other anything contrary to right, which is impossible.

This uniform equality of human beings as subjects of a state is, however, perfectly consistent with the utmost inequality of the mass in the degree of its possessions, whether these take the form of physical or mental superiority over others, or of fortuitous external property and of particular rights (of which there may be many) with respect to others. Thus the welfare of the one depends very much on the will of the other (the poor depending on the rich), the one must obey the other (as the child its parents or the wife her husband), the one serves (the labourer) while the other pays, etc. Nevertheless, they are all equal as subjects *before the law*, which, as the pronouncement of the general will, can only be single in form, and which concerns the form of right and not the material or object in relation to which I possess rights. For no one can coerce anyone else other than through the public law and its executor, the head of state, while everyone else can resist the others in the same way and to the same degree. No one, however, can lose this authority to coerce others and to have rights towards them except through committing a crime. And no one can voluntarily renounce his rights by a contract or legal transaction to the effect that he has no rights but only duties, for such a contract would deprive him of the right to make a contract, and would thus invalidate the one he had already made.

From this idea of the equality of men as subjects in a commonwealth, there emerges this further formula: every member of the commonwealth must be entitled to reach any degree of rank which a subject can earn through his talent, his industry and his good fortune. And his fellow-subjects may not stand in his way by *hereditary* prerogatives or privileges of rank and thereby hold him and his descendants back indefinitely.

All right consists solely in the restriction of the freedom of others, with the qualification that their freedom can co-exist with my freedom within the terms of a general law; and public right in a commonwealth is simply a state of affairs regulated by a real legislation which conforms to this principle and is backed up by power, and under which a whole people live as subjects in a lawful state (*status iuridicus*). This is what we call a civil state, and it is characterized by equality in the effects and counter-effects of freely willed actions which limit one another in accordance with the general law of freedom. Thus the *birthright* of each individual in such a state (i.e. before he has performed any acts which can be judged in relation to right) is absolutely *equal* as regards his authority to coerce others to use their freedom in a way which harmonizes with his freedom. Since birth is not an act on the part of the one who is born, it cannot create any inequality in his legal position and cannot make him submit to any coercive laws except in so far as he is a subject, along with all the others, of the one supreme legislative power. Thus no member of the commonwealth can have a hereditary privilege as against his fellow-subjects; and no one can hand down to his descendants the privileges attached to the rank he occupies in the commonwealth, nor act as if he were qualified as a ruler by birth and forcibly prevent others from reaching the higher levels of the hierarchy (which are *superior* and *inferior*, but never *imperans* and *subiectus*) through their own merit. He may hand down everything else, so long as it is material and not pertaining to his person, for it may be acquired and disposed of as property and may over a series of generations create considerable inequalities in wealth among the members of the commonwealth (the employee and the employer, the landowner and the agricultural servants, etc.). But he may not prevent his subordinates from raising themselves to his own level if they are able and entitled to do so by their talent, industry and good fortune. If this were not so, he would be allowed to practise coercion without himself being subject to coercive counter-measures from others, and would thus be more than their fellow-subject. No one who lives within the lawful state of a commonwealth can forfeit this equality other than through some crime of his own, but never by contract or through military force (*occupatio bellica*). For no legal transaction on his part or on that of anyone else can make him cease to be his own master. He cannot become like a domestic animal to be employed in any chosen capacity and retained therein without consent for any desired period, even with the reservation (which is at times sanctioned by religion, as among the Indians) that he may not be maimed or killed. He can be considered happy in any condition so long as he is aware that, if he does not reach the same level as others, the fault lies either with himself (i.e. lack of ability or serious endeavour) or with circumstances for which he cannot blame others, and not with the irresistible will of any outside party. For as far as right is concerned, his fellow-subjects have no advantage over him.[2]

2. If we try to find a definite meaning for the word *gracious*, as distinct from kind, beneficent, protective etc., we see that it can be attributed only to a person to whom no *coercive rights* apply. Thus only the head of the *state's government*, who enacts and distributes all benefits that are possible within the public laws (for the *sovereign* who provides them is, as it were, invisible, and is not an agent but the personified law itself), can be given the title of *gracious lord*, for he is the

3. The *independence* (*sibisufficientia*) of a member of the common-wealth as a *citizen*, i.e. as a co-legislator, may be defined as follows. In the question of actual legislation, all who are free and equal under existing public laws may be considered equal, but not as regards the right to make these laws. Those who are not entitled to this right are nonetheless obliged, as members of the commonwealth, to comply with these laws, and they thus likewise enjoy their protection (not as *citizens* but as co-beneficiaries of this protection). For all right depends on laws. But a public law which defines for everyone that which is permitted and prohibited by right, is the act of a public will, from which all right proceeds and which must not therefore itself be able to do an injustice to any one. And this requires no less than the will of the entire people (since all men decide for all men and each decides for himself). For only towards oneself can one never act unjustly. But on the other hand, the will of another person cannot decide anything for someone without injustice, so that the law made by this other person would require a further law to limit his legis-lation. Thus an individual will cannot legislate for a common-wealth. For this requires freedom, equality and *unity* of the will of *all* the members. And the prerequisite for unity, since it necessitates a general vote (if freedom and equality are both present), is inde-pendence. The basic law, which can come only from the general, united will of the people, is called the *original contract*.

Anyone who has the right to vote on this legislation is a *citizen*

---

only individual to whom coercive rights do not apply. And even in an aristocratic government, as for example in Venice, the *senate* is the only 'gracious lord'. The nobles who belong to it, even including the *Doge* (for only the *plenary council* is the sovereign), are all subjects and equal to the others so far as the exercise of rights is concerned, for each subject has coercive rights towards every one of them. Princes (i.e. persons with a hereditary right to become rulers) are them-selves called gracious lords only with future reference, an account of their claims to become rulers (i.e. by courtly etiquette, *par courtoisie*). But as owners of property, they are nonetheless fellow-subjects of the others, and even the humblest of their servants must possess a right of coercion against them through the head of state. Thus there can be no more than one gracious lord in a state. And as for gracious (more correctly *distinguished*) ladies, they can be considered entitled to this appellation by their *rank* and their *sex* (thus only as opposed to the *male* sex), and this only by virtue of a refinement of manners (known as gallantry) whereby the male sex imagines that it does itself greater honour by giving the fair sex precedence over itself.

(*citoyen*, i.e. citizen of a state, not *bourgeois* or citizen of a town). The only qualification required by a citizen (apart, of course, from being an adult male) is that he must be his *own master* (*sui iuris*), and must have some *property* (which can include any skill, trade, fine art or science) to support himself. In cases where he must earn his living from others, he must earn it only by *selling* that which is his,[3] and not by allowing others to make use of him; for he must in the true sense of the word *serve* no one but the commonwealth. In this respect, artisans and large or small landowners are all equal, and each is entitled to one vote only. As for landowners, we leave aside the question of how anyone can have rightfully acquired more land than he can cultivate with his own hands (for acquisition by military seizure is not primary acquisition), and how it came about that numerous people who might otherwise have acquired permanent property were thereby reduced to serving someone else in order to live at all. It would certainly conflict with the above principle of equality if a law were to grant them a privileged status so that their descendants would always remain feudal landowners, without their land being sold or divided by inheritance and thus made useful to more people; it would also be unjust if only those belonging to an arbitrarily selected class were allowed to acquire land, should the estates in fact be divided. The owner of a large estate keeps out as many smaller property owners (and their votes) as could otherwise occupy his territories. He does not vote on their behalf, and himself has only *one* vote. It should be left exclusively to the ability, industry and good fortune of each member of the commonwealth to enable

3. He who does a piece of work (*opus*) can sell it to someone else, just as if it were his own property. But guaranteeing one's labour (*praestatio operae*) is not the same as selling a commodity. The domestic servant, the shop assistant, the labourer, or even the barber, are merely labourers (*operarii*), not *artists* (*artifices*, in the wider sense) or members of the state, and are thus unqualified to be citizens. And although the man to whom I give my firewood to chop and the tailor to whom I give material to make into clothes both appear to have a similar relationship towards me, the former differs from the latter in the same way as the barber from the wig-maker (to whom I may in fact have given the requisite hair) or the labourer from the artist or tradesman, who does a piece of work which belongs to him until he is paid for it. For the latter, in pursuing his trade, exchanges his property with someone else (*opus*), while the former allows someone else to make use of him. But I do admit that it is somewhat difficult to define the qualifications which entitle anyone to claim the status of being his own master.

each to acquire a part and all to acquire the whole, although this distinction cannot be observed within the general legislation itself. The number of those entitled to vote on matters of legislation must be calculated purely from the number of property owners, not from the size of their properties.

Those who possess this right to vote must agree *unanimously* to the law of public justice, or else a legal contention would arise between those who agree and those who disagree, and it would require yet another higher legal principle to resolve it. An entire people cannot, however, be expected to reach unanimity, but only to show a majority of votes (and not even of direct votes, but simply of the votes of those delegated in a large nation to represent the people). Thus the actual principle of being content with majority decisions must be accepted unanimously and embodied in a contract; and this itself must be the ultimate basis on which a civil constitution is established.

Conclusion

This, then, is an *original contract* by means of which a civil and thus completely lawful constitution and commonwealth can alone be established. But we need by no means assume that this contract (*contractus originarius* or *pactum sociale*), based on a coalition of the wills of all private individuals in a nation to form a common, public will for the purposes of rightful legislation, actually exists as a *fact*, for it cannot possibly be so. Such an assumption would mean that we would first have to prove from history that some nation, whose rights and obligations have been passed down to us, did in fact perform such an act, and handed down some authentic record or legal instrument, orally or in writing, before we could regard ourselves as bound by a pre-existing civil constitution. It is in fact merely an *idea* of reason, which nonetheless has undoubted practical reality; for it can oblige every legislator to frame his laws in such a way that they could have been produced by the united will of a whole nation, and to regard each subject, in so far as he can claim citizenship, as if he had consented within the general will. This is the test of the rightfulness of every public law. For if the law is such that a whole people could not *possibly* agree to it (for example, if it stated that certain class of *subjects* must be privileged as a hereditary *ruling class*), it is unjust; but if it is at least *possible* that a people could agree to it, it is our duty to consider the law as just, even if the people is at present in such a position or attitude of mind that it would probably refuse its consent if it were consulted.[4] But this restriction obviously applies only to the judgement of the legislator, not to that of the subject. Thus if a people, under some existing legislation, were asked to make a judgement which in all probability would prejudice its happiness, what should it do? Should the people not oppose the measure? The only possible answer is that they can do nothing but obey. For we are not concerned here with any happiness which the subject might expect to derive from the institutions or administration of the commonwealth, but primarily with the rights which would thereby be secured for everyone. And this is the highest principle from which all maxims relating to the commonwealth must begin, and which cannot be qualified by any other principles. No generally valid principle of legislation can be based on happiness. For both the current circumstances and the highly conflicting and variable illusions as to what happiness is (and no one can prescribe to others how they should attain it) make all fixed principles impossible, so that happiness alone can never be a suitable principle of legislation. The doctrine that *salus publica suprema civitatis lex est* [The public welfare is the supreme law of the state] retains its value and authority undiminished; but the public welfare which demands *first* consideration lies precisely in that legal constitution which guarantees everyone his freedom within the law, so that each remains free to seek his happiness in whatever way he thinks best, so long as he does not violate the lawful freedom and rights of his fellow subjects at large. If the supreme power makes laws which are primarily directed towards happiness (the affluence of the citizens, increased population, etc.), this cannot be regarded as the end for

4. If, for example, a war tax were proportionately imposed on all subjects, they could not claim, simply because it is oppressive, that it is unjust because the war is in their opinion unnecessary. For they are not entitled to judge this issue, since it is at least *possible* that the war is inevitable and the tax indispensable, so that the tax must be deemed rightful in the judgement of the subjects. But if certain estate owners were oppressed with levies for such a war, while others of the same class were exempted, it is easily seen that a whole people could never agree to a law of this kind, and it is entitled at least to make representations against it, since an unequal distribution of burdens can never be considered just.

which a civil constitution was established, but only as a means of *securing the rightful state*, especially against external enemies of the people. The head of state must be authorized to judge for himself whether such measures are necessary for the commonwealth's prosperity, which is required to maintain its strength and stability both internally and against external enemies. The aim is not, as it were, to make the people happy against its will, but only to ensure its continued existence as a commonwealth.[5] The legislator may indeed err in judging whether or not the measures he adopts are *prudent*, but not in deciding whether or not the law harmonizes with the principle of right. For he has ready to hand as an infallible *a priori* standard the idea of an original contract, and he need not wait for experience to show whether the means are suitable, as would be necessary if they were based on the principle of happiness. For so long as it is not self-contradictory to say that an entire people could agree to such a law, however painful it might seem, then the law is in harmony with right. But if a public law is beyond reproach (i.e. *irreprehensible*) with respect to right, it carries with it the authority to coerce those to whom it applies, and conversely, it forbids them to resist the will of the legislator by violent means. In other words, the power of the state to put the law into effect is also *irresistible*, and no rightfully established commonwealth can exist without a force of this kind to suppress all internal resistance. For such resistance would be dictated by a maxim which, if it became general, would destroy the whole civil constitution and put an end to the only state in which men can possess rights.

It thus follows that all resistance against the supreme legislative power, all incitement of the subjects to violent expressions of discontent, all defiance which breaks out into rebellion, is the greatest and most punishable crime in a commonwealth, for it destroys its very foundations. This prohibition is *absolute*. And even if the power of the state or its agent, the head of state, has violated the original

5. Measures of this kind might include certain restrictions on imports, so that the means of livelihood may be developed for the benefit of the subjects themselves and not as an advantage to foreigners or an encouragement for their industry. For without the prosperity of the people, the state would not have enough strength to resist external enemies or to preserve itself as a commonwealth.

contract by authorizing the government to act tyrannically, and has thereby, in the eyes of the subject, forfeited the right to legislate, the subject is still not entitled to offer counter-resistance. The reason for this is that the people, under an existing civil constitution, has no longer any right to judge how the constitution should be administered. For if we suppose that it does have this right to judge and that it disagrees with the judgement of the actual head of state, who is to decide which side is right? Neither can act as judge of his own cause. Thus there would have to be another head above the head of state to mediate between the latter and the people, which is self-contradictory. Nor can a right of necessity (*ius in casu necessitatis*) be invoked here as a means of removing the barriers which restrict the power of the people; for it is monstrous to suppose that we can have a right to do wrong in the direst (physical) distress.[6] For the head of state can just as readily claim that his severe treatment of his subjects is justified by their insubordination as the subjects can justify their rebellion by complaints about their unmerited suffering, and who is to decide? The decision must rest with whoever controls the ultimate enforcement of the public law, i.e. the head of state himself. Thus no one in the commonwealth can have a right to contest his authority.

6. There is no *casus necessitatis* except where duties, i.e. an *absolute* duty and another which, however pressing, is nevertheless *relative*, come into conflict. For instance, it might be necessary for someone to betray someone else, even if their relationship were that of father and son, in order to preserve the state from catastrophe. This preservation of the state from evil is an absolute duty, while the preservation of the individual is merely a relative duty (i.e. it applies only if he is not guilty of a crime against the state). The first person might denounce the second to the authorities with the utmost unwillingness, compelled only by (moral) necessity. But if a person, in order to preserve his own life, pushes a shipwrecked fellow away from the plank he grasps, it would be quite false to say that (physical) necessity gives him a right to do so. For it is only a relative duty for me to preserve my own life (i.e. it applies only if I can do so without committing a crime). But it is an absolute duty not to take the life of another person who has not offended me and does not even make me risk my own life. Yet the teachers of general civil law are perfectly consistent in authorizing such measures in cases of distress. For the authorities cannot combine a *penalty* with this prohibition, since this penalty would have to be death. But it would be a nonsensical law which threatened anyone with death if he did not voluntarily deliver himself up to death when in dangerous circumstances.

Nonetheless, estimable men have declared that the subject is justified, under certain circumstances, in using force against his superiors. I need name only Achenwall (1755–6), who is extremely cautious, precise and restrained in his theories of natural right. He says: 'If the danger which threatens the commonwealth as a result of long endurance of injustices from the head of state is greater than the danger to be feared from taking up arms against him, the people may then resist him. It may use this right to abrogate its contract of subjection and to dethrone him as a tyrant.' And he concludes: 'The people, in dethroning its ruler, thus returns to the state of nature' (sections 203–6).

I well believe that neither Achenwall nor any others of the worthy men who have speculated along the same lines as he would ever have given their advice or agreement to such hazardous projects if the case had arisen. And it can scarcely be doubted that if the revolutions whereby Switzerland, the United Netherlands or even Great Britain won their much admired constitutions had failed, the readers of their history would regard the execution of their celebrated founders as no more than the deserved punishment of great political criminals. For the result usually affects our judgement of the rightfulness of an action, although the result is uncertain, whereas the principles of right are constant. But it is clear that these peoples have done the greatest degree of wrong in seeking their rights in this way, even if we admit that such a revolution did no injustice to a ruler who had violated a specific basic agreement with the people, such as the *Joyeuse Entrée*.[7] For such procedures, if made into a maxim, make all lawful constitutions insecure and produce a state of complete lawlessness (*status naturalis*) where all rights cease at least to be effectual. In view of this tendency of so many right-thinking authors to plead on behalf of the people (and to its own detriment), I will only remark that such errors arise in part from the usual fallacy of allowing the principle of happiness to influence the judgement, wherever the principle of right is involved; and partly because these writers have assumed that the idea of an original contract (a basic

7. Charter granted to Brabant by Duke John III in 1354 in which the Duke undertook to maintain the integrity of the Duchy and not to wage war, make treaties or impose taxes without consulting his subjects represented by the municipalities.

postulate of reason) is something which must have taken place *in reality*, even where there is no document to show that any contract was actually submitted to the commonwealth, accepted by the head of state, and sanctioned by both parties. Such writers thus believe that the people retains the right to abrogate the original contract at its own discretion, if, in the opinion of the people, the contract has been severely violated.[8]

It is obvious from this that the principle of happiness (which is not in fact a definite principle at all) has ill effects in political right just as in morality, however good the intentions of those who teach it. The sovereign wants to make the people happy as he thinks best, and thus becomes a despot, while the people are unwilling to give up their universal human desire to seek happiness in their own way, and thus become rebels. If they had first of all asked what is lawful (in terms of *a priori* certainty, which no empiricist can upset), the idea of a social contract would retain its authority undiminished. But it would not exist as a fact (as Danton[9] would have it, declaring that since it does not actually exist, all property and all rights under the existing civil constitution are null and void), but only as a rational principle for judging any lawful public constitution whatsoever. And it would then be seen that, until the general will is there, the people has no coercive right against its ruler, since it can apply coercion legally only through him. But if the will is there, no force can be applied to the ruler by the people, otherwise the people would be the supreme ruler. Thus the people can never possess a right of coercion against the head of state, or be entitled to oppose him in word or deed.

We can see, furthermore, that this theory is adequately confirmed

8. Even if an actual contract of the people with the head of state has been violated, the people cannot reply immediately as a *commonwealth*, but only by forming factions. For the hitherto existing constitution has been destroyed by the people, but a new commonwealth has still to be organized. At this point, the state of anarchy supervenes, with all the terrors it may bring with it. And the wrong which is thereby done is done by each faction of the people to the others, as is clear from the case where the rebellious subjects ended up by trying to thrust upon each other a constitution which would have been far more oppressive than the one they abandoned. For they would have been devoured by ecclesiastics and aristocrats, instead of enjoying greater equality in the distribution of political burdens under a single head of state who ruled them all. [These remarks refer to the French Revolution.]

9. Georges Jacques Danton (1759–94), the French revolutionary leader.

in practice. In the British constitution, of which the people are so proud that they hold it up as a model for the whole world, we find no mention of what the people are entitled to do if the monarch were to violate the contract of 1688.[10] Since there is no law to cover such a case, the people tacitly reserve the right to rebel against him if he should violate the contract. And it would be an obvious contradiction if the constitution included a law for such eventualities, entitling the people to overthrow the existing constitution, from which all particular laws are derived, if the contract were violated. For there would then have to be a *publicly constituted*[11] opposing power, hence a second head of state to protect the rights of the people against the first ruler, and then yet a third to decide which of the other two had right on his side. In fact, the leaders (or guardians – call them what you will) of the British people, fearing some such accusation if their plans did not succeed, *invented* the notion of a voluntary abdication by the monarch they forced out, rather than claim a right to depose him (which would have made the constitution self-contradictory).

While I trust that no one will accuse me of flattering monarchs too much by declaring them inviolable, I likewise hope that I shall be spared the reproach of claiming too much for the people if I maintain that the people too have inalienable rights against the head of state, even if these cannot be rights of coercion.

Hobbes is of the opposite opinion. According to him (1641, chapter 7, section 14), the head of state has no contractual obligations towards the people; he can do no injustice to a citizen, but may act towards him as he pleases. This proposition would be perfectly correct if injustice were taken to mean any injury which gave the injured party a *coercive right* against the one who has done him injustice. But in its general form, the proposition is quite terrifying.

The non-resisting subject must be able to assume that his ruler has

10. This remark refers to the accession of William III of Orange and Mary to the British throne in 1688 (the Glorious Revolution). After James II had been overthrown, Parliament legislated for William's and Mary's accession, restricting the monarchy to the Protestant successors of James I.

11. No right in a state can be tacitly and treacherously included by a secret reservation, and least of all a right which the people claim to be part of the constitution, for all laws within it must be thought of as arising out of a public will. Thus if the constitution allowed rebellion, it would have to declare this right publicly and make clear how it might be implemented.

no *wish* to do him injustice. And everyone has his inalienable rights, which he cannot give up even if he wishes to, and about which he is entitled to make his own judgements. But if he assumes that the ruler's attitude is one of good will, any injustice which he believes he has suffered can only have resulted through error, or through ignorance of certain possible consequences of the laws which the supreme authority has made. Thus the citizen must, with the approval of the ruler, be entitled to make public his opinion on whatever of the ruler's measures seem to him to constitute an injustice against the commonwealth. For to assume that the head of state can neither make mistakes nor be ignorant of anything would be to imply that he receives divine inspiration and is more than a human being. Thus *freedom of the pen* is the only safeguard of the rights of the people, although it must not transcend the bounds of respect and devotion towards the existing constitution, which should itself create a liberal attitude of mind among the subjects. To try to deny the citizen this freedom does not only mean, as Hobbes maintains, that the subject can claim no rights against the supreme ruler. It also means withholding from the ruler all knowledge of those matters which, if he knew about them, he would himself rectify, so that he is thereby put into a self-stultifying position. For his will issues commands to his subjects (as citizens) only in so far as he represents the general will of the people. But to encourage the head of state to fear that independent and public thought might cause political unrest is tantamount to making him distrust his own power and feel hatred towards his people.

The general principle, however, according to which a people may judge negatively whatever it believes was *not decreed* in good will by the supreme legislation, can be summed up as follows: *Whatever a people cannot impose upon itself cannot be imposed upon it by the legislator either*.

For example, if we wish to discover whether a law which declares permanently valid an ecclesiastical constitution (itself formulated at some time in the past) can be regarded as emanating from the actual will or intention of the legislator, we must first ask whether a people is *authorized* to make a law for itself whereby certain accepted doctrines and outward forms of religion are declared permanent, and whether the people may thus prevent its own descendants from making further progress in religious understanding or from correcting any past mistakes. It is clear that any original contract of the people which established such a law would in itself be null and void, for it would conflict with the appointed aim and purpose of mankind. Thus a law of this kind cannot be regarded as the actual will of the monarch, to whom counter-representations may accordingly be made. In all cases, however, where the supreme legislation did nevertheless adopt such measures, it would be permissible to pass general and public judgements upon them, but never to offer any verbal or active resistance.

In every commonwealth, there must be *obedience* to generally valid coercive laws within the mechanism of the political constitution. There must also be a *spirit of freedom*, for in all matters concerning universal human duties, each individual requires to be convinced by reason that the coercion which prevails is lawful, otherwise he would be in contradiction with himself. Obedience without the spirit of freedom is the effective cause of all *secret societies*. For it is a natural vocation of man to communicate with his fellows, especially in matters affecting mankind as a whole. Thus secret societies would disappear if freedom of this kind were encouraged. And how else can the government itself acquire the knowledge it needs to further its own basic intention, if not by allowing the spirit of freedom, so admirable in its origins and effects, to make itself heard?

Nowhere does practice so readily bypass all pure principles of reason and treat theory so presumptuously as in the question of what is needed for a good political constitution. The reason for this is that a legal constitution of long standing gradually makes the people accustomed to judging both their happiness and their rights in terms of the peaceful *status quo*. Conversely, it does not encourage them to value the existing state of affairs in the light of those concepts of happiness and right which reason provides. It rather makes them prefer this passive state to the dangerous task of looking for a better one, thus bearing out the saying which Hippocrates told physicians to remember: *iudicium anceps, experimentum periculosum* ['The judgement is uncertain, and experiments are dangerous']. Thus all constitutions which have lasted for a sufficiently long time, whatever their inadequacies and variations, produce the same result: the people remain content with what they have. If we therefore consider the *welfare of the people*, theory is not in fact valid, for everything depends upon practice derived from experience.

But reason provides a concept which we express by the words *political right*. And this concept has binding force for human beings who coexist in a state of antagonism produced by their natural freedom, so that it has an objective, practical reality, irrespective of the good or ill it may produce (for these can only be known by experience). Thus it is based on *a priori* principles, for experience cannot provide knowledge of what is right, and there is a *theory* of political right to which practice must conform before it can be valid.

The only objection which can be raised against this is that, although men have a mental notion of the rights to which they are entitled, their intractability is such that they are incapable and unworthy of being treated as their rights demand, so that they can and ought to be kept under control by a supreme power acting purely from expediency. But this counsel of desperation (*salto mortale*) means that, since there is no appeal to right but only to force, the people may themselves resort to force and thus make every legal constitution insecure. If there is nothing which commands immediate respect through reason, such as the basic rights of man, no influence can prevail upon man's arbitrary will and restrain his freedom. But if both benevolence and right speak out in loud tones, human nature will not prove too debased to listen to their voice with respect. *Tum pietate gravem meritisque si forte virum quem Conspexere, silent arrectisque auribus adstant* ['If they catch sight of a man respected for his virtues and services, they are silent and stand close with ears alert'] (Virgil, *Aeneid*).

Introduction to the theory of right

1 Definition of the theory of right

The sum total of those laws which can be incorporated in external legislation is termed the *theory of right* (*Ius*). If legislation of this kind actually exists, the theory is one of *positive right*. If a person who is conversant with it or has studied it (*Iuriconsultus*) is acquainted with the external laws in their external function, i.e. in their application to instances encountered in experience, he is said to be experienced in matters of right (*Iurisperitus*). This body of theory may amount to the same as *jurisprudence* (*Iurisprudentia*), but it will remain only the *science of right* (*Iuriscientia*) unless both its elements are present. The latter designation applies to a *systematic* knowledge of the theory of natural right (*Ius naturae*), although it is the student of natural right who has to supply the immutable principles on which all positive legislation must rest.

2 What is right?

The *jurist*, if he does not wish to lapse into tautology or to base his answer on the laws of a particular country at a particular time instead of offering a comprehensive solution, may well be just as perplexed on being asked this as the logician is by the notorious question: '*What is truth?*' He will certainly be able to tell us what is legally right (*quid sit iuris*) within a given context, i.e. what the laws say or have said in a particular place and at a particular time: but whether their provisions are also in keeping with right, and whether they constitute a universal criterion by which we may recognize in general what is right and what is unjust (*iustum et iniustum*), are questions whose answers will remain concealed from him unless he abandons such empirical principles for a time and looks for the sources of these judgements in the realm of pure reason. This will enable him to lay the foundations of all possible positive legislations. And while empirical laws may give him valuable guidance, a purely empirical theory of right, like the wooden head in Phaedrus' fable, may have a fine appearance, but will unfortunately contain no brain.

The concept of right, in so far as it is connected with a corresponding obligation (i.e. the moral concept of right), applies within the following conditions. *Firstly*, it applies only to those relationships between one person and another which are both external and practical, that is, in so far as their actions can in fact influence each other either directly or indirectly. But *secondly*, it does not concern the relationship between the will of one person and the *desires* of another (and hence only the latter's needs, as in acts of benevolence or hardheartedness); it concerns only the relationship between the will of the first and the *will* of the second. And *thirdly*, the will's *material* aspect, i.e. the end which each party intends to accomplish by means of the object of his will, is completely irrelevant in this mutual relationship; for example, we need not ask whether someone who buys goods from me for his own commercial use will gain anything in the process. For we are interested only in the *form* of the relationship between the two wills, in so far as they are regarded as *free*, and in whether the action of one of the two parties can be reconciled with the freedom of the other in accordance with a universal law.

Right is therefore the sum total of those conditions within which the will of one person can be reconciled with the will of another in accordance with a universal law of freedom.

3 The universal principle of right

'Every action which by itself or by its maxim enables the freedom of each individual's will to coexist with the freedom of everyone else in accordance with a universal law is *right*.'

Thus if my action or my situation in general can coexist with the freedom of everyone in accordance with a universal law, anyone who hinders me in either does me an injustice; for this hindrance or resistance cannot coexist with freedom in accordance with universal laws.

It also follows from this that I cannot be required to make this principle of all maxims my own maxim, i.e. *to make it the maxim of my own actions*; for each individual can be free so long as I do not interfere with his freedom by my *external actions*, even although his freedom may be a matter of total indifference to me or although I may wish in my heart to deprive him of it. That I should make it my maxim to *act* in accordance with right is a requirement laid down for me by ethics.

Thus the universal law of right is as follows: let your external actions be such that the free application of your will can coexist with the freedom of everyone in accordance with a universal law. And although this law imposes an obligation on me, it does not mean that I am in any way expected, far less required, to restrict my freedom *myself* to these conditions purely for the sake of this obligation. On the contrary, reason merely says that individual freedom *is* restricted in this way by virtue of the idea behind it, and that it may also be actively restricted by others; and it states this as a postulate which does not admit of any further proof.

If it is not our intention to teach virtue, but only to state what is *right*, we may not and should not ourselves represent this law of right as a possible motive for actions.

4 Right entails the authority to use coercion

Any resistance which counteracts the hindrance of an effect helps to promote this effect and is consonant with it. Now everything that is contrary to right is a hindrance to freedom based on universal laws, while coercion is a hindrance or resistance to freedom. Consequently, if a certain use to which freedom is put is itself a hindrance to freedom in accordance with universal laws (i.e. if it is contrary to right), any coercion which is used against it will be a *hindrance* to a *hindrance of freedom*, and will thus be consonant with freedom in accordance with universal laws – that is, it will be right. It thus follows by the law of contradiction that right entails the authority to apply coercion to anyone who infringes it.

5 In its 'strict' sense, right can also be envisaged as the possibility of a general and reciprocal coercion consonant with the freedom of everyone in accordance with universal laws

This proposition implies that we should not conceive of right as being composed of two elements, namely the obligation imposed by a law, and the authority which someone who obligates another party through his will possesses to coerce the latter into carrying out the obligation in question. Instead, the concept of right should be seen as consisting immediately of the possibility of universal reciprocal coercion being combined with the freedom of everyone. For just as the only object of right in general is the external aspect of actions, right in its strict sense, i.e. right unmixed with any ethical considerations, requires no determinants of the will apart from purely external ones; for it will then be pure and will not be confounded with any precepts of virtue. Thus only a completely external right can be called right in the *strict* (or narrow) sense. This right is certainly based on each individual's awareness of his obligations within the law; but if it is to remain pure, it may not and cannot appeal to this awareness as a motive which might determine the will to act in accordance with it, and it therefore depends rather on the principle of the possibility of an external coercion which can coexist with the freedom of everyone in accordance with universal laws.

Thus when it is said that a creditor has a right to require the debtor to pay his debt, it does not mean that he can make the latter feel that his reason itself obliges him to act in this way. It means instead that the use of coercion to compel everyone to do this can very well be reconciled with everyone's freedom, hence also with the debtor's freedom, in accordance with a universal external law: thus right and the authority to apply coercion mean one and the same thing.

The law of reciprocal coercion, which is necessarily consonant with the freedom of everyone within the principle of universal freedom, is in a sense the *construction* of the concept of right: that is, it represents this concept in pure *a priori* intuition by analogy with the possibility of free movement of bodies within the law of the *equality of action and reaction*. Just as the qualities of an object of pure mathematics cannot be directly deduced from the concept but can only be discovered from its construction, it is not so much the *concept* of right but rather a general, reciprocal and uniform coercion, subject to universal laws and harmonizing with the concept itself, which makes any representation of the concept possible. But while this concept of dynamics (i.e. that of the equality of action and reaction) is based upon a purely formal concept of pure mathematics (e.g. of geometry), reason has taken care that the understanding is likewise as fully equipped as possible with *a priori* intuitions for the construction of the concept of right.

In geometry, the term 'right' (*rectum*), in the sense of '*straight*', can be used either as the opposite of '*curved*' or of '*oblique*'. In the first sense, it applies to a line whose *intrinsic nature* is such that there can be only *one* of its kind between two given *points*. But in the second sense, it applies to an *angle* between two intersecting or coincident *lines* whose nature is such that there can be only *one* of its kind (a right angle) between the given lines. The perpendicular line which forms a right angle will not incline more to one side than to the other, and will divide the area on either side of it into two equal parts. By this analogy, the theory of right will also seek an assurance that each individual receives (with mathematical precision) *what is his due*. This cannot be expected of *ethics*, however, for it cannot refuse to allow some room for exceptions (*latitudinem*).

[Kant then adds some remarks on 'equivocal right'. He does not mean right in the strict sense, but in the wider sense of the word. Only two aspects of right arise here: equity and the right of necessity. Kant remarks of equity that it concerns only such cases as are outside strict right, i.e. where there is no case in law at all. The right of necessity applies to cases where one acts against someone else (for instance, by taking someone else's life because one's own life is in danger). A man cannot be punished with any greater punishment than the loss of life itself. There can be therefore no law punishing a man who acts out of necessity.

Kant explains the division of the theory of right into private and public right. He also distinguishes between innate and acquired rights. In his view, freedom (i.e. independence from the coercive will of another), in so far as it can coexist with the freedom of everyone else in accordance with a universal law, is the sole original right. It belongs to every man by virtue of his humanity. Equality, honesty and the right to act towards others in such a way that their rights are not infringed all derive from this right of freedom. Kant also provides a general division of the metaphysics of morals, distinguishing between those duties which are duties of right and those which are duties of virtue.

In the first section of *The Metaphysical Elements of Right*, Kant deals with private right which is concerned with property. There are two kinds of property: property which one possesses directly through physical possession and property which one only possesses indirectly. Kant examines the philosophical foundations of the law of property, deducing it from the idea of original communal possession of the soil. He also argues that external possession of things of which we are not in physical possession is possible only because we are noumenal beings, not necessarily bound by the limits of mere empirical (phenomenal) possessions. Kant goes on to argue that external possessions are possible only in a state of civil society, whereas in a state of nature, such possession can have only a provisional character.

Subsequently, Kant deals with the right of acquiring things and with various other rights, such as the rights of persons, marriage, parentage, landlords, contract, money, books, inheritance, etc. His discussion of the theory of private right is followed by a discussion of the theory of public right, which is printed below.]

The theory of right: public right
Political right

Public right is the sum total of those laws which require to be made universally public in order to produce a state of right. It is therefore a system of laws for a people, i.e. an aggregate of human beings, or for an aggregate of peoples. Since these individuals or peoples must influence one another, they need to live in a state of right under a unifying will: that is, they require a *constitution* in order to enjoy their rights.

A condition in which the individual members of a people are related to each other in this way is said to be a *civil* one (*status civilis*), and when considered as a whole in relation to its own members, it is called a *state* (*civitas*). Since the state takes the form of a union created by the common interest of everyone in living in a state of right, it is called a *commonwealth* (*res publica latius sic dicta*). In relation to other peoples, however, it is simply called a *power* (*potentia* – hence the word 'potentate'); and if it claims to be united by heredity, it may also call itself a *congeneric nation* (*gens*). Within the general concept of public right, we must therefore include not only *political right* but also *international right* (*ius gentium*). And since the earth's surface is not infinite but limited by its own configuration, these two concepts taken together necessarily lead to the idea of an *international political right* (*ius gentium*) or a *cosmopolitan right* (*ius cosmopolitan*). Consequently, if even only one of these three possible forms of rightful state lacks a principle which limits external freedom by means of laws, the structure of all the rest must inevitably be undermined, and finally collapse.

Experience teaches us the maxim that human beings act in a violent and malevolent manner, and that they tend to fight among themselves until an external coercive legislation supervenes. But it is not experience or any kind of factual knowledge which makes public legal coercion necessary. On the contrary, even if we imagine men to be as benevolent and law-abiding as we please, the *a priori* rational idea of a non-lawful state will still tell us that before a public and legal state is established, individual men, peoples and states can never be secure against acts of violence from one another, since each will have his own right to do *what seems right and good to him*, independently of the opinion of others. Thus the first decision the individual is obliged to make, if he does not wish to renounce all concepts of right, will be to adopt the principle that one must abandon the state of nature in which everyone follows his own desires, and unite with everyone else (with whom he cannot avoid having intercourse) in order to submit to external, public and lawful coercion. He must accordingly enter into a state wherein that which is to be recognized as belonging to each person is allotted to him *by law* and guaranteed to him by an adequate power (which is not his own, but external to him). In other words, he should at all costs enter into a state of civil society.

The state of nature need not necessarily be a *state of injustice* (*iniustus*) merely because those who live in it treat one another solely in terms of the amount of power they possess. But it is a *state devoid of justice* (*status iustitia vacuus*), for if a *dispute* over rights (*ius controversum*) occurs in it, there is no competent judge to pronounce legally valid decisions. Anyone may thus use force to impel the others to abandon this state for a state of right. For although each individual's *concepts of right* may imply that an external object can be acquired by occupation or by contract, this acquisition is only *provisional* until it has been sanctioned by a public law, since it is not determined by any public (distributive) form of justice and is not guaranteed by any institution empowered to exercise this right.

If no one were willing to recognize any acquisition as rightful, not even provisionally so, before a civil state had been established, the civil state would itself be impossible. For in relation to their form, the laws relating to property contain exactly the same things in a state of nature as they would prescribe in a civil state, in so far as we conceive of this state only in terms of concepts of pure reason. The only difference is that in the second case, the conditions under which the laws are applied (in accordance with distributive justice) are given. Thus if there were not even a *provisional* system of external property in the state of nature, there would not be any rightful duties in it either, so that there could not be any commandment to abandon it.

A state (*civitas*) is a union of an aggregate of men under rightful laws. In so far as these laws are necessary *a priori* and follow automatically from concepts of external right in general (and are not just set up by statute), the form of the state will be that of a state in the absolute sense, i.e. as the idea of what a state ought to be according to pure principles of right. This idea can serve as an internal guide (*norma*) for every actual case where men unite to form a commonwealth.

Every state contains three powers, i.e. the universally united will is made up of three separate persons (*trias politica*). These are the *ruling power* (or sovereignty) in the person of the legislator, the *executive power* in the person of the individual who governs in accordance with the law, and the *judicial power* (which allots to everyone what is his by law) in the person of the judge (*potestas legislatoria, rectoria et iudiciaria*). They can be likened to the three propositions in a practical operation of reason: the major premise, which contains the *law* of the sovereign will, the minor premise, which contains the *command* to act in accordance with the law (i.e. the principle of subsumption under the general will), and the conclusion, which contains the *legal decision* (the sentence) as to the rights and wrongs of each particular case.

The legislative power can belong only to the united will of the people. For since all right is supposed to emanate from this power, the laws it gives must be absolutely *incapable* of doing anyone an injustice. Now if someone makes dispositions for *another* person, it is always possible that he may thereby do him an injustice, although this is never possible in the case of decisions he makes for himself (for *volenti non fit iniuria* [no harm is done to a man by an act when he consents to it]). Thus only the unanimous and combined will of everyone whereby each decides the same for all and all decide the same for each – in other words, the general united will of the people – can legislate.

The members of such a society (*societas civilis*) or state who unite for the purpose of legislating are known as *citizens* (*cives*), and the three rightful attributes which are inseparable from the nature of a citizen as such are as follows: firstly, lawful *freedom* to obey no law other than that to which he has given his consent; secondly, civil *equality* in recognizing no one among the people as superior to himself, unless it be someone whom he is just as morally entitled to bind by law as the other is to bind him; and thirdly, the attribute of civil *independence* which allows him to owe his existence and sustenance not to the arbitrary will of anyone else among the people, but purely to his own rights and powers as a member of the commonwealth (so that he may not, as a civil personality, be represented by anyone else in matters of right).

Fitness to vote is the necessary qualification which every citizen must possess. To be fit to vote, a person must have an independent position among the people. He must therefore be not just a part of the commonwealth, but a member of it, i.e. he must by his own free will actively participate in a community of other people. But this latter quality makes it necessary to distinguish between the *active* and the *passive* citizen, although the latter concept seems to contradict the definition of the concept of a citizen altogether. The following examples may serve to overcome this difficulty. Apprentices to merchants or tradesmen, servants who are not employed by the state, minors (*naturaliter vel civiliter* [in either the natural or the political sense]), women in general and all those who are obliged to depend for their living (i.e. for food and protection) on the offices of others (excluding the state) – all of these people have no civil personality, and their existence is, so to speak, purely inherent. The woodcutter whom I employ on my premises; the blacksmith in India who goes from house to house with his hammer, anvil and bellows to do work with iron, as opposed to the European carpenter or smith who can put the products of his work up for public sale; the domestic tutor as opposed to the academic, the tithe-holder as opposed to the farmer; and so on – they are all mere auxiliaries to the commonwealth, for they have to receive orders or protection from other individuals, so that they do not possess civil independence.

This dependence upon the will of others and consequent inequality does not, however, in any way conflict with the freedom and equality of all men as *human beings* who together constitute a people. On the contrary, it is only by accepting these conditions that such a people can become a state and enter into a civil constitution. But all are not equally qualified within this constitution to possess the right to vote, i.e. to be citizens and not just subjects among other subjects.

For from the fact that as passive members of the state, they can demand to be treated by all others in accordance with laws of natural freedom and equality, it does not follow that they also have a right to influence or organize the state itself as *active* members, or to co-operate in introducing particular laws. Instead, it only means that the positive laws to which the voters agree, of whatever sort they may be, must not be at variance with the natural laws of freedom and with the corresponding equality of all members of the people whereby they are allowed to work their way up from their passive condition to an active one.

All of the three powers within the state are dignities, and since they necessarily follow from the general idea of a state as elements essential for its establishment (constitution), they are *political dignities*. They involve a relationship between a universal *sovereign* (who, if considered in the light of laws of freedom, can be none other than the united people itself) and the scattered mass of the people as subjects, i.e. a relationship of *commander* (*imperans*) to him who *obeys* (*subditus*). The act by which the people constitutes a state for itself, or more precisely, the mere idea of such an act (which alone enables us to consider it valid in terms of right), is the *original contract*. By this contract, all members of the people (*omnes et singuli* [together and individually]) give up their external freedom in order to receive it back at once as members of a commonwealth, i.e. of the people regarded as a state (*universi*). And we cannot say that men within a state have sacrificed a *part* of their inborn external freedom for a specific purpose; they have in fact completely abandonced their wild and lawless freedom, in order to find again their entire and undiminished freedom in a state of lawful dependence (i.e. in a state of right), for this dependence is created by their own legislative will.

The three powers in the state are related to one another in the following ways. Firstly, as moral persons, they are co-ordinate (*potestates coordinatae*), i.e. each is complementary to the others in forming the complete constitution of the state (*complementum ad sufficientiam*). But secondly, they are also *subordinate* (*subordinatae*) to one another, so that the one cannot usurp any function of the others to which it ministers; for each has its own principle, so that although it issues orders in the quality of a distinct person, it does so under the condition of a superior person's will. Thirdly, the combination of both relationships described above assures every subject of his rights.

It can be said of these powers, considered in their appropriate dignity, that the will of the *legislator* (*legislatoris*) in relation to external property cannot be reproached (i.e. it is irreprehensible), that the executive power of the supreme *ruler* (*summi rectoris*) cannot be opposed (i.e. it is irresistible), and that the verdict of the supreme *judge* (*supremi iudicis*) cannot be altered (i.e. it is without appeal).

The *ruler* of the state (*rex*, *princeps*) is that moral or physical person who wields the executive power (*potestas executoria*). He is the *agent* of the state who appoints the magistrates, and who prescribes rules for the people so that each may acquire something or retain what is his by law (i.e. by subsuming individual cases under the law). If the ruler is taken to be a moral person, he is called the *directory* or government. His *commands* to the people, the magistrates, and their superiors (ministers) who are responsible for *administering the state* (*gubernatio*), are not laws but ordinances or decrees; for they depend upon decisions in particular cases and are issued subject to revision. A *government* which were also to make *laws* would be called a *despotic* as opposed to a *patriotic* government. This is not to be confused with a *paternal* government (*regimen paternale*); the latter is the most despotic kind of all, for it treats the citizens like children. A patriotic government (*regimen civitatis et patriae*) means that although the state itself (*civitas*) treats its subjects as if they were members of one family, it also treats them as citizens of the state, i.e. in accordance with laws guaranteeing their own independence. Thus each is responsible for himself and does not depend upon the absolute will of anyone equal or superior to him.

The sovereign of the people (the legislator) cannot therefore also be the *ruler*, for the ruler is subject to the law, through which he is consequently beholden to *another* party, i.e. the sovereign. The sovereign may divest the ruler of his power, depose him, or reform his administration, but he cannot *punish* him. (And that is the real meaning of the common English saying that the king – i.e. the supreme executive authority – can do no wrong.) For to punish the ruler would in turn be an act of the executive power, which alone possesses the supreme authority to apply *coercion* in accordance with the law, and such a punishment would mean subjecting the executive power itself to coercion, which is self-contradictory.

Finally, neither the sovereign nor the ruler may *pass judgement*; they can only appoint judges as magistrates. The people judge themselves, through those fellow-citizens whom they have nominated as their representatives, by free election, for each particular juridical act. For a legal decision or sentence is a particular act of public justice (*iustitiae distributivae*) by an administrator of the state (a judge or court of law) upon a subject, i.e. one who belongs to the people, and it does not carry the necessary authority to grant or assign to the subject that which is his. Now since each member of the people is purely passive in his relationship to the supreme authority, it would be possible for either the legislative or the executive power to do him an injustice in any decision it might make in a controversial case involving that which belongs to the subject; for it would not be an action of the people themselves in pronouncing a fellow citizen *guilty* or *not guilty*. After the facts of a legal suit have thus been established, the court of law has the judicial authority to put the law into practice and to ensure, by means of the executive authority, that each person receives his due. Thus only the *people*, albeit through the indirect means of the representatives they have themselves appointed (i.e. the jury), can pass judgement upon anyone of their own number. Besides, it would be beneath the dignity of the head of state to act the part of a judge, i.e. to put himself in a position where he could do some injustice, and thus give cause for an appeal to some higher authority (*a rege male informato ad regem melius informandum* [From a badly trained ruler, to a ruler who is better trained]).

There are thus three distinct powers (*potestas legislatoria, executoria, iudiciaria*) which give the state (*civitas*) its autonomy, that is, which enable the state to establish and maintain itself in accordance with laws of freedom. The *welfare* of the state consists in the union of these powers (*salus reipublicae suprema lex est* [The welfare of the state is the supreme law]). But this welfare must not be understood as synonymous with the *well-being* and *happiness* of the citizens, for it may well be possible to attain these in a more convenient and desirable way within a state of nature (as Rousseau declares), or even under a despotic regime. On the contrary, the welfare of the state should be seen as that condition in which the constitution most closely approximates to the principles of right; and reason, *by a categorical imperative*, obliges us to strive for its realization.

General remarks on the legal consequences of the nature of the civil union

The origin of the supreme power, for all practical purposes, is *not discoverable* by the people who are subject to it. In other words, the subject *ought not* to indulge in *speculations* about its origin with a view to acting upon them, as if its right to be obeyed were open to doubt (*ius controversum*). For since the people must already be considered as united under a general legislative will before they can pass rightful judgement upon the highest power within the state (*summumim perium*), they cannot and may not pass any judgement other than that which is willed by the current head of state (*summus imperans*). Whether in fact an actual contract originally preceded their submission to the state's authority (*pactum subiectionis civilis*), whether the power came first and the law only appeared after it, or whether they ought to have followed this order – these are completely futile arguments for a people which is already subject to civil law, and they constitute a menace to the state. For if the subject, having delved out the ultimate origin, were then to offer resistance to the authority currently in power, he might by the laws of this authority (i.e. with complete justice) be punished, eliminated or banished as an outlaw (*exlex*). A law which is so sacred (i.e. inviolable) that it is practically a crime even to cast doubt upon it and thus to suspend its effectiveness for even an instant, cannot be thought of as coming from human beings, but from some infallible supreme legislator. That is what is meant by the saying that 'all authority comes from God', which is not a *historical derivation* of the civil constitution, but an idea expressed as a practical principle of reason, requiring men to obey the legislative authority now in power, irrespective of its origin.

From this there follows the proposition that the sovereign of a state has only rights in relation to the subject, and no (coercive) duties. Furthermore, if the organ of the sovereign, the ruler, does anything against the laws (e.g. if he infringes the law of equal distribution of political burdens in taxation, recruiting, or the like), the subject may lodge *complaints* (*gravamina*) about this injustice, but he may not offer resistance.

Indeed, even the actual constitution cannot contain any article which might make it possible for some power within the state to resist or hold in check the supreme executive in cases where he violates the constitutional laws. For a person who is supposed to hold the power of the state in check must have more power than (or at least as much power as) the one who is held in check; and if, as a rightful commander, he ordered the subjects to offer resistance, he would also have to be able to *protect* them and to pass legally valid judgements in each particular case which arose, so that he would have to be able to order resistance publicly. But if this were so, the latter instead of the former would be the supreme executive, which is self-contradictory. In such a case, the sovereign would simultaneously be acting through his minister as a ruler, i.e. despotically, and any attempt to pretend that the people (whose power is purely legislative) can hold the executive in check through their deputies cannot conceal the underlying despotism successfully enough to prevent it becoming apparent in the means which the minister employs. The people, who are represented in parliament by their deputies, have in these men guarantors of their freedom and their rights. These deputies, however, will also be actively interested in themselves and their own families, and they will depend upon the minister to supply them with positions in the army, navy or civil service. And even disregarding the fact that there would have to be a prearranged agreement among the people before any resistance could be publicly proclaimed (although such agreements are impermissible in times of peace), we can thus see that the deputies, instead of offering resistance to the pretensions of the government, will always be ready to play into its hands. A so-called 'moderate' political constitution, as a constitution regulating the internal rights of the state, is therefore an absurdity. Far from harmonizing with right, it is merely a clever expedient, designed to make it as easy as possible for the powerful transgressor of popular rights to exercise his arbitrary influence upon the government, disguising this influence as a right of opposition to which the people are entitled.

There can thus be no rightful resistance on the part of the people to the legislative head of state. For a state of right becomes possible only through submission to his universal legislative will. Thus there can be no right of *sedition* (*seditio*), and still less a right of *rebellion* (*rebellio*), least of all a right to *lay hands on* the person of the monarch as an individual, or to take his life on the pretext that he has misused his power (*monarchomachismus sub specie tyrannicidii*). The least attempt to do so is *high treason* (*proditio eminens*), and a traitor of this kind, as one who has tried to *destroy his fatherland* (*parricida*), may be punished with nothing less than death.

The reason why it is the duty of the people to tolerate even what is apparently the most intolerable misuse of supreme power is that it is impossible ever to conceive of their resistance to the supreme legislation as being anything other than unlawful and liable to nullify the entire legal constitution. For before such resistance could be authorized, there would have to be a public law which permitted the people to offer resistance: in other words, the supreme legislation would have to contain a provision to the effect that it is not supreme, so that in one and the same judgement, the people as subjects would be made sovereign over the individual to whom they are subject. This is self-contradictory, and the contradiction is at once obvious if we ask who would act as judge in this dispute between the people and the sovereign (for in terms of right, they are still two distinct moral persons). It then becomes clear that the people would set themselves up as judges of their own cause.[12]

12. It is possible to conceive of a monarch's *dethronement* as a *voluntary* abdication of the crown and a renunciation of his power by giving it back to the people, or as a forfeiture of power, without violation of the monarch's person, whereby he is simply relegated to the rank of a private citizen. And while one might at least appeal to a supposed *right of necessity* (*casus necessitatis*) as an excuse for the people's action in forcibly dethroning the head of state, they can never have the slightest right to punish him for his previous administration. For everything which he previously did in his capacity as head of state must be considered to have been outwardly in keeping with right, and he himself, regarded as the source of all laws, is incapable of any unjust action. But of all the outrages attending a revolution through rebellion, even the *murder* of the monarch is not the worst; for it is still possible to imagine that the people did it because they *feared* that if he were allowed to survive, he might recover his power and mete out to the people the punishment they deserved, in which case their behaviour would not be an act of penal justice but simply an act of self-preservation. It is the formal *execution* of a monarch which must arouse dread in any soul imbued with ideas of human right, and this feeling will recur whenever one thinks of events like the

Any alteration to a defective political constitution, which may certainly be necessary at times, can thus be carried out only by the sovereign himself through *reform*, but not through revolution by the people. And if any such alteration takes place, it can only affect the *executive power*, not the legislature.

A constitution may be arranged in such a way that the people, through their representatives in parliament, are lawfully able to *resist* the executive power and its representative (the minister). This is known as a limited constitution. But even a constitution of this kind cannot permit any active resistance (i.e. an arbitrary association of the people designed to force the government to adopt a certain mode of action, and hence an attempt by the people themselves to act as the executive power). The people may offer only a *negative* form of resistance, in that they may *refuse* in parliament to comply on all occasions with those demands which the executive says must necessarily be met for administrative purposes. In fact, if the people were to comply on all occasions, it would be a sure indication that

---

fate of Charles I or Louis XVI. But how are we to explain this feeling? It is not aesthetic (like that sympathy which comes from imagining oneself placed in the sufferer's situation), but rather moral, being our reaction to the complete reversal of all concepts of right. It is seen as a crime which must always remain as such and which can never be effaced (*crimen immortale, inexpiabile*), and it might be likened to that sin which the theologians maintain can never be forgiven either in this world or the next. The explanation of this phenomenon of the human psyche would seem to lie in the following reflections concerning our own nature, reflections which also cast some light on the principles of political right.

Every transgression of the law can and must be explained only as the result of a maxim of the criminal whereby he makes a rule out of misdeeds like the one in question. For if we were to explain such transgressions in terms of a motive of the senses, the deed could not have been committed by the criminal as a free being, and he could not consequently be held responsible for it. But it is absolutely impossible to explain how the subject is able to formulate a maxim contrary to the clear prohibition of legislative reason, for only those events which follow the mechanism of nature are capable of explanation. Now the criminal can commit his misdeed either by adopting a maxim based on an assumed objective rule (as if it were universally valid), or merely as an exception to the rule (by exempting himself from it as the occasion requires). In the *latter* case, he merely *deviates* (albeit deliberately) from the law, for he may at the same time deplore his own transgression and simply wish to get round the law without formally terminating his obedience to it. But in the *former* case, he rejects the authority of the law itself (although he cannot deny its validity in the light of his own reason), and makes it

they were decadent, their representatives venal, the head of the government a despot through his minister, and the minister himself a traitor to the people.

Furthermore, if a revolution has succeeded and a new constitution has been established, the unlawfulness of its origin and success cannot free the subjects from the obligation to accommodate themselves as good citizens to the new order of things, and they cannot refuse to obey in an honest way the authority now in power. The dethroned monarch, if he survives such a revolution, cannot be taken to task for his earlier management of the state, far less punished for it. This applies so long as he has retired to the status of a citizen, preferring his own peace and that of the state to the hazards of abandoning his position and embarking as a pretender on the enterprise of restoration, whether through secretly instigated counter-revolution or the support of other powers. But if he prefers the latter course, his right to his property remains intact, since the rebellion which deprived him of it was unjust. It must, however, be

---

his rule to act in opposition to it; his maxim is thus at variance with the law not simply through *deficiency* (*negative*); it is actually *contrary* to the law (*contrarie*), or, so to speak, diametrically opposed to it as a contradiction (i.e. virtually hostile to it). So far as can be seen, it is impossible for men to commit a crime of such formal and completely futile malice, although no system of morality should omit to consider it, if only as a pure idea representing ultimate evil.

Thus the reason why the thought of the formal execution of a monarch *by his people* inspires us with dread is that, while his *murder* must be regarded merely as an exception to the rule which the people have taken as their maxim, his *execution* must be seen as a complete *reversal* of the principles which govern the relationship between the sovereign and the people. For it amounts to making the people, who owe their existence purely to the legislation of the sovereign, into rulers over the sovereign, thereby brazenly adopting violence as a deliberate principle and exalting it above the most sacred canons of right. And this, like an abyss which engulfs everything beyond hope of return, is an act of suicide by the state, and it would seem to be a crime for which there can be no atonement. There are therefore grounds for assuming that agreements to perform such executions do not really proceed from any supposed principle of right, but from the people's fear of revenge from the state if it should ever recover, and that such formalities are introduced only in order to give the deed an air of penal justice and of *rightful procedure* (with which murder, on the other hand, could not be reconciled). But this disguise is futile, since any such presumption on the part of the people is more atrocious than murder itself, for it in fact embodies a principle which must make it impossible for an overthrown state to be reconstituted.

left to international right to decide whether other powers have the right to join in an association for the benefit of this fallen monarch simply in order that the people's crime should not go unpunished or remain as a scandal in the eyes of other states, and whether they are entitled or called upon to overthrow a constitution established in any other state by revolution, and to restore the old one by forcible means.

Can the sovereign be regarded as the supreme proprietor of the land, or must he be regarded only as one who exercises supreme command over the people by means of laws? Since the land is the ultimate condition under which it is alone possible to possess external objects as one's own, while the possession and use of such objects in turn constitutes the primary hereditary right, all such rights must be derived from the sovereign as *lord of the land*, or rather as the supreme proprietor (*dominus territorii*). The people, as a mass of subjects, also belong to him (i.e. they are his people), although they do not belong to him as an owner by the right of property, but as a supreme commander by the right of persons.

But this supreme ownership is only an idea of the civil union, designed to represent through concepts of right the need to unite the private property of all members of the people under a universal public owner; for this makes it possible to define particular ownership by means of the necessary formal principle of *distribution* (division of the land), rather than by principles of *aggregation* (which proceeds empirically from the parts to the whole). The principles of right require that the supreme proprietor should not possess any land as private property (otherwise he would become a private person), for all land belongs exclusively to the people (not collectively, but distributively). Nomadic peoples, however, would be an exception to this rule, for they do not have any private property in the shape of land. Thus the supreme commander cannot own any *domains*, i.e. land reserved for his private use or for the maintenance of his court. For since the extent of his lands would then depend on his own discretion, the state would run the risk of finding all landed property in the hands of the government, and all the subjects would be treated as serfs bound to the soil (*glebae adscripti*) or holders of what always remained the property of someone else; they would consequently appear devoid of all freedom (*servi*). One can thus say of a lord of the land that he *possesses nothing* of his own (except his own person). For if he owned something on equal terms with anyone else in the state, he could conceivably come into conflict with this other person without there being any judge to settle it. But it can also be said that he *possesses everything*, because he has the right to exercise command over the people, to whom all external objects (*divisim*) belong, and to give each person whatever is his due.

It follows from this that there can be no corporation, class or order within the state which may as an owner hand down land indefinitely, by appropriate statutes, for the exclusive use of subsequent generations. The state can at all times repeal such statutes, with the one condition that it must compensate those still alive. The *order of knights* (either as a corporation or simply as a class of eminently distinguished individual persons) and the *order of the clergy* (i.e. the church) can never acquire ownership of land to pass on to their successors by virtue of the privileges with which they have been favoured; they may acquire only the temporary use of it. Either the land tenure of the military orders or the estates of the church can be suspended without hesitation, so long as the above-named condition is fulfilled. This could happen to the military orders if public opinion no longer wished to use *military honour* as a means of protecting the state against indifference in matters of defence, or alternatively to the church if the public no longer wished to use masses for the dead, prayers and a host of men employed as spiritual advisers as means of urging on the citizens to preserve them from eternal fire. Those who are affected by such a reform cannot complain of being expropriated, for *public opinion* was the only ground on which their previous possessions were based, and they remained legitimate so long as this opinion remained constant. But as soon as public opinion changes (above all in the judgement of those who, by virtue of their merit, have the strongest claim to lead it), the pretended ownership must cease as if by public appeal to the state (*a rege male informato ad regem melius informandum* [from a badly trained ruler to a ruler who is better trained]).

From this basic right of ownership as it was originally acquired, the supreme commander (as the supreme proprietor or lord of the land) derives his right to *tax* the private landowners, i.e. to impose levies in the shape of land taxes, excises and customs duties, or to require work such as military service. But it must be done in such a way that the people tax themselves, for this alone would be in keeping with laws of right. It is therefore done through the corps of deputies of the people, although it may be permissible to impose an enforced loan (i.e. a loan not provided for in the law as it has hitherto stood) by the right of majesty in cases where the state is threatened with dissolution.

From the same source, the rights of economic and financial administration and of the police force are derived. The police look after public *security, convenience* and also *propriety*; for it makes it much easier for the government to perform its business of governing the people by laws if the public sense of propriety (*sensus decori* – a negative taste) is not dulled by affronts to the moral sense such as begging, uproar in the streets, offensive smells and public prostitution (*venus volgivaga*).

A third kind of right is necessary for the preservation of the state – the right of *inspection* (*ius inspectionis*). This requires that no association which could influence the *public* welfare of society (*publicum*), such as an association of political or religious *illuminati*, may be kept secret; at the request of the police, it must not refuse to disclose its constitution. But only in cases of emergency may the police search anyone's private residence, and in each case, they must be authorized to do so by a higher authority.

Indirectly, i.e. in so far as he takes the duty of the people upon himself, the supreme commander has the right to impose taxes upon the people for their own preservation, e.g. for the *care of the poor*, for *foundling hospitals* and *church activities*, or for what are otherwise known as charitable or pious institutions.

For the general will of the people has united to form a society which must constantly maintain itself, and to this end, it has subjected itself to the internal power of the state so as to preserve those members of the society who cannot do so themselves. The nature of the estate thus justifies the government in compelling prosperous citizens to provide the means of preserving those who are unable to provide themselves with even the most rudimentary necessities of nature. For since their existence itself is an act of submission to the protection of the commonwealth and to the care it must give them to enable them to live, they have committed themselves in such a way that the state has a right to make them contribute their share to maintaining their fellow citizens. This may be done by taxing the citizens' property or their commercial transactions, or by instituting funds and using the interest from them – not for the needs of the state (for it is rich), but for the needs of the people. The contributions should not be purely *voluntary* (for we are here concerned only with the *rights* of the state as against the subjects), they must in fact be compulsory political impositions. Some voluntary contributions such as lotteries, which are made from profit-seeking motives, should not be permitted, since they create greater than usual numbers of poor who become a danger to public property.

It might at this point be asked whether the poor ought to be provided for by *current contributions* so that each generation would support its own members, or by gradually accumulated *capital funds* and *pious foundations* at large (such as widows' homes, hospitals, etc.). Funds must certainly not be raised by begging, which has close affinities with robbery, but by lawful taxation. The first arrangement (that of current contributions) must be considered the only one appropriate to the rights of the state, for no one who wishes to be sure of his livelihood can be exempt from it. These contributions increase with the numbers of poor, and they do not make poverty a means of support for the indolent (as is to be feared in the case of pious foundations), so that the government need not impose an *unjust* burden on the people.

As for the support of children abandoned through need or through shame (and who may even be murdered for such reasons), the state has a right to make it a duty for the people not to let them perish knowingly, even although they are an unwelcome increase to the state's population. But whether this can justly be done by taxing bachelors of both sexes (i.e. single persons of *means*) as a class which is partly responsible for the situation, using the proceeds to set up foundling hospitals, or whether any other method is preferable (although it is scarcely likely that any means of preventing the evil can be found) – this is a problem which has not yet been successfully solved without prejudice to right or to morality.

The *church*, as an institution for public *divine service* among the people whose opinions or convictions created it, must be carefully distinguished from religion, which is an inward attitude of mind quite outside the sphere of influence of the civil power. As such, the church fulfils a genuine political necessity, for it enables the people to regard themselves as subjects of an *invisible* supreme power to which they must pay homage and which may often come into very unequal conflict with the civil powers. The State certainly has no right to legislate on the internal constitution of the Church, to arrange church affairs to suit its own advantage, or to issue directions and commands to the people in matters of faith and liturgical forms; for all this must be left entirely to the teachers and supervisors whom the people have themselves elected. It has only a *negative* right to prevent the public teachers of religion from exercising any influence on the *visible* political commonwealth such as might threaten the public peace, and to ensure that internal conflicts within the church or conflicts between different churches do not endanger civil concord. That is, it has a right like that of the police. It would be *beneath the dignity* of the ruling authority to interfere in church affairs by requiring that a church should have a certain belief and by laying down which belief it should have, or by demanding that it should preserve this belief without alteration and never attempt to reform itself. For by becoming involved in a scholastic quarrel, the supreme power would be placing itself on an equal footing with the subjects and the monarch setting himself up as a priest. The subjects may tell him outright that he does not understand the affairs in question, especially if he attempts to prohibit internal reforms, for anything which the entire people cannot decide for itself cannot be decided for the people by the legislator either. But no people can decide never to make further progress in opinions relating to its faith (i.e. in enlightenment), nor can it decide never to undertake reforms in affairs of the church, for this would be contrary to humanity as represented in the person of the people, hence also to the people's highest rights. Thus no ruling authority may make such a decision for the people. But for precisely the same reason, the onus of paying the costs of maintaining the church cannot fall upon the state; they must be met by that portion of the people which follows one or other particular creed, i.e. by the congregation.

References

ACHENWALL, G. (1755–6), *Ius naturae in usum auditorum*, Göttinger, 7th edn, 1781.
HOBBES, T. (1642), *De Cive*, Amsterdam.
HOBBES, T. (1651), Leviathan, London.

7 J. Viner

Bentham and J. S. Mill: The Utilitarian Background

J. Viner, 'Bentham and J. S. Mill', *American Economic Review*, vol. 39, 1949, March, pp. 360–82.

The one-hundredth anniversary of the publication of Mill's *Principles of Political Economy* falls in the year 1948, and the American Economic Association in the programming of its meetings takes advantage of anniversaries of births, deaths, and dates of publication to remind its members that our discipline has a past. This is a proper occasion, therefore, for a paper on Mill. The inclusion of Bentham in the scope of my paper is of my own contriving, but perhaps I can technically legitimatize it by appeal to the fact that British learned circles have been celebrating during 1948 the two-hundredth anniversary of Bentham's birth. There is no intellectual difficulty, however, in associating Bentham with Mill. The intellectual history of Mill is in large part a history, first, of faithful discipleship, then of rebellion from, and finally of substantial return, to the Benthamite set of doctrines.

The general lines of Bentham's thought were wholly of the eighteenth century, as I could demonstrate if there were time. Of English intellectuals who have had great influence, Bentham was perhaps the least original in his stock of general ideas, but clearly the most original in finding means and devices for putting his philosophy to practical use. To the nineteenth century Bentham was important as a carrier of eighteenth century thought and, still more, as a translator of this thought into a program of social reform. It was the seventeenth century which was the Age of Genius. The philosophers of the eighteenth century were, nonetheless, fertile in ideas. They were, however, almost completely devoid of zeal for the application of these ideas to change of institutions, or even of zeal in generating ideas which would call for change in existing institutions.

We economists like to think of Adam Smith as an exception in this regard, but he was so only to a moderate extent. The one social issue on which Adam Smith was a zealot was the issue of freedom of trade *versus* mercantilism. But Smith had little confidence in the ability of ideas to move worlds. It is often overlooked that it was with reference to internal as well as to international free trade that Adam Smith made his famous statement that 'To expect, indeed, that the freedom of trade should ever be entirely restored in Great Britain, is as absurd as to expect that an Oceana or Utopia should ever be established in it', and this although when he wrote, by obsolescence rather than by deliberate repeal, the restrictions on internal freedom of trade had already become largely inoperative. There is no evidence that Smith was more optimistic about the prospects for international than for domestic free trade, or that, beyond writing his book and preparing a few memoranda for the government when called upon, he ever felt moved to do anything, and especially to resort to anything rude or, in the eighteenth-century meaning of the term, to 'enthusiasm', to obtain acceptance and execution of his reforming ideas.

The eighteenth century, in Britain if not in France, and before the American and the French Revolutions if not after, was the age of social complacency, political, economic, moral, of satisfaction with the *status quo* at least to the extent of belief that the costs of substantial change would exceed the benefits of removal of moderation of whatever evils were recognized to prevail. British eighteenth-century government was oligarchic, corrupt, inefficient, though it was generally not tyrannical in intent and usually too lax, too inert, too decentralized, and too sceptical to be seriously tyrannical in effect. Until the end of the century there was no major figure who even mildly suggested the need for major political reform. Whether the economic condition of the masses of the people was improving or deteriorating, and whatever its trend, whether it was desperately bad or moderately good as compared to later standards, I frankly have no idea. We may rest assured, however, that it was not idyllic, if only because it never is.

Nevertheless, there was not until the very last moments of the century either a single major political debate which turned on the economic conditions of the poor or a single major writer who had important suggestions as to how to improve them, with the sole exception of Adam Smith's plea for freedom of trade. It was even a common doctrine of the century that the poor should never be relieved of their poverty above the level of a bare subsistence plus perhaps a few crumbs of cake, and it was at least the quasi-official doctrine of the Church of England that the poverty of the poor – and the prosperity of the bishops – were in accordance with the Divine Will.

Bentham and the Benthamites, on the other hand, were never complacent about the condition of the people of England. They were 'Radical Reformers', and they worked hard at their reforms: by working out detailed blueprints for them; by propaganda, agitation, intrigue, conspiracy; and, if truth be told, by encouragement to revolutionary movements up to – but not beyond – the point where resort to physical force would be the next step. Bentham, moreover, was a successful social reformer, more successful perhaps than anyone else in history except Karl Marx – I have in mind here only the realization and not the merits of programs of change – if he is given credit for those changes which came after his death as the result largely of the efforts of his disciples.

The list of reforms in England which derive largely from Bentham is a truly impressive one, and I present it here only in part: fundamental law reform in many of its branches; prison reform; adult popular suffrage, including woman suffrage; free trade; reform in colonial government; legalization of trade unions; general education at public expense; free speech and free press; the secret ballot; a civil service appointed and promoted on merit; repeal of the usury laws; general registration of titles to property; reform of local government; a safety code for merchant shipping; sanitary reform and preventive medicine at public expense; systematic collection of statistics; free justice for the poor. Bentham was the first person to propose birth-control as a measure of economic reform, and this *before* Malthus had published his first *Essay on the Principle of Population* (Bentham, 1797; see also Himes, 1936). The Ministry of Health which he proposed would be made responsible not only for general sanitation and routine public health work, but also for smoke prevention, local health-museums, and the policing of the medical profession to prevent their formation of monopolies.

Related to the conditions of the time when these reforms were proposed, Bentham's program was comprehensive, radical, and progressive without being visionary. The modern 'democratic socialist' would find it wanting, since Bentham did not approve of tampering with the system of private property except through inheritance taxation and insisted on 'compensation' where reform measures would involve violation of 'reasonable expectations'. He apparently never formulated any concrete proposals for social security on an insurance basis, but he approved in principle of government-administered and government-subsidized insurance against every conceivable type of social hazard for which individual prudence could not make adequate provision. It was too early for proposals to stabilize employment through monetary or fiscal measures, although Bentham did explore the possibility of increasing real investment and production through the 'forced frugality' induced by the issue of paper money.[1] Pronounced individualist though he was, his specific program of reforms in both the content and the processes of legislation, in governmental organization, and in public administration, made him a major source of inspiration for the Fabian socialists as well as for the *laissez-faire* liberals.

To belief in political democracy Bentham came only slowly, and only as their failure to adopt his proposals eroded his faith in the good intentions of the British aristocratic politicians. The Benthamite case for political democracy was first elaborately expounded by James Mill in his famous essay on Government first published in 1820. It turned out to be an embarrassment for Bentham and his other disciples because by the scholastic formalism of its argument and the extreme lengths to which it carried Bentham's doctrine it was seriously vulnerable to rebuttal and, even worse, to ridicule. Starting out from the proposition that the sole proper purpose of government is to promote the greatest happiness of mankind, Mill proceeded by pure *a priori* analysis, without any reference to history or to contemporary fact, from the premise that legislators served *only* their 'sinister interests' – a stock Benthamite term for the self-interest of rulers or a ruling class – to the conclusion that good

1. Bentham's treatment of this still remains in large part in manuscript. Extracts from these unpublished manuscripts and comments by Ricardo on them have recently been published by Silberner (1940), and were then also already in page proof in Piero Sraffa's long-forthcoming edition of Ricardo's works.

government was therefore obtainable only by making it, through popular suffrage and frequent elections, the self-interest of the elected to serve the interests of the electors.

Bentham, writing in the 1780s, had conceded that if at any time legislators 'have suffered the nation to be preyed upon by swarms of idle pensioners, or useless place-men, it has rather been from negligence and imbecility, than from any settled plan for oppressing and plundering of the people', but in 1814 he appended a note withdrawing the concession: 'So thought Anno 1780 and 1790.—Not so Anno 1814, J. Bentham' (1838–43a). By that time he had adopted the doctrine of 'sinister interests'. But Mill carried the doctrine further than was necessary to meet Bentham's requirements and probably further than Bentham's belief in it. As Tawney has remarked: 'To [James Mill] the State is not a band of brothers, but a mutual detective society: the principal advantage of popular government is that there are more detectives, and therefore, presumably, fewer thieves' (1920, p. 21). Bentham always, but Mill rarely, if ever, conceded that men, even legislators, could not only be influenced by the praise and blame of other men, but could even display some measure of pure benevolence. As Barker has commented, '. . . while all – or nearly all – of the theorems of Mill's article may be found in Bentham, they have undergone a change. The egoism is more egoistic; the negativism is more negative' (1937, p. 15), and it may be added the *a priori* analysis more 'high *priori*'. In the seventeenth century Harrington had denied that Hobbes could work the miracle of 'making you a king by geometry'. Macaulay was now to deny that the Benthamites could depose an aristocracy by geometry.

Macaulay, a young man anxiously seeking fame by his fluent and facile pen, found the opportunity in James Mill's essay on Government. Reviewing in 1829, in the magisterial *Edinburgh Review*, a reprint of this essay of James Mill, Macaulay raked it high and low, primarily on the basis of its use, without benefit of historical induction or of reference to contemporary facts, of the *a priori* or, in the language of the time and earlier, the geometrical method, but also on the more concrete ground that the proposition that legislators *always* and *invariably* act in terms of their selfish interests was preposterous whatever the method by which it was attempted to establish it (1891, preface, pp. 9–11; and p. 160 ff.).

The Benthamites were shaken by the attack, and John Stuart Mill most so, as we shall see later. But Macaulay himself, without withdrawing anything of what he had written, soon thereafter made his peace with James Mill and from then on was an exponent of political democracy on the basis of a line of argument which Paxton in his *Civil Polity* had already presented in 1703, and which should have been the original and was to become the standard line of the Benthamites, namely, that only by democratic voting could there be an adequate guarantee that legislators would *always* or predominantly serve the general interest, without denial that they might sometimes do so even in the absence of democracy.

I come now to deal more systematically with the most difficult and the most controverted aspect of Benthamism, namely, its psychological and ethical justifications for utilitarianism as legislative policy.

Bentham's main concern with ethics was with the ethics which should be followed by moral leaders, not with the ethics of the ordinary man, not with private morals, except as they were data to be operated on by the elite. 'The science,' he said, 'whose foundations we have explored can appeal only to lofty minds with whom the public welfare has become a passion' (Atkinson, 1914, section 2, p. 337). And by them, Bentham held, its lessons should be pressed on legislators, whether *their* minds were lofty ones or not. As Bentham acknowledged,[2] he sometimes overlooked this, and wrote as if what he had to say was directed at private morals, and critics have made much of this oversight without treating it merely as a lapse from his fundamental purposes. It was Benthamism interpreted as a system of private ethics, didactic as well as descriptive, that has aroused the most violent and the most emotional antagonism. Even as private ethics, however, Benthamism has seemed so vulnerable a target to *odium theologicum* and *odium ethicum* only because the private ethics of the critics permitted them to attack Bentham's words without taking pains to ascertain what the thoughts were which these words were intended to communicate.

2. Cf. for example, the preface, first added to the 1823 edition, of his *Introduction to the Principles of Morals and Legislation*, where he says that 'an introduction to a plan of a penal code' would have been a title better indicating the nature of its contents.

Bentham starts from the standard eighteenth-century proposition, common to theologians and to sceptical philosophers alike, that man operates 'under the governance of two sovereign masters, pain and pleasure'. Happiness is a net sum or aggregate of individually experienced pleasures and pains.[3] Man, he claims, acts only in response to his 'interests', by which he usually, and fundamentally, means whatever men are interested in, but, unfortunately, frequently allows to mean what men regard as in their self-interest. Men normally are interested to some extent in the happiness of others than themselves, and in exceptional cases are capable of 'universal benevolence', or a dominating concern with the happiness of mankind at large, but generally, if they are left to themselves, there will be serious discrepancy between the actual behavior of individuals and the behavior which would conduce to 'the greatest happiness of the greatest number'. It is the function of legislation to coerce or bribe individuals to make their behaviour coincide with that required by the greatest-happiness principle, and of education and moral leaders to mould men's desires so that they spontaneously associate the happiness of others with their own happiness.

Bentham nowhere attempts or asserts the possibility of a positive demonstration that greatest happiness, whether as hedonism or as eudaemonism, is the proper moral objective for the common man, the moral leader, or the legislator, and his only argument in support of the greatest-happiness principle is the negative one that the rival principles proposed by other ethical systems are either resolvable upon scrutiny to verbal variants of the utility principle, or are sheer *ipse dixitism*, or are meaningless patterns of words.

'Pleasure' and 'happiness' were to Bentham widely inclusive terms, involving not only the pleasures of the senses but also those of the heart and the mind. Pleasures, moreover, which in their 'simple' or primary form, genetically speaking, were pleasures of self could by 'association of ideas' become associated with the pleasures of others. Man, by living in society, by education, and by acts of parliament, could be made good. The eighteenth-century

3. Cf. 'Gamaliel Smith' [=Jeremy Bentham] (1823), p. 394: 'happiness, to be anything, must be composed of pleasures: and, be the man who he may, of what it is that gives pleasure to him, he alone can be judge.'

utilitarians may have traded, as a German philosopher has put it, 'in the small wares of usefulness (*Nutzlichkeitskrämerei*)'. Or it may be that to accept the pursuit of pleasure as a proper end of man is 'swinish doctrine', if it be proper to assume that man pursues swinish pleasures. But a utilitarian does not have to be a Philistine. If in Bentham's exposition of his psychology there was often undue stress on the selfish sentiments, this fault – which was much more evident in James Mill than in Bentham – was the result of lack of imagination and of feeling, or of faulty observation – itself the consequence of these lacks – rather than any inherent incompatibility of broader views with the logic of his system. One important manifestation of this – systematic on the part of James Mill but only occasional and incidental on the part of Bentham – was the assumption that even when one's own pleasure had through association of ideas become involved in the pleasure of other persons, the affectionate sentiments toward others still contained an element of conscious reference back to one's own pleasures. This, by implication at least, was a proclamation of the universal prevalence of psychological hedonism.[4]

The eighteenth century is often termed the 'Age of Reason', and it is correctly so termed if by the phrase is meant that it was the age in which philosophers held that the credibility of all things should be tested by reason. But from the point of view of its prevailing psychological doctrines, it could more properly be called the 'Age of the Passions' because of its stress on the emotions and the instincts, the affections and aversions, and its playing down of the role of reason in the behaviour of the ordinary man. Hume was writing in the spirit of his times when he declared that: 'Reason is and ought only to be the slave of the passions, and can never pretend to any other office than to serve and obey them.' The normal role of reason was that of an obedient servant of the passions, a passive agent for the comparison of their relative intensities and for the justification of the choices made between them. 'So convenient a thing,' said Franklin, in his autobiography, 'it is to be a reason-

4. In notes to his edition of James Mill (1869) J. S. Mill, without fully admitting that his father had held this doctrine, points out passages which could be interpreted as implying it, see section 2, 217, note; section 2, 233 ff., note; section 2, 286 ff. note, etc.

able creature, since it enables one to find or make a reason for everything one has a mind to do'.

For the moral philosopher and the properly conditioned legislator, however, Bentham assigned more important roles to reason, first, that of moulding the passions of individuals so that they would contribute more to the augmentation of general happiness, and second, that of providing a technique for the comparison of passions of individuals with a view to making a socially oriented choice between them and where choice had to be or could be made. It was for this social purpose, and not for the routine behaviour of routine individuals, that Bentham endeavoured to construct what he at different times labelled as a 'moral thermometer', a 'moral arithmetic', a 'felicific calculus'.

Much amusement has been derived from Bentham's attempt to develop a technique by which the quantities of pleasure and pain could be measured by the legislator or the benevolent philosopher. Mitchell's well-known essay on 'Bentham's Felicific Calculus' (1937, pp. 177–202), is the fullest and the least unsympathetic account I am acquainted with of Bentham's position on this question. Mitchell points out the excessive degree of hedonism attributed by Bentham to mankind, and comments penetratingly on Bentham's attempt to find a common denominator through money for the pleasures of different persons. Mitchell says that in fact Bentham used the calculus not as an instrument of calculation, but as a basis of ordinal classification. 'It pointed out to him what elements should be considered in a given situation, and among these elements *seriatim* he was often able to make comparisons in terms of greater and less.' I think this is a somewhat misleading description of Bentham's method. The 'classification' was not *seriatim*, was not in terms of higher and lower, but merely of pro and con, of pleasure and pain, and was wholly preliminary to, rather than part of, the calculus. The 'calculus' as he actually used it was merely a mental comparison of the comparative weights of the pros and cons, a technique which neither calls for fancy labels nor is properly conducive either to merriment or to measurement.

Bentham did not invent the concept or the terminology of 'moral arithmetic'. Play with the idea of measuring the unmeasurable and resort to the language of measurement where it was silly to attempt to apply it goes back to at least the seventeenth century, when the prestige of geometry and later of algebra tended to trap all philosophers with scientific pretensions into casting their analysis into pseudo-mathematical form. Mandeville, as early as 1730, laughed at physicians who studied mathematics because it was fashionable, and cited one who had advised that for certain diseases 'the doses of the medicines are to be as the Squares of the Constitutions'.[5] Reid, in his *Essay on Quantity* of 1748, questioned the possibility of reducing to measurement such things as sensations, beauty, pleasure, and the affections and appetites of the mind, even though they 'are capable of more and less', and he warned that to apply mathematical language to non-measurable things is 'to make a show of mathematical reasoning, without advancing one step in real knowledge' (Hamilton, 1852, p. 717).

Bentham never went far afield for the sources of his ideas, and I suspect that Benjamin Franklin was his source, direct or indirect, for this idea of classification by 'bipartition' plus 'measurement' of the relative weight of the two classes. Franklin a few years earlier, in 1772, had been expounding it in private correspondence with Joseph Priestly and Richard Price – with all three of whom Bentham had personal contacts – in very much the same terms as Bentham was later to use, and under the similar, and already old, label of 'moral or prudential algebra' (*The Monthly Repository*, 1817, p. 13; *Proceedings of the Massachusetts Historical Society*, 1903, p. 264).

None of Bentham's immediate disciples showed any interest in this aspect of Bentham's thought, and it was not until Jevons drew attention to it and made it the basis of his subjective theory of economic value that it had any influence, for good or bad. I like to think, more so probably than Mitchell would have appreciated, that Bentham's felicific calculus was merely one more manifestation of the inferiority complex which practitioners of the social 'sciences' had in the eighteenth century, and have reacquired in the twentieth, towards mathematics, towards the exact sciences, and towards quantification as one of the higher virtues. Since with the application of 'political arithmetic' to 'moral arithmetic' we now all accept without protest the derivation of measured 'propensities' from correlations between psychologically and otherwise promiscuous

5. Mandeville (1730, p. 184). Compare the history of 'Lullism'.

statistical aggregates compiled catch-as-catch-can on anything up to global scale, our readiness to laugh at Bentham's modest and wholly platonic gestures in this direction excites my propensity for amazement.

There remains one question, specially important for economics, where the influence of Bentham on John Stuart Mill is obvious, the question of *laissez-faire*, or the economic role of government. Halévy, in his great but tendentious work on the Benthamites (1901-4), has made much of the existence in Bentham's system of a conflict between his juristic and his economic doctrines. According to Halévy, Bentham in his juristic theory makes it the primary function of government to create an *artificial* harmony between the interests of individuals and the public interest, whereas in his economic theory he reaches *laissez-faire* conclusions on the basis of an implied natural or spontaneous harmony of interests. This has become a stereotype of present-day comments on Bentham, and although there may be exceptions to the natural law which proclaims that stereotypes in the field of the history of ideas provide a light which blinds rather than guides, this is not one of them.

Bentham did interpret the function of government, under the influence largely of Helvétius, as that of creating, through the application of rewards and punishments, an approach to harmony between the interests of individuals and the social interests. He did prescribe limits for the field for governmental intervention in economic matters, but these limits were not, as we shall see, very narrow ones, and in any case were not so narrow as to give scope for a doctrine of natural harmony of interests, in the sense of a harmony preordained or inherent in the nature of man living in a society unregulated by government. Of explicit formulation by Bentham of a doctrine of natural harmony I can find not the slightest trace in his writings, and such a doctrine would be in basic conflict not only with his juristic theories but with his whole cosmological outlook. Faith in natural harmony always stems from either faith in the continuous intervention of a beneficent 'author of nature' or faith in the workings of a natural evolutionary process, and the Benthamites rejected the former and had not yet heard of the latter.

It has been common since Adam Smith's day to take for granted *in economics* the role of the state with reference to the protection of legal property rights and the enforcement of contract, leaving it to juristic inquiry to explore the problems of theory and of practice in this field. Such was also the procedure of Bentham, and in his juristic writings he keeps very much in mind that 'passion ... from the excesses of which, by reason of its strength, constancy, and universality, society has most to apprehend; I mean that which corresponds to the motive of pecuniary interest' (1838–43b, pp. 90–91). Here he deals with the problem of 'repression' of harmful economic activity by means of civil and penal law. If Bentham believed that there was a natural harmony of private and public interests in the economic field, it was one, therefore, which would prevail only after the magistrate and the constable had performed their duties.[6]

But Bentham does not advocate anything like 'anarchy plus the constable'. His most general proposition of a *laissez-faire* character is as follows:

With the view of causing an increase to take place in the mass of national wealth, or with a view to increase of the means either of subsistence or enjoyment, without some special reasons, the general rule is, that nothing ought to be done or attempted by government. The motto, or watchword of government, on these occasions, ought to be – *Be Quiet* (1838–43d, p. 33).

This may sound like a sweeping enough support of *laissez-faire*, if, as is common though rarely desirable practice in such matters, it be read carelessly and out of its context. There are important qualifications, explicit or implied, within this apparently emphatic text. First, the text deals with 'encouragement' and not with 'repression' of economic activity. As I have already pointed out, Bentham deals with the problem of repression of harmful economic activity as a problem in law and not in economics. Second, the general rule of doing nothing positive is applicable only if there is no special reason to the contrary. A rule is not equivalent for him to a principle, nor a 'motto' to a dogma.

Bentham (1838–43d) presents three grounds for the general rule against governmental activity of a positive kind in the economic

6. Bentham deals briefly with the relations between political economy and law in *Works* (1838–43c, pp. 203–4).

field: (1) in this field, individuals know their own interest better than government can; (2) individuals operate more ardently and more skilfully in pursuit of their own interests than government can or will operate on their behalf; (3) governmental intervention means coercion, either directly or indirectly through taxation, and coercion involves 'pain' and therefore is an evil.

Bentham is ready to approve of any departure from the general rule, however, if a case can be made for such departure on utility grounds. 'Indiscriminate generalizations' are an error, he says, and 'In laying down general rules, [even] fortuitous and transient cases ought not to be forgotten.' And he lives up to his doctrine as, for instance, when he says that 'what ought not to be done with the intention of supporting an unprofitable branch of trade, may yet be proper for preventing the ruin of the workmen employed in such business', or, when opposing in general any restrictions on the introduction of labour-saving machinery, he approves, however, of transitory aid to workmen injured economically by such introduction.

Bentham does not, moreover, limit his exceptions from the nonintervention rule to fortuitous and transient cases, but presents an elaborate analysis of the circumstances under which government should not ('non-agenda') and those under which it should ('agenda') intervene. The argument may, to some tastes, be weighted too heavily on the side of *non-agenda*, but it is free from any dogma except the utilitarian one with which it is supposed by Halévy to clash.

Whether government should intervene, says Bentham, should depend on the extent of the power, intelligence, and inclination, and therefore the spontaneous initiative, possessed by the public, and this will vary as between countries. 'In Russia, under Peter the Great, the list of *sponte acta* being a blank, that of *agenda* was proportionately abundant.' Government has special responsibilities for providing security against food shortages as well as military security. He approves of government aid in the construction of roads, canals, iron railways, of public hospitals for the sick, hurt and helpless, of public establishments for the 'occasional maintenance and employment of able-bodied poor', and, as we have seen, of public health activities on a scale still unknown. He was an ardent advocate of general education at public expense and he urged the extension of governmental registration services to make fraud more hazardous – and also of the systematic collection of economic statistics, but with a proviso which I suspect saps his concession of most of its virtue for modern statisticians, namely, that 'no institution should be set on foot for the furnishing any such articles, without a previous indication of the benefit derivable from such knowledge, and a conviction that it will pay for the expense'.

Whatever its merits or defects, this treatment of the economic role of government is not in manner or substance doctrinaire, is not in any detail, as far as I can see, inconsistent with his general 'principle of utility', and does not have in it, explicitly or implicitly, any trace of a doctrine of natural harmony of interests. It is to be borne in mind, moreover, that the best Bentham hopes for after all that can be done artificially to harmonize private interests with the public interest will still be far from perfect harmony. This has, indeed, been made the basis from another point of view of attack by moral philosophers of other faiths against utilitarianism: it is taken to task for failing to build a bridge between individual and general happiness. But this would be a valid criticism only if either it had professed to have succeeded in doing so and failed, or if it were a proper demand of *any* moral philosophy that it should provide a *practicable* scheme of perfect harmony of interests. Bentham did not completely bridge the gulf between private interests and the general interest, but neither did he deny the existence of such a gulf, and he did propose two ways, education and government, by which the gulf could be somewhat narrowed – with religion, though grudgingly, accepted as a useful part of education in so far as it educates for virtue. Does anyone know of a third way?

I turn now to John Stuart Mill. His famous *Autobiography* – revealing, but not as much so as he no doubt intended – made generally known the extraordinary intellectual regime to which he had been subjected as a boy by his father, and the precocity which resulted from it. In 1822, at the age of sixteen, he was engaging the redoubtable Robert Torrens in battle in the pages of an important newspaper about the theory of (economic) value. Before he was twenty he had edited Bentham's five-volumed work on the *Rationale of Evidence*, had published at least seven major articles in important periodicals on economic, political, and legal matters, had pointed out with great assurance and even less reverence the literary, political, economic, philosophical, and ethical shortcomings of the august *Edinburgh Review*, and had been arrested for distributing birth-control pamphlets.

In the first stage of his career, drilled to a rigid adherence to the Benthamite canon, John Stuart Mill was a zealous exponent of Bentham's and of his father's moral and political doctrines and of Ricardo's economics. In 1826, however, when still in his twentieth year, he underwent a mental crisis, which continued intermittently for several years and which brought him sieges of mental depression, as well as an intellectual conversion which he was later, in his *Autobiography*, to describe as akin to a religious 'conviction of sin', the sin being in effect Benthamism.

It is conceivable that John Stuart Mill's main trouble was primarily due to overwork, but his own explanation was that the sudden realization that the Benthamite doctrines left the nobler human feelings too much out of account and did not offer a sufficiently full prospect for human happiness had proved more than he could take. During these and subsequent years, he manifested the characteristic which was to remain prominent in all the rest of his career, his susceptibility to influence from widely diverse ideas or, as he was later to put it in his *Autobiography*, his 'great readiness and eagerness to learn from everybody, and to make room in my opinions for every new acquisition by adjusting the old and the new to one another'. New winds of doctrine were impinging on his mind, which was then as open as a prairie: Wordsworth's nature poetry, with its reverence for beauty and its revelation – for a Benthamite – that there were other fruitful sources of impressions than those provided by syllogisms; the reading of one of Comte's early works and personal associations with Saint-Simonians, which brought him into contact with the new historical approach to social thought; Macaulay's refutation in the *Edinburgh Review* of his father's *a priori* demonstration of the superiority of democracy to aristocratic government; the conservative political views and the more-or-less orthodox religious views of his friends John Sterling and Frederick Maurice; the feudalistic and pre-fascistic doctrines being expounded with fiery moral passion by Carlyle; and so forth. From all of them he borrowed something, although never as much as he then supposed, and for the most part not for keeps.

For a time, while his dour and magerful father still lived, the younger Mill did not break openly with the Benthamites, but his personal relations with the school became strained – more so, in fact, than he was ever to be aware of. Bentham, however, died in 1832 and James Mill in 1836, and freed from the restraint of their disapproval and evident disappointment, John Stuart Mill began to explore the new ground on which he not too firmly stood by the hazardous procedure of putting his thoughts in print for the public to read.

The break was sharpest in the field of private ethics, where Bentham's and James Mill's interest had been least. In his economics, John Stuart Mill remained faithful to the Ricardian doctrines as he understood them – and, to some extent, improved upon them in the process of interpreting them. In any case, the Ricardian economics was not wholly acceptable to Bentham, nor Bentham's economics at all acceptable to Ricardo. In the fields of politics and of law, John Stuart Mill proclaimed some major departures in his thinking from the views of Bentham, but he never specified what they were. I think that, apart from some wavering as to the virtues of political democracy and some approaches to the benevolent Toryism of Coleridge, Wordsworth, Sterling, and Maurice, these were mainly methodological, loss of faith in the adequacy of the 'geometrical' method in politics, rather than substantive.[7] With his father's writing he never, it seems to me, dealt with complete frankness, and he reserved for Bentham blows which could more justly have been directed against James Mill. The harshness and vehemence of the attack on Bentham was no doubt a subconscious manifestation of the urge he was under to free himself from what he had come to feel was an intellectual straitjacket, but it had been his father rather than Bentham who had placed it on him.

The attacks on Benthamism began in 1833, while his father was still living but after Bentham had died, with critical 'Remarks on Bentham's Philosophy' included, under cover of anonymity, as an

7. For his attempt to substitute, under Saint-Simonian influence, a philosophy-of-history approach, see his series of essays (1831) with a characteristically learned and penetrating introduction by Hayek (1942).

appendix to Bulwer Lytton's *England and the English*. In 1838, or two years after his father's death, he published in the *London and Westminster Review* his famous full-dress article on Bentham, again anonymous, but with the authorship inevitably known at once to friends and foes. In 1840, he published in the same *Review* an article on Coleridge, which, by its sympathetic treatment of the latter's ethical and political views, was indirectly a criticism of Benthamism.

Meanwhile, in 1835, in a review in the *London and Westminster* of a book by Adam Sedgwick which criticized utilitarian ethics as expounded by Paley, he had defended the principle of utility when properly expounded, but without mentioning any names had remarked that for a full exposition of it additional materials were needed beyond those already to be found in the writings of philosophers.

In these articles Mill was clearly endeavouring to salvage, or at least shrinking from abandoning, a utilitarian system of ethics while rejecting such features of Bentham's system as he could no longer tolerate. There was high praise, therefore, for Bentham as well as sharp blame. His main criticism of Bentham related to his treatment of private morals and of psychology, and especially the stress Bentham put on the role played in human behavior by calculation of gain or loss. He objected also that Bentham, by shifting from a technical (or broad) meaning of terms – and especially of the term 'interest' – to a popular (or narrow) meaning, often slid into an account of human behavior which pictured it as inherently selfish. He explained this – unkindly – in terms of Bentham's personality. Bentham, said Mill, intellectually recognized the possibility of generous action, of benevolence, but 'the incompleteness of his own mind as a representative of universal human nature' led him to regard genuine benevolence as rare and therefore unimportant in real life.

In many of the most natural and strongest feelings of human nature he had no sympathy; from many of its graver experiences he was altogether cut off; and the faculty by which one mind understands a mind different from itself, and throws itself into the feelings of that other mind, was denied him by his deficiency of Imagination (1875a).

There was a basis for Mill's criticisms. That Bentham frequently fell into language which pictured human behavior as if it consisted almost solely of action based on calculations of personal gain and that his imagination was deficient with respect to the possible range of human emotions is beyond dispute. But Mill goes further in his criticism at some points than the texts he cites, or their context, justify, and in doing so disregards peculiarities of the Benthamite terminology which at other times, when his attitude had changed, he was to invoke against misinterpretations of Bentham at other hands. I can here deal with only one of these misinterpretations. Mill points out that if in Bentham's *Table of the Springs of Action* we find such words as 'conscience', 'principle', 'moral rectitude', 'moral duty', which in the mouths of others represent recognition of such a thing as conscience as a thing distinct from philanthropy, affection, or self-interest in this world or the next, it is as synonymous for 'love of reputation', and that the word 'self-respect' appears not at all either here or in any of Bentham's writings (1875). The critics of Bentham who have since made the same criticism and cited his *Table of the Springs of Action* as evidence are beyond enumeration.

There is only too much ground for criticism of Bentham for not using words quite as other men do, provided that deviation on his part from the common use of terms is not taken as reliable evidence of deviation from the common run of thought on the questions with which these words are usually associated. But Mill, who should have known better, makes use here of this kind of argument against the one person of all who by his discussions of the logic of language had made himself least vulnerable to it. Moreover, Bentham in his writings does use 'conscience' and 'duty' very much as other men do, and if he did not use 'self-respect', his stock of synonyms was adequate to fill the void.

The *Table of the Springs of Action*, however, itself provides a more direct, though only a partial, answer to Mill's criticism. The psychology of Hartley and of James Mill from which Bentham started distinguished between 'simple' pleasures, and 'complex' or 'compound' pleasures derived from the 'simple' ones genetically by the processes of 'association of ideas'. Benevolence, generosity, duty, justice, conscience, and so forth would be 'compound' pleasures. But Bentham expressly says of the *Table* – which is sufficiently formidable as it stands – that: 'The pleasures and pains here brought to view are, every one of them, *simple* and *elementary*' (1838–43a, p. 207). He does cite a few 'compound pleasures', as illustrative of one broad category of such excluded from the table. One of these, 'love of justice', has as one of its components 'sympathy for community at large, in respect of the interest which it has in the maintenance of justice'. Mill was later to emphasize love of justice as one of the major virtues. His present refusal to be satisfied with Bentham's recognition of it as one of the 'springs of action' was perhaps a not too captious suspicion that the words added to it by Bentham made of it a less admirable virtue than if Bentham had written merely 'love of justice (period)'. But it was common ground among the Benthamites, including John Stuart Mill, that the tone and moral significance of 'compound pleasures' could be radically different from the tone and original significance of their component elements, the 'simple pleasures' from which they had been compounded.

By the time Mill was working on his *Principles of Political Economy*, he had swung back a large part though not all of the way to Bentham's political theory and moral philosophy. What was left of his revolt was confined mostly to a continued insistence on recognition of the complete range of human feelings and a consequent endeavour to avoid exaggerating the role of rationalistic hedonism in human behaviour.

William Whewell, an anti-utilitarian professor of moral philosophy at Cambridge University where an even narrower type of utilitarianism with hell-fire trimmings – 'theological utilitarianism', it was later to be labeled – had until his advent reigned unchallenged for over a century, in 1838, on the appearance of Mill's article on Bentham, had in private correspondence with a friend welcomed Mill's recantation, but complained – with some justice – of its manner:

It is certainly very encouraging to see on all sides strong tendencies to a reform of the prevalent system of morals. The article [by Mill] in the *London Review* is an indication of this, and appears to me to be in many important points right, and at any rate right in the vigorous rejection of Bentham's doctrines and keen criticism of his character. But I confess I do not look with much respect upon a body of writers, who, after habitually showering the most bitter abuse on those who oppose Bentham's principles, come round to the side of their opponents, without a single word of apology, and with an air of imperturbable complacency, as if they had been right before and after the change. Nor do I see any security, in their present creed, against a change of equal magnitude hereafter (Douglas, 1881, pp. 270–71).

This was real prescience on Whewell's part. In 1843, in conversation about the surviving disciples of Bentham, Mill made the remark which 'though smilingly uttered . . . was not at all a jest' that as for himself: 'And I am Peter, who denied his Master' (Masson, 1908, p. 553). In 1852 Mill was to write a critical review of Whewell's *Lectures on the History of Moral Philosophy in England*, published in the same year. Conceding very little error in the Benthamite doctrine, Mill rejected vehemently Whewell's objections to utilitarian ethics in general and to Bentham in particular, even when they were very similar indeed to his own criticism of Bentham in 1838.

The final stage in Mill's presentation of his ethical views was in 1863, when his essays on Utilitarianism appeared. In form, these still represented an adherence to the doctrine, but so modified by the admission without obvious absorption of foreign elements that they have been the despair of its friends and the delight of its critics ever since. Acts were to be morally appraised solely in terms of their consequences for happiness – a strictly Benthamite proposition. *All* consequences, however, were to be taken into account, including the effects on the character of the agent – an early doctrine of Mill's, which he derived from Coleridge and which he regarded as contrary to Bentham's views, mistakenly, I think. Happiness was conceived broadly enough to cover every type of wish or aspiration man could experience. Mill – unwisely, I think – went a step further than Bentham ever ventured by offering a 'proof' that happiness was the proper criterion of virtue: namely, that competent judges accepted it as such, a type of proof which eighteenth century critics of the 'moral sense' school of ethics had exposed to ridicule for its circularity.

Mill now attempted also to incorporate into utilitarianism a novel element for it and one which many moral philosophers hold to be incompatible with it, namely, the recognition of non-homogeneity of pleasures and consequently the existence of qualitative differences of a hierarchial nature, as well as quantitative differences, between pleasures:

It is quite compatible with the principle of utility to recognize the fact, that some *kinds* of pleasure are more desirable and more valuable than others. It would be absurd that while, in estimating all other things, quality is considered as well as quantity, the estimation of pleasures should be supposed to depend on quantity alone (Mill, 1867, pp. 11–12).

The test of quality as between two pleasures was the preference 'by those who are competently acquainted with both' of the one above the other despite the fact that the other represented a much greater quantity of pleasure.[8]

I venture to suggest: (1) that the problem as Mill presents it, that is, within the limits of utilitarianism, is a spurious one; (2) that what he proffers as a solution is even more spurious; and (3) that Bentham and his predecessors to some extent and modern economists using utility theory to a larger extent, have provided a technique which, while it does not solve any fundamental moral problem, suffices to show that a dichotomy and possible clash between ratings of values on the basis of quality and their rating on the basis of quantity is not one of the fundamental moral problems.

Pleasures – or desires – are of course not homogeneous with respect to every conceivable quality they may possess – any more than are any other objects of human attention except abstract numbers. Comparison is – or should be – always with respect to specified qualities of objects, and if there is possibility of and proper occasion for measurement the measurement is also with reference to these specified qualities.

Mill confuses the issue by attempting at the same time to give predominant importance to the ordering of *classes* of pleasures on a higher–lower scale and to leave room for legitimate preference in particular cases of a pleasure of a lower order over one of a higher.

8. Mill, 1867, p. 12. In an undated manuscript 'On Social Freedom', found in Mill's house at Avignon after his death, and published, among other places, in *Living Age* (1907), pp. 323–36, there is a stronger statement of the higher-lower thesis with the order of rank made a pure matter of 'feeling', not subject to demonstration or to argument – a complete swing back to the eighteenth century 'moral sense' school.

This is the famous and ancient false dilemma of the water-*versus*-diamonds problem in economics, extended to the whole field of values. Whatever may be the case for didactic purposes, for actual behavior – including 'moral' behavior – the issues arise in the form of necessary choices between units and not between classes of objects. Bentham's famous dictum 'Quantum of pleasure being equal, pushpin [a children's game] is as good as poetry' would meet all the proper requirements of the utilitarian principle if restated somewhat as follows: 'Desire being equal at the margin of choice, a marginal unit of pushpin is as good as a marginal unit of poetry.' The utilitarian but didactic moralist would still be free to insist that since in fact experienced choosers don't plump for even a first unit of pushpin until they are gorged with poetry, *in that sense* poetry as a class is higher on the scale of values than pushpin as a class.

I come now at long last to Mill's *Principles of Political Economy*. He wrote this two-volume book in less than two years, and when he began it he expected it to take only a few months to write. For at least ten years prior to this, he had not given much attention to economics. It was designed to do for Mill's time what Adam Smith had done for his, and to present what was known of the 'principles of political economy' as a science, together with their applications to concrete problems and, in the words of its title page, 'some of their Applications to Social Philosophy'. By the 'science' of political economy Mill meant a body of deductive analysis, resting on psychological premises derived from introspection and observation of one's neighbors, and even with respect to these premises abstracting from all aspects of human behavior except those most intimately and most generally associated with the business of buying and selling. When Malthus, in 1824, objected that the 'new school' of Ricardians had 'altered the theories of Adam Smith upon pure speculation', Mill had replied: 'it would, indeed, have been somewhat surprising if they had altered them on any other ground'.[9] Later, as the result of Comtean influence and of his investigations in logical method, Mill was more receptive in principle to the possibilities of historical induction. But it is clear that he never assigned to it the right to an independent role in the 'science' of political

9. In a review (1825) of the article by Malthus (1824) criticizing McCulloch's article, in the *Encyclopaedia Britannica*.

economy. Writing in 1835 with respect to the historical form of the inductive method, he had said:

History is not the foundation, but the verification, of the social science; it corroborates, and often suggests, political truths, but cannot prove them. The proof of them is drawn from the laws of human nature; ascertained through the study of ourselves by reflection, and of mankind by actual intercourse with them. . . . The usefulness of history depends upon its being kept in the second place (Mill, 1875a, pp. 112–13).

This was, of course, standard methodological doctrine, and to a large extent practice, in English social thought since Hobbes. Inquiry was to be pursued by means of deductive reasoning resting on psychological premises obtained empirically, but chiefly through introspection – which, it should always be remembered, was universally regarded in the past, whatever may be the fashion today, as an 'empirical' technique of investigation, and sharply distinguished from intuition, or 'innate ideas'. But in Mill, as methodological doctrine, it has less significance than for most of his predecessors, since he confines it to the 'scientific' part of political economy, stresses the importance of 'applications' which can proceed by a wider range of logical methods, gives repeatedly at least platonic warnings that any abstraction from reality must be allowed for before the results of such analysis are made the basis for pronouncements on policy, and rejects it for every other established branch of social thought.

Of his earlier rebellion against the psychology of Bentham and of his father, the most important residue for his economics was probably his repeated emphasis on the importance of custom as a rival to the competitive principle, especially in connection with land-tenure and the relations of landlord and tenant. Here he showed the influence of Richard Jones, one of the pioneer advocates of resort to systematic induction in economics. But this presented Mill with somewhat of a methodological dilemma, which he never succeeded in resolving. 'It is unphilosophical,' he wrote, 'to construct a science out of a few of the agencies by which the phenomena are determined, and leave the rest to the routine of practice or the sagacity of conjecture' (1848, p. 472). On the other hand, 'only through the principle of competition has political economy any pretension to the character of a science' (1848, book 2, chapter 4), a proposition which Edgeworth was later in effect to repeat, when he wrote that if monopoly should prevail over a large part of the economic order:

Among those who would suffer by the new regime there would be [included] . . . the abstract economists, who would be deprived of their occupation, the investigation of the conditions which determine value. There would survive only the empirical school, flourishing in a chaos congenial to their mentality (1925, pp. 138–9).

We seem, however, to have found another alternative, that of becoming amateur lawyers.

Mill thus had no technique for dealing systematically with the analysis of economic process where competition was encroached upon either by custom or by monopoly, and when he did mention custom – or monopoly – he left it to the reader to estimate its importance and to make the necessary corrections in the conclusions he had reached on the basis of abstractions from these complicating factors. For himself, he assumed the responsibility only for that 'uncertain and slippery intermediate region', between 'ultimate aims' and 'the immediately useful and practically attainable' (1813, p. 189). Logicians and physical scientists have the right, I suppose, to jeer at Mill's failure to extricate himself from this plight. For those among us, however, upon whom the redeeming grace has not as yet been bestowed of that special ideology which takes the form of faith in the capacity of statistical method to perform logical miracles, humility is prescribed, since we are all in the same fix.

The *Principles* thus has no single methodological character. As is the case with the *Wealth of Nations* of Adam Smith, some portions are predominantly abstract and *a priori*; in others, there is a substantial measure of factual data and of inference from history. Its wide range of subject matter; the success with which the lucidity of its style and the nobility of its outlook on life divert attention from its lack of logical rigor; the patent honesty and open mindedness with which controversial issues are treated; these and other qualities made it probably the longest-lived textbook our discipline has ever had or ever will have. It was the text used in the first college course in economics I took, over sixty years after its first publication.

Francis Walker's *Political Economy* was also assigned to us, and I think we showed good judgement when we labeled the course, as students will, 'milk and water'. Writing in 1832, Mill had presented a forceful case in defence of ambiguity in language, on the ground that it was for many persons the price which would have to be paid if important ideas, which by their richness and variety of content it is difficult to make clear, were not to be sacrificed on the altar of logical clarity (1832). The *Principles*, I think, demonstrate that for Mill himself this was good doctrine; it would have been an inferior book, much less rich in content – and much smaller in size – if Mill had thrown out all that was ambiguous and lacking in strict logical consistency.

What most struck his contemporaries in the contents of the *Principles* was the sympathetic manner in which Mill dealt with proposals for radical change along socialist lines in the economic structure of society. The sympathy was in large degree platonic, for in no major concrete instance did Mill actually commit himself to the desirability of a specific drastic change. Mill aspired after the millennium, but he found abundant reason why it was not and should not be wished to be imminent. He looked forward, mostly on ethical and humanitarian grounds, to substantial socialization of the institution of property at some time in the vague future. Meanwhile, however, he warned against any weakening of the institutions of private property, free competition, and the rule of the market. This combination of hard-headed rules and utopian aspirations was just exactly the doctrine that Victorians of good will yearned for, and it made a large contribution to the popular success of the book.

Mill's handling of the problem of *laissez-faire* was a case in point. Except for the difference in tone and feeling, the fuller expression of lofty ideals and impracticable aspirations, it was subsequently similar in method of analysis and nature of conclusions to Bentham's treatment. Like Bentham, and like all the other major classical economists except perhaps Senior – who was not a Benthamite – Mill gave only a very qualified adherence to *laissez-faire*. It was for him only a rule of expediency, always subordinate to the principle of utility, and never a dogma. The dogmatic exponents of *laissez-faire* of the time were the Manchester School, and Mill – like Torrens before him and Cairnes, Jevons, Sidgwick, Marshall, Edgeworth and others after him – denied repeatedly, and forcefully almost to the point of blasphemy, that the Cobdenites had either authority or logic to support them when they invoked the 'Laws of Political Economy' to stop government from coming to the relief of distress.

It is, fortunately, not part of my assignment to appraise the technical economics of Mill's *Principles*. What I have tried to do is to show the intellectual relations between two men important in the history of our discipline. From these two men several generations of British and American – and above all Canadian – economists, and to some extent also 'liberal' continental economists, derived in large part the psychological, ethical, political, and methodological presuppositions upon which they built their economic analysis. With the ebbing of liberalism in the profession, the importance of knowing what its intellectual foundations were has become chiefly historical, and to those under fifty the historical is not obviously important. But for those *over* fifty, a comment of Tawney's is relevant. 'It is a wise philosopher,' he writes, the flatterer really meaning 'economist', 'who knows the source of his own premises' (1929). I would go even further. It is an unusually alert economist who knows what his premises are, regardless of their source. For those over fifty study of Bentham and of Mill can do something to remedy both of these lacks. Beyond this remark, I make no attempt to draw any moral from what I have said. But I believe that in exercising this unaccustomed measure of self-restraint I am conforming to the 'principle of utility' if broadly enough interpreted.

References

ATKINSON, C. M. (ed.) (1914), *Theory of Legislation*, section 2, London.

BARKER, E. SIR (1937), Preface to his edition of James Mill, *Essay on Government*, Cambridge.

BENTHAM, J. (1797), 'Situation and relief of the poor', *Annals of Agriculture*, vol. 29, pp. 422–3.

BENTHAM, J. (1823), *Not Paul, but Jesus*, London.

BENTHAM, J. (1838–43a), 'Principles of morals and legislation', *Works*, vol. 1.

BENTHAM, J. (1838–43b), 'Introduction to the principles of morals and legislation', *Works*, vol. 1.

BENTHAM, J. (1838–43c), 'A general view of a complete code of laws', *Works*, vol. 3.

BENTHAM, J. (1838–43d), 'Manual of political economy', *Works*, vol. 3.

DOUGLAS, S. (1881), *Life of William Whewell*, London.

EDGEWORTH, F. Y. (1925), 'The pure theory of monopoly (1897)', in *Papers Relating to Political Economy*, vol. 1, London.

HALÉVY, E. (1901–4), *La Formation du Radicalisme Philosophique*, 3 vols, Paris.

HAMILTON, W. SIR (ed.) (1852), *The Works of Sir Thomas Reid*, 3rd edn, Edinburgh.

HIMES, N. E. (1936), 'Jeremy Bentham and the genesis of English neo-Malthusianism', *Econ. Hist.* (supplement of *econ. J.*), vol. 3, pp. 267–76.

Living Age (1907), 7th series, vol. 36.

MACAULAY, LORD (1891), *The Miscellaneous Writings and Speeches of Lord Macaulay*, popular edition, London.

MCCULLOCH, J. R., 'Political economy', in supplement to *Encyclopaedia Britannica*, 4th edn.

MALTHUS, T. R. (1824), *Q. Rev.*, vol. 30, January.

MANDEVILLE, B. (1730), *A Treatise of the Hypochondriack and Hysterick Diseases*, 2nd edn, London.

MASSON, D. (1908), 'Memories of London in the "Forties"', *Blackwood's*, vol. 183.

MILL, J. (1869), *Analysis of the Phenomena of the Human Mind*, London.

MILL, J. S. (1825), review, *Westminster Review*, vol. 3, p. 213.

MILL, J. S. (1831), 'The spirit of the age', *Examiner*; reprinted in 1942, University of Chicago Press.

MILL, J. S. (1832), 'Review of G. C. Lewis's "Use and abuse of political terms"' *Tait's Edinburgh Magazine*, vol. 1, p. 164.

MILL, J. S. (1867), *Utilitarianism*, 3rd edn.

MILL, J. S. (1863), *Autobiography*, London.

MILL, J. S. (1850), *A System of Logic*, 3rd edn, vol. 2, Longman.

MILL, J. S. (1848), *Principles of Political Economy*, 5th edn, Longman.

MILL, J. S. (1875a), 'Bentham', reprinted in *Dissertations and Discussions*, 3rd edn.

MILL, J. S. (1875b), 'Professor Sedgwick's discourse on the studies of the University of Cambridge', *Dissertations and Discussions*, vol. 1.

MITCHELL, W. C. (1937), *The Backward Art of Spending Money*, New York.

Monthly Repository (1817), vol. 12.

Proceedings of the Massachusetts Historical Society (1903), 2nd series, vol. 17.

SILBENER, E. (1940), 'Un manuscrit inédit de David Ricardo sur le problème monétaire', *Revue d'Histoire Économique et Sociale*, vol. 25, pp. 195–259.

TAWNEY, R. H. (1920), Preface to *Life and Struggle of William Lovett*, new edn, New York.

TAWNEY, R. H. (1929), Introduction to R. W. Firth, *Primitive Economics of the New Zealand Maori*, New York.

8 H. Sidgwick

The Reasonableness of Utilitarianism

H. Sidgwick, excerpts from *The Method of Ethics*, Macmillan, 1907, 7th edn.

Can we then, between this Scylla and Charybdis of ethical inquiry,
avoiding on the one hand doctrines that merely bring us back to common opinion with all its imperfections, and on the other hand doctrines that lead us round in a circle, find any way of obtaining
self-evident moral principles of real significance? It would be dis-
heartening to have to regard as altogether illusory the strong instinct
of common sense that points to the existence of such principles, and
the deliberate convictions of the long line of moralists who have
enunciated them. At the same time, the more we extend our knowledge of man and his environment, the more we realize the vast variety
of human natures and circumstances that have existed in different
ages and countries, the less disposed we are to believe that there is any
definite code of absolute rules, applicable to all human beings without
exception. And we shall find, I think, that the truth lies between these
two conclusions. There are certain absolute practical principles, the
truth of which, when they are explicitly stated, is manifest; but they
are of too abstract a nature, and too universal in their scope, to
enable us to ascertain by immediate application of them what we
ought to do in any particular case; particular duties have still to be
determined by some other method.

Some underlying principles

One such principle was given in chapter 1, section 3 of this book
(1907); where I pointed out that whatever action any of us judges to
be right for himself, he implicitly judges to be right for all similar
persons in similar circumstances. Or, as we may otherwise put it,
'if a kind of conduct that is right (or wrong) for me is not right (or
wrong) for some one else, it must be on the ground of some differ-

ence between the two cases, other than the fact that I and he are different persons'. A corresponding proposition may be stated with equal truth in respect of what ought to be done *to* – not *by* – different individuals. These principles have been most widely recognized, not in their most abstract and universal form, but in their special application to the situation of two (or more) individuals similarly related to each other: as so applied, they appear in what is popularly known as the golden rule, 'Do to others as you would have them do to you.' This formula is obviously unprecise in statement; for one might wish for another's cooperation in sin, and be willing to reciprocate it. Nor is it even true to say that we ought to do to others only what we think it right for them to do to us; for no one will deny that there may be differences in the circumstances – and even in the natures – of two individuals, *A* and *B*, which would make it wrong for *A* to treat *B* in the way in which it is right for *B* to treat *A*. In short the self-evident principle strictly stated must take some such negative form as this; 'it cannot be right for *A* to treat *B* in a manner in which it would be wrong for *B* to treat *A*, merely on the ground that they are two different individuals, and without there being any difference between the natures or circumstances of the two which can be stated as a reasonable ground for difference of treatment'. Such a principle manifestly does not give complete guidance – indeed its effect, strictly speaking, is merely to throw a definite *onus probandi* on the man who applies to another a treatment of which he would complain if applied to himself; but common sense has amply recognized the practical importance of the maxim: and its truth, so far as it goes, appears to me self-evident.

A somewhat different application of the same fundamental principle that individuals in similar conditions should be treated similarly finds its sphere in the ordinary administration of law, or (as we say) of 'justice'. Accordingly in section 1 of chapter 5 of this book (1907) I drew attention to 'impartiality in the application of general rules', as an important element in the common notion of justice; indeed, there ultimately appeared to be no other element which could be intuitively known with perfect clearness and certainty. Here again it must be plain that this precept of impartiality is insufficient for the complete determination of just conduct, as it does not help us to decide what kind of rules should be thus impartially applied; though all admit the importance of excluding from government, and human conduct generally, all conscious partiality and 'respect of persons'.

The principle just discussed, which seems to be more or less clearly implied in the common notion of 'fairness' or 'equity', is obtained by considering the similarity of the individuals that make up a logical whole or genus. There are others, no less important, which emerge in the consideration of the similar parts of a mathematical or quantitative whole. Such a whole is presented in the common notion of the good – or, as is sometimes said, 'good on the whole' – of any individual human being. The proposition 'that one ought to aim at one's own good' is sometimes given as the maxim of 'rational self-love' or prudence: but as so stated it does not clearly avoid tautology; since we may define 'good' as 'what one ought to aim at'. If, however, we say 'one's good on the whole', the addition suggests a principle which, when explicitly stated, is, at any rate, not tautological. I have already referred to this principle (see 1907, p. 124, note) as that 'of impartial concern for all parts of our conscious life': – we might express it concisely by saying 'that hereafter *as such* is to be regarded neither less nor more than now'. It is not, of course, meant that the good of the present may not reasonably be preferred to that of the future on account of its greater certainty: or again, that a week ten years hence may not be more important to us than a week now, through an increase in our means or capacities of happiness. All that the principle affirms is that the mere difference of priority and posteriority in time is not a reasonable ground for having more regard to the consciousness of one moment that to that of another. The form in which it practically presents itself to most men is 'that a smaller present good is not to be preferred to a greater future good' (allowing for difference of certainty): since prudence is generally exercised in restraining a present desire (the object or satisfaction of which we commonly regard as *pro tanto* 'a good'), on account of the remoter consequences of gratifying it. The commonest view of the principle would no doubt be that the present *pleasure* or *happiness* is reasonably to be foregone with the view of obtaining greater pleasure or happiness hereafter: but the principle need not be restricted to a hedonistic application; it is equally applicable to any other interpretation of 'one's own good', in which good is conceived as a mathematical whole, of which the integrant parts are realized in different parts or moments of a lifetime. And therefore it is perhaps better to distinguish it here from the principle 'that pleasure is the sole ultimate good', which does not seem to have any logical connection with it.

So far we have only been considering the 'good on the whole' of a single individual: but just as this notion is constructed by comparison and integration of the different 'goods' that succeed one another in the series of our conscious states, so we have formed the notion of 'universal good' by comparison and integration of the goods of all individual human – or sentient – existences. And here again, just as in the former case, by considering the relation of the integrant parts to the whole and to each other, I obtain the self-evident principle that the good of any one individual is of no more importance, from the point of view (if I may say so) of the universe, than the good of any other; unless, that is, there are special grounds for believing that more good is likely to be realized in the one case than in the other. And it is evident to me that as a rational being I am bound to aim at good generally – so far as it is attainable by my efforts – not merely at a particular part of it.

From these two rational intuitions we may deduce, as a necessary inference, the maxim of benevolence in an abstract form: viz. that each one is morally bound to regard the good of any other individual as much as his own, except in so far as he judges it to be less, when impartially viewed, or less certainly knowable or attainable by him. I before observed that the duty of benevolence as recognized by common sense seems to fall somewhat short of this. But I think it may be fairly urged in explanation of this that *practically* each man, even with a view to universal good, ought chiefly to concern himself with promoting the good of a limited number of human beings, and that generally in proportion to the closeness of their connection with him. I think that a 'plain man', in a modern civilized society, if his conscience were fairly brought to consider the hypothetical question, whether it would be morally right for him to seek his own happiness on any occasion if it involved a certain sacrifice of the greater happiness of some other human being – without any counter-balancing gain to any one else – would answer unhesitatingly in the negative.

I have tried to show how in the principles of justice, prudence, and rational benevolence as commonly recognized there is at least a self-evident element, immediately cognizable by abstract intuition; depending in each case on the relation which individuals and their particular ends bear as parts to their wholes, and to other parts of these wholes. I regard the apprehension, with more or less distinctness, of these abstract truths, as the permanent basis of the common conviction that the fundamental precepts of morality are essentially reasonable. No doubt these principles are often placed side by side with other precepts to which custom and general consent have given a merely illusory air of self-evidence: but the distinction between the two kinds of maxims appears to me to become manifest by merely reflecting upon them. I know by direct reflection that the propositions, 'I ought to speak the truth', 'I ought to keep my promises' – however true they may be – are not self-evident to me; they present themselves as propositions requiring rational justification of some kind. On the other hand, the propositions, 'I ought not to prefer a present lesser good to a future greater good', and 'I ought not to prefer my own lesser good to the greater good of another',[1] do present themselves as self-evident; as much (e.g.) as the mathematical axiom that 'if equals be added to equals the wholes are equal'.

It is on account of the fundamental and manifest importance, in my view, of the distinction above drawn between (1) the moral maxims which reflection shows not to possess ultimate validity, and (2) the moral maxims which are or involve genuine ethical axioms, that I refrained at the outset of this investigation from entering at length into the psychogonical question as to the origin of apparent moral intuitions. For no psychogonical theory has ever been put forward professing to discredit the propositions that I regard as really axiomatic, by showing that the causes which produced them were such as had a tendency to make them false: while as regards the former class of maxims, a psychogonical proof that they are untrustworthy when taken as absolutely and without qualification true is in my view, superfluous: since direct reflection shows me they have no claim to be so taken. On the other hand, so far as psychogonical

1. To avoid misapprehension I should state that in these propositions the consideration of the different degrees of *certainty* of present and future good, own and others' good respectively, is supposed to have been fully taken into account *before* the future or alien good is judged to be greater.

theory represents moral rules as, speaking broadly and generally, means to the ends of individual and social good or well-being, it obviously tends to give a general support to the conclusions to which the preceding discussion has brought us by a different method: since it leads us to regard other moral rules as subordinate to the principles of prudence and benevolence. . . .[2]

The meaning of utilitarianism

. . . The term utilitarianism is, at the present day, in common use, and is supposed to designate a doctrine or method with which we are all familiar. But on closer examination, it appears to be applied to several distinct theories, having no necessary connection with one another, and not even referring to the same subject-matter. It will be well, therefore, to define, as carefully as possible, the doctrine that is to be denoted by the term in the present book: at the same time distinguishing this from other doctrines to which usage would allow the name to be applied, and indicating, so far as seems necessary, its relation to these.

By utilitarianism is here meant the ethical theory, that the conduct which, under any given circumstances, is objectively right, is that which will produce the greatest amount of happiness on the whole; that is, taking into account all whose happiness is affected by the conduct. It would tend to clearness if we might call this principle, and the method based upon it, by some such name as 'universalistic hedonism': and I have therefore sometimes ventured to use this term, in spite of its cumbrousness.

The first doctrine from which it seems necessary to distinguish this, is the egoistic hedonism expounded and discussed in book 2 of this treatise. The difference, however, between the propositions (1) that each ought to seek his own happiness, and (2) that each ought to seek the happiness of all, is so obvious and glaring, that instead of dwelling upon it we seem rather called upon to explain how the two ever came to be confounded, or in any way included under one notion. This question and the general relation between the two

2. It may, however, be thought that in exhibiting this aspect of the morality of common sense, psychogonical theory leads us to define in a particular way the general notion of 'good' or 'well-being', regarded as a result which morality has a demonstrable natural tendency to produce.

doctrines were briefly discussed in a former chapter.[3] Among other points it was there noticed that the confusion between these two ethical theories was partly assisted by the confusion with both of the psychological theory that in voluntary actions every agent does, universally or normally, seek his own individual happiness or pleasure. Now there seems to be no *necessary* connection between this latter proposition and any ethical theory: but in so far as there is a natural tendency to pass from psychological to ethical hedonism, the transition must be – at least primarily – to the egoistic phase of the latter. For clearly, from the fact that every one actually does seek his own happiness we cannot conclude, as an immediate and obvious inference, that he ought to seek the happiness of other people.[4]

Nor, again, is utilitarianism, as an ethical doctrine, necessarily connected with the psychological theory that the moral sentiments are derived, by 'association of ideas' or otherwise, from experiences of the non-moral pleasures and pains resulting to the agent or to others from different kinds of conduct. An intuitionist might accept this theory, so far as it is capable of scientific proof, and still hold that these moral sentiments, being found in our present conscious-ness as independent impulses, ought to possess the authority that they seem to claim over the more primary desires and aversions from which they have sprung: and an egoist on the other hand might fully admit the altruistic element of the derivation, and still hold that these and all other impulses (including even universal benevolence) are properly under the rule of rational self-love: and that it is really only reasonable to gratify them in so far as we may expect to find our private happiness in such gratification. In short, what is often called the 'utilitarian' theory of the origin of the moral sentiments cannot by itself provide a proof of the ethical doctrine to which I in this treatise restrict the term utilitarianism. I shall, however, hereafter try to show that this psychological theory has an important though subordinate place in the establishment of ethical utilitarianism (cf. 1907, book 4, chapter 4).

3. Book 1, chapter 6. It may be worthwhile to notice, that in Mill's well-known treatise on utilitarianism this confusion, though expressly deprecated, is to some extent encouraged by the author's treatment of the subject.

4. I have already criticized the mode in which Mill attempts to exhibit this inference (book 3, chapter 13).

Finally, the doctrine that universal happiness is the ultimate *standard* must not be understood to imply that universal benevolence is the only right or always best *motive* of action. For, as we have before observed, it is not necessary that the end which gives the criterion of rightness should always be the end at which we consciously aim: and if experience shows that the general happiness will be more satisfactorily attained if men frequently act from other motives than pure universal philanthropy, it is obvious that these other motives are reasonably to be preferred on utilitarian principles.

Let us now examine the principle itself somewhat closer. I have already attempted (book 2, chapter 1) to render the notion of greatest happiness as clear and definite as possible; and the results there obtained are of course as applicable to the discussion of universalistic as to that of egoistic hedonism. We shall understand, then, that by greatest happiness is meant the greatest possible surplus of pleasure over pain, the pain being conceived as balanced against an equal amount of pleasure, so that the two contrasted amounts annihilate each other for purposes of ethical calculation. And of course, here as before, the assumption is involved that all pleasures included in our calculation are capable of being compared quantitatively with one another and with all pains; that every such feeling has a certain intensive quantity, positive or negative (or, perhaps, zero), in respect of its desirableness, and that this quantity may be to some extent known: so that each may be at least roughly weighed in ideal scales against any other. This assumption is involved in the very notion of maximum happiness; as the attempt to make 'as great as possible' a sum of elements not quantitatively commensurable would be a mathematical absurdity. Therefore whatever weight is to be attached to the objections brought against this assumption must of course tell against the present method.

We have next to consider who the 'all' are, whose happiness is to be taken into account. Are we to extend our concern to all the beings capable of pleasure and pain whose feelings are affected by our conduct? Or are we to confine our view to human happiness? The former view is the one adopted by Bentham and Mill, and (I believe) by the utilitarian school generally: and is obviously most in accordance with the universality that is characteristic of their principle. It is the good *universal*, interpreted and defined as 'happiness' or 'pleasure', at which a utilitarian considers it his duty to aim: and it seems arbitrary and unreasonable to exclude from the end, as so conceived, any pleasure of any sentient being.

It may be said that by giving this extension to the notion, we considerably increase the scientific difficulties of the hedonistic comparison, which have already been pointed out (book 2, chapter 3): for if it be difficult to compare the pleasures and pains of other men accurately with our own, a comparison of either with the pleasures and pains of brutes is obviously still more obscure. Still, the difficulty is at least not greater for utilitarians than it is for any other moralists who recoil from the paradox of disregarding altogether the pleasures and pains of brutes. But even if we limit our attention to human beings, the extent of the subjects of happiness is not yet quite determinate. In the first place, it may be asked, how far we are to consider the interests of posterity when they seem to conflict with those of existing human beings? It seems, however, clear that the time at which a man exists cannot affect the value of his happiness from a universal point of view; and that the interests of posterity must concern a utilitarian as much as those of his contemporaries, except in so far as the effect of his actions on posterity – and even the existence of human beings to be affected – must necessarily be more uncertain. But a further question arises when we consider that we can to some extent influence the number of future human (or sentient) beings. We have to ask how, on utilitarian principles, this influence is to be exercised. Here I shall assume that, for human beings generally, life on the average yields a positive balance of pleasure over pain. This has been denied by thoughtful persons: but the denial seems to me clearly opposed to the common experience of mankind, as expressed in their commonly accepted principles of action. The great majority of men, in the great majority of conditions under which human life is lived, certainly act as if death were one of the worst of evils, for themselves and for those whom they love: and the administration of criminal justice proceeds on a similar assumption.[5]

5. Those who held the opposite opinion appear generally to assume that the appetites and desires which are the mainspring of ordinary human action are in themselves painful: a view entirely contrary to my own experience, and, I believe, to the common experience of mankind. So far as their argument is not a development of this psychological error, any plausibility it has seems to me to be obtained

Assuming, then, that the average happiness of human beings is a positive quantity, it seems clear that, supposing the average happiness enjoyed remains undiminished, utilitarianism directs us to make the number enjoying it as great as possible. But if we foresee as possible that an increase in numbers will be accompanied by a decrease in average happiness or *vice versa*, a point arises which has not only never been formally noticed, but which seems to have been substantially overlooked by many utilitarians. For if we take utilitarianism to prescribe, as the ultimate end of action, happiness on the whole, and not any individual's happiness, unless considered as an element of the whole, it would follow that, if the additional population enjoy on the whole positive happiness, we ought to weigh the amount of happiness gained by the extra number against the amount lost by the remainder. So that, strictly conceived, the point up to which, on utilitarian principles, population ought to be encouraged to increase, is not that at which average happiness is the greatest possible – as appears to be often assumed by political economists of the school of Malthus – but that at which the product formed by multiplying the number of persons living into the amount of average happiness reaches its maximum.

It may be well here to make a remark which has a wide application in utilitarian discussion. The conclusion just given wears a certain air of absurdity to the view of common sense; because its show of exactness is grotesquely incongruous with our consciousness of the inevitable inexactness of all such calculations in actual practice. But, that our practical utilitarian reasonings must necessarily be rough, is no reason for not making them as accurate as the case admits; and we shall be more likely to succeed in this if we keep before our mind as distinctly as possible the strict type of the calculation that we

by dwelling onesidedly on the annoyances and disappointments undoubtedly incident to normal human life, and on the exceptional sufferings of small minorities of the human race, or perhaps of most men during small portions of their lives.

The reader who wishes to see the paradoxical results of pessimistic utilitarianism seriously worked out by a thoughtful and suggestive writer, may refer to Professor Macmillan's book (1890). The author considers that 'the philosophical world is pretty equally divided between optimists and pessimists', and his own judgement on the question at issue between the two schools appear to be held in suspense.

should have to make, if all the relevant considerations could be estimated with mathematical precision.

There is one more point that remains to be noticed. It is evident that there may be many different ways of distributing the same quantum of happiness among the same number of persons; in order, therefore, that the utilitarian criterion of right conduct may be as complete as possible, we ought to know which of these ways is to be preferred. This question is often ignored in expositions of utilitarianism. It has perhaps seemed somewhat idle, as suggesting a purely abstract and theoretical perplexity, that could have no practical exemplification; and no doubt, if all the consequences of actions were capable of being estimated and summed up with mathematical precision, we should probably never find the excess of pleasure over pain exactly equal in the case of two competing alternatives of conduct. But the very indefiniteness of all hedonistic calculations, which was sufficiently shown in book 2, renders it by no means unlikely that there may be no *cognizable* difference between the quantities of happiness involved in two sets of consequences respectively; the more rough our estimates necessarily are, the less likely we shall be to come to any clear decision between two apparently balanced alternatives. In all such cases, therefore, it becomes practically important to ask whether any mode of distributing a given quantum of happiness is better than any other. Now the utilitarian formula seems to supply no answer to this question: at least we have to supplement the principle of seeking the greatest happiness on the whole by some principle of just or right distribution of this happiness. The principle which most utilitarians have either tacitly or expressly adopted is that of pure equality – as given in Bentham's formula, 'everybody to count for one, and nobody for more than one'. And this principle seems the only one which does not need a special justification; for, as we saw, it must be reasonable to treat any one man in the same way as any other, if there be no reason apparent for treating him differently. . . .[6]

6. It should be observed that the question here is as to the distribution of *happiness*, not the *means of happiness*. If more happiness on the whole is produced by giving the same means of happiness to *B* rather than to *A*, it is an obvious and incontrovertible deduction from the utilitarian principle that it ought to be given to *B*, whatever inequality in the distribution of the *means* of happiness this may involve.

The proof of utilitarianism

... In book 2, where we discussed the method of egoistic hedonism, we did not take occasion to examine any proof of its first principle: and in the case of universalistic hedonism also, what primarily concerns us is not how its principle is to be proved to those who do not accept it, but what consequences are logically involved in its acceptance. At the same time it is important to observe that the principle of aiming at universal happiness is more generally felt to require some proof, or at least (as Mill puts it) some 'considerations determining the mind to accept it', than the principle of aiming at one's own happiness. From the point of view, indeed, of abstract philosophy, I do not see why the egoistic principle should pass unchallenged any more than the universalistic. I do not see why the axiom of prudence should not be questioned, when it conflicts with present inclination, on a ground similar to that on which egoists refuse to admit the axiom of rational benevolence. If the utilitarian has to answer the question, 'Why should I sacrifice my own happiness for the greater happiness of another?' it must surely be admissible to ask the egoist, 'Why should I sacrifice a present pleasure for a greater one in the future? Why should I concern myself about my own future feelings any more than about the feelings of other persons?' It undoubtedly seems to common sense paradoxical to ask for a reason why one should seek one's own happiness on the whole; but I do not see how the demand can be repudiated as absurd by those who adopt the views of the extreme empirical school of psychologists, although those views are commonly supposed to have a close affinity with egoistic hedonism. Grant that the ego is merely a system of coherent phenomena, that the permanent identical 'I' is not a fact but a fiction, as Hume and his followers maintain; why, then, should one part of the series of feelings into which the ego is resolved be concerned with another part of the same series, any more than with any other series?

However, I will not press this question now; since I admit that common sense does not think it worth while to supply the individual with reasons for seeking his own interest.[7] Reasons for doing his

7. The relation of egoistic to universalistic hedonism is further examined in the concluding chapter.

duty – according to the commonly accepted standard of duty – are not held to be equally superfluous: indeed we find that utilitarian reasons are continually given for one or other of the commonly received rules of morality. Still the fact that certain rules are commonly received as binding, though it does not establish their self-evidence, renders it generally unnecessary to prove their authority to the common sense that receives them: while for the same reason a utilitarian who claims to supersede them by a higher principle is naturally challenged, by intuitionists no less than by egoists, to demonstrate the legitimacy of his claim. To this challenge some utilitarians would reply by saying that it is impossible to 'prove' a first principle; and this is of course true, if by proof we mean a process which exhibits the principle in question as an inference from premises upon which it remains dependent for its certainty; for these premises, and not the inference drawn from them, would then be the real first principles. Nay, if utilitarianism is to be *proved* to a man who already holds some other moral principles – whether he be an intuitional moralist, who regards as final the principles of truth, justice, obedience to authority, purity, etc., or an egoist who regards his own interest as the ultimately reasonable end of his conduct – it would seem that the process must be one which establishes a conclusion actually *superior* in validity to the premises from which it starts. For the utilitarian prescriptions of duty are *prima facie* in conflict, at certain points and under certain circumstances, both with rules which the intuitionist regards as self-evident, and with the dictates of rational egoism; so that utilitarianism, if accepted at all, must be accepted as overruling intuitionism and egoism. At the same time, if the other principles are not throughout taken as valid, the so-called proof does not seem to be addressed to the intuitionist or egoist at all. How shall we deal with this dilemma? How is such a process – clearly different from ordinary proof – possible or conceivable? Yet there certainly seems to be a general demand for it. Perhaps we may say that what is needed is a line of argument which on the one hand allows the validity, to a certain extent, of the maxims already accepted, and on the other hand shows them to be not absolutely valid, but needing to be controlled and completed by some more comprehensive principle.

Such a line of argument, addressed to egoism, was given in

chapter 13 of the foregoing book. It should be observed that the applicability of this argument depends on the manner in which the egoistic first principle is formulated. If the egoist strictly confines himself to stating his conviction that he ought to take his own happiness or pleasure as his ultimate end, there seems no opening for any line of reasoning to lead him to universalistic hedonism as a first principle;[8] it cannot be proved that the difference between his own happiness and another's happiness is not *for him* all-important. In this case all that the utilitarian can do is to effect as far as possible a reconciliation between the two principles, by expounding to the egoist the *sanctions* of rules deduced from the universalistic principle – i.e. by pointing out the pleasures and pains that may be expected to accrue to the egoist himself from the observation and violation respectively of such rules. It is obvious that such an exposition has no tendency to make him accept the greatest happiness of the greatest number as his ultimate end; but only as a means to the end of his own happiness. It is therefore totally different from a *proof* (as above explained) of universalistic hedonism. When, however, the egoist puts forward, implicitly or explicitly, the proposition that his happiness or pleasure is good, not only *for him* but from the point of view of the universe – as (e.g.) by saying that 'nature designed him to seek his own happiness' – it then becomes relevant to point out to him that *his* happiness cannot be a more important part of good, taken universally, than the equal happiness of any other person. And thus, starting with his own principle, he may be brought to accept universal happiness or pleasure as that which is absolutely and without qualification good or desirable: as an end, therefore, to which the action of a reasonable agent as such ought to be directed.

This, it will be remembered, is the reasoning[9] that I used in chapter 13 of the preceding book in exhibiting the principle of rational benevolence as one of the few intuitions which stand the test of rigorous criticism. It should be observed, however, that as

8. It is to be observed that he may be led to it in other ways than that of argument: i.e. by appeals to his sympathies, or to his moral or quasi-moral sentiments.
9. I ought to remind the reader that the argument in chapter 13 only leads to the first principle of utilitarianism, if it be admitted that happiness is the only thing ultimately and intrinsically good or desirable. I afterwards in chapter 14 endeavoured to bring common sense to this admission.

addressed to the intuitionist, this reasoning only shows the utilitarian first principle to be *one* moral axiom: it does not prove that it is *sole* or *supreme*. The premises with which the intuitionist starts commonly include other formulae held as independent and self-evident. Utilitarianism has therefore to exhibit itself in the twofold relation above described, at once negative and positive, to these formulae. The utilitarian must, in the first place, endeavour to show to the intuitionist that the principles of truth, justice,[10] etc. have only a dependent and subordinate validity: arguing either that the principle is really only affirmed by common sense as a general rule admitting of exceptions and qualifications, as in the case of truth, and that we require some further principle for systematizing these exceptions and qualifications; or that the fundamental notion is vague and needs further determination, as in the case of justice;[10] and further, that the different rules are liable to conflict with each other, and that we require some higher principle to decide the issue thus raised; and again, that the rules are differently formulated by different persons, and that these differences admit no intuitional solution, while they show the vagueness and ambiguity of the common moral notions to which the intuitionist appeals.

This part of the argument I have perhaps sufficiently developed in the preceding book. It remains to supplement this line of reasoning by developing the positive relation that exists between utilitarianism and the morality of common sense: by showing how utilitarianism sustains the general validity of the current moral judgements, and thus supplements the defects which reflection finds in the intuitive recognition of their stringency; and at the same time affords a principle of synthesis, and a method for binding the unconnected and occasionally conflicting principles of common moral reasoning into a complete and harmonious system. If systematic reflection upon the morality of common sense thus exhibits the utilitarian principle as that to which common sense naturally appeals for that further development of its system which this same reflection shows to be necessary, the proof of utilitarianism seems as complete as it can be made. And since, further – apart from the question of proof – it is important in considering the method of utilitarianism to

10. That is, so far as we mean by justice anything more than the simple negation of arbitrary inequality.

determine exactly its relation to the commonly received rules of morality, it will be proper to examine this relation at some length in the following chapter. . . .

Utilitarianism and common sense

. . . I pass to consider another group of duties, often contrasted with those of benevolence, under the comprehensive notion of justice.

'That justice is useful to society,' says Hume, 'it would be a superfluous undertaking to prove': what he endeavours to show at some length is 'that public utility is the *sole* origin of justice': and the same question of origin has occupied the chief attention of John Stuart Mill (1867, chapter 5). Here, however, we are not so much concerned with the growth of the sentiment of justice from experiences of utility, as with the utilitarian basis of the mature notion; while at the same time if the analysis previously given be correct, the justice that is commonly demanded and inculcated is something more complex than these writers have recognized. What Hume (e.g.) means by justice is rather what I should call order, understood in its widest sense: the observance of the actual system of rules, whether strictly legal or customary, which bind together the different members of any society into an organic whole, checking malevolent or otherwise injurious impulses, distributing the different objects of men's clashing desires, and exacting such positive services, customary or contractual, as are commonly recognized as matters of debt. And though there have rarely been wanting plausible empirical arguments for the revolutionary paradox quoted by Plato, that 'laws are imposed in the interest of rulers', it remains true that the general conduciveness to social happiness of the habit of order or law-observance, is, as Hume says, too obvious to need proof; indeed it is of such paramount importance to a community, that even where particular laws are clearly injurious it is usually expedient to observe them, apart from any penalty which their breach might entail on the individual. We saw, however, that common sense sometimes bids us refuse obedience to bad laws, because 'we ought to obey God rather than men' (though there seems to be no clear intuition as to the kind or degree of badness that justifies resistance); and further allows us, in special emergencies, to violate rules generally good, for 'necessity has no law', and '*salus populi suprema lex*'.

These and similar common opinions seem at least to suggest that the limits of the duty of law-observance are to be determined by utilitarian considerations. While, again, the utilitarian view gets rid of the difficulties in which the attempt to define intuitively the truly legitimate source of legislative authority involved us (cf. 1907, book 3, chapter 6, sections 2, 3); at the same time that it justifies to some extent each of the different views current as to the intrinsic legitimacy of governments. For, on the one hand, it finds the moral basis of any established political order primarily in its effects rather than its causes; so that, generally speaking, obedience will seem due to any *de facto* government that is not governing very badly. On the other hand, in so far as laws originating in a particular way are likely to be (1) better, or (2) more readily observed, it is a utilitarian duty to aim at introducing this mode of origination: and thus in a certain stage of social development it may be right that (e.g.) a 'representative system' should be popularly demanded, or possibly (in extreme cases) even introduced by force: while, again, there is expediency in maintaining an ancient mode of legislation, because men readily obey such: and loyalty to a dispossessed government may be on the whole expedient, even at the cost of some temporary suffering and disorder, in order that ambitious men may not find usurpation too easy. Here, as elsewhere, utilitarianism at once supports the different reasons commonly put forward as absolute, and also brings them theoretically to a common measure, so that in any particular case we have a principle of decision between conflicting political arguments.

As was before said, this law-observance, in so far at least as it affects the interests of other individuals, is what we frequently mean by justice. It seems, however (cf. book 3, chapter 5), that the notion of justice, exhaustively analysed, includes several distinct elements combined in a somewhat complex manner: we have to inquire, therefore, what latent utilities are represented by each of these elements.

Now, first, a constant part of the notion, which appears in it even when the just is not distinguished from the legal, is impartiality or the negation of arbitrary inequality. This impartiality, as we saw (book 3, chapter 13, section 3) (whether exhibited in the establishment or in the administration of laws), is merely a special application of the wider maxim that it cannot be right to treat two persons differently if their cases are similar in all material circumstances. And utilitarianism, as we saw, admits this maxim no less than other systems of ethics. At the same time, this negative criterion is clearly inadequate for the complete determination of what is just in laws, or in conduct generally; when we have admitted this, it still remains to ask, 'What are the inequalities in laws, and in the distribution of pleasures and pains outside the sphere of law, which are not arbitrary and unreasonable? and to what general principles can they be reduced?'

Here in the first place we may explain, on utilitarian principles, why apparently arbitrary inequality in a certain part of the conduct of individuals is not regarded as injustice or even – in some cases – as in any way censurable. For freedom of action is an important source of happiness to the agents, and a socially useful stimulus to their energies: hence it is obviously expedient that a man's free choice in the distribution of wealth or kind services should not be restrained by fear of legal penalties, or even of social disapprobation, beyond what the interests of others clearly require; and therefore, when distinctly recognized claims are satisfied, it is *pro tanto* expedient that the mere preferences of an individual should be treated by others as legitimate grounds for inequality in the distribution of his property or services. Nay, as we have before seen, it is within certain limits expedient that each individual should practically regard his own unreasoned impulses as reasonable grounds of action: as in the rendering of services prompted by such affections as are normally and properly spontaneous and unforced.

Passing to consider the general principles upon which 'just claims' as commonly recognized appear to be based, we notice that the grounds of a number of such claims may be brought under the general head of 'normal expectations'; but that the stringency of such obligations varies much in degree, according as the expectations are based upon definite engagements, or on some vague mutual understanding, or are merely such as an average man would form from past experience of the conduct of other men. In these latter cases common sense appeared to be somewhat perplexed as to the validity of the claims. But for the utilitarian the difficulty has ceased to exist. He will hold any disappointment of expectations to be *pro tanto* an evil, but a greater evil in proportion to the previous security of the expectant individual, from the greater shock thus given to his reliance on the conduct of his fellow-men generally: and many times greater in proportion as the expectation is generally recognized as normal and reasonable, as in this case the shock extends to all who are in any way cognizant of his disappointment. The importance to mankind of being able to rely on each other's actions is so great, that in ordinary cases of absolutely definite engagements there is scarcely any advantage that can counterbalance the harm done by violating them. Still, we found (book 3, chapter 4) that several exceptions and qualifications to the rule of good faith were more or less distinctly recognized by common sense: and most of these have a utilitarian basis, which it does not need much penetration to discern. To begin, we may notice that the superficial view of the obligation of a promise which makes it depend on the assertion of the promiser, and not, as utilitarians hold, on the expectations produced in the promisee, cannot fairly be attributed to common sense: which certainly condemns a breach of promise much more strongly when others have acted in reliance on it, than when its observance did not directly concern others, so that its breach involves for them only the indirect evil of a bad precedent – as when a man breaks a pledge of total abstinence. We see, again, how the utilitarian reasons for keeping a promise are diminished by a material change of circumstances (cf. book 3, chapter 6, section 8), for in that case the expectations disappointed by breaking it are at least not those which the promise originally created. It is obvious, too, that it is a disadvantage to the community that men should be able to rely on the performance of promises procured by fraud or unlawful force, so far as encouragement is thereby given to the use of fraud or force for this end.[11] We saw, again, that when the performance would be injurious to the promisee, common sense is disposed to admit that its obligation is superseded; and is at least doubtful whether the promise should be kept, even when it is only the promiser who would be injured, if the harm be extreme – both which qualifications are in harmony with utilitarianism. And similarly for the other qualifications and exceptions: they all turn out to be as clearly utilitarian, as the general utility of keeping one's word is plain and manifest.

11. In the case of force, however, there is the counterbalancing consideration that the unlawful aggressor may be led to inflict worse injury on his victim, if he is unable to rely on the latter's promise.

But further, the expediency of satisfying normal expectations, even when they are not based upon a definite contract, is undeniable; it will clearly conduce to the tranquillity of social existence, and to the settled and well-adjusted activity on which social happiness greatly depends, that such expectations should be as little as possible baulked. And here utilitarianism relieves us of the difficulties which beset the common view of just conduct as something absolutely precise and definite. For in this vaguer region we cannot draw a sharp line between valid and invalid claims; 'injustice' shades gradually off into mere 'hardship'. Hence the utilitarian view that the disappointment of natural expectations is an evil, but an evil which must sometimes be incurred for the sake of a greater good, is that to which common sense is practically forced, though it is difficult to reconcile it with the theoretical absoluteness of justice in the intuitional view of morality.

The gain of recognizing the relativity of this obligation will be still more felt, when we consider what I distinguished as ideal justice, and examine the general conceptions of this which we find expressed or latent in current criticisms of the existing order of society.

We have seen that there are two competing views of an ideally just social order – or perhaps we may say two extreme types between which the looser notions of ordinary men seem to fluctuate – which I called respectively individualistic and socialistic. According to the former view an ideal system of law ought to aim at freedom, or perfect mutual non-interference of all the members of the community, as an absolute end. Now the general utilitarian reasons for leaving each rational adult free to seek happiness in his own way are obvious and striking: for, generally speaking, each is best qualified to provide for his own interests, since even when he does not know best what they are and how to attain them, he is at any rate most keenly concerned for them: and again, the consciousness of freedom and concomitant responsibility increases the average effective activity of men: and besides, the discomfort of constraint is directly an evil and *pro tanto* to be avoided. Still, we saw (book 3, chapter 4, section 4) that the attempt to construct a consistent code of laws, taking maximum freedom (instead of happiness) as an absolute end, must lead to startling paradoxes and insoluble puzzles: and in fact the practical interpretation of the notion 'freedom', and the limits within which its realization has been actually sought, have always – even in the freest societies – been more or less consciously determined by considerations of expediency. So that we may fairly say that in so far as common sense had adopted the individualistic ideal in politics, it has always been as subordinate to and limited by the utilitarian first principle.[12]

It seems, however, that what we commonly demand or long for, under the name of ideal justice, is not so much the realization of freedom, as the distribution of good and evil according to desert: indeed it is as a means to this latter end that freedom is often advocated; for it is said that if we protect men completely from mutual interference, each will reap the good and bad consequences of his own conduct, and so be happy or unhappy in proportion to his deserts. In particular, it has been widely held that if a free exchange of wealth and services is allowed, each individual will obtain from society, in money or other advantages, what his services are really worth. We saw, however, that the price which an individual obtains under a system of perfect free trade, for wealth or services exchanged by him, may for several reasons be not proportioned to the social utility of what he exchanges: and reflective common sense seems to admit this disproportion as to some extent legitimate, under the influence of utilitarian considerations correcting the unreflective utterances of moral sentiments.

To take a particular case: if a moral man were asked how far it is right to take advantage in bargaining of another's ignorance, probably his first impulse would be to condemn such a procedure altogether. But reflection, I think, would show him that such a censure would be too sweeping: that it would be contrary to common sense to 'blame A for having, in negotiating with a stranger B, taken advantage of B's ignorance of facts known to himself, provided that A's superior knowledge had been obtained by a legitimate use of diligence and foresight, which B might have used with equal success. . . . What prevents us from censuring in this and similar cases is, I conceive, a more or less conscious apprehension of the indefinite loss to the wealth of the community that is likely to result from any

12. In another work (1883, book 3, chapter 2) I have tried to show that complete *laissez-faire*, in the organization of industry, tends in various ways to fall short of the most economic production of wealth.

effective social restrictions on the free pursuit and exercise' of economic knowledge. And for somewhat similar reasons of general expediency, if the question be raised whether it is fair for a class of persons to gain by the unfavourable economic situation of any class with which they deal, common sense at least hesitates to censure such gains – at any rate when such unfavourable situation is due 'to the gradual action of general causes, for the existence of which the persons who gain are not specially responsible'.[13]

The general principle of 'requiting good desert', so far as common sense really accepts it as practically applicable to the relations of men in society, is broadly in harmony with utilitarianism; since we obviously encourage the production of general happiness by rewarding men for felicific conduct; only the utilitarian scale of rewards will not be determined entirely by the magnitude of the services performed, but partly also by the difficulty of inducing men to perform them. But this latter element seems to be always taken into account (though perhaps unconsciously) by common sense: for, as we have been led to notice (compare book 3, chapter 2, section 1), we do not commonly recognize merit in right actions, if they are such as men are naturally inclined to perform rather too much than too little. Again, in cases where the intuitional principle that ill-desert lies in wrong intention conflicts with the utilitarian view of punishment as purely preventive, we find that in the actual administration of criminal justice common sense is forced, however reluctantly, into practical agreement with utilitarianism. Thus after a civil war it demands the execution of the most purely patriotic rebels; and after a railway accident it clamours for the severe punishment of unintentional neglects, which, except for their consequences, would have been regarded as very venial.

If, however, in any distribution of pleasures and privileges, or of pains and burdens, considerations of desert do not properly come in (i.e. if the good or evil to be distributed have no relation to any conduct on the part of the persons who are to receive either) – or if it is practically impossible to take such considerations into account – then common sense seems to fall back on simple equality as the

13. The quotations are from Sidgwick (1883, book 3, chapter 9), where these questions are discussed at somewhat greater length.

principle of just apportionment.[14] And we have seen that the utilitarian, in the case supposed, will reasonably accept equality as the only mode of distribution that is not arbitrary; and it may be observed that this mode of apportioning the means of happiness is likely to produce more happiness on the whole, not only because men have a disinterested aversion to unreason, but still more because they have an aversion to any kind of inferiority to others (which is much intensified when the inferiority seems unreasonable). This latter feeling is so strong that it often prevails in spite of obvious claims of desert; and it may even be sometimes expedient that it should so prevail.

For, finally, it must be observed that utilitarianism furnishes us with a common standard to which the different elements included in the notion of justice may be reduced. Such a standard is imperatively required: as these different elements are continually liable to conflict with each other. The issue, for example, in practical politics between conservatives and reformers often represents such a conflict: the question is, whether we ought to do a certain violence to expectations arising naturally out of the existing social order, with the view of bringing about a distribution of the means of happiness more in accordance with ideal justice. Here, if my analysis of the common notion of justice be sound, the attempt to extract from it a clear decision of such an issue must necessarily fail: as the conflict is, so to say, permanently latent in the very core of common sense. But the utilitarian will merely use this notion of justice as a guide to different kinds of utilities; and in so far as these are incompatible, he will balance one set of advantages against the other, and decide according to the preponderance.

14. I have before observed that it is quite in harmony with utilitarian principles to recognize a sphere of private conduct within which each individual may distribute his wealth and kind services as unequally as he chooses, without incurring censure as unjust.

References

MACMILLAN, M. (1890), *Promotion of General Happiness*, Swan Sonnenschein and Co.
MILL, J. S. (1867), *Utilitarianism*, Doubleday, 1961.
SIDGWICK, H. (1907), *The Method of Ethics*, 7th edn, Macmillan.
SIDGWICK, H. (1883), *Principles of Political Economy*, Macmillan.

9 M. Fleming

A Cardinal Concept of Welfare

M. Fleming, 'A cardinal concept of welfare', *Quarterly Journal of Economics*, vol. 66, 1952, October.

1 Introduction

I hope to show that, given any ethical system which conforms to certain conditions (of a sort to which many ethical systems do in fact conform) it is in principle possible to assign numbers to the different degrees of general welfare obtaining in different hypothetical situations, and to the different degrees of well-being which the several individuals experience in these situations, in such a manner as to ensure that welfare is the sum of individual well-beings. The indicators of welfare and individual well-being which permit of this additive relationship are unique: the numbers assigned to the different degrees of welfare and well-being may all be altered by a common proportion but in no other way. Ethical systems which meet the prescribed conditions yield a concept of welfare as an extensive or additive magnitude, susceptible of fundamental measurement.

By this I do not mean that these ethical systems necessarily postulate a concept of welfare based on some other property (e.g., happiness) which is independently and empirically measurable. I mean that they themselves provide a way of measuring welfare through the process of ethical evaluation. All reasoning which presupposes an ethical system of this type may legitimately speak of welfare as in the fullest sense a cardinal magnitude. This applies, for example, to any brand of welfare economics which may be based on an ethical system of this type. And it can, I believe, be shown that to be able to treat welfare as cardinal is, if not a necessity, at least, a considerable convenience for any such welfare economics. At the end of this paper I briefly indicate the directions in which I believe this convenience to lie.

What do we mean when we dispute whether any property (e.g., welfare, utility, happiness) is ordinal or cardinal? The contrast is less sharp than is sometimes supposed. In order to be cardinal, or in the fullest sense measurable, a property has to be able to meet a certain number of requirements. Some properties satisfy some of these requirements and fail to satisfy others.[1]

Consider the property 'blankness'. The first requirement of cardinality is that the property must arise out of ordinal relations between pairs of 'objects' (or however one may term that to which the property applies) so that one can say 'A is blanker than B (B is less blank than A)'. Secondly, this relationship must be asymmetrical, so that if A is blanker than B, B is not blanker than A. Thirdly, the relationship must be transitive, so that, if A is blanker than B, and B is blanker than C, A is blanker than C. Fourthly, if A and B are of the same degree of blankness (if neither is A blanker than B nor B blanker than A), and if A is blanker than C, B must be blanker than C. It follows that if A is as blank as B, and B as blank as C, A is as blank as C.

If all of these requirements are met, we may speak of blankness as an ordinal magnitude, different degrees of which may be distinguished, occupying different positions in a linear order. Numbers can then be assigned to the degrees of blankness possessed respectively by different objects, in such a way that the same number will be assigned to objects of the same degree of blankness, and that the blanker of two objects will always be assigned the higher number. Such numbers may be regarded as particular values, corresponding to particular degrees of blankness, of a continuous function, or indicator providing a cardinal representation of the property 'blankness'.

Any property which meets only those requirements discussed above, and fails to meet those discussed below, can, however, be represented by any one of a family of indicators whose only connection is that they are increasing functions one of another throughout their entire range. Such numerical indication falls short of measurement. If k_1, k_2, k_3 and k_4, are descending degrees of blankness it is meaningless to compare the 'distance' between k_1 and k_2 with that

1. The following five paragraphs are much influenced by Campbell (1928) and Cohen and Nagel (1934), chapter 15. The idea of 'mutual measurement', however, is, so far as I know, my own.

between k_2 and k_3. Still the 'distance' between k_1 and k_4 may be considered as 'greater than' that between k_2 and k_3, in the sense that whatever indicator may be used to represent blankness, k_1 *minus* k_4 will exceed k_2 *minus* k_3.

The fifth requirement of cardinality is that it should be possible to limit the range of admissible indicators of blankness so that any admissible indicator differs from another only with respect to origin or zero-point, and proportionate scale. The criterion of an admissible indicator is that it should simplify the mathematical expression of the relationship between blankness and other properties (magnitudes). That is, it should enable this relationship to be expressed in the form of a simple numerical equation (law). Where the class of admissible indicators is thus limited blankness may be said to be a measurable magnitude, though possibly only an intensive one. Where the other magnitudes in question are themselves measured by an independent process, the measurement of blankness may be said to be 'derived'. It is possible, however, that the criterion of mathematical simplicity may enable suitably limited classes of indicators to be selected simultaneously for a number of magnitudes not otherwise measurable. This I would call 'mutual measurement'.

The sixth and final requirement for a cardinal blankness is that (1) among the objects to which blankness appertains there should be some which, if only by convention, can be regarded as collections or combinations of parts which are themselves capable of existence as independent objects, and (2) a process of mutual measurement is possible whereby the blankness of the complex objects can be expressed as the sum of the blanknesses of their parts. If blankness meets this requirement also it is measurable by the fundamental process and may be regarded as a truly extensive or cardinal magnitude. We can say 'A is three times as blank as B' meaning that A is as blank as a complex object C which is composed of objects D, E, and F, each of which is as blank as B.

The property whose cardinality is in question may be one which is believed to manifest itself in the world of experience or it may be one which is implicit in a conceptual scheme or theory. In the former case all the requirements of cardinality have to be fulfilled empirically. For example, the numerical equation referred to above has to be a scientific law. In the latter case, on the other hand, the various requirements have to be shown by deductive reasoning to be implicit in the postulated conceptual scheme or theory. An example of a cardinal magnitude of the first kind would be length as found in nature. An example of a cardinal magnitude of the second kind would be length as defined in certain geometries.

My cardinalization of welfare is of the second type. It is my contention that all ethical systems which obey certain not very exacting conditions – and not only, as is frequently assumed, those which are explicitly based on some property, such as 'pleasure' believed to be measurable in an empirical sense – yield a concept of welfare which fulfils all the six requirements of cardinality discussed above.

Though I regard welfare as an ethical concept and its cardinality as dependent on ethical presuppositions, I hope that this cardinality may prove useful for the purpose of welfare economics. This does not mean that I wish to bring value judgements into economics – quite the contrary. Though no ethical relativist, I think economic science had better be *wertfrei*. But welfare economics is inevitably concerned with values in the sense that it represents the application of economic science, in itself *wertfrei*, to the service of a *postulated* set of ethical ends. There are, in principle, as many systems of welfare economics as there are systems of ethical ends. But economic analysis is more serviceable to certain systems of ends than to others (e.g., to those emphasizing individual happiness rather than those emphasizing moral righteousness) and my contention is that if an ethical system permits of a cardinal concept of welfare, that fact is likely to make economic analysis still more serviceable to it.

The ethical postulates set forth below do not purport to constitute a complete ethical system. They do not even define the minimum conditions which any ethical system must meet if welfare is to be measurable. All they do is to give an example of a set of propositions which, if included explicitly or implicitly in any ethical system, will suffice to ensure that the welfare concept characteristic of that ethical system will be susceptible of fundamental measurement. I choose this particular set of sufficient conditions partly because they can be expressed in terms analogous to those with which economists are familiar, and partly because they appear to be satisfied by most of the ethical systems which I personally regard as intellectually respectable!

2 Basic ethical postulates

Postulate A. Let us mean by a 'situation' a hypothetical past and future of the universe. Then *behaviour should be determined, at least in part, by expectations as to the situations which would result, respectively, from the adoption of each of the various alternative courses of action.* Let us mean by '*A* is more desirable than *B*' that, to the (not negligible) extent that behaviour should be determined by consequences, a course of action resulting with certainty in situation *A* should be preferred to one resulting with certainty in situation *B*. Then we can formulate Postulate A as: *the relation 'more desirable than' exists in some instances as between situations.* From its definition, this relation must be asymmetrical, thus fulfilling the first requirement of cardinality (see p. 246).

Postulate B. The ethic is self-consistent. *If A is more desirable than B and B is more desirable than C, then A is more desirable than C.* This fulfills the second requirement of cardinality.

Postulate C. In principle (i.e. given certain knowledge) there is no indeterminacy as to the relative desirability of situations. *If A is as desirable as B* (neither more nor less desirable than *B*) *and B is as desirable as C, A is as desirable as C.* This fulfils the third requirement of cardinality. It follows from Postulates A, B, and C that situations are arranged, with respect to their relative desirability, in a linear order of precedence. Desirability or welfare (see below) may thus be considered an ordinal magnitude.

Postulate D. (What follows is rather long and complicated but is best treated as a single postulate since the rejection of its initial steps would entail its rejection as a whole. On the other hand, ethical systems to which this postulate is repugnant may nevertheless be compatible with some other postulate which, because of its formal analogy with this, will serve the same purpose so far as the measurement of welfare is concerned, and may be substituted at this point).

Let us define a 'mental state' as 'the experience of a sentient being or individual over a moment of time, i.e. over a period of time short enough for any such experience to be homogeneous'. In considering situations as ends of moral action attention must be paid (according to this postulate) not to the external or physical aspects of the situations but to the mental states which they contain or engender. In assessing the relative desirability of the various possible situations one is really evaluating the various possible mental states in their various possible combinations.

Let us define an 'elementary' situation as one in which only a single mental state exists or in which no mental state exists. Then the same properties, whatever they are, which make the elementary situation associated with some particular mental state a relatively desirable one will tend to enhance the desirability of any situation of which that mental state forms a part.

Let us define 'welfare (in any situation A)' as 'the desirability of situation A'. And let us define 'the well-being of individual x at moment t (in situation A)' as 'the desirability of a hypothetical elementary situation containing a mental state identical with that which exists (as part of situation A) in individual x at moment t'. Postulate D then affirms (1) that if each individual at each moment of time has the same degree of well-being in situation A as in situation B, the two situations have the same degree of welfare, and (2) that if all individual-moments save one have the same degree of well-being in situation A as in situation B, and if that one has a higher degree of well-being in situation A than in situation B, situation A will have a higher degree of welfare than situation B. More briefly, *welfare is an increasing function of the well-being of each individual at each moment of time.* If D is any indicator of welfare and $x, y, z, ...$ are any indicators of individual-momentary well-beings, then $D = D(x, y, z, ...)$,[2] and $D'_r > 0$, when $r = x, y, z, ...$ and D'_r is the partial derivative of D with respect to r.[3]

2. From our method of deriving well-being from the welfare of elementary situations it might reasonably be assumed that the choice of an indicator for welfare would *ipso facto* determine the indicators of the various well-beings and establish a relationship between them which would not exist if the well-beings had been independently derived. In order to make our argument cover interpretations of the welfare function using an independent concept of well-being, it is assumed in the subsequent treatment that separate indicators are initially chosen, independently and arbitrarily, for each of the several well-beings and for welfare.

3. There seems to be no justification for treating welfare as a function of well-beings which is not at the same time a justification for treating it as an *increasing* function of well-beings. It was, however, not strictly necessary to introduce the latter assumption explicitly at this point since it could have been deduced as a corollary of postulate E.

I have identified well-being with the welfare of elementary situations. What the above equation does is to describe a certain internal relationship which is posited to exist within the welfare ordering of situations, according to which the welfare-rating of complex situations depends on that of elementary situations. All this may seem a little abstract, for I have said nothing about what determines the welfare-rating of elementary situations, and hence the various well-beings. That depends on the particular ethical system which one assumes. In one system well-being may be correlated with 'happiness' (whether conceived as an ordinal or as a cardinal property of states of mind), in another with 'righteousness' somehow conceived, in another with 'knowledge', or with 'intensity of consciousness' – these being different ways of conceiving goodness-as-an-end. Or there might be no single mental property with which well-being is correlated. A man may be quite unable to say what makes him regard one mental state as better (as an end) than another. From the standpoint of the measurability of welfare and well-being it does not in the least matter what a man's conception of well-being is so long as his ordering of situations with respect to desirability depends on his ordering of states of mind in the manner described in postulates D and E.

I spoke, on p. 249, of the possibility of substituting for postulate D some analogous postulate. An ethical system might base its ordering of alternative courses of action not on the nature of the mental states that are expected to result from the respective courses of action, but on the orderings of these courses of action by a (somehow selected) set of individuals. These individual orderings might themselves have an ethical or a non-ethical character. If by welfare we now mean the position of a course of action in the general ordering, and by well-being the position of the same course of action in an individual ordering, we can then formulate the analogue of postulate D in almost the same language, viz., that welfare should be an increasing function of individual well-beings. Though the underlying meaning has changed substantially, it is still quite plausible that ethical systems of this type would conform to this analogue of postulate D.[4] They are perhaps less likely to take the next hurdle, postulate E.

4. Bergson constructs his welfare function on this assumption, see (1938).

Postulate E. In assessing the relative desirability or welfare of any two situations no account need be taken of states of mind which are common to the two situations. If situations *A* and *B* are identical with respect to the states of mind of certain individual-moments and different with respect to the states of mind of other individual-moments, and if *A'* and *B'* are identical with situations *A* and *B* respectively, except that they do not contain the states of mind which are common to *A* and *B* (because the individuals who experience the same states of mind in *A* as in *B* are non-existent at the moments in question both in *A'* and in *B'*), then *A* will be more, equally, or less desirable than *B* according as *A'* is more, equally, or less desirable than *B'*.

I would maintain that, in practice, everyone who seeks to assess the desirability of 'situations' at all (i.e. everyone whose ethic requires him to take account of the results of alternative courses of action) does and must accept this postulate implicitly. For example, we all exclude the past from our ethical calculations. I am sure that most readers' eyebrows were raised when, on p. 249, I defined a situation, for the purpose of ethical evaluation, as including the past as well as the future. I entirely agree that the past is irrelevant in this context. But the only justification for excluding it from our consideration is that past states of mind are there for good and all and cannot be affected by what we may now decide. Again, in considering policies affecting the inhabitants of this planet we do not feel hampered by our ignorance regarding states of mind which prevail among the inhabitants of Mars. And in cases where a course of action can be presumed to exhaust its effects within a short period of time, we normally refrain from speculation as to the condition of mankind in some remote future. There is, however, no logical stopping place in this process. If we are content to ignore individual-moments which are past, or remote in time and space, because they are unaffected by our decisions, we must be prepared to ignore individual-moments in all cases in which they are unaffected by our decisions.

It was assumed, in postulate D, that situational changes which leave unaffected the well-being of each individual-moment, have no effect on welfare. From this, and from the last paragraph but one, it follows that, in comparing two situations for welfare, not only can those individual-moments whose states of mind are the same in both situations be left out of account but also those whose states of mind, though they may be different in one situation from what they are in the other, are of the same well-being in the two situations. *The desirability of any situational change (the sign of the change in welfare) depends on the levels of well-being, in the two situations, of those individual-moments whose well-beings are affected by the change.* Symbolically we may express this as follows:

Sign $dD = f(dx, dy,...:x, y,...)$ $dx \neq 0; dy \neq 0$.

It should be noted that the above proposition does not imply that the well-being of any individual at any time may not be psychologically affected by what he believes the states of mind and well-beings of other people to be, or by what he remembers of his own past states of mind. What we are concerned with here is the ethical evaluation of a situational change after all psychological as well as physical interconnections have been taken into account.

As already observed for postulate D it makes no difference as regards conformity to postulate E what the substantive content of well-being is deemed to be. If well-being is correlated with happiness then postulate E requires that all those whose happiness is unaffected by any situational change should be ignored in the evaluation of that change. If well-being depends on loving-kindness, it is those whose level of loving-kindness is left unchanged who should be ignored.

Let us revert for a moment to the subsidiary line of thought developed earlier in which welfare relates to a general ordering not of 'situations' but of courses of action, and in which well-being relates not to a general ordering of individual states of mind (or rather of the associated elementary situations) but to individual orderings of courses of action. In such a conceptual scheme the analogue of postulate E would be a requirement that whether one course of action is deemed more or less desirable than another should depend solely on the respective ratings given to the two courses of action in the orderings of those individuals who are not indifferent as between the two. This seems to me a fairly plausible condition to which many systems of general ordering based on individual orderings may conform. But it cannot claim support from what I regard as the compelling arguments of the last paragraph but three, which relate to a different class of ethical systems.

The list of ethical postulates is now complete. My impression is that in the case of ethical systems which evaluate situations on the basis of the states of mind which they contain, the only postulate which is at all likely to give trouble is postulate D, which may be repugnant to systems which attach importance to the *pattern* or combination of states of mind within a situation as well as to the states of mind themselves. In the case of systems of general ordering based on individual orderings or preferences the stumbling block, if any, is more likely to be postulate E.

Corollary to postulate E. Consider situational changes which leave unaffected the well-beings of all individual-moments save two. Let x and y be the two well-beings affected by the changes, while z represents all the unaffected well-beings. We know from postulate D that if there is some situational change which raises x-well-being from a specific level x_1 to another x_2, and which leaves welfare unaffected, it must reduce the level of y-well-being. We also know from the same postulate that if there is some situational change which raises x-well-being from x_1 to x_2 and reduces y-well-being from y_1 to y_2 and leaves welfare unaffected, any other change at the same level of z-well-being which raises x from x_1 to x_2, starts from y_1, and leaves welfare unaffected, must reduce y to y_2. So that, with respect to the assumed level of z-well-being, the increase in x-well-being from x_1 to x_2 may be deemed equal in its effect on welfare to the increase of y-well-being from y_2 to y_1. Moreover from postulate E we know that if a situational change which raises x from x_1 to x_2 and lowers y from y_1 to y_2, leaves welfare unaffected *at a given level of z-well-being*, then a change with the same effect on x and y, *at a different level of z-well-being*, will also leave welfare unaffected. So that the increase in x from x_1 to x_2 is equal, in its effect on welfare, to the increase in y from y_2 to y_1 irrespective of the level of z-well-being.

If numerical indicators are selected at random for x, y, and z, the amount of the fall in y which will offset, in its effect on welfare, a unit increase in x will vary with the initial levels of x and y but will be independent of z. For infinitesimal changes the rate at which y must fall as x rises in order to keep welfare constant will be equal to the ratio of the partial derivative of welfare with respect to x to the partial derivative of welfare with respect to y. By analogy with the marginal utility of commodities we might term this ratio that of the 'marginal welfare of x-well-being' to the 'marginal welfare of y-well-being'. Using 'a well-being' to mean 'the well-being of an individual moment', we conclude that *the ratio of the marginal welfares of any two well-beings depends solely on the amounts of the two well-beings in question and is independent of the amount of any other well-being*. In symbols:

$$\frac{\partial(D'_x/D'_y)}{\partial z} = \frac{\partial(D'_y/D'_z)}{\partial x} = \frac{\partial(D'_z/D'_x)}{\partial y} = 0.$$

While the above equations will hold true irrespective of the choice of indicators for the various well-beings, any alteration in the indicators will alter the numerical values of the marginal welfare ratios as well as of the well-beings themselves.

3 Mutual measurement of welfare and well-beings

The next step is to show that, for any ethical system which is compatible with postulates A to E, it is possible so to measure (i.e. assign indicators to) welfare and individual-momentary well-beings that welfare is the sum of well-beings, and that the measurements so arrived at are unique save for proportionate scale.

We have seen that, where D is any cardinal indicator of welfare and x, y, z any cardinal indicators of individual momentary well-beings,

$$D = D(x, y, z), \tag{1}$$

$$D'_r > 0 \quad (r = x, y, z), \tag{2}$$

$$\frac{\partial(D'_x/D'_y)}{\partial z} = \frac{\partial(D'_y/D'_z)}{\partial x} = \frac{\partial(D'_z/D'_x)}{\partial y} = 0. \tag{3}$$

We want to find new indicators of welfare and well-beings, W, d, e, f, which are increasing functions of D, x, y, z, respectively and such that

$$W(D) = d(x) + e(y) + f(z). \tag{4}$$

Now, it is easy to show that equations **1** to **3** must be satisfied if equation **4** is satisfied.[5] What we have to show, however, is that if equations **1** to **3** are satisfied, equation **4** must be satisfied. This can be proved by demonstrating the actual process whereby, starting from indicators D, x, y, z, which satisfy equations **1** to **3**, one can arrive at indicators W, d, e, f, satisfying equation **4**.

The essence of the procedure adopted is to take a specific infinitesimal change in the well-being of some particular individual-moment (such as would result from a specific situational change) and to use this as a yardstick for measuring out units of well-being for all individual-moments. All increments in well-being which have an effect on welfare equivalent to that of the yardstick are regarded as numerically equal.

Operation 1. Starting from a particular level of z-well-being, $z = m$, consider an increment in z-well-being amounting to one (infinitesimal) unit as measured by the original arbitrary scale of z-well-being. This is the yardstick.

Operation 2. Starting from the arbitrary zero-point $y = 0$, mark out on the original arbitrary scale of y-well-being successive infinitesimal positive increments, dy, such that the effect on welfare of a y-increment is equal to the effect of a unit increment of z at $z = m$. Since these increments are infinitesimal, the effect on welfare of any such increment dy will be equal to dy *times* the marginal welfare of y at the point in question D'_y, and this will be equal to the marginal welfare of z at the point $z = m$, $D'_{z=m}$. It follows that dy, in terms of the original y-scale, will be equal to the ratio of the marginal welfare of z at $z = m$ to the marginal welfare of y (i.e. $dy = D'_{z=m}/D'_y$). From the corollary to postulate E we know that this ratio is a function of y alone and is independent of x. There is therefore no ambiguity about the amounts of the successive increments dy as we move up the y-scale.

5. $D = f(W) = f(d+e+f) = D(x, y, z).$ **1**

Thus $D'_x = \dfrac{dD}{dW} W'_x = \dfrac{dD}{dW} \dfrac{dd}{dx}$,

and since $\dfrac{dD}{dW} > 0$ and $\dfrac{dd}{dx} > 0$,

it follows that $D_x > 0$.   **2**

We can thus write $\dfrac{\partial(D_x/D'_y)}{\partial z} = \dfrac{\partial}{\partial z} \left\{ \dfrac{(dD/dW)(dd/dx)}{(dD/dW)(de/dy)} \right\} = 0.$ **3**

Coming back to $y = 0$, mark off negative increments on the y-scale each of which is equal, in its effect on welfare, to the negative of a unit increment of z at $z = m$.

Construct a new indicator of y-well-being called b in which each of the dy increments, marked off according to the process described above, will correspond to a unit increment in b. b will have the same zero point as y and will be a monotone increasing function of y. Since the units of b have been so chosen that a unit increment of b at any level will have the same effect on welfare as a unit increment of z at $z = m$, and since all these unit increments are infinitesimal it follows that the marginal welfare of b, D'_b, will be equal, for all values of b and of x, to the marginal welfare of z at $z = m$, $D'_{z=m}$.

Operation 2 is not complete when it has been performed on y-well-being alone. The same kind of transformation has to be applied to the original indicators of all well-beings other than that of z, a unit increment of z from the point $z = m$ always being used as the yardstick. Thus in the case of indicator x we mark out successive increments each equal to the ratio $D'_{z=m}/D'_x$ and constitute these the units of a new indicator a, which is an increasing function of x with the same zero point, and with D'_a equal to $D'_{z=m}$ for all values of a and b.

Operation 3. We now apply operation 2 in reverse. Take as yardstick a unit increment on the b-scale of y-well-being, starting from any arbitrary level, $b = n$. Then, in precisely the same manner as before, transform the original indicator z into a new indicator c having the property that, for all levels of c and a, the marginal welfare of c, D'_c, is equal to the marginal welfare of b at the point $b = n$, viz., $D'_{b=n}$. Let t be the level of c corresponding to our original starting point $z = m$. This, of course, will be the one level of z-well-being at which marginal welfare is unaffected by the transformation of z into c (i.e. $D'_{c=t} = D'_{z=m}$).

It can easily be shown that, for all values of a, b, and c (i.e. for all situations), the marginal welfare of a is equal to that of b which is equal to that of c. $D'_a \equiv D'_b \equiv D'_c$.[6]

6. (a) When $c = t$, $D'_a = D'_b = D'_{c=t}$ for all values of a and b. But D'_a/D'_b is independent of c. Therefore $D'_a \equiv D'_b$ for all values of a, b, and c.

(b) When $b = n$, $D'_a = D'_{b=n}$ for all values of a and c. Also, since, as we have seen, $D'_a \equiv D'_b$ it follows that when $b = n$, $D'_a = D'_{b=n} = D'_c$, for all values of

Operation 4. We are now in a position to transform the initial welfare indicator, D, into a new indicator which will be equal to the sum of the well-beings, a, b, and c *plus* an arbitrary constant. Start from the level of welfare at which $D = 0$. Since, as we have seen, the marginal welfares of a, b, and c, are equal whatever the values of a, b, and c, the increase in D which would result from raising a by one unit will be the same as that which would result from raising b, or c, by one unit. Mark off such an increment on the D-scale, and continue up the scale marking off adjacent intervals each of which represents the effect of increasing the level of a (or of b, or of c) by a single unit. Going back to $D = 0$, mark off, in an analogous way, adjacent reductions in D, each of which represents the effect of reducing the level of a (or of b, or of c) by a single unit.

We can now establish a new indicator of welfare, U, with the same zero-point as D, and having the property that each of the intervals marked out in the D indicator, in the manner described above, corresponds to a single unit of U. Then the marginal welfare of a (or of b, or of c) in terms of the new indicator will always be unity, for all values of a, b, and c. $U_a' = U_b' = U_c' = 1$. And this means that U is a linear function of a, b, and c. $U = a+b+c+K$, a constant.

The final step is to eliminate the constant K by adjusting the zero-points of the welfare and well-being indicators while keeping the unit-intervals unchanged. Fortunately this can be done in a way which will give the new zero-points a definite significance. From postulate E it can be deduced that if, in any situation R, each of the elementary situations which correspond respectively to the various well-beings has the same welfare as a situation S in which no mental state exists, then situation R will have the same welfare as situation S. Let us now (a) assign a zero value to any well-being of which the associated elementary situation has the same welfare as situation S, (b) assign a zero value to the level of welfare of situation S, and (c) adjust the existing welfare and well-being indicators U, a, b, c, by subtracting from each the values previously assigned to the

---

a and c. But D_a'/D_c' is independent of b. Therefore $D_a' \equiv D_c'$ for all values of $a, b,$ and c.

(c) Since $D_a' \equiv D_b'$, and $D_a' \equiv D_c'$, therefore $D_b' \equiv D_c'$ for all values of a, b, and c.

new zero points. Then we shall find that in the case of situation R, (zero) welfare will equal the sum of (zero) well-beings, so that the new constant replacing K must be zero. If W is the new indicator of welfare obtained by adjusting U in this way, and if d, e, and f are the new indicators of well-being obtained by adjusting a, b, and c, respectively, we can now represent welfare simply as the sum of the individual-momentary well-beings. $W = d+e+f$.[7]

Starting with an arbitrary set of indicators of welfare and well-beings, and using as a yardstick an arbitrary increment in one of the well-beings we have arrived at a particular set of indicators which meet our requirement that the relation between welfare and well-beings should be additive. Using a different yardstick we would have arrived at a different set of indicators. But the class of admissible indicators is limited. They may differ only in respect of proportionate scale in the sense that if the measurement of some particular level of some particular well-being is altered by x per cent, all the measurements of all the well-beings and of welfare must also be altered by x per cent.[8]

4 Fundamental measurement of welfare

We have arrived at a simple additive relationship between welfare and well-beings. Welfare relates to situations, well-being to individual-moments. But the well-being of an individual-moment has

7. On the alternative interpretation of the welfare function in which welfare represents a general ordering and well-being an individual ordering of courses of action there seems to be no particularly 'natural' basis for choosing zero points. The constant K can be eliminated by taking any particular course of action and regarding as zero both its position in the general ordering and its position in each of the individual orderings.

8. Let there be two sets of welfare and well-being orderings W, d, e, f and V, p, q, z, respectively, such that

$W = d+e+f$ and $V(W) = p(d)+q(e)+r(f)$,

where $V'(W) > 0$, $p'(d) > 0$, $q'(e) > 0$, $r'(f) > 0$.

Then $V'(W) = p'(d) = q'(e) = r(f) = k$.

However $\partial q'(e)/\partial d = 0$,

thus $p''(d) = q''(e) = r''(f) = 0$, i.e. k is constant,

and since the two sets of indicators have identical zero points

$V/W = p/d = q/e = r/f = k$.

been defined as the welfare of an elementary situation containing a single state of mind. Now by a not very strained convention, complex situations containing several states of mind can be regarded as combinations of elementary situations each containing one of the states of mind. Thus our additive relationship between the welfare of any complex situation and that of the elementary situations of which it is composed is in effect an additive relationship between the welfare of a whole and that of its parts. This is sufficient to constitute welfare a fundamentally measurable magnitude. It is legitimate to say that the welfare of situation *A* is three times that of situation *B*. What this means is that if each of the states of mind existing in situation *B* were available in triplicate and all were combined in a single situation *B*, then *B* would have the same welfare as situation *A*.

On the alternative mode of interpreting the welfare function in which welfare measures the degree of preference given to a particular course of action in a general or social ordering, while well-being measures the preference given to it by some individual, it is not clear to me that fundamental measurement is possible. The property measured relates to courses of action which are not divisible or combinable in any significant sense within the conceptual framework. For purposes of application, however (see section 7), measurement of welfare by the 'mutual' process as described in the preceding section appears to serve as well as fundamental measurement.

5 Other ways of measuring welfare

I have nowhere claimed that postulates A to E are necessary conditions for measuring welfare. It appears likely, however, that something analogous to them must be found if the criterion for the true measurement of welfare is to be that it enables welfare to be regarded as the sum of well-being. Equations 1 to 3, p. 255, are, as we have seen, necessary conditions for this. Of course, a wide variety of interpretations can be given to 'welfare' and 'well-being'.

It seems fairly clear, on the analogy of the Neumann–Morgenstern cardinalization of utility, that welfare could be measured on the basis of certain postulates regarding ethical behaviour with respect to uncertainty. Let us define a prospect as a probability distribution of a certain variety of outcomes, and the welfare of an outcome as the desirability of a prospect containing a 100 per cent probability of a particular outcome. The criterion of 'true' measurement both of prospect-desirability and of welfare would then be that prospect-desirability should equal the sum of the welfares of the different possible outcomes weighted by their respective probabilities. While the criterion is rather more complicated than that used in this paper it seems to me likely, though I have not gone into the matter, that the necessary conditions for this type of cardinalization would be somewhat analogous, at least, to those discussed in this paper.

6 The relation of cardinal welfare to cardinal utility

It is important to distinguish the question of the measurability of welfare from that, more discussed in economic literature, of the measurability of utility. 'Utility' is an ambiguous concept. It is sometimes used to mean welfare or 'desirability', sometimes 'desiredness' (ophelimity), and sometimes a vague intermediate category – 'that which it would be rational to desire'. Taking utility in the sense of 'desiredness', the measurement of utility can be achieved only if some restrictive assumptions can be made regarding the preferences, as manifested by the behaviour, of individuals acting on the market, just as measurement of welfare is only possible if some restrictive assumptions can be made regarding ethical judgements.

One way of measuring utility to an individual implies that the marginal rate at which he would be willing to substitute the consumption of any one commodity for that of any other is independent of the amounts of remaining commodities which he consumes. Another method implies that the marginal rate at which the individual would be prepared to substitute consumption at one time-point for consumption at another, is independent of his consumption at the remaining time-points. A third method implies that the individual chooses between uncertain prospects as if he had a cardinal scale of utility applicable to various possible outcomes and as if he were trying to maximize the mathematical expectation of this utility.

Such assumptions are, of course, open to empirical verification. I doubt whether anyone would claim for them more than an approximate validity, which implies that at best utility could only be regarded as 'more or less' cardinal. Where more than this is claimed it is because people have in mind not actual but some sort of ideal behaviour.

As is evident from the argument of this paper the measurability of welfare depends on the characteristics of the ethical system in question and not on the validity of behaviouristic assumptions such as would enable us to derive a measurement for individual utility, in the sense of 'desiredness'. Nevertheless empirically measurable individual utilities might be of assistance in the application of an ethic. For example, suppose that through a scrutiny of an individual's behaviour in choosing between different combinations of present and future income, his utility could be expressed as the sum of magnitudes each of which is a function of the income of a different future period. Then *if* the individual can be assumed to choose as the ethic would have him choose, save in his neglect of effects on the well-beings of others, increments in his utility might reasonably be assumed to be proportional to increments in the sum of his true momentary well-beings.[9] Assuming no significant external economies or diseconomies of consumption[10] this would serve to indicate the slope of the marginal welfare of the individual's income at various points of time, though it would still shed no light on the relative marginal welfare of the incomes of different individuals.

7 Uses of a cardinal welfare

Granted that welfare can meaningfully be regarded as cardinal, the question remains whether any practical advantage is to be reaped by so regarding it. For my own part I should not have thought it worthwhile to engage in a cardinalization of welfare as a pure exercise in moral philosophy if it had not seemed to me to serve a useful purpose in relation to welfare economics. In effect certain of the rules of prescriptive economics can be more clearly and help-

9. In the assumed circumstances the individual's utility must be an increasing function of the sum of his true momentary well-beings. The only alternative to assuming that increments in his utility are proportionate to increments in the sum of his well-beings is to assume that any increment to his income at any given time-point effects a uniform proportionate increase or reduction in the marginal well-beings of his income at all other time-points. This seems unplausible.

10. In the sense that the consumption of one person has no significant direct effect on the welfare of another. Much recent work (e.g., Duesenberry (1947), emphasizing the influence exercised by the consumption of one person on the consumption behaviour of another makes any such assumption extremely questionable.

fully formulated if it is permissible to refer to welfare as measurable. Admittedly some of the operations for which a cardinal welfare appears to me useful would be considered by the purists to be outside the scope of welfare economics proper. Others could scarcely be excluded by the strictest canon. An adequate treatment of these questions must be reserved for a separate paper. For the present the following brief indications must suffice.

The concepts of welfare and well-being as discussed thus far in this paper could not, as they stand, be made the basis of any type of welfare economics. For that they would have to acquire additional substantive content. Moreover, unless this content is such as to permit of some correlation between well-being and individual preference, it is unlikely that economic theory as we know it would have much to contribute to the attainment of the welfare in question. An extreme example of such a correlation would be to postulate a perfect correspondence between individual well-being and individual preference. A truer conception (in my opinion), though a more old fashioned one, is to regard individual-momentary well-being as an increasing function of happiness, so that a situational change will enhance the well-being of an individual at a moment of time if it makes him happier at that moment. On this view we may still assume some correspondence between individual well-being and individual preference, though only an approximate one.

Let us decompose situational changes, as has been customary in welfare economics, into (a) a productional component, which either shifts everyone to a more preferred position or everyone to a less preferred position, and (b) a distributional component, which 'improves' the position of some and 'worsens' that of others. Then the first and most obvious application of a cardinal welfare concept is in the evaluation of distributional components. It is difficult to see how else one could set about assessing the merits of a distributional change than by imagining the effects of the change on the various individuals or classes of individuals concerned, measuring them by the yardstick of some specific well-being difference, probably drawn from one's own remembered experience, and adding the results. The process of measuring the effect on any individual consists essentially in estimating how many intermediate degrees of well-being, such that the difference between each degree of well-being and the next is ethically equivalent to the yardstick, could be interposed between the pre-change and the post-change levels of well-being of the individual in question. This is a purely subjective process, and a difficult one, but it will be rendered less arduous if the evaluator is not hampered by doubts as to its legitimacy.

Another application of cardinal welfare is in correcting the bias of individual choice in respect of time-preference. I think it difficult to handle the question of optimal saving, for example, without assuming a specific indicator of welfare.

Finally – and this brings us into the indubitable sphere of welfare-economics – reference to a specific indicator of welfare appears to be necessary in evaluating the productional component of certain types of large situational changes. What I have in mind is something akin to Marshall's use of producers' and consumers' surpluses in the evaluation of the productional component of sizeable changes such as the building of a bridge or the imposition of a tax. When such changes are in question the least unsatisfactory test of productional desirability is one which has reference to the areas (over the relevant intervals) of product-demand curves and factor-supply curves drawn on specific assumptions. But this test can be justified only if one can assume that the marginal welfare-yield of money to the average spender is constant over the relevant intervals of these demand and supply curves.

Admittedly Professor Hicks has shown that even without invoking a cardinal welfare one can have a satisfactory measure of the productional component, and can employ a test of the type discussed above, provided that income effects can be assumed to be virtually absent with respect to those products and factors whose prices change substantially. But I would contend (a) that even where the Hicksian solution is applicable, the conception of constancy in the marginal utility (welfare) of money, if conceptually admissible as we have argued, is preferable because simpler than that of absence of income effects, and (b) that there are cases where it is not permissible to assume absence of income-effects but where it may nevertheless be permissible to assume constancy of marginal utility (welfare) of money to the average individual. Such cases – which arise when the distributional elements in the change predominate over the productional elements, so that it is precisely those products and factors most susceptible to income effects whose prices are most affected – can, I think, be handled only with the aid of a cardinal concept of welfare.

References

BERGSON, A. (1938), 'A reformulation of certain aspects of welfare economics', *Q. J. Econ.*, vol. 52, pp. 310–34, reprinted in A. Bergson, *Essays in Normative Economics*, Harvard University Press, 1966, pp. 1–49.

CAMPBELL, N. R. (1928), *Principles of Measurement and Calculation*, Longmans.

COHEN, M. R., and NAGEL, E. (1934), *Introduction to Logic and Scientific Method*, Harcourt, Brace Jovanovich.

DUESENBERRY, J. S. (1949), *Incomes, Saving and Theory of Consumer Behavior*, Harvard, University Press.

10 J. C. Harsanyi

Cardinal Welfare, Individualistic Ethics and Interpersonal
Comparisons of Utility

J. C. Harsanyi, 'Cardinal welfare, individualistic ethics and interpersonal
comparisons of utility', *Journal of Political Economy*, 1955, August.

1

The naïve concept of social welfare as a sum of intuitively measurable and comparable individual cardinal utilities has been found
unable to withstand the methodological criticism of the Pareto
school. Professor Bergson (1938 and 1939, especially pp. 412–20) has
therefore recommended its replacement by the more general concept
of a social welfare function, defined as an arbitrary mathematical
function of economic (and other social) variables, of a form freely
chosen according to one's personal ethical (or political) value judgements. Of course, in this terminology everybody will have a social
welfare function of his own, different from that of everybody else,
except to the extent to which different individuals' value judgements
happen to coincide with one another. Actually, owing to the prevalence of individualistic value judgements in our society, it has
been generally agreed that a social welfare function should be an
increasing function of the utilities of individuals: if a certain situation, X, is preferred by an individual to another situation, Y, and
if none of the other individuals prefers Y to X, then X should be
regarded as socially preferable to Y. But no other restriction is to be
imposed on the mathematical form of a social welfare function.

Recently, however, Professor Fleming[1] (Reading 9) has shown
that if one accepts one further fairly weak and plausible ethical
postulate, one finds one's social welfare function to be at once
restricted to a rather narrow class of mathematical functions so as to
be expressible (after appropriate monotone transformation of the

1. For a different approach to the same problem see Goodman and Markovitz
(1952).

social welfare and individual utility indexes if necessary) as the weighted sum of the individuals' utilities. This does not mean, of course, a return to the doctrine that the existence of an additive cardinal utility function is intuitively self-evident. The existence of such a function becomes, rather, the consequence of the ethical postulates adopted and is wholly dependent on these postulates. Still, Fleming's results do in a sense involve an unexpected revival of some views of the pre-Pareto period.

In this paper I propose, first of all, to examine the precise ethical meaning of Fleming's crucial postulate and to show that it expresses an *individualistic* value judgement going definitely beyond the generally adopted individualistic postulate mentioned earlier, though it represents, as I shall argue, a value judgement perfectly acceptable according to common ethical standards (section 2). I shall also attempt to show that, if both social and individual preferences are assumed to satisfy the von Neumann–Morgenstern–Marschak axioms about choices between uncertain prospects, even a much weaker ethical postulate than Fleming's suffices to establish an additive cardinal social welfare function (section 3). In effect, it will be submitted that a mere logical analysis of what we mean by value judgements concerning social welfare and by social welfare functions leads, without any additional ethical postulates, to a social welfare function of this mathematical form (section 4). Finally, I shall turn to the problem of interpersonal comparisons of utility, which gains new interest by the revival of an additive cardinal welfare concept, and shall examine what logical basis, if any, there is for such comparisons (section 5).

2

Fleming expresses his ethical postulates in terms of two alternative conceptual frameworks: one in terms of an *'ideal utilitarianism'* of G. E. Moore's type, the other in terms of a *preference* terminology more familiar to economists. Though he evidently sets greater store by the first approach, I shall adopt the second, which seems to be freer of unnecessary metaphysical commitments. I have also taken the liberty of rephrasing his postulates to some extent.

Postulate A (asymmetry of social preference). If 'from a social stand-point'[2] situation X is preferred to situation Y, then Y is not preferred to X.

Postulate B (transivity of social preference). If from a social standpoint X is preferred to Y, and Y to Z, then X is preferred to Z.

Postulate C (transitivity of social indifference). If from a social standpoint neither of X and Y is preferred to the other, and again neither of Y and Z is preferred to the other, then likewise neither of X and Z is preferred to the other.

These three postulates are meant to insure that 'social preference' establishes a *complete ordering* among the possible social situations, from which the existence of a social welfare function (at least of an ordinal type) at once follows. (Actually, two postulates would have sufficed if, in the postulates, 'weak' preference, which does not exclude the possibility of indifference, had been used instead of 'strong' preference.)

Postulate D (positive relation of social preferences to individual preferences). If a given individual i prefers situation X to situation Y, and none of the other individuals prefers Y to X, then X is preferred to Y from a social standpoint.

As already mentioned postulate D expresses a generally accepted individualistic value judgement.

Finally, Fleming's postulate E states essentially that on issues on which two individuals' interests (preferences) conflict, all other individuals' interests being unaffected, social preferences should depend exclusively on comparing the relative social importance of the interests at stake of each of the two individuals concerned. In other words, it requires that the distribution of utilities between each pair of individuals should be judged separately on its own merits, independently of how utilities (or income) are distributed among the other members of the community.

2. Of course, when I speak of preferences 'from a social standpoint', often abbreviated to 'social' preferences and the like, I always mean preferences based on a given individual's value judgements concerning 'social welfare'. The foregoing postulates are meant to impose restrictions on *any* individual's value judgements of this kind, and thus represent, as it were, value judgements of the second order, that is, value judgements concerning value judgements. Later I shall discuss the concept of 'preferences from a social standpoint' at some length and introduce the distinctive term 'ethical preferences' to describe them (in section 4). But at this stage I do not want to prejudice the issue by using this terminology.

Postulate E (independent evaluation of the utility distribution[3] between each pair of individuals). (1) There are at least three individuals. (2) Suppose that individual i is indifferent between situations X and X' and also between situations Y and Y', but prefers situations X and X' to situations Y and Y'. Suppose, further, that individual j is also indifferent between X and X' and between Y and Y', but (unlike individual i) prefers Y and Y' to X and X'. Suppose also that all other individuals are indifferent between X and Y, and likewise between X' and Y'.[4] Then social preferences should always go in the same way between X and Y as they do between X' and Y' (that is, if from a social standpoint X is preferred to Y, then X' should also be preferred to Y'; if from a social standpoint X and Y are regarded as indifferent, the same should be true of X' and Y'; and if from a social standpoint Y is preferred to X, then Y' should also be preferred to X').

Postulate E is a natural extension of the individualistic value judgement expressed by postulate D. Postulate D already implies that if the choice between two situations X and Y happens to affect the interests of the individuals i and j only, without affecting the interests of anybody else, social choice must depend exclusively on i's and j's interests – provided that i's and j's interests *agree* in this matter. Postulate E now adds that in the assumed case social choice must depend exclusively on i's and j's interests (and on weighing these two interests one against the other in terms of a consistent ethical standard), even if i's and j's interests are in *conflict*. Thus both postulates make social choice dependent solely on the *individual* inte-

3. The more general term 'utility distribution' is used instead of the term 'income distribution', since the utility enjoyed by each individual will, in general, depend not only on his own income but also, owing to external economies and diseconomies of consumption, on other people's incomes.

4. It is not assumed, however, that the other individuals are (like i and j) indifferent between X and X' and between Y and Y'. In effect, were this restrictive assumption inserted into postulate E, this latter would completely lose the status of an independent postulate and would become a mere corollary of postulate D.

5. In view of consumers' notorious 'irrationality', some people may feel that these postulates go too far in accepting the consumers' sovereignty doctrine. These people may reinterpret the terms in the postulates referring to individual preferences as denoting, not certain individuals' actual preferences, but rather their 'true' preferences, that is, the preferences they *would* manifest under 'ideal conditions', in possession of perfect information, and acting with perfect logic

rests directly affected.[5] They leave no room for the separate interests of a superindividual state or of impersonal cultural values[6] (except for the ideals of equity incorporated in the ethical postulates themselves).

At first sight, postulate E may look inconsistent with the widespread habit of judging the 'fairness' or 'unfairness' of the distribution of income between two individuals, not only on the basis of these two people's personal conditions and needs, but also on the basis of comparing their incomes with the incomes of the other members of their respective social groups. Thus people's judgements on the income distribution between a given worker and his employer will also depend on the current earnings of other similar workers and employers. But the conflict with postulate E is more apparent than real. In a society with important external economies and diseconomies of consumption, where the utility of a given income depends not only on its absolute size but also on its relation to other people's incomes, it is not inconsistent with postulate E that, in judging the income distribution between two individuals, other people's incomes should also be taken into account. An income distribution between a given worker and a given employer, which in the original situation seemed perfectly 'fair' in terms of a given ethical standard, may require adjustment in the worker's favour, once wages have generally gone up, since the worsening of this worker's position relative to that of his fellows must have reduced him to a lower level of utility.

Postulate E requires that the distribution of *utility* between two individuals (once the utility levels of the two individuals are given) should always be judged independently of how utility and income

and care. With some ingenuity it should not be too difficult to give even some sort of 'operational' meaning to these ideal conditions, or to some approximation of them, acceptable for practical purposes. (Or, alternatively, these terms may be reinterpreted as referring even to the preferences that these individuals *ought* to exhibit in terms of a given ethical standard. The latter interpretation would, of course, deprive the postulates of most of their individualistic meaning.)

6. These postulates do not exclude, however, the possibility that such consideration may influence the relative weights given to different individuals' utilities within the additive social welfare function. Even by means of additional postulates, this could be excluded only to the extent to which the comparison of individual utilities can be put on an objective basis independent of individual value judgements (see section 5).

are distributed among other members of the society. In the absence of external economies and diseconomies of consumption, this would necessarily also mean judging the distribution of *income* between two individuals independently of the incomes of others. In the presence of such economies and diseconomies, however, when the utility level of any person depends not only on his own income but also on other persons' incomes, it is not inconsistent with postulate E that our value judgement on the distribution of income between two individuals should be influenced by the income distribution in the rest of the society – in so far as the income distribution in the rest of the society affects the utility levels of these two individuals them-selves and consequently the distribution of utility between them. Postulate E demands only that, once these effects have been allowed for, the distribution of income in the rest of the society must not have any further influence on our value judgement.

3

In accordance with prevalent usage in welfare economics, Fleming's postulates refer to social or individual preferences between *sure prospects* only. However, it seems desirable to have both sorts of preferences defined for choices between *uncertain prospects* as well. More often than not, we have to choose in practice between social policies that promise given definite results only with larger or smaller probabilities. On the other hand, if we subscribe to some sort of individualistic ethics, we should like to make social attitude towards uncertainty somehow dependent on individual attitudes toward it (at least if the latter do not manifest too patent and too great an inconsistency and irrationality).

Since we admit the possibility of external economies and dis-economies of consumption, both social and individual prospects will, in general, specify the amounts of different commodities con-sumed and the stocks of different goods held by all individuals at different future dates (up to the time horizon adopted), together with their respective probabilities.

As the von Neumann–Morgenstern axioms (1947) or the Marschak postulates (1950)[7] equivalent to them (which latter I shall adopt) are

7. Marschak's postulates can be summarized as follows. *Postulate 1 (complete ordering)*: The relation of preference establishes a complete ordering among all

essential requirements for rational behaviour, it is natural enough to demand that both social and individual preferences[8] should satisfy them. This gives us:

Postulate a. Social preferences satisfy Marschak's Postulates 1, 2, 3', and 4.

Postulate b. Individual preferences satisfy the same four postulates.

In addition, we need a postulate to secure the dependence of social preferences on individual preferences:

Postulate c. If two prospects P and Q are indifferent from the standpoint of every individual, they are also indifferent from a social standpoint.

Postulate c once more represents, of course, an individualistic value judgement – though a very weak one, comparable to Fleming's postulate D rather than to his postulate E.

I propose to show that postulate c suffices to establish that the cardinal social welfare function defined by postulate a can be obtained as a weighted sum of the cardinal individual utility functions defined by postulate b (on the understanding that the zero point of the social welfare function is appropriately chosen).

Theorem 1. There exists a social welfare function such that its actuarial value is maximized by choices conformable to the social

---

prospects. *Postulate 2* (continuity): If prospect P is preferred to prospect R, while prospect Q has an intermediate position between them (being preferred to R but less preferred than P), then there exists a mixture of P and R, with appropriate probabilities, such as to be exactly indifferent to Q. *Postulate 3'* (*sufficient number of nonindifferent prospects*): There are at least four mutually nonindifferent prospects. *Postulate 4* (*equivalence of mixture of equivalent prospects*): If prospects Q and Q' are indifferent, then, for any prospect P, a given mixture of P and Q is indifferent to a similar mixture of P and Q', (that is, to a mixture of P and Q' which has the same probabilities for the corresponding constituent prospects).

Postulate 1 is needed to establish the existence of even an *ordinal* utility (or welfare) function, while the other three postulates are required to establish the existence of a *cardinal* utility (or welfare) function. But, as postulates 2 and 3 are almost trivial, Postulate 4 may be regarded as being decisive for cardinality as against mere ordinality.

8. There are reasons to believe that, in actuality, individual preferences between uncertain prospects do not always satisfy these postulates of rational behaviour (for example, owing to a certain 'love of danger'; see Marschak, 1950, pp. 137–41). In this case we may fall back again upon the preferences each individual *would* manifest under 'ideal conditions' (see note 3).

.preferences given. This social welfare function is unique up to linear transformation.

Theorem 2. For each individual there exists a utility function such that its actuarial value is maximized by choices conformable to the individual's preferences. This utility function is unique up to linear transformation.

Both theorems follow from Marschak's argument.

Let W denote a social welfare function satisfying theorem 1 and U_i denote a utility function of the i'th individual, satisfying theorem 2. Moreover, let W be chosen so that $W = 0$ if for all the n individuals $U_1 = U_2 = \dots = U_n = 0$.

Theorem 3. W is a single-valued function of $U_1, U_2, \dots, U_n$. This follows, in view of theorems 1 and 2, from postulate c.

Theorem 4. W is a homogeneous function of the first order of U_1 $U_2, \dots, U_n$.

Proof. We want to show that, if the individual utilities $U_1 = u_1$; $U_2 = u_2; \dots$; $U_n = u_n$ correspond to the social welfare $W = w$, then, the individual utilities $U_1 = k u_1$; $U_2 = k u_2; \dots$; $U_n = k u_n$ correspond to the social welfare $W = k w$.

This will be shown first for the case where $0 \leqslant k \leqslant 1$. Suppose that prospect O represents $U_1 = U_2 = \dots = U_n = 0$ for the different individuals and consequently represents $W = 0$ for society, while prospect P represents $U_1 = u_1$; $U_2 = u_2; \dots$; $U_n = u_n$ for the former and $W = w$ for the latter. Moreover, let Q be the mixed prospect of obtaining either prospect O (with the probability $1-p$) or prospect P (with the probability p). Then, obviously, Q will represent $U_1 = p u_1$; $U_2 = p u_2; \dots$; $U_n = p u_n$ for the individuals and $W = p w$ for society. Now, if we write $k = p$, a comparison between the values of the variables belonging to prospect P and those belonging to prospect Q will, in view of theorem 3, establish the desired result for the case where $0 \leqslant k \leqslant 1$ (p, being a probability, cannot be < 0 or > 1).

Next let us consider the case where $k < 0$. Let us choose prospect R so that prospect O becomes equivalent to the mixed prospect of obtaining either prospect R (with the probability p) or prospect P (with the probability $1-p$). A little calculation will show

J. C. Harsanyi 273

that in this case prospect R will represent $U_1 = (1-1/p)u_1$; $U_2 = (1-1/p)u_2;...; U_n = (1-1/p)u_n$ for the different individuals and $W = (1-1/p)w$ for society. If we now write $k = 1-1/p$, a comparison between the variables belonging to R and those belonging to P will establish the desired result for the case $k < 0$ (by an appropriate choice of the probability p, we can make k equal to any negative number).

Finally, the case where $k > 1$ can be taken care of by finding a prospect S such that prospect P becomes equivalent to the mixed prospect of obtaining either S (with a probability p) or O (with a probability $1-p$). Then this prospect S will be connected with the values $U^1 = (1/p)u^1$; $U_2 = (1/p)u_2;...; U_n = (1/p)u_n$ and $W = (1/p)w$. If we now write $k = 1/p$ we obtain the desired result for the case where $k > 1$ (by an appropriate choice of p we can make k equal to any number >1).

Theorem 5. W is a weighted sum of the individual utilities, of the form

$$W = \sum a_i U_i,$$

where a_i stands for the value that W takes when $U_i = 1$ and $U_j = 0$ for all $j \neq i$.

Proof. Let S_i be a prospect representing the utility U_i to the ith individual and the utility zero to all other individuals. Then, according to theorem 4, for S_i we have $W = a_i \cdot U_i$.

Let T be the mixed prospect of obtaining either S_1 or S_2 or...S_n, each with probability $1/n$. Then T will represent the individual utilities $U_1/n, U_2/n,...,U_n/n$ and the social welfare

$$W = \frac{1}{n} \sum a_i U_i.$$

In view of theorem 4, this directly implies that if the individual utility functions take the values $U_1, U_2,...,U_n$, respectively, the social welfare function has the value

$$W = \sum a_i U_i,$$

as desired.[9]

9. If we want a formal guarantee that no individual's utility can be given a negative weight in the social welfare function, we must add one more postulate (for instance, postulate D of section 2).

4

In the pre-Pareto conceptual framework, the distinction between social welfare and individual utilities was free of ambiguity. Individual utilities were assumed to be directly given by introspection, and social welfare was simply their sum. In the modern approach, however, the distinction is far less clear. On the one hand, our social welfare concept has come logically nearer to an individual utility concept. Social welfare is no longer regarded as an objective quantity, the same for all, by necessity. Rather, each individual is supposed to have a social welfare function of his own, expressing his own individual values – in the same way as each individual has a utility function of his own, expressing his own individual taste. On the other hand, our individual utility concept has come logically nearer to a social welfare concept. Owing to a greater awareness of the importance of external economies and diseconomies of consumption in our society, each individual's utility function is now regarded as dependent not only on this particular individual's economic (and noneconomic) conditions but also on the economic (and other) conditions of all other individuals in the community— in the same way as a social welfare function is dependent on the personal conditions of all individuals.

At the same time, we cannot allow the distinction between an individual's social welfare function and his utility function to be blurred if we want (as most of us do, I think) to uphold the principle that a social welfare function ought to be based not on the utility function (subjective preferences) of *one* particular individual only (namely, the individual whose value judgements are expressed in this welfare function), but rather on the utility functions (subjective preferences) of *all* individuals, representing a kind of 'fair compromise' among them.[10] Even if both an individual's social welfare function and his utility function in a sense express his own individual preferences, they must express preferences of different sorts: the former must express what this individual prefers (or, rather, would prefer) on the basis of impersonal social considerations alone, and the latter must express what he actually prefers,

10. This principle is essentially identical with Professor Arrow's 'nondictatorship' postulate (1951a) (see also note 9).

whether on the basis of his personal interests or on any other basis. The former may be called his 'ethical' preferences, the latter his 'subjective' preferences. Only his 'subjective' preferences (which define his utility function) will express his preferences in the full sense of the word as they actually are, showing an egoistic attitude in the case of an altruist. His 'ethical' preferences (which define his social welfare function) will, on the other hand, express what can in only a qualified sense be called his 'preferences': they will, be definition, express what he prefers only in those possibly rare moments when he forces a special impartial and impersonal attitude upon himself.[11]

In effect, the ethical postulates proposed in sections 2 and 3 – namely, postulates D, E, and c – can be regarded as simply an implicit definition of what sort of 'impartial' or 'impersonal' attitude is required to underlie 'ethical' preferences: these postulates essentially serve to exclude nonethical subjective preferences from social welfare functions. But this aim may also be secured more directly by explicitly defining the impartial and impersonal attitude demanded.

I have argued elsewhere (Harsanyi, 1953, pp. 434–5) that an individual's preferences satisfy this requirement of impersonality if they indicate what social situation he would choose if he did not know what his personal position would be in the new situation

11. Little's objection to Arrow's nondictatorship postulate (see Little's review article, Reading 5) loses its force, once the distinction between 'ethical' and 'subjective' preferences is noted. It does, then, make sense that an individual should morally *disapprove* (in terms of his 'ethical' preferences) of an unequal income distribution which benefits him financially, and should still *prefer* it (in terms of his 'subjective' preferences) to a more egalitarian one or should even *fight* for it – behaviour morally regrettable but certainly not logically inconceivable.

Arrow's distinction between an individual's 'tastes' (which order social situations only according to their effects on his own consumption) and his 'values' (which take account also of external economies and diseconomies of consumption and of ethical considerations, in ordering social situations) does not meet the difficulty, since it does not explain how an individual can without inconsistency accept a social welfare function conflicting with his own 'values'. This can be understood only if his social welfare functions represents preferences of another sort than his 'values' do. (Of course, in my terminology Arrow's 'values' fall in the class of 'subjective' preferences and not in the class of 'ethical' preferences, as is easily seen from the way in which he defines them.)

chosen (and in any of its alternatives) but rather had an equal *chance* of obtaining any of the social positions[12] existing in this situation, from the highest down to the lowest. Of course, it is immaterial whether this individual does not in fact know how his choice would affect his personal interests or merely disregards this knowledge for a moment when he is making his choice. As I have tried to show (1953), in either case an impersonal choice (preference) of this kind can in a technical sense be regarded as a choice between 'uncertain' prospects.

This implies, however, without any additional ethical postulates that an individual's impersonal preferences, if they are rational, must satisfy Marschak's axioms and consequently must define a cardinal social welfare function equal to the arithmetical mean[13] of the utilities of all individuals in the society (since the arithmetical mean of all individual utilities gives the actuarial value of his uncertain prospect, defined by an equal probability of being put in the place of any individual in the situation chosen).

More exactly, if the former individual has any objective criterion for comparing his fellows' utilities with one another and with his own (see section 5), his social welfare function will represent the unweighted mean of these utilities, while in the absence of such an objective criterion it will, in general, represent their weighted mean, with arbitrary weights depending only on his personal value judgements. In the former case social welfare will in a sense be an objective quantity, whereas in the latter case it will contain an important subjective element; but even in this latter case it will be something very different from the utility function of the individual concerned.[14]

12. Or, rather, if he had an equal chance of being 'put in the place of' any individual member of the society, with regard not only to his objective social (and economic) conditions, but also to his subjective attitudes and tastes. In other words, he ought to judge the utility of another individual's position not in terms of his own attitudes and tastes but rather in terms of the attitudes and tastes of the individual actually holding this position.

13. Obviously, the (unweighted or weighted) *mean* of the individual utilities defines the same social welfare function as their *sum* (weighted by the same relative weights), except for an irrelevant proportionality constant.

14. The concept of ethical preferences used in this section implies, of course, an ethical theory different from the now prevalent subjective attitude theory, since it makes a person's ethical judgements the expression, not of his subjective attitudes in general, but rather of certain special unbiased impersonal attitudes

5

There is no doubt about the fact that people do make, or at least attempt to make, interpersonal comparisons of utility, both in the sense of comparing different persons' total satisfaction and in the sense of comparing increments or decrements in different persons' satisfaction.[15] The problem is only what logical basis if any, there is for such comparisons.

In general, we have two indicators of the utility that *other* people attach to different situations: their preferences as revealed by their actual choices, and their (verbal or nonverbal) expressions of satisfaction in each situation. But while the use of these indicators for comparing the utilities that a *given* person ascribes to different situations is relatively free of difficulty, their use for comparing the utility that *different* persons ascribe to each situation entails a special problem. In actual fact, this problem has two rather different aspects, one purely metaphysical and one psychological, which have not, however, always been sufficiently kept apart.

The *metaphysical* problem would be present even if we tried to compare the utilities enjoyed by different persons with identical preferences and with identical expressive reactions to any situation. Even in this case, it would not be inconceivable that such persons should have different susceptibilities to satisfaction and should attach different utilities to identical situations, for, in principle, identical preferences may well correspond to different absolute levels of utility (as long as the ordinal properties of all persons' utility functions are the same),[16] and identical expressive reactions

---

only. I shall set out the philosophic case for this ethical theory in a forthcoming publication. (For a similar view, see Findlay, 1954, pp. 145–61.)

15. See Little (1950), chapter 4. I have nothing to add to Little's conclusion on the *possibility* of interpersonal comparisons of utility. I only want to supplement his argument by an analysis of the *logical basis* of such comparisons. I shall deal with the problem of comparisons between total utilities only, neglecting the problem of comparisons between differences in utility, since the social welfare functions discussed in the previous sections contain only total utilities of individuals.

16. Even identical preferences among uncertain prospects (satisfying the Marschak axioms) are compatible with different absolute levels of utility, since they do not uniquely determine the zero points and the scales of the corresponding cardinal utility functions.

may well indicate different mental states with different people. At the same time, under these conditions this logical possibility of different susceptibilities to satisfaction would hardly be more than a metaphysical curiosity. If two objects or human beings show similar behaviour in *all* their relevant aspects open to observation, the assumption of some unobservable hidden difference between them must be regarded as a completely gratuitous hypothesis and one contrary to sound scientific method.[17] (This principle may be called the 'principle of unwarranted differentiation'.) In the last analysis, it is on the basis of this principle that we ascribe mental states to other human beings at all: the denial of this principle would at once lead us to solipsism (Little, 1950, pp. 56–7). Thus in the case of persons with similar preferences and expressive reactions we are fully entitled to assume that they derive the same utilities from similar situations'.

In the real world, of course, different people's preferences and their expressive reactions to similar situations may be rather different, and this does represent a very real difficulty in comparing the utilities enjoyed by different people – a difficulty in addition to the metaphysical difficulty just discussed and independent of it. I shall refer to it as the *psychological* difficulty, since it is essentially a question of how psychological differences between people in the widest sense (for example, differences in consumption habits, cultural background, social status, and sex and other biological conditions, as well as purely psychological differences, inborn or acquired) affect the satisfaction that people derive from each situation. The problem in general takes the following form. If one individual prefers situation X to situation Y, while another prefers Y to X, is this so because the former individual attaches a *higher* utility to situation X, or because he attaches a *lower* utility to situation Y, than does the latter – or is this perhaps the result of both these factors at the same time? And, again, if in a given situation one individual gives more forcible signs of satisfaction or dissatisfaction than another, is this so because the former feels more intense satisfaction or

17. By making a somewhat free use of Professor Carnap's distinction, we may say that the assumption of different susceptibilities of satisfaction in this case, even though it would not be against the canons of *deductive* logic, would most definitely be against the canons of *inductive* logic.

dissatisfaction, or only because he is inclined to give stronger expression to his feelings?

This psychological difficulty is accessible to direct empirical solution to the extent to which these psychological differences between people are capable of change, and it is therefore possible for some individuals to make direct comparisons between the satisfactions open to one human type and those open to another.[18] Of course, many psychological variables are not capable of change or are capable of change only in some directions but not in others. For instance, a number of inborn mental or biological characteristics cannot be changed at all, and, though the cultural patterns and attitudes of an individual born and educated in one social group can be considerably changed by transplanting him to another, usually they cannot be completely assimilated to the cultural patterns and attitudes of the second group. Thus it may easily happen that, if we want to compare the satisfactions of two different classes of human beings, we cannot find any individual whose personal experiences would cover the satisfactions of both these classes.

Interpersonal comparisons of utility made in everyday life seem, however, to be based on a different principle (which is, of course, seldom formulated explicitly). If two individuals have opposite preferences between two situations, we usually try to find out the psychological differences responsible for this disagreement and, on the basis of our general knowledge of human psychology, try to increase or decrease their satisfaction derived from each situation. For example, if one individual is ready at a given wage rate to supply more labour than another, we tend in general to explain this mainly by his having a lower disutility for labour if his physique is much more robust than that of the other individual and if there is no ascertainable difference between the two individuals' economic needs; we tend to explain it mainly by his having a higher utility for income (consumption goods) if the two individuals' physiques are similar and if the former evidently has much greater economic needs (for example, a larger family to support).

Undoubtedly, both these methods of tackling what we have

18. On the reliability of comparisons between the utility of different situations before a change in one's 'taste' (taken in the broadest sense) and after it, see the first two sections of Harsanyi (1953–4, pp. 204–8).

called the 'psychological difficulty' are subject to rather large margins of error.[19] In general, the greater the psychological, biological, cultural, and social differences between two people, the greater the margin of error attached to comparisons between their utility.

Particular uncertainty is connected with the second method, since it depends on our general knowledge of psychological laws, which is still in a largely unsatisfactory state.[20] What is more, all our knowledge about the psychological laws of satisfaction is ultimately derived from observing how changes in different (psychological and other) variables affect the satisfactions an individual obtains from various situations. We therefore have no direct empirical evidence on how people's satisfactions are affected by the variables that, for any particular individual, are *not* capable of change. Thus we can, in general, judge the influence of these 'unchangeable' variables only on the basis of the correlations found between these and the 'changeable' variables, whose influence we can observe directly. For instance, let us take sex as an example of 'unchangeable' variables (disregarding the few instances of sex change) and abstractive ability as an example of 'changeable' variables. We tend to assume that the average man finds greater satisfaction than the average woman does in solving mathematical puzzles *because*, allegedly, men in general have greater abstractive ability than women. But this reasoning depends on the implicit assumption that differences in the 'unchangeable' variables, if unaccompanied by differences in the 'changeable' variables, are in themselves immaterial. For example, we must assume that men and women equal in abstractive ability (and the other relevant characteristics) would tend to find the same satisfaction in working on mathematical problems.

19. Though perhaps it would not be too difficult to reduce these margins quite considerably (for example, by using appropriate statistical techniques), should there be a need for more precise results.

20. Going back to our example, for instance, the disutility of labour and the utility of income are unlikely to be actually independent variables (as I have tacitly assumed), though it may not always be clear in which way their mutual influence actually goes. In any case, income is enjoyed in a different way, depending on the ease with which it has been earned, and labour is put up with in a different spirit, depending on the strength of one's need for additional income.

Of course, the assumption that the 'unchangeable' variables in themselves have no influence is *ex hypothesi* not open to direct empirical check. It can be justified only by the *a priori* principle that, when one variable is alleged to have a certain influence on another, the burden of proof lies on those who claim the existence of such an influence.[21] Thus the second method of interpersonal utility comparison rests in an important sense on empirical evidence more indirect[22] than that underlying the first method. On the other hand, the second method has the advantage of also being applicable in those cases where no one individual can possibly have wide enough personal experience to make direct utility comparisons in terms of the first method.

In any case, it should now be sufficiently clear that interpersonal comparisons of utility are not value judgements based on some ethical or political postulates but rather are factual propositions based on certain principles of inductive logic.

At the same time, Robbins (1953, pp. 99–111, especially p. 109; 1948, chapter 6; 1938, pp. 635–41) is clearly right when he maintains that propositions which purport to be interpersonal comparisons of utility often contain a purely *conventional* element based on ethical or political value judgements. For instance, the assumption that different individuals have the same susceptibility to satisfaction often expresses only the egalitarian value judgement that all individuals

21. This principle may be called the 'principle of unwarranted correlation' and is again a principle of inductive logic, closely related to the principle of unwarranted differentiation referred to earlier.

22. There is also another reason for which conclusions dependent on the principle of unwarranted correlation have somewhat less cogency than conclusions dependent only on the principle of unwarranted differentiation. The former principle refers to the case where two individuals differ in a certain variable X (in our example, in sex) but where there is no special evidence that they differ also in a certain other variable Y (in susceptibility to satisfaction). The latter principle, on the other hand, refers to the case where there is no ascertainable difference at all between the two individuals in any observable variable whatever, not even in X (in sex). Now, though the assumption that these two individuals differ in Y (in susceptibility to satisfaction) would be a gratuitous hypothesis in either case, obviously it would be a less unnatural hypothesis in the first case (where there is some observed difference between the two individuals) than in the second case (where there is none).

should be treated equally rather than a belief in a factual psychological equality between them. Or, again, different people's total satisfaction is often compared on the tacit understanding that the gratification of wants regarded as 'immoral' in terms of a certain ethical standard shall not count. But in order to avoid confusion, such propositions based on ethical or political restrictive postulates must be clearly distinguished from interpersonal comparisons of utility without a conventional element of this kind.

It must also be admitted that the use of conventional postulates based on personal value judgements may sometimes be due not to our free choice but rather to our lack of the factual information needed to give our interpersonal utility comparisons a more objective basis. In effect, if we do not know anything about the relative urgency of different persons' economic needs and still have to make a decision, we can hardly avoid acting on the basis of personal guesses more or less dependent on our own value judgements.

On the other hand, if the information needed is available, individualistic ethics consistently requires the use, in the social welfare function, of individual utilities not subjected to restrictive postulates. The imposition of restrictive ethical or political conventions on the individual utility functions would necessarily qualify our individualism, since it would decrease the dependence of our social welfare function on the actual preferences and actual susceptibilities to satisfaction, of the individual members of the society, putting in its place a dependence on our own ethical or political value judgements (see notes 3 and 4).

To sum up, the more complete our factual information and the more completely individualistic our ethics, the more the different individuals' social welfare functions will converge toward the same objective quantity, namely, the unweighted sum (or rather the unweighted arithmetic mean) of all individual utilities. This follows both from (either of two alternative sets of) ethical postulates based on commonly accepted individualistic ethical value judgements and from the mere logical analysis of the concept of a social welfare function. The latter interpretation also removes certain difficulties connected with the concept of a social welfare function, which have been brought out by Little's criticism of certain of Arrow's conclusions.

Of course, the practical need for reaching decisions on public policy will require us to formulate social welfare functions – explicitly or implicitly – even if we lack the factual information needed for placing interpersonal comparisons of utility on an objective basis. But even in this case, granting the proposed ethical postulates (or the proposed interpretation of the concept of a social welfare function), our social welfare function must take the form of a weighted sum (weighted mean) of all individual utility functions, with more or less arbitrary weights chosen according to our own value judgements.

There is here an interesting analogy with the theory of statistical decisions (and, in general, the theory of choosing among alternative hypotheses). In the same way as in the latter, it has been shown[23] that a rational man (whose choices satisfy certain simple postulates of rationality) must act *as if* he ascribed numerical subjective probabilities to all alternative hypotheses, even if his factual information is insufficient to do this on an objective basis – so in welfare economics we have also found that a rational man (whose choices satisfy certain simple postulates of rationality and impartiality) must likewise act *as if* he made quantitative interpersonal comparisons of utility, even if his factual information is insufficient to do this on an objective basis.

Thus if we accept individualistic ethics and set public policy the task of satisfying the preferences of the individual members of the society (deciding between conflicting preferences of different individuals according to certain standards of impartial equity), our social welfare function will always tend to take the form of a sum (or mean) of individual utilities; but whether the weights given to these individual utilities have an objective basis or not will depend wholly on the extent of our factual (psychological) information.

23. See Marschak's discussion of what he calls 'Ramsey's norm' (1954). For a survey of earlier literature see Arrow (1951, pp. 404–37, especially pp. 431–32, and the references there quoted).

References

ARROW, K. J. (1951a), *Social Choice and Individual Values*, 2nd edn, 1963, Wiley.
ARROW, K. J. (1951b), 'Alternative approaches to the theory of choice in risk-taking situations', *Econometrica*, vol. 19.

BERGSON, A. (1938), 'A reformulation of certain aspects of welfare economics', *Q. J. Econ.*, vol. 52, pp. 310–34.

BERGSON, A. (1949), 'Socialist economics', in H. S. Ellis (ed.), *A Survey of Contemporary Economics*, Philadelphia.

FINDLAY, J. N. (1954), 'The justification of attitudes', *Mind*, new series, vol. 63, April.

GOODMAN, L., and MARKOVITZ, H. (1952), 'Social welfare functions based on individual rankings', *Amer. J. Sociol.*, vol. 58, November.

HARSANYI, J. C. (1953), 'Cardinal utility in welfare economics and in the theory of risk-taking', *J. polit. Econ.*, vol. 61, October, pp. 434–5.

HARSANYI, J. C. (1953–4), 'Welfare economics of variable tastes', *Rev. econ. Stud.*, vol. 21.

LITTLE, I. M. D. (1950), *A Critique of Welfare Economics*, Oxford University Press.

MARSCHAK, J. (1950), 'Rational behaviour, uncertain prospects and measurable utility', *Econometrica*, vol. 18, pp. 111–41.

MARSCHAK, J. (1954), 'Probability in the social sciences', in P. F. Lazarsfeld (ed.), *Mathematical Thinking in the Social Sciences*, section 1, Glencoe, reprinted as no. 82, of Cowles Commission Papers, new series.

ROBBINS, L. (1938), 'Interpersonal comparisons of utility', *econ. J.*, vol. 43.

ROBBINS, L. (1948), *An Essay on the Nature and Significance of Economic Science*, 2nd edn, Macmillan.

ROBBINS, L. (1953), 'Robertson on utility and scope', *Economica*, new series, vol. 20.

VON NEUMANN, J., and MORGENSTERN, O. (1947), *Theory of Games and Economic Behaviour*, 2nd edn, Princeton.

11 W. S. Vickrey

Risk, Utility and Social Policy

W. S. Vickrey, 'Risk, utility and social policy', *Social Research*, 1961, Summer.

Utility is the technical term that economists have settled on to designate the degree to which individuals attain the goals they are presumably pursuing when they choose among alternative courses of action. Originally conceived of as rather closely approaching a measure of subjective satisfaction or pleasure, it has in the hands of many modern authors been almost completely purged of this experiential content, and has come to mean more nearly 'what individuals tend to maximize in making choices', much as in physics a gravitational potential is what a body tends to minimize when allowed to move in a gravitational field.

In addition to differences over the psychic content of the utility concept, there have been more tangible differences, regarding the degree to which it is conceived to be measurable. Bentham advanced a 'felicific calculus' in terms of the intensity, duration, purity, and other qualities of pleasures and pains, strongly implying that if direct measurement in terms of these parameters was not yet an accomplished fact, it was just around the corner. Pareto, however, valiantly wielding Occam's Razor, asserted that if all that can be objectively observed is the choices that individuals do make among alternatives, then it suffices to know when the utility of one state is greater than that of another, and it is operationally meaningless to inquire by how much greater, or whether state B provides an individual with 10 per cent more utility than A, since the objective choice would be the same regardless of the answer. Indeed, to emphasize his objection to the 'cardinally measurable' utility of Bentham, he coined the term *ophélimité* for his version of the concept, and thus became the father of the 'ordinalist' school.

Although the term ophelimity never caught on, the ordinalist view thus introduced did, and it gained ground rapidly until, in 1944, von Neumann and Morgenstern, for purposes of their theory of games, resurrected an idea tracing back to Daniel Bernoulli in 1738. This idea is that for an individual faced with choices involving uncertain outcomes it would be rational to maximize 'moral expectation', defined as a weighted average of the utilities associated with the different possible outcomes resulting from a given choice, the weights being proportional to the probabilities of these outcomes. If utility is thus defined as that of which individuals attempt to maximize the expectation, it becomes 'cardinally' defined 'to within linear transformations'. This means that we can take the utility of two states A and B as calibration points, analogous to defining a temperature scale in terms of the freezing and boiling points of water, and that if $U(A) = 100$ and $U(B) = 200$, the utility of C is determined by finding that probability p such that the individual is just on the margin of indifference between choosing the certainty of C as against an alternative that promises B with probability p and A with probability $1-p$; given such a p, we have $U(C) = 100(1+p)$.

Partly because this resurrection of the Bernoullian theory was associated with the formidable mathematics of the theory of games, partly because of observations of behaviour that seemed incompatible with the assumption that individuals can be considered, even in an average sense, to exhibit the kind of rationality assumed by this theory, and partly for other reasons, acceptance of this form of utility function as relevant to the 'welfare' to be pursued as a social and political policy has been very slow, and many economists have explicitly denied that there is or can be any connection. Professor Baumol has recently joined his voice to those who would deny that an index thus defined in terms of risky choice can have any status as a measure of satisfaction or any role as a predictor of choice in risky situations – thus following the stand that has been taken with varying degrees of vigour by Ellsberg (1954) and Friedman–Savage (1952), among others (Baumol, 1958). The opposite view is represented by casual identification rather than by explicit statement, and it probably would not be fair to impute a definite view to authors on such scanty evidence. Even Sir Dennis Robertson, after having a good look at the von Neumann and Morgenstern baby, now a strapping youth of seventeen years, rather thinks that it is not the sort of child he wants to adopt as his own (1954). The present article is an attempt to provide a basis for according somewhat greater status to this index, even to the extent of making it a major pillar of normative economics.

Methods for cardinal measurement of utility

On taking a first look at the risk-utility function of the theory of games, which we shall call U_G, many were inclined to identify it without further ado with the introspectively and intuitively postulated 'utility', 'happiness', or 'joy' that had been discussed, but never effectively measured, by Bentham, Jevons, Marshall, and others. Baumol, however, appears to place U_G in a category intermediate between the purely ordinal ophelimity of Pareto, U_P, and the conceptually cardinal utility or happiness, U_B, that Bentham was seeking to maximize in terms of its algebraic sum over the entire population. There have of course been other attempts at an operational definition of utility, and it is perhaps worthwhile for completeness to mention here the Fisher-Frisch cardinal utility U_F, derived from the assumption that it is possible to find a pair of commodities or commodity groups such that it can be asserted on *a priori* grounds that the marginal utility of one does not depend on the quantity of the other (1932). There is also the individual-utility measure U_R, which can be considered to be contained in the Rothenberg (ordinal) social-utility or welfare function $W = f(U_{R1}, U_{R2}, \ldots U_{Rn})$, where W can be thought of as that function of individual utilities which authorities attempt to maximize in making their policy decisions, much in the same sense in which U_P can be defined as that which the individual attempts to maximize in making his personal decisions (Rothenberg, 1953). Further operational variants of the utility concept will be encountered as we proceed.

The identification of the theory-of-games utility, U_G, with 'old-fashioned "cardinal" joy,' U_B is characterized by Baumol as naïve, in that it assumes that the marginal utility of successive increments in the probability of winning a specified prize is constant. In terms of the U_G utility index this marginal utility is of course constant, as a logical consequence of the definition; in terms of U_B it is perhaps a little difficult to see directly why it should be, yet in certain circumstances, a bridge can be constructed indicating a close similarity, if not identity, between U_G and U_B.

To be sure, there are some interpretations of U_B that provide no foundations for this bridge. If we consider U_B to be identical with a hypothetical U_R that would serve, in Rothenberg's scheme, to rationalize the observed actions of a specific parliament, there may be no basis for a bridge. But surely Bentham was trying to indicate to Parliament how it should act, rather than merely to provide a rationale in terms of which the way a parliament is observed to act can be explained, so we may dismiss U_R as irrelevant. Similarly, there is grave doubt as to whether the observed preference patterns are such as to be compatible with an 'independence of utilities' function U_F, let alone whether, if such a pattern were to be found, the proposition of utility independence could be maintained *a priori*. While it is true that many of the Benthamite writings are couched in terms that could be taken to imply independently additive joys, it is surely in the spirit of his line that once interdependence is recognized at all, it should be admitted generally.

Indeed, it might well be considered that it is the approach of the psychophysicists that lies in the most direct line of descent from Bentham, via Jevons and Marshall, in that direct appeal is made to the judgement of the subjects. Experimenters have had a certain degree of success in producing reasonably uniform results by simply asking a naïve subject naïve questions. However, an attempt to import these techniques into economics for the construction of utility functions raises questions that may seriously impair the validity of the techniques.

In the threshold-of-discrimination techniques the experimenter achieves a certain degree of objectivity by ascertaining at various levels of the stimulus just what difference in the magnitude of two similar stimuli will enable the subject to discern, with say 90 per cent accuracy, which of the two is the greater. Even in the best of experimental conditions the method has its pitfalls, in that wide variations in the circumstances surrounding the presentation of the stimuli may affect the results; for example, different 'JNDs' (just noticeable differences) may be generated according to whether the subject is lifting two weights from the table in front of him or must go to the other end of the room in order to lift the second.

In the measurement of utility it is difficult to imagine, even in principle, how such an experiment could be carried out in a meaningful way. It is not feasible, in practice, actually to cause the subject to experience successively two alternative levels of income. Even if this were feasible, the results would be difficult to interpret, since, as Boulding so well emphasizes, much of the joy we obtain from an event occurs not while the event is taking place but from anticipation and planning, on the one hand, and recollection (and retelling!) on the other. We are therefore forced to fall back on hypothetical choice based on description. To be sure, the choice may be motivated by arranging that upon the occurrence of some random event with a small but positive probability, the choice will be converted by the experimenter to a real one; but the choice itself is still necessarily made on the basis of description. Everything then depends on the terms of the description, and on how close the alternatives are to each other in directions other than in line with the origin.

If the only difference between two alternatives is expressed as the difference between two sums of money, discrimination is likely to be nearly perfect, except for subjects who really do not understand the questions in the first place, and hence yield no utility measure. It is no use asking about preferences between A, Y and A, Y' where A is an apartment on 12th Street and Y and Y' are two sums of money to be spent on groceries: the larger sum of money will be preferred with near certainty, no matter how small the differential. On the other hand, if we consider another similar apartment B, also on 12th Street, with sums Z and Z' to be spent on groceries, and ascertain for what Z the combination B, Z will be chosen 90 per cent of the time over A, Y, and for what Z' the combination A, Y will be preferred to B, Z' 90 per cent of the time, we may say that $U_J(B, Z) - U_J(A, Y) = U_J(A, Y) - U_J(B, Z') = 1$ JND. But if we now consider what sums W and W' in combination with C, an apartment on 136th Street, will result in A, Y being chosen rather than C, W and C, W' with 90 and 10 per cent probability, respectively, we are likely to find that $W - W'$ considerably exceeds $Z - Z'$, and the hypothesis that $U_J(C, W) = U_J(B, Z)$ and $U_J(C, W') = U_J(C, W')$ becomes untenable.

Perhaps considerably closer to Bentham's intent would be a technique analogous to that in which the subject is asked to adjust sound stimulus A until it is 'twice as loud' as sound stimulus B. In the utility case the corresponding question 'what income would make you twice as happy as you are now?' might evoke an embarassingly large number of responses to the effect that no mere increment of income could accomplish this; on the other hand, to ask 'what income would make you 10 per cent better off' might evoke an even larger number of responses asking 'what do you mean, "10 per cent better off"?' Nevertheless, it is probably time that economists took such possible approaches a little more seriously; psychophysicists using comparable techniques have obtained results that are at least reasonably self-consistent, in spite of the ordinalist's characterizing them as essentially meaningless. Somewhat more definite responses might be obtained by asking questions of the form 'what increment to your income would be necessary to increase your happiness by as much as a decrease of $100 would lower it?' While this precise question might result in answers severely polarized by considerations of the frictional cost of changes in either direction in the standard of living, other more complicated questions could in principle be devised that would get over such a hurdle – though probably at considerable cost in terms of the difficulty of getting the question understood by the respondent.

A more pervasive difficulty, which may be impossible to overcome completely, is that the satisfactions associated with levels of income in the neighbourhood of that currently or recently experienced are the most vivid in the mind of the respondent, and that he may therefore tend to exaggerate the gradient of the utility function in the neighbourhood of his actual income, and understate the gradient for more remote regions. On the other hand, as pointed out by Friedman and Savage (1948), there may also be a 'threshold effect', whereby the utility loss or gain associated with small changes in income is overwhelmed by the inherent uncertainties in the relationship between income and utility; or is diminished by the frictions that inhibit small changes in living standards or constrain them to less effective channels; or is so small as to escape conscious consideration. In such cases there may be a systematic tendency to understate the utility differential for a small income change, such as that derived from a successful lottery ticket, as compared with that for a large change, such as would be associated with a winning sweepstakes ticket. At best, what is obtained is an estimate of the function representing the utility that the subject associates at a given point of time with different hypothetical incomes, which is not necessarily the best available estimate of the actual satisfaction that would in fact be obtained. Whether there is any close relationship between such a U_N (obtained by naïve questioning) and a U_G (derived from choices among gambles) is in principle subject to experimental verification; the *a priori* grounds for expecting such a relationship to emerge may seem fairly weak.

Utility functions and social policy

Yet more fundamentally, when the Benthamite utility function is considered in relation to the application intended to be made of it, there may be a closer relation between U_B and U_G than even between U_B and U_N. One may, for example, imagine a situation in which two separate expeditions are being formed to found colonies in Terra Australia Incognita. The leadership of the two expeditions may be considered to be in the hands of older men 'without hope of posterity'. The remainder of each expedition is to be recruited from a population that is homogeneous as to utility function and as to presently evident capabilities. It is from this homogeneous population and its descendants that the eventual population of the colonies will derive, but there is no way of predicting which of the embarking colonists is most likely to fill any particular role after the retirement of the present leadership. The articles of association are to specify in great detail how the national product is to be redistributed via various social schemes, and thus the prospective colonists will have a clear picture of their chance of attaining various levels of income.

In this situation – given a utility function and a relation between the distribution of income, the consequent intensity of economic incentives, and the attainable aggregate national income – the selection of a social policy for the colony can be made with the aim of maximizing the aggregate utility. Profiting from the experience of Roanoke and other experiments with extreme egalitarianism, the policy-makers will presumably introduce some inequality, but probably not so much as would eventuate from a policy of complete individualism. The question is what utility function is appropriate to use for such a purpose?

The test that seems relevant in this case is whether the utility function leads, via application of the maximization-of-aggregate-utility principle, to the adoption of that social policy for the colony-to-be which makes the venture most attractive to the prospective colonists. Indeed, one might attempt to deduce a new utility function, specialized to this purpose, by constructing the indifference map of the colonists among all the varieties of social policy that might be offered, and determining the utility function, U_C, that would rationalize this indifference map. But if this procedure is either too time-consuming or too complex for the impatient leaders of the expeditions, is there not some information they can draw from the utility functions U_G, U_N or U_F, assuming that surveys have already established these functions for the population under consideration.

On examination it appears that the choice confronting the prospective colonists is not so very much different from a choice between alternative gambles in which the prizes are incomes corresponding to the net incomes anticipated for the various roles in the new colonies, while the probabilities of the various prizes are proportional to the number of such anticipated roles in the population. The notion of choosing among gambles in such a way as to maximize expected utility is closely isomorphic with the problem of choosing between two alternative colonies on the basis of the maximum per capita utility, which for colonies of the same aggregate population will be the same as choosing the colony with the largest aggregate utility. There is thus very strong reason to believe that a U_G derived from choices among gambles would correspond very closely to the U_C that would be appropriate for choosing a social-welfare policy for such a colony, if indeed the two would not be indistinguishable. There is thus considerable warrant for identifying the U_G derived from risky choices with the U_B that is to be used as a criterion for the selection of a social policy, at least in the peculiar circumstances of our hypothetical example.

It is possible, to be sure, to claim that attitudes toward pure gambles based on purely random events, such as the drawing of a lottery, may differ substantially from attitudes toward gambles involving one's own prowess, even though there may be no more *a priori* evidence of one's suitability for life in the new world than there is of the way a lottery will turn out. Or there may be some who feel that the element of adventure presented by the possibility of achieving different degrees of eminence is sufficient spice in itself, and does not require the addition of the further element of a wide range of incomes; if they are asked about a lottery under stay-at-home conditions they may feel much more in need of the insertion of a chance element into their otherwise drab lives. This particular difficulty might perhaps be surmounted by imputing a psychic income to each role, in addition to the money income, though to find any objective basis for doing this might prove difficult. But in so far as U_G is assumed to rationalize risky choice in areas of skill and judgement – such as racetrack and pool betting, bridge, or poker – as well as in insurance and lotteries, it should be equally capable of rationalizing the choice between alternative social policies for the colonies.

The intended parallel between the choice of social policy for a new colony by its promoters and the choice of a social policy for an existing social order by a legislature is obvious. There is, however, one important difference: U_C is influenced to the maximum possible extent by whatever preference or aversion for uncertainty *per se* is present in the preference scheme of the individuals concerned, whereas this element is largely absent when policy decisions are limited to changing the income distribution without disturbing the ranking of individuals in a rigidly stratified and immobile society, as when the only question is one of setting income-tax rates; changes in policy will then have little or no effect on the range of uncertainty of individual income expectations. The importance of this divergence between a policy based on U_C and a policy appropriate to a given situation will depend on the degree of social mobility prevailing: in effect the colonial example presented was at the extreme of social mobility, for there was explicitly assumed to be no evidence available at the moment of decision as to where the individual would land in the eventual distribution of incomes. Thus the use of U_C as a standard for social policy would be somewhat more appropriate in a highly mobile society, such as that of the

United States, than in a more rigidly stratified society like that of India.

In one respect, however, U_G is essentially inadequate in guiding social-welfare policy, whether of a prospective colony or of an existing and stable social order: it takes no explicit account of external economies and diseconomies of income dispersion, such as are evidenced by the attention accorded Buckingham Palace and Hollywood. This factor of vicarious enjoyment or entertainment, to the extent that it is conceded to be legitimate rather than one to be dismissed as an impure or unworthy sort of satisfaction, would appear to call for an income distribution slightly more dispersed in the upper ranges and less so in the lower ranges than would otherwise be indicated. But then none of the utility functions that have as arguments only the income or other personal circumstances of the individual would take this factor into account, whereas U_C in principle would, as would probably U_B.

Conclusions

Where does all this leave us? I cannot help feeling that of all the utility functions proposed, U_G is the only one that holds out any strong hope for reasonably reliable measurement, though even here the reliability to be expected leaves much to be desired. With U_G it is at least possible, though difficult, to motivate serious answers by promising to turn a hypothetical choice into a real one upon the occurrence of some random event with a suitable positive (but not necessarily measurable) probability. How far the investigator could or should go, pragmatically or ethically, in misrepresenting this probability to the subject, or in promising more than could or would be carried out in the event of a specified occurrence, is a question that may be crucial in deciding whether or not adequate motivation can be provided in this way at a cost that will be within the limits set by the value of the derived information.

The experiment, to be meaningful, would have to be on a full scale covering a significant range of lifetime incomes. Experiments of the Mosteller-Nogee type (1951), carried on at full 'strength' (that is, 100 per cent execution of choices) but on a very limited scale in terms of income range, carry little weight for major policy decisions on income distribution, and must be regarded as merely pilot studies. For example, the fact that one group of subjects showed increasing marginal utility over the range covered by the experiment can, I think, be considered a merely local phenomenon. The behaviour of a group of college students, showing significantly declining marginal utility, is in a sense more disturbing: the number whose behaviour was consistent with the nearly linear utility one would expect over the narrow range of the experiment was very small. Such results cast doubt on the extent to which the procedure induces choice in accordance with perceived orthodoxy or perhaps with an extreme short-run point of view. This is the more so in that the experiment in question involved possible losses of only $0·05 per choice, or $1 per session, as compared to gains of $10 in some instances. For a subject in an extremely illiquid position it is much easier to rationalize sharply increasing short-run utility in terms of a crucial opportunity for using $10 that will be missed if not availed of immediately than it is to rationalize a sharply declining utility in the face of the evident possibility of setting the $10 aside until a good use can be found for it.

In any case, I think it would be feasible to carry out a sufficiently persuasive inquiry along U_G lines. If the results were to persist in showing an increasing marginal utility I would be induced to conclude that my own introspectively evaluated utility function differs fundamentally from that of the bulk of my fellows, and that my egalitarian predilections are a personal prejudice that is insufficiently generally held to warrant the espousal of a corresponding policy as an acceptable social choice. I might indeed look hard for loopholes before retreating in such fashion, but, given the facts, I think I could be forced to retreat eventually, rather than merely declaring my neutrality with an invocation of 'de gustibus non disputandum est' or a sour-grapes comment that I really had something else in mind all the time.

Of course all of this says nothing about the vexing matter of interpersonal comparisons. The colonization example evades this issue by its assumption of identical tastes and complete long-run mobility. But the problem of interpersonal comparisons, together with the operationally insignificant aspects of a related problem – that is, whether there is any relation whatever between U_G, on the one hand, or any other U that economists may play with, and, on the other hand, contentment, joy, happiness, peace of mind, or any other concepts of absolute individual human felicity – had best be left, I think, to theologians and metaphysicians, until such time as someone thinks up a new way of defining them operationally. There are also other intractable problems that economists will be generally glad to leave to others. For example, if A is shown to be a less efficient 'pleasure machine' than B, congenitally and through no fault of his own, should utility be maximized by concentrating income in the hands of B, or should A be compensated for this misfortune by giving him a larger share?

Indeed, justice, like beauty, is often in the eye of the beholder, and if Justice Holmes could declare that criminals should be punished in the same spirit that conscripts are sent into battle, not to mete out justice but to preserve society, then cardinal measurement of utility becomes relevant to social policy only to the extent that the use of this concept contributes to social stability. This in turn comes close to saying that utility is what people who are concerned about utility (by whatever name) think it is. For the present, I consider that U_G has as much cardinality and relevance for purposes of determining social policy as any measure of individual economic welfare we are likely to find.

References

BAUMOL, W. J. (1958), 'The cardinal utility which is ordinal', *econ. J.*, vol. 68, December, pp. 665–72.

ELLSBERG, D. (1954), 'Classical and current notions of measurable utility', *econ. J.*, vol. 64, September, pp. 528–56.

FRIEDMAN, M., and SAVAGE, L. J. (1948), 'The utility analysis of choices involving risk', *J. polit. Econ.*, vol. 56, pp. 279–304.

FRIEDMAN, M., and SAVAGE, L. J. (1952), 'The expected utility hypothesis and measurement of utility', *J. polit. Econ.*, vol. 60, December, pp. 463–74.

FRISCH, R. (1932), 'New methods of measuring marginal utility', in *Beitrage sur Ökonomische Theorie*, Tübingen.

MOSTELLER, F., and NOGEE, P. (1951), 'An experimental measurement of utility', *J. polit. Econ.*, vol. 59, pp. 371–404.

ROBERTSON, D. H. (1954), 'Utility and all what?', *econ. J.*, vol. 64, December, pp. 665–78.

ROTHENBERG, J. (1953), 'Conditions for a social welfare function', *J. polit. Econ.*, vol. 61, pp. 389–405.

12 P. K. Pattanaik

Risk, Impersonality and the Social Welfare Function

P. K. Pattanaik, 'Risk, impersonality and the social welfare function', *Journal of Political Economy*, 1968, December.

In the recent literature on welfare economics it has been held by some writers (for example, Arrow, 1964, pp. 9–10, and Friedman and Savage, 1948, p. 283, note 11) that individual preferences among risky prospects have little or no relevance for constructing a pattern of social preferences for non-risky social states. In contrast, other writers have expressed the opinion that not only are individual preferences among risky prospects relevant, but also they have a certain logical connection with the intuitive concept of social welfare. The purpose of this note is to examine some of these formulations, to clarify the basic concepts involved, and to assess their bearing on the Arrowian problem of constructing a social ordering by aggregating the individual preferences. The formulations examined are those of Harsanyi (1953, 1955)[1] and Vickrey (1960). Section 1 gives the main propositions advanced by these writers, section 2 analyses their ethical bases, and section 3 suggests how some of Harsanyi's concepts can be used to deal with Arrow's problem. Finally in section 4 we indicate some of the difficulties likely to be met in our attempt to use Harsanyi's concepts for deriving a social welfare function of the Arrow type.

1

The intuitive notion of a relation between 'fairness' and a certain type of risk is very old. If a cake is to be divided between two persons, it has usually been considered 'fair' if one of the persons, say

---

1. Harsanyi (1955) has two models. One of them is different from that in Harsanyi (1953). For convenience this will be called model A. The other is identical with that in Harsanyi (1953). This will be called model B. For a brief statement of the result established by model B, see section 3 below.

A, divides it into two parts and the other person, B, chooses whichever part he likes (see Steinhaus, 1948). Thus, A has to divide the cake without knowing which part he will get. Something similar to this underlies the formulations of Vickrey and Harsanyi. Vickrey, for example, considers a prospective immigrant weighing the relative attractiveness of different communities into which he can immigrate. The preference pattern of all individuals in all communities is exactly similar to that of the immigrant. Individuals, however, differ in talents (although each community enjoys the same distribution of talents), and this produces inequality in the distribution of income within each community. The immigrant is uncertain of the position that he can occupy in the various communities. Under these conditions, 'he may, . . ., make his decisions on the basis of maximizing his expected utility, the alternative utilities in question being those of the various members of a given community. . . . If we identify the social welfare with the attractiveness of the various communities to this prospective immigrant, we see that the social welfare function takes the form of a weighted sum of the individual utilities. If the immigrant is completely ignorant as to what role he will fill in the new community and weights the roles of all individuals equally, we get the Benthamite summation of individual utilities with the utilities being Bernoullian' (Vickrey, 1960, pp. 524–5). Let the social state, represented by the ith community having n individuals, be S_i. Let X_{ij} be the social position of the jth individual in S_i. The prospective immigrant is thus evaluating the uncertain prospects S_i composed of the positions X_{ij} $(j = 1,...,n)$, all having equal probability. If the individual preferences are assumed to satisfy the von Neumann–Morgenstern axioms, the utility W_i of the social state S_i for this immigrant (this utility is identified with social welfare) will be

$$W_i = \frac{1}{n} \sum_{j=1}^{n} U(X_{ij}),$$

where $U(X_{ij})$ refers to the immigrant's evaluation of X_{ij}. Since all the individuals involved (including the prospective immigrant) are assumed to have exactly the same preference patterns,[2]

2. As will be seen below, it is necessary to interpret 'preference patterns' to include attitude toward risk.

$$W_t = \frac{1}{n} \sum_{j=1}^{n} U_j(X_{ij}),$$

where $U_j(X_{ij})$ refers to the jth individual's evaluation of his position in the social state S_i. In other words, except for a multiplicative constant, social welfare is equal to the sum of the individual utilities.

But, of course, the assumption of identical preference patterns is drastic and rules out all the complications which arise in connection with interpersonal comparisons of utility. Any genuine attempt at evaluating social welfare must take into account the differences in preference patterns of individuals. And it is precisely here that Harsanyi's model B differs from that of Vickrey. Harsanyi does not make the restrictive assumption of identical preferences. Still, Harsanyi's social welfare function[3] gives social welfare as a weighted sum of what he calls[4] the individual utilities. Just as social welfare is identified in Vickrey with the evaluation of the prospective immigrant, it is identified in Harsanyi with the individual's evaluation of the social state under certain conditions. Each social state facing the evaluating individual is assumed to be an uncertain prospect composed of equal chances of the individual's being each of the other individuals in their respective positions. To make the concept more precise, let the social alternative S_i be a set of n positions X_{ij} $(j = 1, 2,..., n)$ corresponding to the n individuals in the society. Let (X_{ij}, Y_j) refer to the sure prospect of being the jth individual in the objective position X_{ij}. The expression Y_j may be interpreted as the aggregate of subjective features of the jth individual. Social welfare of S_i is identified with the individual's evaluation of the risky prospect composed of the alternatives (X_{i1}, Y_1), (X_{i2}, Y_2),..., (X_{in}, Y_n), all the alternatives having equal probability. If it is now assumed that individual preferences among alternatives of the type (X_{ij}, Y_j) satisfy the Marschak axioms (Marschak, 1950), it follows that the individual's evaluation of the uncertain prospect S_i will be equal to the arithmetic mean of $U(X_{ij}, Y_j)$ $(j = 1, 2,..., n)$, where

3. The phrase 'social welfare function' as used by Harsanyi refers to 'preferences based on a given individual's value judgements concerning "social welfare"' (Harsanyi, 1955, p. 310, note 4). This point will be further discussed below.
4. The meaning of this qualifying phrase will be clarified later.

$U(X_{ij}, Y_j)$ indicates the utility attached by the *evaluating individual* to (X_{ij}, Y_j). This, Harsanyi thinks, is the same as saying that the social welfare of a particular social state is the arithmetic mean of the utilities of different individuals in that state, provided the individual has some 'objective criterion for comparing his fellows' utilities with one another and with his own.' As a corollary, it follows that if such an objective criterion were available, social welfare evaluation arrived at by each individual would be the same.

In the next two sections we attempt to clarify the ethical basis of this formulation and to show that while the ethical foundation is appealing, one *cannot* derive from it the conclusion that social welfare is the arithmetic mean of the individual utilities, or that, given full factual information about other people's utility, the process outlined above gives us social welfare as a magnitude which will be the same irrespective of whoever happens to be the evaluator. It will also be seen that this remark does not apply to Vickrey's model.

2

A point that has caused some misunderstanding is the nature of the uncertain prospects involved in Harsanyi's model *B*. As pointed out above, the elements of the uncertain prospect S_i are not X_{i1}, X_{i2},..., X_{in}, but (X_{i1}, Y_1), (X_{i2}, Y_2),...,(X_{in}, Y_n), that is, the alternatives involved comprise not only the objective positions but also the subjective features of the respective individuals. This seems to have created some confusion. Rothenberg (1961, pp. 268–69), for example, writes:

Why should he *become* some other concrete individual in order to experience one position or another? No one individual is uniquely suited to any one social niche. . . . If the evaluator must *become* others, then the procedure is purely and simply one in which the choice criterion is the average of everybody's pay off in some particular social state. There is no uncertainty about anybody's position – certainly not the evaluator's. But if there is no uncertainty, then the evaluator's choice has nothing to do with maximization of *his* utility. So the assumption of von Neumann–Morgenstern rationality does not suffice to determine his choice.

This criticism involves two propositions: (1) If the individuals are not 'uniquely suited' to their respective positions, it is not necessary for any individual to undergo a transformation of personality so as to experience another individual's position. (2) If, on the other hand, we assume that the different individuals are 'uniquely suited' to their respective positions so that a transformation of personality is necessary for the individual to experience another individual's position, there is no uncertainty and therefore the question of maximizing utility does not arise. But what is meant by an individual's being 'uniquely suited' to his position? The only reasonable meaning one can assign to it is that it is inconceivable that a particular individual should occupy the position of another individual while remaining himself. But this is obviously absurd. We are therefore obliged to fall back on the first proposition. And the first proposition is true. If the individuals can be conceived to occupy a position different from what they are occupying now while retaining their own identity, it is certainly not necessary for them to undergo a transformation of personality to experience it. But Harsanyi's purpose is *not* merely to put several *objective* positions as the uncertain outcomes before the evaluating individual. In fact, the entire criticism seems to be based on a misunderstanding of the elements involved in the uncertain prospects and a failure to appreciate their full significance. The elements are not X_{i1}, $X_{i2},...,X_{in}$, but (X_{i1},Y_1), $(X_{i2},Y_2),...,(X_{in},Y_n)$. Since being a particular individual means possessing the features of his personality, it is clear that the procedure implies putting the subjective characteristics of an individual on the same basis as the more 'objective' items in his possession.[5] Once we consider the possession of an individual to comprise not only his 'objective' position but also his subjective features, it becomes self-evident why a transformation of personality is required so as to experience another individual's possessions (as defined above). Nor is this requirement of the imaginative perception of utility that can be realized in the other man's position with the other man's personality 'gratuitous and destructive of the sense of the procedure,' as Rothenberg would like us to believe. On the contrary, it serves a definite purpose and increases the ethical appeal of the formulation. This we will discuss later, but first it is necessary to analyse the role of risk in this type of model.

5. Cf. Arrow (1964, p. 115) for an interesting discussion of what he calls 'extended sympathy', meaning thereby a comparison between alternatives of the type (X_{ij},Y_j).

Risk here is intimately linked to the concept of impersonality or objectivity, which is explicitly postulated in Harsanyi's discussion of the social welfare function and which seems to be implicit in Vickrey's formulation. In Harsanyi particularly, the social welfare function is visualized as a process of second order evaluation of social alternatives by the individual, its crucial characteristic being 'impersonality' or 'impartiality'. The first-order evaluation expresses the 'subjective preferences' of the evaluating individual, being based on the utility of that *one* individual only, while the second-order evaluation expresses the 'ethical preferences,' being based on a 'fair compromise' of the utilities of *all* individuals:

Even if both an individual's social welfare function and his utility function in a sense express his own individual preferences, they must express preferences of a different sort: the former must express what this individual prefers (or rather would prefer) on the basis of impersonal social considerations alone, and the latter must express what he actually prefers, whether on the basis of his personal interests or on any other basis. The former may be called his 'ethical' preference, the latter his 'subjective' preferences [Harsanyi, 1955, p. 315].[6]

Model *B* of Harsanyi is an attempt to provide a precise meaning of this impersonality. Harsanyi's reasoning seems to be that the subjective preferences of the individual have no moral force at all (and therefore cannot be elevated to the height of a social welfare function), since they may be based on judgements like 'Slavery is good, I being a slave-owner'. It is only when the individual can say, 'Slavery is good, even though I do not know whether I am going to be a slave or a slave-owner', that this statement acquires a moral sanctity. This is closely similar to the school of thought which views moral judgements as basically universal prescriptive judgements. It has been held, for example, that the moral judgement, 'You ought not to be rude to your friends', is ultimately backed by a universal prescriptive judgement, 'No one ought to be rude to one's friends.'[7] Similarly, my statement that slavery is good becomes a moral judgement only when it is universalizable – only if I can say it

6. This is reminiscent of Kant's distinction between pragmatic and moral imperatives.

7. Cf. Hare (1961) for a detailed exposition of this view regarding the universalizability of ethical judgements.

irrespective of my position. Harsanyi's position, however, differs somewhat from this, for in Harsanyi the statement, 'Slavery is good', becomes a moral judgement, not when I can say it irrespective of my position, but when I say it even though I do not know what my position is going to be or, to be more precise, even though I know that there is an equal chance of my being a slave or a slave-owner.[8] Thus risk and universalizability together give us Harsanyi's concept of impersonality, which he holds to be the defining feature of the social welfare function of the individual.

But it can further be asked why extended sympathy should have been brought in. Is it not enough for the evaluating individual to be presented with an uncertain prospect where the elements are only the objective positions X_{i1}, Xi_2,..., X_{in}? Some such question seems to be implied in the passage quoted from Rothenberg above. But there seem to be good reasons why it is not enough to take uncertain prospects having X_{i1}, X_{i2}, and so on, for their elements. It can be seen that, without sympathetic identification or some such assumption, the analysis may lead to some odd results. Take, for example, a situation where individual A (who hates oranges but likes peaches) gets ten peaches and B (who in turn hates peaches and loves oranges) gets ten oranges. If A were to evaluate the positions in terms of his own subjective preferences, his social welfare function may prescribe that B (who hates peaches) should get some peaches and he himself should get some oranges!

But what is more important, this formulation does not correspond to our idea of justice as much as does Harsanyi's. For we would surely not call somebody a good judge if in deciding cases he takes into account only the facts of the objective situation and does not consider the subjective states of the individuals by means of some kind of sympathetic identification. Similarly, an evaluation which completely ignores other people's attitudes could hardly be called a

8. One is reminded of Rawls (1958), who elaborates the concept of justice as fairness by visualizing a group of rational egoists deliberating as to the rules of decision-making in the case of conflicts, when they are uncertain about the relation in which they will stand to others in the conflicts that are likely to occur in the future. In particular, compare the following remark of Rawls (1958, pp. 172–3): 'Having a morality is analogous to having made a firm commitment in advance; for one must acknowledge the principles of morality even when to one's disadvantage.'

social welfare function. It is interesting to note the similarity between Harsanyi's concept of impersonality in this respect and Rawls's concept of a 'competent judge': 'A competent judge . . . must not consider his own *de facto* preferences as the necessarily valid measure of the actual worth of those interests which come before him, but that he be both able and anxious to determine, by imaginative appreciation, what those interests mean to persons who share them, and to consider them accordingly' (Rawls, 1951, p. 179).[9]

One last question: Is such comparison possible? This raises a point of logic and a point of fact. Without entering into any philosophical depth, it may be remarked that logically there does not seem to be any reason why the individual cannot choose between the alternatives (X_{i1}, Y_1) and (X_{i2}, Y_2). Although I as an individual possess a bundle of characteristics and am identified by (some or all of) them, there is no logical reason why I should not be able to conceive of myself as possessing another such bundle of consistent subjective characteristics. And if I can do this, there is no logical reason why I cannot choose and compare alternatives of the type (X_{ij}, Y_j). As regards the point of fact, that such comparisons are fairly widespread is evidenced by our daily experience when we frequently make comments such as, 'I would rather be myself in my humble position than be Mr X for all his wealth.'[10]

3

Harsanyi's concept of ethical preference is a persuasive one, but, as will be argued in this section, it does not in itself solve Arrow's problem of constructing a social ordering by aggregating individual preferences. It should be noted that the term 'social preference' is used by Harsanyi in a sense different from Arrow's. Harsanyi is concerned with the social welfare function in the sense of some given individual's evaluation of social welfare, whereas Arrow's social welfare function (Arrow, 1964, pp. 23–4) refers to the process by which a social ordering of the alternatives is arrived at on the basis of individual orderings. In other words, Harsanyi (like Bergson,

9. This imaginative appreciation, however, is only one of the features of Rawls's competent judge.

10. For an interesting example of such extended sympathy, see the inscription quoted by Arrow (1964, p. 14).

1938, 1948) explicates the notion of social welfare through the welfare judgements of individuals. There can therefore be as many social welfare functions as there are individuals in the community. The problem of aggregating these *individual* social welfare functions into a *social* social welfare function has not been undertaken by Harsanyi. In fact, this further problem of aggregation would be superfluous if Harsanyi's conclusions were correct. For Harsanyi thinks that his model B gives social welfare as an arithmetic mean of individual utilities, and if full factual information were available to the evaluating individual about other people's utility, this would be the same for each individual.

The conclusion that the social welfare indexes constructed in Harsanyi fashion will be the same for different individuals implies at least that the ethical orderings (that is, the orderings corresponding to ethical preferences) will be identical for all individuals. This conclusion, however, cannot be sustained: even under 'ideal conditions' the ethical ordering will not necessarily be the same, for the simple reason that the risk attitudes of different individuals will, in general, be different, and that the von Neumann–Morgenstern utility indexes are affected by attitudes to risk. As an example, consider a society of two individuals indicated by the subscripts 1 and 2. Let the social states under consideration be S_1 and S_2. Let $\bar{U}_k(X_{ij}, Y_j)$ indicate the *introspective* utility of the kth individual from (X_{ij}, Y_j), and let $U_k(X_{ij}, Y_j)$ indicate the von Neumann–Morgenstern utility index for (X_{ij}, Y_j) with respect to the kth individual. Now consider the introspective utilities from the basic alternatives (X_{11}, Y_1), (X_{12}, Y_2), (X_{21}, Y_1) and (X_{22}, Y_2). These will be identical for the two individuals. There would be no meaning in distinguishing, for example, between $\bar{U}_1(X_{11}, Y_1)$ and $\bar{U}_2(X_{11}, Y_1)$. All possible grounds of distinction are irrelevant because of the presence of Y_1 (standing for the subjective features of individual 1) in the alternatives. The introspective utility of individual 2 from (X_{11}, Y_1) must be the same as that of individual 1 since, to experience the alternative (X_{11}, Y_1) at all, individual 2 has to transform himself through imagination into individual 1. The subscripts of $\bar{U}$ are therefore superfluous, and we can simply write $\bar{U}(X_{ij}, Y_j)$. But from this it does not follow that the preference orderings (among all the prospects, risky as well as certain) will be the same for both individuals. Let us suppose that $\bar{U}(X_{11}, Y_1) = \bar{U}(X_{12}, Y_2) = \bar{U}'$. Let $\bar{U}(X_{21}, Y_1)$ be very much higher than $\bar{U}'$ and $\bar{U}(X_{22}, Y_2)$ be very much lower than $\bar{U}'$. Now present the social states S_1 and S_2 before each individual in the Harsanyi fashion. Will the ordering of the two individuals between the uncertain prospects S_1 and S_2 be the same? Not necessarily. For the ordering of each individual will depend not only on his introspective utilities from the basic alternatives involved but also on his risk attitude. Although the introspective utilities from the basic alternatives are identical for both individuals, their risk attitudes, in general, will be different. Suppose one of the individuals is a risk-lover and the other is a risk-averter. It is likely that the risk-lover will prefer S_2 to S_1 and the risk-averter will prefer S_1 to S_2. Thus, even though the introspective utilities (and, therefore, the orderings) of the two individuals are identical for the basic (certain) alternatives, their orderings of the uncertain prospects will differ if their risk attitudes are different. Therefore, if the choices of the individuals can be rationalized at all in terms of von Neumann–Morgenstern utility indexes, it can be done only by assigning to them different sets of indexes implying different orderings of the prospects.[11] This stricture, however, does not apply to Vickrey's result. For Vickrey's immigrant by assumption has a preference pattern (which presumably includes risk attitudes) exactly the same as that of any other individual involved. In Vickrey's model, therefore, social welfare evaluations would be the same for all individuals (in the sense explained above), and there would be no problem of aggregation. But the very problem of group preference loses most of its significance if we assume all the individuals to have identical preferences.

Once we allow differences in risk attitudes, ethical preferences (identified with the individual social welfare evaluations) no longer remain the same for all individuals even if we introduce sympathetic

11. The ethical preference index of the kth individual for S_i will, indeed, be

$$W_{ik} = \frac{1}{n} \sum_{j=1}^{n} U_k(X_{ij}, Y_j).$$

But, as is clear from what has been said above, this is quite different from saying that

$$W_{ik} = \frac{1}{n} \sum_{j=1}^{n} U_j(X_{ij}, Y_j).$$

identification as in Harsanyi, and Arrow's problem crops up again. How to aggregate these individual social welfare functions so as to get a social social welfare function?[12] Harsanyi's formulation of ethical preferences in itself does not provide a solution. But as noted above, there is an alternative model (which we call model A) in Harsanyi's paper. By combining the result of model A with that of model B, it seems possible to utilize the highly appealing concept of ethical preferences to derive the social preferences in Arrow's sense. Model A is based on the following postulates: (1) social preferences satisfy the Marschak axioms of expected utility, (2) individual preferences also satisfy the same axioms, and (3) if two prospects P and Q are indifferent from the standpoint of every individual, they are also indifferent from the social standpoint. On the basis of these postulates, the conclusion is deduced that the social welfare function is of the form

$$W = \sum_{j=1}^{n} a_j U_j,$$

where U_j refers to the utility of the jth individual and a_j to the weight to be attached to a unit change in the jth individual's utility. With full factual information about different persons' utilities with complete individualistic ethics, we get

$$W = \sum_{j=1}^{n} U_j.$$

This is an interesting result in view of the fact that the ethical judgement embodied in postulate (3) is a weak one and is likely to be generally acceptable. It should be noted, however, that the individual preferences and social preferences referred to in the postulates both refer to individual evaluations, although of a different order; they correspond to the subjective preferences and ethical preferences, respectively. What we want to suggest here is that the individual preferences in postulate (2) should be interpreted as ethical preferences and the social preferences referred to in postulate (1) should be interpreted in Arrow's sense. Thus, social preferences of

12. As we have seen earlier, Harsanyi's use of the term 'social welfare function' differs from that of Arrow. What we call the 'social social welfare function' refers to Arrow's social welfare function, while the 'individual social welfare function' refers to Harsanyi's use of the term.

Arrow are to be derived by aggregating ethical preferences of individuals and not their subjective preferences. It will be seen below that this interpretation has an inherent attractiveness due to the persuasive quality of the concept of ethical preference.

There are thus three distinct concepts: (1) subjective preferences of the individuals, (2) ethical preferences of the individuals (that is, Harsanyi's social preferences), and (3) Arrow's social preferences. To avoid confusion, we shall henceforth use the term 'ethical preference' to indicate Harsanyi's social preferences and reserve the term 'social preference' for the concept used by Arrow. Three different problems of derivation are particularly interesting:

(a) Subjective preferences → ethical preferences.
(b) Subjective preferences → social preferences.
(c) Ethical preferences → social preferences.

Derivation (a) corresponds to Harsanyi's Model B. Derivation (b) corresponds to Arrow's method of deriving the social preferences. Derivation (c) is the one advocated here. The hierarchy of preferences under the interpretation suggested here is schematically represented in Figure 1. Harsanyi's formulation confines itself to Stages 1 and 2 and never undertakes the aggregation of Stage 3 (presumably because it would not be necessary under his conclusions, which, however, are based on very strong assumptions, as we have seen earlier). Arrow's analysis passes directly from individual values to social preferences, thus omitting the intermediate step of deriving ethical preferences. The interpretation suggested here comprises all three stages.

In dealing with Arrow's problem, we have the choice of taking either the subjective preferences or the ethical preferences as arguments of the social welfare function. It would, however, seem more reasonable to base social evaluation on the balanced and unegoistic evaluations of individuals rather than on the subjective preferences which may reflect the extreme egoism of selfish individuals. This is not to say that we should reject the procedure of basing social preferences on individual preferences. All that is maintained is that individual preferences may be at different levels of objectivity and that it seems more reasonable to base social preferences on a higher-order individual evaluation – ethical preferences – rather than on a

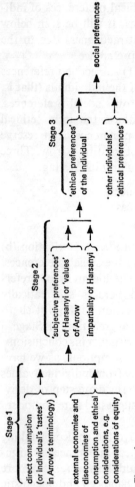

Figure 1

Stage 1

direct consumption
(or individual's 'tastes'
in Arrow's terminology)

external economies and
diseconomies of
consumption and ethical
considerations, e.g.
considerations of equity

Stage 2

'subjective preferences'
of Harsanyi or 'values'
of Arrow

impartiality of Harsanyi

Stage 3

'ethical preferences'
of the individual

'other individuals'
'ethical preferences'

social preferences

lower-order evaluation – subjective preferences. Unless some such procedure is adopted, the individual interests of the egoistic individuals will have too great a weight in a cardinal social welfare

Table 1

Social states	Shares of individuals in terms of units of X			Utilities			Sum of utilities	Social choice
	A	B	C	A	B	C		
S_1	80	10	10	0	0	0	0	
S_2	$33\frac{1}{3}$	$33\frac{1}{3}$	$33\frac{1}{3}$	100	50	80	230	
S_3	40	35	25	80	60	50	190	
S_4	15	50	35	50	100	100	250	S_4

function, and the more altruistic individuals are likely to be penalized precisely because of their altruism. The following example will illustrate the point. Let A, B, and C be the three individuals in the society, let S_1, S_2, S_3, and S_4 be four social states, and let there be a single commodity X. The individual preferences are represented by utility indexes, the best and the worst alternatives for each individual being given the values 100 and 0, respectively,[13] for that individual. Table 1 summarizes the choice situation. The social state selected is S_4. But in S_4, A gets only fifteen units. As can be seen from the example, B and C are the more egoistic individuals and A is more altruistic. Had A been egoistic like B and C and given the lowest valuation to S_4, some other alternative might have been chosen. But thanks to the altruism of A, he ends up with only fifteen units of X. It is, of course, possible to fix up (by additional value judgements) what relative social weight a unit change in the utility of different individuals should have in the social preference. But such value judgements are extremely difficult to make, and a much more palatable procedure would be to take the ethical preferences of all individuals, which are more or less on the same level of objectivity, and to aggregate them into social preferences.

13. These indexes are assumed to reflect *introspective* utilities corresponding to subjective preferences of the individuals. It is also assumed that the scales have been standardized so as to make interpersonal comparisons possible. The question as to how we could arrive at such indexes need not concern us here.

4

So far it has been taken for granted that the von Neumann–Morgenstern index for ethical preferences exists and that the use of this index for deriving social preferences is justified. We have now to examine some of the difficulties likely to be faced in these respects. These difficulties are broadly of two types. First, individual preferences, particularly in the context of social choice, may not satisfy the von Neumann–Morgenstern or Marschak axioms, and in that case we may not be able to construct such an index at all. Second, the use of such an index (granting that it exists) in the social welfare function has been held to be illegitimate. The former question is entirely of an empirical nature, while the latter involves value judgements and is more difficult to decide.

The limitations of the axioms of the expected utility hypothesis have been dealt with extensively in the literature.[14] What needs to be particularly mentioned here is that these difficulties are likely to be enhanced in the context of social choice, especially if the alternatives involved are of the Harsanyi type. Even if we take it for granted that they will be satisfied by subjective preferences, it is by no means sure that ethical preferences will also satisfy them. In particular, further difficulties are likely to arise in connection with the axiom of complete pre-ordering and that of 'reduction of compound lottery'.[15] According to the axiom of complete pre-ordering, the individual's preference relationship R among all types of prospects satisfies the properties of reflexivity (xRx), connectedness (for all $x \neq y$, xRy or yRx), and transitivity $\big(\text{for all } x, y \text{ and } z, (xRy$ and $yRz) \to xRz\big)$. How likely is it that ethical preferences satisfy the property of transitivity? There seem to be certain difficulties here, inherent in the nature of the alternatives involved. In a stimulating paper, May (1954) cites a number of evidences of 'irrational' or intransitive behaviour and suggests a rationalization of such behaviour. Basically, the thesis is that 'intransitivity is a natural result of the necessity of choosing among alternatives according

14. For a lucid discussion, see Luce and Raiffa (1957).

15. The properties of connectedness and transitivity entailed by complete pre-ordering, constitute axioms (3:A:a) and (3:A:b), respectively, in von Neumann and Morgenstern (1953, p. 26). The rule for reduction of compound lottery con , stitutes their axiom (3:C:b).

to conflicting criteria.' The individual while comparing multi-dimensional objects is faced with a large number of simultaneously relevant critera, and the ranking of different objects on the basis of different criteria will differ. This is held to be responsible for intransitive behaviour in such a context.[16] It is clear that the likelihood of such intransitivity will be greater, the greater the variety of criteria that are employed to judge overall desirability and the more conflicting the rankings according to these criteria. The variety, as well as the conflict, among criteria is likely to be immensely greater when the alternatives to be evaluated comprise not only the objective situations but also the personalities of the respective individuals. For, whereas in the usual case the individual evaluates each objective situation (which, of course, has several dimensions) combined with a uniform set of subjective features (his own subjective features), in Harsanyi's formulation the subjective features associated with the objective situations also vary from situation to situation. It will be no wonder, therefore, if one finds intransitivity to be an almost universal phenomenon in this type of evaluation.[17]

16. May's rationalization takes advantage of the formal framework of Arrow's general possibility theorem. Individual preferences (starting from the individual's evaluation according to different criteria) are held to satisfy conditions practically identical with those of social preferences of Arrow (starting from individual preferences), and the result is therefore an intransitive pattern of individual preferences. It may, however, be observed that while Arrow's condition 3 may have a certain appeal in the context of social choice because of the difficulties of interpersonal comparisons of utility, it is not appropriate when viewed as an empirically testable hypothesis about the nature of individual preferences. It may not be insuperably difficult for the single individual to take into account the *intensity* of desirability according to different criteria and to weight them in assessing overall desirability, and the difficulty is not comparable with that of interpersonal comparison of preference intensity.

17. The other property of a complete pre-ordering – connectedness – may also not be satisfied. Can the individual in practice really compare *all* pairs of alternatives such as (X_{ij}, Y_j) even if he can compare *all* pairs of the type X_{ij}? The relevance of this question can be appreciated if we remember that in Harsanyi's formulation the individual is required to compare the subjective features *together with* the objective positions of all pairs of individuals in the society, and that to imagine oneself as possessing the subjective characteristics of another individual is much more difficult than to imagine oneself in the objective situation of another individual. It seems highly probable that there will be a failure of imagination for at least some pairs of alternatives.

The axiom regarding the reduction of compound lotteries into simple lotteries is also likely to be violated. Suppose we confront a particular individual with half-and-half probabilities of getting (X_{l1}, Y_1) and (X_{l2}, Y_2). But the alternatives (X_{l1}, Y_1) and (X_{l2}, Y_2) themselves may be risky prospects. For example, (X_{l1}, Y_1) may be a risky prospect involving the alternatives of success and failure with the probabilities $\frac{1}{3}$ and $\frac{2}{3}$, respectively. Let these two alternatives be indicated by $(X_{l1}, Y_1)^{I}$ and $(X_{l1}, Y_1)^{II}$, respectively. Similarly, (X_{l2}, Y_2) may be a risky prospect involving the outcomes $(X_{l2}, Y_2)^{I}$ and $(X_{l2}, Y_2)^{II}$ with the probabilities $\frac{1}{4}$ and $\frac{3}{4}$, respectively. The axiom about the reduction of compound lotteries requires the individual to be indifferent between the original compound risky prospect and a simple risky prospect in which we offer to the individual the alternatives $(X_{l1}, Y_1)^{I}$, $(X_{l1}, Y_1)^{II}$, $(X_{l2}, Y_2)^{I}$ and $(X_{l2}, Y_2)^{II}$ with the probabilities $\frac{1}{6}$, $\frac{1}{3}$, $\frac{1}{8}$, and $\frac{3}{8}$, respectively. But is it reasonable to expect him to be indifferent between the two? In the case of the compound prospect, he first puts himself in the shoes of the other two individuals and then, with *their* attitude toward risk, he views the alternatives $(X_{l1}, Y_1)^{I}$, and so on. In the case of the simple prospect, however, he faces these alternatives directly, and it is with *his* attitude toward risk – and his attitude only – that he judges the uncertain prospect. If individuals 1 and 2 are risk-lovers and the evaluating individual is a risk-averter, there seems to be good reason to expect that the evaluating individual will not be indifferent between the compound prospect and the simple prospect derived from the compound one by the familiar rules of operating with probabilities. The difficulty would seem to be inherent in the fact that in applying the rules for reduction of compound prospects, what we are actually doing is to combine attitudes of risk of more than one person, and although the single individual's choice among risky prospects may satisfy the rules of consistency posited by the expected utility axioms, there is no reason to expect such consistency in the case where more than one person's attitudes are involved.

The other problem – that regarding the welfare significance of the von Neumann–Morgenstern index – is more of a conceptual nature. As regards the nature of preference intensities revealed by such an index and their ethical significance for social choice, it has been argued that these utility indexes are constructed in a situation involving risk and, since the choices offered to the individual are risky prospects, the utility numbers attached to these alternatives will inevitably reflect attitude to risk. From this it is concluded that the cardinalism of these indexes has no relevance for social choice in a context where no risk is involved. Arrow (1964, p. 10), for example, writes:

This theorem does not, as far as I can see, give any special ethical significance to the particular utility scale found. For instead of using the utility scale found by von Neumann and Morgenstern, we could use the square of that scale; then behaviour is described by saying that the individual seeks to maximize the expected value of the square root of his utility ... it has nothing to do with welfare considerations, particularly if we are interested primarily in making a social choice among alternative policies in which no random elements enter. To say otherwise would be to assert that the distribution of the social income is to be governed by the tastes of individuals for gambling.

The passage quoted gives two reasons why the von Neumann–Morgenstern utility index should not be used as an index of individual welfare. The first reason is that no special ethical significance attaches to such an index since we could as well rationalize the individual's behaviour by taking the square of the scale adopted. This is no doubt true. But as Arrow himself recognizes, one of the tests for judging among alternative scientific hypotheses is that of simplicity. If two hypotheses serve equally well to explain, it is scientific practice to accept the simpler of the two and reject the other. It is on this ground that we accept the von Neumann–Morgenstern scale rather than its square or square root. But once we accept a certain hypothesis as 'correct' in this sense in positive economics, it seems difficult to see why one should have qualms in using it as the basis of welfare judgements *provided* it is not objectionable in any other way.

The second reason cited by Arrow is that the von Neumann–Morgenstern index will reflect the individual's tastes for 'gambling' and is therefore irrelevant for social choice among sure prospects. In the context of our specific problem, it would mean that the preference intensities revealed by such an index constructed for ethical preferences among S_i are affected by the individual's attitude toward risk. This is true; all the same, such attitude toward risk *is* relevant for social choice among sure prospects provided we accept the contention that it is more reasonable to base social preferences on ethical preferences than on subjective preferences. In the models we have examined, risk is the device through which an impersonal evaluation is distilled from the subjective preferences of individuals; the attitude toward risk cannot therefore be rejected in the context of social choice among sure prospects simply because it is attitude toward risk (or gambling, as Arrow would put it). More convincing arguments would seem to be required to justify such rejection.

The real difficulty in the use of such an index (granting that it exists) for deriving a social ordering seems to lie somewhere else. The mere construction of a cardinal utility index to represent the ethical preferences of each individual is not enough. It is necessary to reduce the scales to a comparable basis before they can be aggregated. For each individual there exists an infinite set of von Neumann–Morgenstern indexes, all linear transforms of each other. The crucial problem is that of choosing one from a set of indexes for each individual. Whatever practical procedure we may follow is likely to be more or less arbitrary, and it is difficult to see how one can escape this arbitrariness.[18]

18. Cf. Arrow (1964), Vickrey (1960), and Sen (1966). Sen (1966) shows that the ordering which results from aggregation of individual preferences by means of Harsanyi's model A will differ, depending on the procedure followed to standardize the scales of different individuals. Sen is concerned with the problem of aggregating subjective preferences into social preferences in Harsanyi's sense. But his conclusion regarding non-uniqueness of the result of aggregation applies equally well to our problem, namely, that of aggregating ethical preferences into Arrowian social preferences. Vickrey (1960, pp. 526–30) makes a detailed investigation into the undesirable consequences of the different practical procedures that can be followed to render the scales comparable. Arrow (1964, pp. 32–3) illustrates these difficulties in the specific case where the utility numbers 1 and 0 are assigned to the best and worst alternatives, respectively, for each individual. The examples given by Arrow are meant to illustrate how the use of the von Neumann–Morgenstern index leads to violation of his condition of independence of irrelevant alternatives. However, it is not only the violation of this condition as such but also the nature of such violation which is disturbing.

5

The main conclusions of our argument may now be summed up as follows:

1. The concept of 'ethical preferences' as developed by Harsanyi (1955) is persuasive enough to justify the qualification 'ethical,' and it is the combination of risk and the 'extended sympathy' type of comparison which accounts for this persuasiveness. Ethical preferences can be used as the ingredients for deriving social preferences, and in some respects this procedure is more appealing than the Arrowian procedure (Arrow, 1964) of deriving social preferences directly from the individual's 'subjective preferences.'

2. Granted that individual 'ethical preferences' can be represented by von Neumann–Morgenstern utility indexes this in itself does not solve the problem of deriving social preferences by aggregating the individual preferences. This is because 'ethical preferences' will not necessarily be identical for different individuals, as claimed by Harsanyi (1955).

3. In the context of Harsanyi's 'ethical preferences,' the use of von Neumann–Morgenstern utility indexes for deriving social preferences is less open to Arrow's objection about its implicit use of people's attitudes toward risk, for risk here is an integral part of the concept of impersonality. The ethical significance of attitudes toward risk comes out especially in the context of 'universalizability' of value judgements as proposed by Hare (1961) and the concept of 'justice' as developed by Rawls (1958).

4. The problem of reducing different individuals' welfare indexes to a comparable basis is serious in view of the uniqueness only up to linear transformation of the von Neumann–Morgenstern indexes. This has been noted by Arrow. But no less serious is the fact that Harsanyi's 'ethical preferences' may not at all satisfy the von Neumann–Morgenstern or the Marschak axioms. In particular, the axioms of 'reduction of compound lottery' and of 'complete ordering' are open to serious doubts of a type that does not arise with the 'subjective preferences'. Thus even individual preferences of the 'ethical' type may not be cardinalizable in the sense of von Neumann and Morgenstern and of Marschak, and this is a basic difficulty with Harsanyi's approach.

References

ARROW, K. J. (1964), *Social Choice and Individual Values*, 2nd edn, Wiley.

BERGSON, A. (1938), 'A reformulation of certain aspects of welfare economics' *Q.J. Econ.*, vol. 52, pp. 310–34.

BERGSON, A. (1948), 'Socialist economics', in H. S. Ellis (ed.), *A Survey of Contemporary Economics*, Blackiston.

FRIEDMAN, M., and SAVAGE, J. (1948), 'The utility analysis of choices involving risk', *J. polit. Econ.*, vol. 56, August, pp. 279–304.

HARE, R. M. (1961), *The Language of Morals*, Oxford University Press.

HARSANYI, J. C. (1953), 'Cardinal utility in welfare economics and in the theory of risk-taking', *J. polit. Econ.*, vol. 61, October, pp. 434–5.

HARSANYI, J. C. (1955), 'Cardinal welfare, individualistic ethics, and interpersonal comparisons of utility', *J. polit. Econ.*, vol. 63, no. 4, pp. 309–21.

LUCE, R. D., and RAIFFA, H. (1957). *Games and Decisions*, Wiley.

MARSCHAK, J. (1950), 'Rational behaviour, uncertain prospects, and measurable utility', *Econometrica*, vol. 18, no. 2, pp. 111–41.

MAY, K. O. (1954), 'Intransitivity, utility and the aggregation of preference patterns', *Econometrica*, vol. 22, no. 1, January, pp. 1–13.

RAWLS, J. (1951), 'Outline of a decision procedure for ethics', *philosoph. Rev.*, vol. 60, no. 1, pp. 177–97.

RAWLS, J. (1958), 'Justice as fairness', *philosoph. Rev.*, vol. 67, no. 164–94.

ROTHENBERG, J. (1961), *The Measurement of Social Welfare*, Prentice-Hall.

SEN, A. K. (1966), 'Planners' preferences: optimality, distribution, and social welfare', presented at the International Economic Association Round Table on the Economics of the Public Sector at Biarritz, September, to be published by the International Economic Association.

STEINHAUS, H. (1948), 'The problem of fair division', *Econometrica*, vol. 16, January, pp. 101–4.

VICKREY, W. (1960), 'Utility, strategy and social decision rules', *Q.J. Econ.*, vol. 74, November, pp. 507–35.

VON NEUMANN, J., and MORGENSTERN, O. (1953), *Theory of Games and Economic Behavior*, 3rd edn, Princeton University Press.

13 J. Rawls[1]

Distributive Justice

J. Rawls, 'Distributive justice', in P. Laslett and W. G. Runciman (eds.),
Philosophy, Politics and Society, Blackwell, 1967, third series, pp. 58–82; and
J. Rawls, 'Distributive justice: some addenda', in *Natural Law Reform*,
vol. 13, 1968.

1

We may think of a human society as a more or less self-sufficient
association regulated by a common conception of justice and aimed
at advancing the good of its members. As a cooperative venture for
mutual advantage, it is characterized by a conflict as well as an
identity of interests. There is an identity of interests since social
cooperation makes possible a better life for all than any would have
if everyone were to try to live by his own efforts; yet at the same
time persons are not indifferent as to how the greater benefits produced by their joint labours are distributed, for in order to further
their own aims each prefers a larger to a lesser share. A conception
of justice is a set of principles for choosing between the social
arrangements which determine this division and for underwriting
a consensus as to the proper distributive shares.

Now at first sight the most rational conception of justice would
seem to be utilitarian. For consider: each person in realizing his
own good can certainly balance his own losses against his own gains.
We can impose a sacrifice on ourselves now for the sake of a greater
advantage later. An individual quite properly acts, as long as others

1. This essay, as presented here, includes the whole of 'Distributive justice'
(1967) and the main part of 'Distributive justice: some addenda'. Allowing for
some deletions to reduce repetition, substantially all of the second essay, except
for the first and last sections, has been placed between sections 5 and 6 of the
first essay as originally published. Thus, as numbered in the text above, sections
1–4 and 11–14 are from 'Distributive justice' and sections 5–10 are from 'Some
Addenda'. I have interpolated a few brief passages here and there to connect the
inserted sections; but while I have made a few small changes, I have not tried to
revise the essays as first printed. A fuller account of the ideas they contain can be
found in Rawls (1971).

are not affected, to achieve his own greatest good, to advance his ends as far as possible. Now, why should not a society act on precisely the same principle? Why is not that which is rational in the case of one person right in the case of a group?

Surely the simplest and most direct conception of the right, and so of justice, is that of maximizing the good. This assumes a prior understanding of what is good, but we can think of the good as already given by the interests of rational individuals. Thus just as the principle of individual choice is to achieve one's greatest good, to advance so far as possible one's own system of rational desires, so the principal of social choice is to realize the greatest good (similarly defined) summed over all the members of society. We arrive at the principle of utility in a natural way: by this principle a society is rightly ordered, and hence just, when its institutions are arranged so as to realize the greatest sum of satisfactions.

The striking feature of the principle of utility is that it does not matter, except indirectly, how this sum of satisfactions is distributed among individuals, any more than it matters, except indirectly, how one person distributes his satisfactions over time. Since certain ways of distributing things affect the total sum of satisfactions, this fact must be taken into account in arranging social institutions; but according to this principle the explanation of common-sense precepts of justice and their seemingly stringent character is that they are those rules which experience shows must be strictly respected and departed from only under exceptional circumstances if the sum of advantages is to be maximized. The precepts of justice are derivative from the one end of attaining the greatest net balance of satisfactions. There is no reason in principle why the greater gains of some should not compensate for the lesser losses of others; or why the violation of the liberty of a few might not be made right by a greater good shared by many. It simply happens, at least under most conditions, that the greatest sum of advantages is not generally achieved in this way. From the standpoint of utility the strictness of common-sense notions of justice has a certain usefulness, but as a philosophical doctrine it is irrational.

If, then, we believe that as a matter of principle each member of society has an inviolability founded on justice which even the welfare of everyone else cannot override, and that a loss of freedom for some is not made right by a greater sum of satisfactions enjoyed by many, we shall have to look for another account of the principles of justice. The principle of utility is incapable of explaining the fact that in a just society the liberties of equal citizenship are taken for granted, and the rights secured by justice are not subject to political bargaining nor to the calculus of social interests. Now, the most natural alternative to the principle of utility is its traditional rival, the theory of the social contract. The aim of the contract doctrine is precisely to account for the strictness of justice by supposing that its principles arise from an agreement among free and independent persons in an original position of equality and hence reflect the integrity and equal sovereignty of the rational persons who are the contractees. Instead of supposing that a conception of right, and so a conception of justice, is simply an extension of the principle of choice for one person to society as a whole, the contract doctrine assumes that the rational individuals who belong to society must choose together, in one joint act, what is to count among them as just and unjust. They are to decide among themselves once and for all what is to be their conception of justice. This decision is thought of as being made in a suitably defined initial situation one of the significant features of which is that no one knows his position in society, nor even his place in the distribution of natural talents and abilities. The principles of justice to which all are forever bound are chosen in the absence of this sort of specific information. A veil of ignorance prevents anyone from being advantaged or disadvantaged by the contingencies of social class and fortune; and hence the bargaining problems which arise in everyday life from the possession of this knowledge do not affect the choice of principles. On the contract doctrine, then, the theory of justice, and indeed ethics itself, is part of the general theory of rational choice, a fact perfectly clear in its Kantian formulation.

Once justice is thought of as arising from an original agreement of this kind, it is evident that the principle of utility is problematical. For why should rational individuals who have a system of ends they wish to advance agree to a violation of their liberty for the sake of a greater balance of satisfactions enjoyed by others? It seems more plausible to suppose that, when situated in an original position of equal right, they would insist upon institutions which returned compensating advantages for any sacrifices required. A rational individual would not accept an institution merely because it maximized the sum of advantages irrespective of its effect on his own interests. It appears, then, that the principle of utility would be rejected as a principle of justice, although I shall not try to argue this important question here. Rather, my aim is to give a brief sketch of the conception of distributive shares implicit in the principles of justice which, it seems, would be chosen in the original position. The philosophical appeal of utilitarianism is that it seems to offer a single principle on the basis of which a consistent and complete conception of right can be developed. The problem is to work out a contractarian alternative in such a way that it has comparable if not all the same virtues.

2

In this discussion I shall make no attempt to derive the two principles of justice which I shall examine; that is, I shall not try to show that they would be chosen in the original position.[2] It must suffice that it is plausible that they would be, at least in preference to the standard forms of traditional theories. Instead we shall be mainly concerned with three questions: first, how to interpret these principles so that they define a consistent and complete conception of justice; second, whether it is possible to arrange the institutions of a constitutional democracy so that these principles are satisfied,

2. This question is discussed in *A Theory of Justice*, especially chapters 3–4. The intuitive idea is as follows. Given the circumstances of the original position, it is rational for a person to choose as if he were designing a society in which his enemy is to assign him his place. Thus, in particular, given the complete lack of knowledge (which makes the choice one under uncertainty), the fact that the decision involves one's life-prospects as a whole and is constrained by strict obligations to third parties (e.g. one's descendants) and duties to certain values (e.g. to religious truth), it is rational to be conservative and so to choose in accordance with an analogue of the maximin principle. One way to make this plausible is to note that, since we must guarantee our personal and spiritual liberties, 'marginal utility' is infinite, and this leads to the greatest risk aversion and so to maximin, at least with respect to these liberties. Viewing the situation in this way, the interpretation given to the principles of justice in section 4 is perhaps natural enough. Moreover, it seems clear how the principle of utility can be interpreted: it is the analogue of the Laplacean principle for choice uncertainty.

at least approximately; and third, whether the conception of distributive shares which they define is compatible with common-sense notions of justice. The significance of these principles is that they allow for the strictness of the claims of justice; and if they can be understood so as to yield a consistent and complete conception, the contractarian alternative would seem all the more attractive.

The two principles of justice which we shall discuss may be formulated as follows: first, each person engaged in an institution or affected by it has an equal right to the most extensive liberty compatible with a like liberty for all; and second, inequalities as defined by the institutional structure or fostered by it are arbitrary unless it is reasonable to expect that they will work out to everyone's advantage and provided that the positions and offices to which they attach or from which they may be gained are open to all. These principles regulate the distributive aspects of institutions by controlling the assignment of rights and duties throughout the whole social structure, beginning with the adoption of a political constitution in accordance with which they are then to be applied to legislation. It is upon a correct choice of a basic structure of society, its fundamental system of rights and duties, that the justice of distributive shares depends.

The two principles of justice apply in the first instance to this basic structure, that is, to the main institutions of the social system and their arrangement, how they are combined together. Thus the structure includes the political constitution and the principal economic and social institutions which together define a person's liberties and rights and affect his life-prospects, what he may expect to be and how well he may expect to fare. The intuitive idea here is that those born into the social system at different positions, say in different social classes, have varying life-prospects determined, in part, by the system of political liberties and personal rights, and by the economic and social opportunities which are made available to these positions. In this way the basic structure of society favours certain individuals over others, and these are the basic inequalities, the ones which affect their whole life-prospects. It is inequalities of this kind, presumably inevitable in any society, with which the two principles of justice are primarily designed to deal.

Now the second principle holds that an inequality is allowed only if there is reason to believe that the institution with the inequality, or permitting it, will work out for the advantage of every person engaged in it. In the case of the basic structure this means that all inequalities which affect life-prospects, say the inequalities of income and wealth which exist between social classes, must be to the advantage of everyone. Since the principle applies to institutions, we interpret this to mean that inequalities must be to the advantage of the representative person for each relevant social position; they should improve each such person's expectation. Here we assume that it is possible to attach to each position an expectation, and that this expectation is a function of the whole institutional structure: it can be raised and lowered by reassigning rights and duties throughout the system. Thus the expectation of any position depends upon the expectations of the others, and these in turn depend upon the pattern of rights and duties established by the basic structure. But it is not clear what is meant by saying that inequalities must be to the advantage of every representative person, and hence our first question.

3

One possibility is to say that everyone is made better off in comparison with some historically relevant benchmark. An interpretation of this kind is suggested by Hume.[3] He sometimes says that the institutions of justice, that is, the rules regulating property and contracts, and so on, are to everyone's advantage, since each person can count himself the gainer on balance when he considers his permanent interests. Even though the application of the rules is sometimes to his disadvantage, and he loses in the particular case, all gain in the long-run by the steady administration of the whole system of justice. But Hume seems to mean by this only that everyone is better off in comparison with the situation of human beings in the state of nature, understood either as some primitive condition or as the circumstances which would obtain at any time if the existing institutions of justice were to break down. While this sense of everyone's being made better off is perhaps clear enough, Hume's interpretation is surely unsatisfactory. For even if all persons including slaves are made better off by a system of slavery than they

3. For this observation I am indebted to Brian Barry.

would be in the state of nature, it is not true that slavery makes everyone (even a slave) better off, at least not in a sense which makes the arrangement just. The benefits and burdens of social cooperation are unjustly distributed even if everyone does gain in comparison with the state of nature; this historical or hypothetical benchmark is simply irrelevant to the question of justice. In fact, any past state of society other than a recent one seems irrelevant offhand, and this suggests that we should look for an interpretation independent of historical comparisons altogether. Our problem is to identify the correct hypothetical comparisons defined by currently feasible changes.

Now the well-known criterion of Pareto[4] offers a possibility along these lines once it is formulated so as to apply to institutions. Indeed, this is the most natural way of taking the second principle (or rather the first part of it, leaving aside the requirement about open positions). This criterion says that group welfare is at an optimum when it is impossible to make any one person better off without at the same time making at least one other person worse off. Applying this criterion to allocating a given bundle of goods among given individuals, a particular allocation yields an optimum if there is no redistribution which would improve one individual's position without worsening that of another. Thus a distribution is optimal when there is no further exchange which is to the advantage of both parties, or to the advantage of one and not to the disadvantage of the other. But there are many such distributions, since there are many ways of allocating commodities so that no further mutually beneficial exchange is possible. Hence the Pareto criterion, as important as it is, admittedly does not identify the best distribution, but rather a class of optimal, or efficient, distributions. Moreover, we cannot say that a given optimal distribution is better than any non-optimal one; it is only superior to those which it dominates. The criterion is at best an incomplete principle for ordering distributions.

Pareto's idea can be applied to institutions. We assume, as remarked above, that it is possible to associate with each social position an expectation which depends upon the assignment of rights and duties in the basic structure. Given this assumption, we get a

4. Introduced by him in his *Manuel d'économie politique* (1909) and long since a basic principle of welfare economics.

principle which says that the pattern of expectations (inequalities in life-prospects) is optimal if and only if it is impossible to change the rules, to redefine the scheme of rights and duties, so as to raise the expectations of any representative person without at the same time lowering the expectations of some other representative person. Hence the basic structure satisfies this principle when it is impossible to change the assignment of fundamental rights and duties and to alter the availability of economic and social opportunities so as to make some representative better off without making another worse off. Thus, in comparing different arrangements of the social system, we can say that one is better than another if in one arrangement all expectations are at least as high, and some higher, than in the other. The principle gives grounds for reform, for if there is an arrangement which is optimal in comparison with the existing state of things, then, other things equal, it is a better situation all around and should be adopted.

The satisfaction of this principle, then, defines a second sense in which the basic structure makes everyone better off; namely, that from the standpoint of its representative persons in the relevant positions, there exists no change which would improve anyone's condition without worsening that of another. Now we shall assume that this principle would be chosen in the original position, for surely it is a desirable feature of a social system that it is optimal in this sense. In fact, we shall suppose that this principle defines the concept of efficiency for institutions, as can be seen from the fact that if the social system does not satisfy it, this implies that there is some change which can be made which will lead people to act more effectively so that the expectations of some at least can be raised. Perhaps an economic reform will lead to an increase in production with given resources and techniques, and with greater output someone's expectations are raised.

It is not difficult to see, however, that while this principle provides another sense for an institution's making everyone better off, it is an inadequate conception of justice. For one thing, there is the same incompleteness as before. There are presumably many arrangements of an institution and of the basic structure which are optimal in this sense. There may also be many arrangements which are optimal with respect to existing conditions, and so many reforms which would be improvements by this principle. If so, how is one to choose between them? It is impossible to say that the many optimal arrangements are equally just, and the choice between them a matter of indifference, since efficient institutions allow extremely wide variations in the pattern of distributive shares.

Thus it may be that under certain conditions serfdom cannot be significantly reformed without lowering the expectations of some representative individual, say that of landowners, in which case serfdom is optimal. But equally it may happen under the same conditions that a system of free labour could not be changed without lowering the expectations of some representative individual, say that of free labourers, so that this arrangement likewise is optimal. More generally, whenever a society is relevantly divided into a number of classes, it is possible, let's suppose, to maximize with respect to any one of its representatives at a time. These maxima give at least this many optimal positions, for none of them can be departed from to raise the expectations of any individual without lowering those of another, namely the individual with respect to whom the maximum is defined. Hence each of these extremes is optimal. All this corresponds to the obvious fact that, in distributing particular goods to given individuals, those distributions are also optimal which give the whole stock to any one person; for once a single person has everything, there is no change which will not make him worse off.

We see, then, that social systems which we should judge very differently from the standpoint of justice may be optimal by this criterion. This conclusion is not surprising. There is no reason to think that, even when applied to social systems, justice and efficiency come to the same thing. These reflections only show what we knew all along, which is that we must find another way of interpreting the second principle, or rather the first part of it. For while the two principles taken together incorporate strong requirements of equal liberty and equality of opportunity, we cannot be sure that even these constraints are sufficient to make the social structure acceptable from the standpoint of justice. As they stand the two principles would appear to place the burden of ensuring justice entirely upon these prior constraints and to leave indeterminate the preferred distributive shares.

4

There is, however, a third interpretation which is immediately suggested by the previous remarks, and this is to choose some social position by reference to which the pattern of expectations as a whole is to be judged, and then to maximize with respect to the expectations of this representative man consistent with the demands of equal liberty and equality of opportunity. Now, the one obvious candidate is the representative of those who are least favoured by the system of institutional inequalities. Thus we arrive at the following idea: the basic structure of the social system affects the life-prospects of typical individuals according to their initial places in society, say the various income classes into which they are born, or depending upon certain natural attributes, as when institutions make discriminations between men and women or allow certain advantages to be gained by those with greater natural abilities. The fundamental problem of distributive justice concerns the differences in life-prospects which come about in this way. We interpret the second principle to hold that these differences are just if and only if the greater expectations of the more advantaged, when playing a part in the working of the whole social system, improve the expectations of the least advantaged. The basic structure is just throughout when the advantages of the more fortunate promote the well-being of the least fortunate, that is, when a decrease in their advantages would make the least fortunate even worse off than they are. The basic structure is perfectly just when the prospects of the least fortunate are as great as they can be.

In interpreting the second principle (or rather the first part of it which we may, for obvious reasons, refer to as the difference principle), we assume that the first principle requires a basic equal liberty for all, and that the resulting political system, when circumstances permit, is that of a constitutional democracy in some form. There must be liberty of the person and political equality as well as liberty of conscience and freedom of thought. There is one class of equal citizens which defines a common status for all. We also assume that there is equality of opportunity and a fair competition for the available positions on the basis of reasonable qualifications. Now, given this background, the differences to be justified are the various economic and social inequalities in the basic structure which must inevitably arise in such a scheme. These are the inequalities in the distribution of income and wealth and the distinctions in social prestige and status which attach to the various positions and classes. The difference principle says that these inequalities are just if and only if they are part of a larger system in which they work out to the advantage of the most unfortunate representative individual. The just distributive shares determined by the basic structure are those specified by this constrained maximum principle.

Thus, consider one chief problem of distributive justice, that concerning the distribution of wealth as it affects the life-prospects of those starting out in the various income groups. These income classes define the relevant representative individuals from which the social system is to be judged. Now, a son of a member of the entrepreneurial class (in a society with private ownership of the means of production) has a better prospect than that of the son of an unskilled labourer. This will be true, it seems, even when the social injustices which presently exist are removed and the two men are of equal talent and ability; the inequality cannot be done away with as long as something like the family is maintained. What, then, can justify this inequality in life-prospects? According to the second principle it is justified only if it is to the advantage of the representative individual who is worst off, in this case the representative unskilled labourer. The inequality is permissible because lowering it would, let's suppose, make the working man even worse off than he is. Presumably, given the principle of open offices (the second part of the second principle), the greater expectations allowed to entrepreneurs has the effect in the longer run of raising the life-prospects of the labouring class. The inequality in expectation provides an incentive so that the economy is more efficient, industrial advance proceeds at a quicker pace, and so on, the end result of which is that greater material and other benefits are distributed throughout the system. Of course, all of this is familiar, and whether true or not in particular cases, it is the sort of thing which must be argued if the inequality in income and wealth is to be acceptable by the difference principle.

We should now verify that this interpretation of the second principle gives a natural sense in which everyone may be said to be made better off. Let us suppose that inequalities are chain-connected:

that is, if an inequality raises the expectations of the lowest position, it raises the expectations of all positions in between. For example, if the greater expectations of the representative entrepreneur raises that of the unskilled labourer, it also raises that of the semi-skilled. Let us further assume that inequalities are closeknit: that is, it is impossible to raise (or lower) the expectation of any representative individual without raising (or lowering) the expectations of every other representative individual, and in particular, without affecting one way or the other that of the least fortunate. There is no loose-jointedness, so to speak, in the way in which expectations depend upon one another. Now, with these assumptions, everyone does benefit from an inequality which satisfies the difference principle, and the second principle as we have formulated it reads correctly. For the representative individual who is better off in any pairwise comparison gains by being allowed to have his advantage, and the person who is worse off benefits from the contribution which all inequalities make to each position below. Of course, chain-connection and closeknitness may not obtain; but in this case those who are better off should not have a veto over the advantages available for the least advantaged. The stricter interpretation of the difference principle should be followed, and all inequalities should be arranged for the advantage of the most unfortunate even if some inequalities are not to the advantage of those in middle positions. Should these conditions fail, then, the second principle would have to be stated in another way.

It may be observed that the difference principle represents, in effect, an original agreement to share in the benefits of the distribution of natural talents and abilities, whatever this distribution turns out to be, in order to alleviate as far as possible the arbitrary handicaps resulting from our initial starting places in society. Those who have been favoured by nature, whoever they are, may gain from their good fortune only on terms that improve the well-being of those who have lost out. The naturally advantaged are not to gain simply because they are more gifted, but only to cover the costs of training and cultivating their endowments and for putting them to use in a way which improves the position of the less fortunate. We are led to the difference principle if we wish to arrange the basic social structure so that no one gains (or loses) from his luck in the natural lottery of talent and ability, or from his initial place in society, without giving (or receiving) compensating advantages in return. (The parties in the original position are not said to be attracted by this idea and so agree to it; rather, given the symmetries of their situation, and particularly their lack of knowledge, and so on, they will find it to their interest to agree to a principle which can be understood in this way.) And we should note also that when the difference principle is perfectly satisfied, the basic structure is optimal by the efficiency principle. There is no way to make anyone better off without making someone else worse off, namely, the least fortunate representative individual. Thus the two principles of justice define distributive shares in a way compatible with efficiency, at least as long as we move on this highly abstract level. If we want to say (as we do, although it cannot be argued here) that the demands of justice have an absolute weight with respect to efficiency, this claim may seem less paradoxical when it is kept in mind that perfectly just institutions are also efficient.

5

I should now like to digress a bit and to make a few further comments about the principles of justice, and in particular about the second principle. First of all, the formulation of the principles assumes that we can usefully divide the social structure into two more or less distinct parts, the first principle applying to one, the second to the other. We are to distinguish between those aspects of the social system that define and secure the equal liberties and opportunities of citizenship and those aspects that establish or permit social and economic inequalities. The fundamental freedoms, that is, the main political rights, liberty of conscience and freedom of thought, the basic civil rights, and the like – these are all required to be equal by the first principle. The second principle applies to the distribution of income and wealth, and to the structure of political and economic institutions in so far as these involve differences in organizational authority.

What is to be emphasized here is that we are to try to design a system of rights and duties such that, assuming the scheme to be properly carried out, the resulting distribution of income to particular individuals and the allocation of particular items are just (or at least not unjust) whatever it turns out to be. The system includes an element of pure procedural justice.

A closely related consideration is this. The problem of distributive justice is not that of sharing out a given batch of things to particular individuals with known tastes and preferences. We should not take as the typical case instances of allocative justice, for example, situations in which, say, a wealthy person is deciding how to divide his estate given a knowledge of the desires and needs of the various individuals who are the possible objects of his beneficence. In this case a knowledge about particular persons is relevant to the decision; and, moreover, their desires and needs are taken as fixed, whereas in determining the justice of the social system as a whole, we want to consider only general facts, that is, the general features of politics, economics, and psychology, and so on, as these are expressed by the laws established by the corresponding sciences. One is attempting to set up a workable and just system, and since this system will itself affect the wants and preferences that persons come to have, their wants and preferences cannot be taken as given. Indeed, one must choose between social systems in part according to the desires and needs which they generate and encourage. To judge these desires and needs, certain standards are necessary, and it is here that the conception of justice has a role along with other moral principles.

Finally, we need some way of defining the expectations of representative individuals, since expectations determine what is to their advantage. Now I shall assume that expectations are specified by the expected pattern of primary goods, that is, things which rational persons may be presumed to want whatever else they want. Human beings have an interest in having these goods however various their more particular ends. For example, among the primary goods are liberty and opportunity, income and wealth, health and educated intelligence. Perhaps the most important primary good is self-respect, a confident conviction of the sense of one's own value, a firm assurance that what one does and plans to do is worth doing. Later on, the good of self-respect plays a part in showing the merits of the two principles; but for simplicity the discussion is often in terms of the other primary goods. Thus I shall say that when a representative person can reasonably expect a larger index of primary goods, say a preferred pattern of liberty and opportunity, income and wealth, he is better off. Inequalities are to everyone's advantage if they increase each representative person's expectations understood in this sense.

6

I now want to consider some further aspects of the second principle of justice. In order to do this, I shall take up in sequence three interpretations of this principle which specifies the conditions under which social and economic inequalities are justified. To make things more manageable, we may provisionally think of these inequalities as those of income and wealth, but eventually a more comprehensive account is necessary. The first principle of equal liberty is assumed to have the same sense throughout, and therefore the several interpretations arise from the various meanings of the two parts of the second principle.

Now both parts of the second principle have at least two natural senses; and since these senses are independent of one another, there are four possible interpretations of the two principles. These are indicated in this diagram:

(a) 'everyone's advantage' / (b) 'equally open'	principle of efficiency (Pareto optimality)	difference principle (principle of mutual advantage)
equality as careers open to talents	system of natural liberty	natural aristocracy
equality as equal opportunity under similar conditions	liberal equality	democratic equality

Figure 1

I shall examine in sequence these three interpretations: the system of natural liberty, liberal equality, and democratic equality. In some respects this sequence represents the more intuitive development, but the second sequence via the interpretation of natural aristocracy is not without interest, and I shall comment upon it having set out the first sequence. As a problem of interpreting the conception of justice as fairness, the question is which of these four interpretations is to be preferred. I have already suggested in section 4 that one should adopt that of democratic equality. By considering these possibilities in order I wish to bring out some further reasons for this choice.

The first interpretation (in either sequence) I shall refer to as the system of natural liberty. In this rendering the first part of the second principle is understood as the principle of efficiency (Pareto optimality) adjusted so as to apply to social institutions, or, in our case, to the basic structure of society; and (b) the second part is understood as an open social system in which, to use the traditional phrase, careers are open to talents. It is also assumed in this, and also in the other interpretations, that the first principle is satisfied and that the economy is roughly a free market system, although the means of production may or may not be privately owned. The system of natural liberty assumes, then, that a basic structure satisfying the principle of efficiency and in which positions are open to those able and willing to compete for them will lead to a just distribution. Assigning rights and duties in this way is thought to give a scheme which allocates wealth and income, authority and responsibility, in a fair way whatever this allocation turns out to be. The doctrine includes an important element of pure procedural justice which is carried over to the other interpretations.

We have already discussed the meaning of the principle of efficiency. In order to apply this principle to institutions I assume, as already remarked in section 2, that it is possible to associate with each relevant social position an expectation which depends upon the assignment of rights and duties in the basic structure. But this principle, as previously observed, does not by itself determine a unique distribution. Even when we apply it to the basic structure, there are presumably many arrangements that satisfy it. Thus the question arises as to how the system of natural liberty chooses among the efficient distributions. Now let's suppose that we know from economic theory that under the standard assumptions defining a competitive free market system, income and wealth will be distributed in an efficient way and that the particular optimal distribution which results in any period of time is determined by the initial distribution of assets, that is, by the initial distribution of income and wealth, and of natural talents and abilities. With each initial distribution, a different efficient outcome is arrived at. Thus if we are to accept the outcome as just, and not as merely efficient, we must accept the basis upon which over time the initial distribution of assets is determined.

Now in the system of natural liberty the initial distribution is regulated by the arrangements implicit in the conception of careers open to talents as earlier defined. These arrangements presuppose a background of equal liberty (as defined by the first principle) and a free market economy. They require a formal equality of opportunity in that all have at least the same legal rights of access to all advantaged social positions. But since there is no effort to preserve an equality, or a similarity, of social conditions, except in so far as this is necessary to preserve the required background institutions, the initial distribution of assets for any period of time is strongly influenced by natural and social contingencies. The existing distribution of income and wealth, say, is the cumulative effect of prior distributions of natural assets, that is, natural talents and abilities, as these have been affected and their use favoured or disfavoured over time by social circumstances and such chance contingencies as accident and good fortune, and so on. The injustice of the system of natural liberty is that it permits distributive shares to be improperly influenced by these factors.

The liberal interpretation, as I shall refer to it, modifies the system of natural liberty by adding to the requirement of careers open to talents the requirement of the principle of fair equality of opportunity. The thought here is that positions should not only be open to all in a formal sense, but that all should have a fair chance to attain them. Offhand it is not clear precisely what the desired equality entails, but assuming that the analogy with games is relevant, we might say that those with similar abilities and skills should have similar life chances. More specifically, assuming that there is a distribution of natural assets, those at the same level of talent and ability and who have the same willingness to use them, should have the same prospects of success regardless of their initial place in the social system, that is, irrespective of the class into which they were born. In all sectors of society there should be roughly equal prospects of culture and achievement for everyone similarly endowed and motivated. The expectations of those with the same abilities and aspirations should not be affected by their social class.[5]

The liberal conception of the two principles seeks, then, to mitigate the influence of social contingencies on distributive shares. To accomplish this end it is necessary to impose certain basic structural conditions on the social system. One has to set free market arrangements within a framework of political and legal institutions that regulates the overall trends of economic activity and preserves the social conditions necessary for fair equality of opportunity. The elements of this framework are familiar enough, and I sketch them later in section 11.

While the liberal conception is clearly preferable to the system of natural liberty, it is still defective. For one thing, even if it works to perfection in eliminating the influence of social contingencies, it still allows the resulting distribution of wealth and income to be singled out by the natural distribution of abilities and talents. Within the limits allowed by the background arrangements, distributive shares are decided by the outcome of the natural lottery; and this outcome is also arbitrary from a moral point of view. There is no more reason to permit the distribution of wealth and income to be settled by the distribution of natural assets than by historical accident and social fortune. Furthermore the principle of fair opportunity can only be imperfectly carried out, at least as long as we accept the institution of the family, as I have been assuming. The extent to which natural capacities develop and reach fruition is affected by all kinds of social conditions and class attitudes. Even the willingness to make an effort, to try, and so to be deserving in the ordinary sense is itself dependent on fortunate family and social circumstances. It is impossible in practice to secure equal chances of achievement and culture for those similarly endowed, and therefore we need to adopt a principle which recognizes this fact and which also mitigates the arbitrariness of the natural lottery itself. That the liberal conception fails to do this is its chief weakness from the standpoint of interpreting the two principles of justice as fairness.

5. This definition follows a suggestion of Sidgwick's; see (1907, p. 285 n); see also Tawney (1952, chapter 3, section 2).

Our problem clearly is to find an interpretation of the two principles under which distributive shares are not improperly influenced by the arbitrary contingencies of social fortune and the lottery of natural assets. The liberal conception is a step in the right direction but it does not go far enough. Now we have already interpreted the first part of the second principle in the following way. Assuming the framework of institutions required by fair equality of opportunity to obtain, the higher expectations of those better situated in the basic structure are just if and only if they work as part of a scheme which improves the expectations of the least advantaged members of society. The intuitive idea is that the social order should not establish and secure the more attractive prospects of those better off unless doing so is to the advantage of those less fortunate. Thus the case for the democratic interpretation as I have called it, rests on the fact that when it is satisfied distributive shares are not improperly influenced either by social contingencies or by the lottery in natural assets. So understood, the two principles define a fair way of dealing with accidental social circumstances and the arbitrary distributions of nature (see section 4, last para.); and in this respect they are superior to other conceptions.

I should now comment on the second sequence via the conception of natural aristocracy. On this view no attempt is made to regulate the effects of social contingencies beyond what is required by formal equality of opportunity, but the advantages of persons with greater natural endowments are to be limited to those that further the good of the poorer sections of society. The aristocratic ideals is applied to a social system at least formally open, and the better situation of those favoured by it can be justified only by radiating benefits and on the condition that were less given to those above, less would be attained by those beneath them.[6] In this way the idea of *noblesse oblige* is carried over to the conception of natural aristocracy. Now it should be noted that both the liberal view and that of natural aristocracy are unstable. For, once we are troubled by the influence of either social contingencies or natural chance on the determination of distributive shares, we are bound, on reflection, to be equally

6. This formulation is derived from Santayana's description of aristocracy (1906), in the last part of chapter 4.

concerned by the influence of the other. So however we move away from the system of natural liberty, we cannot stop short of the democratic conception. Indeed, as soon as we try to formulate an interpretation of the two principles of justice which treats everyone equally as moral persons, and which does not weight individuals' share in the benefits of social cooperation according to happenstance and accident, and in particular by their good social fortune or their luck in the natural lottery, it is clear that the democratic rendering is the only possible choice among the four alternatives. I now wish to support this conclusion by presenting further reasons in support of the difference principle.

8

At first sight the difference principle seems unworkable if not eccentric. A necessary step in removing this impression is to keep in mind that it applies to the basic structure of society and to representative groups defined by it. The crucial point is that the difference principle can be regarded as an agreement to consider the distribution of natural assets as common property and to share in the benefits of this distribution whatever it turns out to be. Those who have been favoured by nature, whoever they are, may gain from their good fortune only on terms that improve the situation of those who have done less well. Moreover, this principle has a number of special features that deserve mention. One of these features is that it gives some weight to the considerations singled out by the principle of redress. This is the principle that undeserved inequalities call for redress; and since inequalities of birth and natural endowment are undeserved, these inequalities are to be somehow compensated for (Spiegelberg, 1944; Raphael, 1950–51). Thus the principle of redress holds that in order to treat all persons equally, to provide genuine equality of opportunity, society must give more attention to those with fewer native assets and to those born into the less favourable social positions. The idea is to redress the bias of contingencies in the direction of equality. In pursuit of this principle greater resources might be spent on the education of the less rather than the more intelligent, at least over a certain time of life, say, the earlier years of school.

The principle of redress has not, to my knowledge, been proposed as the sole criterion of justice, as the single aim of the social order. It is plausible, as most such principles are, as a prima facie principle, one that has to be weighed in the balance with others. For example, we are to weigh it against the principle to improve the average standard of life, or to advance the common good (Spiegelberg, 1944, pp. 120.) But whatever other principles we hold, the claims of the principle of redress are to be taken into account. It is thought to represent one of the elements in our conception of justice.

Now the difference principle is not, of course, the principle of redress. It does not require society to move in the direction of an equality of natural assets. We are not to try to even our handicaps as if all were expected to compete on a fair basis in the same race. But the difference principle would allocate resources in education, say, so as to improve the long-term expectation of the least favoured. If this end is attained by giving more attention to the better endowed, it is permissible; otherwise not. And in making this decision, the value of education should not be assessed only in terms of its productivity effects, that is, its realizing a person's capacity to acquire wealth. Equally important, if not more so, is the role of education in enabling a person to enjoy the culture of his society and to take part in its affairs, and in this way to provide everyone with a secure sense of his own worth.

Thus, although the difference principle is not the same as that of redress, it does achieve some of the intent of the latter principle. It transforms the aims of the basic structure so that the total scheme of institutions no longer emphasizes social efficiency and technocratic values. The ideal of equal opportunity ceases to be the right to leave the less fortunate behind, and hence the callous aspects of a meritocratic regime are avoided.

9

Another feature of the difference principle is that it provides an interpretation of the principle of fraternity. In comparison with liberty and equality, the idea of fraternity has had a lesser place in democratic theory. It is thought to be less specifically a political concept, not in itself defining any of the democratic rights but conveying instead the attitudes of mind without which the values expressed by these rights would be lost sight of (see Pennock, 1950, p. 94). Or closely related to this, fraternity is held to represent a certain equality of social esteem manifest in various public conventions and in the absence of manners of deference and servility (Perry, 1944, chapter 19, section 8). No doubt fraternity implies these things as well as a sense of civic friendship and solidarity, but so far it expresses no definite requirement. The difference principle, however, corresponds to a natural meaning of fraternity: namely, to the idea of not wanting to have greater advantages unless this is for the benefit of others who are less well off. In the ideal conception of the family, the principle of maximizing the sum of advantages is rejected, and no one wishes to gain unless he does so in ways that further the interests of others less well situated. But wanting to act on the difference principle has precisely this consequence. Those better circumstanced are willing to have their greater advantages only under a scheme in which this works out for the welfare of the less fortunate.

The idea of fraternity is sometimes thought to involve ties of sentiment and feeling which it is unrealistic to expect between the members of society. But if it is interpreted as incorporating the requirements of the difference principle, it is not an impracticable criterion. It does seem that the institutions and policies which we most confidently think to be just satisfy its demands, at least in the sense that the inequalities permitted by them contribute to the well-being of the less favoured. On this interpretation the principle of fraternity is a feasible standard to follow. We can now associate the ideas of liberty, equality, and fraternity with the democratic interpretation of the two principles of justice as follows: liberty corresponds to the first principle, equality with equality of fair opportunity, and fraternity with the difference principle. We have found a place for the notion of fraternity in the democratic interpretation of the two principles, and we see that it imposes a definite requirement on the basic structure of society.

It is also possible to use the difference principle to give an explication of the Kantian idea that persons are always to be treated as ends and never as means only (Kant, 1786, p. 66). I shall not examine Kant's view here; instead, I shall freely render this notion in the light of the two principles. Now this suggestion of Kant's obviously needs interpretation. Certainly we cannot say that it comes to no more than treating everyone by the same general principles. This interpretation makes it equivalent to formal justice, that similar cases (as defined by the system of principles, whatever it is) are to be treated similarly; but even a caste or slave society can meet this condition. In accordance with the conception of justice as fairness we could say that treating persons always as ends and never as means only signifies at the very least dealing with them as required by those principles to which they would consent in an original position of equality. For in this situation individuals have equal representation as moral persons who regard themselves as ends, and the principles they accept will be rationally designed to protect the claims of their person. This conception of justice, then, gives a sense to the Kantian idea. But this interpretation is abstract, and the question arises as to whether this idea is expressed by any substantive principle; or put another way, if the contracting parties wished to express visibly in the structure of their institutions that they wanted always to regard each other as ends and never as means only, what principle would they acknowledge in the original position?

Now it seems that the two principles of justice on the democratic interpretation achieve this aim: for all have an equal liberty, and the difference principle insists that none gain from basic inequalities in the social system except in ways that further the advantage of the less fortunate. The difference principle explicates a distinction between treating persons as means only and treating them as ends in themselves. To regard a person as an end in himself in the basic design of society is to agree to forego those gains which do not contribute to his expectations. By contrast, to regard a person as a means only is to be prepared to impose upon him lower prospects of life for the sake of sufficiently compensating higher expectations of others and so to promote a greater sum of advantages. The principle of utility subordinates individuals to the common good, or to the end of attaining the greatest net balance of satisfaction, in a way that the conception of justice as fairness excludes. For this principle allows, at least in theory, that the greater gains of some, even when they are better off, may offset the losses of others less fortunate.

The utilitarian may object to this that his principle also gives a meaning to the Kantian idea, namely, the meaning provided by Bentham's formula (attributed to him by J. S. Mill) 'everybody to count for one, nobody for more than one' (1867, chapter 5, paragraph 36). This implies, as Mill remarks, that one person's happiness assumed to be equal in degree to another person's is to be counted exactly as much. The weights in the additive function that represents the utility principle are the same for all individuals, and it is natural to take them as one. Therefore the utilitarian can say that his principle treats all persons always as ends and never as means only, since the well-being of all is given the same weight, and no one's happiness is counted for naught.

There is no reason to deny that utilitarianism can give this interpretation. Rather, the two principles of justice with the difference principle provide a more plausible rendering, or at least a stricter one. For it seems that a natural sense of treating others as means is to require them to have less, to make still further sacrifices, for the purpose of raising the prospects of others who are more favoured. To ask someone to accept less for the sake of improving the welfare of others whose situation is already better than his is to treat him as a means to their well-being. The principle of utility, one might say, treats persons both as means and as ends. It treats them as ends by assigning the same weight to the welfare of each; it treats them as means by allowing the benefits to some to counterbalance the losses of others, especially when those who lost out are the less advantaged. The difference principle provides a stricter interpretation to the Kantian idea by ruling out even the tendency to regard persons as means to one another's welfare. It gives a meaning to a more stringent variant of the notion, namely, always to treat them solely as ends and never in any way as means.

10

A further consideration in support of the difference principle is that it satisfies a reasonable standard of reciprocity. Indeed, it constitutes a principle of mutual benefit, for, when it is met, each representative person can accept the basic structure as designed to advance his interests. The social order can be justified to everyone, and in particular to those who are least favoured. By contrast with the principle of utility, it is excluded that any one worse off than another should be asked to accept less so that the more advantaged can have more. This condition seems an essential part of the notion of reciprocity, and the difference principle fulfils it whereas utilitarianism does not.

It is necessary, however, to discuss in more detail how the condition of mutual benefit is satisfied. Consider any two representative individuals A and B, and let B be the one who is worse off. Actually, since we are most interested in the comparison with the least favoured, let's assume that B is this individual. Now clearly B can accept A's being better off since A's advantages have been gained in ways that improve B's prospects. If A were not permitted to win his better position, B would be even worse off than he is. The difficulty, if there is one, is to show that A has no grounds for complaint. Perhaps he is required to have less than he might since from it there would be no additional benefit to B. Now, viewing things from the standpoint of the original position, what can be said to the more favoured individual? First of all, it is clear that everyone's well-being depends upon a scheme of social cooperation without which no one could have a satisfactory life. Second, such a scheme should draw forth the willing cooperation of everyone taking part in it, and this can be asked for only if reasonable terms are proposed. The difference principle, then, seems to be a fair basis on which those better endowed, or more fortunate in their social circumstances, could expect the willing cooperation of others when some workable scheme is a necessary condition of every one's welfare.[7] If we look at the situation from the perspective of the original position, we shall benefit either way from the distribution of natural assets. Should we be less favoured, we gain from the efforts of others; should we be more favoured, we gain still more if we use our assets in socially fruitful ways.

There is a natural inclination to object that those better situated deserve their greater advantages whether or not they are to the benefit of others. But at this point it is necessary to be clear about the notion of desert. It is perfectly true that given a just system of cooperation as a scheme of public rules and the expectations set up by it, those who with the prospect of improving their condition have done what the system announces that it will reward are entitled

7. For this suggestion I am indebted to Allan Gibbard.

to their advantages. In this sense the more fortunate deserve their better situation; their claims are legitimate expectations established by social institutions, and the community is obligated to meet them. But this sense of desert presupposes the existence of the cooperative scheme; it is irrelevant as to how in the first place the scheme is to be designed, whether in accordance with the difference principle or some other criterion.

Perhaps some will think that the person with greater natural endowments deserves those assets and the superior character that made their development possible. Because he is more worthy in this sense, he deserves the greater advantages that he could achieve with them. This view, however, is surely incorrect. It seems widely agreed that no one deserves his place in the distribution of native endowments, any more than one deserve's one's initial starting place in society. Also a person's deserving the superior character that enabled him to cultivate his abilities is equally problematic; for this character depends upon fortunate family and social circumstances for which he can claim no credit. The notion of desert seems not to apply to these cases. Thus the more advantaged representative individual cannot say, and being reasonable, will not say, that he deserves and therefore has a right to a scheme of cooperation in which he is permitted to acquire benefits in ways that do not contribute to the welfare of others. There is no basis upon which he can make this claim.

The difference principle should be acceptable, then, no matter whether we think we will be the more advantaged or the less advantaged party. The principle of mutual benefit applies to each increment of gain for the more favoured individual, a unit increase, so to speak, that improves the situation of this individual being allowed provided that it contributes to the prospects of the least fortunate. The principle of reciprocity applies each step of the way, the increments for the better situated continuing until the mutual benefit ceases. It is evident that, in general, the principle of utility does not satisfy the principle of reciprocity; there is no definite sense in which everyone necessarily benefits from the inequalities that are authorized by the utilitarian conception. It seems irrelevant to say that everyone is better off than he would be in a state of nature, or if social co-operation were to break down altogether, or even that all are better off than they were in comparison with some historical benchmark. We want to be able to say that as the social system now works, the inequalities it allows contribute to the welfare of each.

Now the fact that the two principles of justice embody this reciprocity principle is important for the stability of this conception. A conception of justice is stable if, given the laws of human psychology and moral learning, the institutions which satisfy it tend to generate their own support, at least when this fact is publicly recognized. Stability means that just arrangements bring about in those taking part in them the corresponding sense of justice, that is, a desire to apply and to act upon the appropriate principles of justice. Assuming as a basic psychological principle that we tend to cherish what affirms our good and to reject what does us harm, all those living in a basic structure satisfying the two principles of justice will have an attachment to their institutions regardless of their position. This is the case since all representative persons benefit from the scheme. In a utilitarian society, however, this is not guaranteed; and therefore to the extent that this psychological principle holds, the principle of utility is likely to be a less stable conception. This consideration is reinforced by the fact that a social system acknowledging the stronger variant of the Kantian idea, that is, the idea of always treating persons solely as ends and never in any ways as means, is bound to underwrite a more secure foundation for individuals' sense of their own worth, a firm confidence that what they do and plan to do is worth doing. For our self-respect, which mirrors our sense of our own worth, depends in part upon the respect shown to us by others; no one can long possess an assurance of his own value in the face of the enduring contempt or even the indifference of others. But it is precisely by publicly affirming the two principles of justice on the democratic interpretation that a society acts on the Kantian idea and makes visible in its institutions the respect that its citizens have for one another as moral persons. Since a sense of our worth is perhaps the most important primary good, these considerations constitute strong arguments for the democratic interpretation, as well as for the two principles of justice in preference to the principle of utility.

It is remarkable that Mill appears to agree with this conclusion. In *Utilitarianism* he notes that with the advance of civilization individuals come more and more to recognize that society between human beings is manifestly impossible on any other basis than that the interests of all are to be consulted. The improvement of political institutions removes the opposition of interests and the barriers and inequalities that encourage citizens to disregard one another's claims. The natural end to this development is a state of the human mind in which each person has a feeling of unity with others. This state of mind, if perfect, makes an individual 'never think of, or desire, any beneficial condition for himself, in the benefits of which they are not included.' One of the individual's natural wants is that 'there should be harmony between his feelings and aims and those of his fellow creatures'. He desires to know that 'his real aim and theirs do not conflict; that he is not opposing himself to what they really wish for, namely their own good, but is, on the contrary, promoting it.' (1867, chapter 3, paragraphs 10–11). Now the desire Mill characterizes here is a desire to act upon the difference principle and not a desire to act on the principle of utility. Certainly it is curious that Mill does not notice this discrepancy; in any case, however, he seems intuitively to recognize that a perfectly just society in which persons' aims are harmoniously reconciled would be one that followed the concept of reciprocity expressed by the difference principle. A stable conception of justice which generates its own support and elicits the natural sentiments of unity and fellow feeling is more likely to follow this ideal than the utilitarian standard.

11

The force of these arguments shows, I believe, that the democratic interpretation of the two principles is a reasonable conception of justice. It turns out that, despite its initial implausibility, the difference principle expresses a number of aspects of the democratic ideal. I should now like to turn to the second question we set out to consider (see section 2, first paragraph), namely whether it is possible to arrange the institutions of a constitutional democracy so that the two principles of justice are satisfied, at least approximately. We shall try to show that this can be done provided the government regulates a free economy in a certain way. More fully, if law and government act effectively to keep markets competitive, resources fully employed, property and wealth widely distributed over time, and to maintain the appropriate social minimum, then if there is equality of opportunity underwritten by education for all, the resulting distribution will be just. Of course, all of these arrangements and policies are familiar. The only novelty in the following remarks, if there is any novelty at all, is that this framework of institutions can be made to satisfy the difference principle. To argue this, we must sketch the relations of these institutions and how they work together. I assume throughout that the framework described is consistent with a liberal socialist regime, as well as with a property-owning democracy.

First of all, the basic social structure is controlled by a just constitution which secures the various liberties of equal citizenship. Thus the legal order is administered in accordance with the principle of legality, and liberty of conscience and freedom of thought are taken for granted. The political process is conducted, so far as possible, as a just procedure for choosing between governments and for enacting just legislation. From the standpoint of distributive justice, it is also essential that there be equality of opportunity in several senses. Thus, we suppose that, in addition to maintaining the usual social overhead capital, government provides for equal educational opportunities for all, either by subsidizing private schools or by operating a public school system. It also enforces and underwrites equality of opportunity in commercial ventures and in the free choice of occupation. This result is achieved by policing the behaviour of firms and by preventing the establishment of barriers and restriction to the desirable positions and markets. Lastly, there is a guarantee of a social minimum which the government meets by family allowances and special payments in times of unemployment, or by a negative income tax.

In maintaining this system of institutions the government may be thought of as divided into four branches. Each branch is represented by various agencies (or activities thereof) charged with preserving certain social and economic conditions. These branches do not necessarily overlap with the usual organization of government, but should be understood as purely conceptual. Thus the allocation branch is to keep the economy feasible competitive, that is, to prevent the formation of unreasonable market power. Markets are competitive in this sense when they cannot be made more so consistent with the requirements of efficiency and the acceptance of the facts of consumer preferences and geography. The allocation branch is also charged with identifying and correcting, say by suitable taxes and subsidies wherever possible, the more obvious departures from efficiency caused by the failure of prices to measure accurately social benefits and costs. The stabilization branch strives to maintain reasonably full employment so that there is no waste through failure to use resources and the free choice of occupation and the deployment of finance is supported by strong effective demand. These two branches together are to preserve the efficiency of the market economy generally.

The social minimum is established through the operations of the transfer branch. Later on we shall consider at what level this minimum should be set, since this is a crucial matter; but for the moment, a few general remarks will suffice. The main idea is that the workings of the transfer branch take into account the precept of need and assign it an appropriate weight with respect to the other common-sense precepts of justice. A market economy ignores the claims of need altogether. Hence there is a division of labour between the parts of the social system as different institutions answer to different common-sense precepts. Competitive markets (properly supplemented by government operations) handle the problem of the efficient allocation of labour and resources and set a weight to the conventional precepts associated with wages and earnings (the precepts of each according to his work and experience, or responsibility and the hazards of the job, and so on), whereas the transfer branch guarantees a certain level of well-being and meets the claims of need. Thus it is obvious that the justice of distributive shares depends upon the whole social system and how it distributes total income, wages plus transfers. There is with reason strong objection to the competitive determination of total income, since this would leave out of account the claims of need and of a decent standard of life. From the standpoint of the original position it is clearly rational to insure oneself against these contingencies. But now, if the appropriate minimum is provided by transfers, it may be perfectly fair that the other part of total income is competitively determined. Moreover, this way of dealing with the claims of need is doubtless more efficient, at least from a theoretical point of view, than trying to regulate prices by minimum wage standards and so on. It is preferable to handle these claims by a separate branch which supports a social minimum. Henceforth, in considering whether the second principle of justice is satisfied, the answer turns on whether the total income of the least advantaged, that is, wages plus transfers, is such as to maximize their long-term expectations consistent with the demands of liberty.

Finally, the distribution branch is to preserve an approximately just distribution of income and wealth over time by affecting the background conditions of the market from period to period. Two aspects of this branch may be distinguished. First of all, it operates a system of inheritance and gift taxes. The aim of these levies is not to raise revenue, but gradually and continually to correct the distribution of wealth and to prevent the concentrations of power to the detriment of liberty and equality of opportunity. It is perfectly true, as some have said, see for example, Van Hayek (1960, p. 90), that unequal inheritance of wealth is no more inherently unjust than unequal inheritance of intelligence; as far as possible the inequalities founded on either should satisfy the difference principle. Thus, the inheritance of greater wealth is just as long as it is to the advantage of the worst off and consistent with liberty, including equality of opportunity. Now by the latter we do not mean, of course, the equality of expectations between classes, since differences in life-prospects arising from the basic structure are inevitable, and it is precisely the aim of the second principle to say when these differences are just. Instead, equality of opportunity is a certain set of institutions which assures equally good education and chances of culture for all and which keeps open the competition for positions on the basis of qualities reasonably related to performance, and so on. It is these institutions which are put in jeopardy when inequalities and concentrations of wealth reach a certain limit; and the taxes imposed by the distribution branch are to prevent this limit from being exceeded. Naturally enough where this limit lies is a matter for political judgement guided by theory, practical experience, and plain hunch; on this question the theory of justice by itself has nothing to say.

The second part of the distribution branch is a scheme of taxation for raising revenue to cover the costs of public goods, to make transfer payments, and the like. This scheme belongs to the distribution branch since the burden of taxation must be justly shared. Although we cannot examine the legal and economic complications involved, there are several points in favour of proportional expenditure taxes as part of an ideally just arrangement. For one thing, they are preferable to income taxes at the level of common-sense precepts of justice, since they impose a levy according to how much a person takes out of the common store of goods and not according to how much he contributes (assuming that income is fairly earned in return for productive efforts). On the other hand, proportional taxes treat everyone in a clearly defined uniform way (again assuming that income is fairly earned) and hence it is preferable to use progressive rates only when they are necessary to preserve the justice of the system as a whole, that is, to prevent large fortunes hazardous to liberty and equality of opportunity, and the like. If proportional expenditure taxes should also prove more efficient, say because they interfere less with incentives, or whatever, this would make the case for them decisive provided a feasible scheme could be worked out (Kaldor, 1955). Yet these are questions of political judgement which are not our concern; and, in any case, a proportional expenditure tax might be part of an idealized scheme which we are describing. It does not follow that even steeply progressive income taxes, given the injustice of existing systems, do not improve justice and efficiency all things considered. In practice we must usually choose between unjust, or second best, arrangements and then it is a matter of finding the least unjust scheme.

Whatever form the distribution branch assumes, the argument for it is to be based on justice: we must hold that once it is accepted the social system as a whole – the competitive economy surrounded by a just constitutional and legal framework – can be made to satisfy the principles of justice with the smallest loss in efficiency. The long-term expectations of the least advantaged are raised to the highest level consistent with the demands of equal liberty. In discussing the choice of a distribution scheme I have made no reference to the traditional criteria of taxation according to ability to pay or benefits received; nor have I mentioned any of the variants of the sacrifice principle. These standards are subordinate to the two principles of justice; once the problem is seen as that of designing a whole social system, they assume the status of secondary precepts with no more independent force than the precepts of common sense in regard to wages. To suppose otherwise is not to take a sufficiently comprehensive point of view. In setting up a just distribution branch these precepts may or may not have a place depending upon the requirements of the two principles of justice when applied to the entire system.

12

Our problem now is whether the whole system of institutions which has been described, the competitive economy surrounded by the four branches of government, can be made to satisfy the two principles of justice. It seems intuitively plausible that this can be done, but we must try to make sure. We assume that the social system as a whole meets the demands of liberty; it secures the rights required by the first principle and the principle of open offices. Thus the question is whether, consistent with these liberties, there is any way of operating the four branches of government so as to bring the inequalities of the basic structure in line with the difference principle.

Now, quite clearly the thing to do is to set the social minimum at the appropriate level. So far we have said nothing about how high this minimum should be. Common sense might be content to say that the right level depends on the average wealth of the country, and that, other things equal, the minimum should be higher if this average is higher; or it might hold that the proper level depends on customary expectations. Both of these ideas are unsatisfactory. The first is not precise enough since it does not state how the minimum should depend on wealth and it overlooks other relevant considerations such as distribution; and the second provides no criterion for when customary expectations are themselves reasonable. Once the difference principle is accepted, however, it follows that the minimum should be set at the level which, taking wages into account, maximizes the expectations of the lowest income class. By adjusting the amount of transfers, and the benefits from public goods which improve their circumstances, it is possible to increase or decrease the total income of the least advantaged (wages plus transfers plus benefits from public goods). Controlling the sum of transfers and benefits, thereby raising or lowering the social minimum, gives sufficient leeway in the whole scheme to satisfy the difference principle.

Now, offhand it might appear that this arrangement requires a very high minimum. It is easy to imagine the greater wealth of those better off being scaled down until eventually all stand on nearly the same level. But this is a misconception. The relevant expectation of the least advantaged is their long-term expectation extending over all generations; and hence over any period of time the economy must put aside the appropriate amount (possibly zero) of real capital accumulation. Assuming for the moment that this amount is given, the social minimum is determined in the following way. Suppose, for simplicity, that transfer payments and the benefits from public goods are supported by expenditure (or income) taxes. Then raising the minimum entails raising the constant proportion at which consumption (or income) is taxed. Now presumably as this proportion is increased there comes a point beyond which one of two things happens: either the savings required cannot be made or the increased taxes interfere so much with the efficiency of the economy that the expectations of the lowest class for that period no longer improve but begin to decline. In either case the appropriate level for the minimum has been reached and no further increase should be made.

In order to make the whole system of institutions satisfy the two principles of justice, a just savings principle is presupposed. Hence we must try to say something about this difficult question. Unfortunately there are no very precise limits on what the rate of saving should be; how the burden of real saving should be shared between generations seems to admit of no definite answer. It does not follow, however, that certain general bounds cannot be prescribed which are ethically significant. For example, it seems clear that the classical principle of utility, which requires us to maximize total well-being over all generations, results in much too high a rate of saving, at least for the earlier generations. On the contract doctrine the question is approached from the standpoint of the parties in the original position who do not know to which generation they belong, or what comes to the same thing, they do not know the stage of economic advance of their society. The veil of ignorance is complete in this respect. Hence the parties ask themselves how much they would be willing to save at each stage on the assumption that other generations save at the same rates. That is, a person is to consider his willingness to save at every phase of development with the understanding that the rates he proposes will regulate the whole span of accumulation. Since no one knows to which generation he belongs, the problem is looked at from the standpoint of each. Now it is immediately obvious that all generations, except possibly the first, gain from a reasonable rate of accumulation being maintained. Once the saving process is begun, it is to the advantage of all later generations. Each generation passes on to the next a fair equivalent in real capital as defined by a just savings principle, this equivalent being in return for what is received from previous generations and enabling the later ones to have a higher standard of life than would otherwise be possible. Only those in the first generation do not benefit, let's suppose; while they begin the whole process, they do not share in the fruits of their provision. At this initial stage, then, in order to obtain unanimity from the point of view of generations, we must assume that fathers, say, are willing to save for the sake of their sons, and hence that, in this case at least, one generation cares for its immediate descendants. With these suppositions, it seems that some just savings principle would be agreed to.

Now a just savings principle will presumably require a lower rate of saving in the earlier stages of development when a society is poor, and a greater rate as it becomes wealthier and more industrialized. As their circumstances become easier individuals would find it reasonable to save more since the real burden is less. Eventually, perhaps, there will come a point beyond which the rate of saving may decline or stop altogether, at least if we suppose that there is a level of wealth when a society may concentrate on other things and it is sufficient that improvements in productive techniques be introduced only to the extent covered by depreciation. Here we are referring to what a society must save as a matter of justice; if it wishes to save for various grand projects, this is another matter.

We should note a special feature of the reciprocity principle in the case of just savings. Normally this principle applies when there is an exchange of advantages, that is, when each party gives something to the other. But in the accumulation process no one gives to those from whom he has received. Each gives to subsequent generations and receives from his predecessors. The first generation obtains no benefits at all, whereas the last generations, those living when no further saving is required, gain the most and give the least. Now this may appear unjust; and contrary to the formulation of the difference principle, the worst off save for those better off. But although this relation is unusual, it does not give rise to any difficulty. It simply expresses the fact that generations are spread out in time and exchanges between them can take place in only one direction. Therefore, from the standpoint of the original position, if all are to gain, they must agree to receive from their predecessors and to pass along a fair equivalent to those who come after them. The criterion of justice is the principle which would be chosen in the original position; and since a just savings principle would, let's suppose, be agreed to, the accumulation process is just. The savings principle may be reconciled with the difference principle by assuming that the representative person in any generation required to save belongs to the lowest income class. Of course, this saving is not done so much, if at all, by taking an active part in the investment process; rather it takes the form of approving of the economic arrangements which promote accumulation. The saving of those worse off is undertaken by accepting, as a matter of political judgement, those policies designed to improve the standard of life, thereby abstaining from the immediate advantages which are available to them. By supporting these arrangements and policies the appropriate savings can be made, and no representative man regardless of generation can complain of another for not doing his part.

Of the nature of the society at which the saving process aims we can give only the most general description. It is a society of persons enjoying the benefits of the greatest equal liberty under economic conditions reached immediately after the highest average income *per capita* at which any saving at all is required. All of this is, unfortunately, terribly vague. But, in any case, this general conception specifies a horizon of sorts at which the savings process aims so that the just savings principle is not completely indeterminate. That is, we suppose that the intention is to reach a certain social state, and the problem of the proper rate of accumulation is how to share fairly in the burdens of achieving it. The contractarian idea is that if we look at this question from the perspective of those in the original position, then, even though the savings principle which results is inevitably imprecise, it does impose ethically significant bounds. What is of first importance is that the problem of just savings be approached in the right way; the initial conception of what we are to do determines everything else. Thus, from the standpoint of the original position, representatives of all generations, so to speak, must agree on how to distribute the hardships of building and preserving a just society. They all gain from adopting a savings principle, but also they have their own interests which they cannot sacrifice for another.

13

The sketch of the system of institutions satisfying the two principles of justice is now complete. For once the just rate of savings is determined, at least within broad limits, we have a criterion for setting the level of the social minimum. The sum of transfers should be that which maximizes the expectations of the lowest income class consistent with the appropriate savings being undertaken and the system of equal liberties maintained. This arrangement of institutions working over time results in a definite pattern of distributive shares, and each receives a total income (wages plus transfers) to which he is entitled under the rules upon which his legitimate expectations are founded. Now an essential feature of this whole scheme is that it contains an element of pure procedural justice. That is, no attempt is made to specify the just distribution of particular goods and services to particular persons, as if there were only one way in which, independently of the choices of economic agents, these things should be shared. Rather, the idea is to design a scheme such that the resulting distribution, whatever it is, which is brought about by the efforts of those engaged in cooperation and elicited by their legitimate expectations, is just.

The notion of pure procedural justice may be explained by a comparison with perfect and imperfect procedural justice. Consider the simplest problem of fair division. A number of men are to divide a cake: assuming that a fair division is an equal one, which procedure will give this outcome? The obvious solution is to have the man who divides the cake take the last piece. He will divide it equally, since in this way he assures for himself as large a share as he can. Now in this case there is an independent criterion for which is the fair division. The problem is to devise a procedure, a set of rules for dividing the cake, which will yield this outcome. The problem of fair division exemplifies the features of perfect procedural justice. There is an independent criterion for which the outcome is just; and we can design a procedure guaranteed to lead to it.

The case of imperfect procedural justice is found in a criminal trial. The desired outcome is that the defendant should be declared guilty if and only if he has committed the offence as charged. The trial procedure is framed to search for and to establish this result, but we cannot design rules guaranteed to reach it. The theory of trial procedures examines which rules of evidence, and the like, are best calculated to advance this purpose in ways consistent with other ends. Different procedures may reasonably be expected in different circumstances to yield the right result, not always, but at least much of the time. Hence a trial is a case of imperfect procedural justice. Even though the law may be carefully followed, and the trial fairly and properly conducted, it may reach the wrong outcome. An innocent man may be found guilty, a guilty man may be set free. In such cases we speak of a miscarriage of justice: the injustice springs from no human fault but from a combination of circumstances which defeats the purpose of the rules.

The notion of pure procedural justice is illustrated by gambling. If a number of persons engage in a series of fair bets, the distribution of cash after the last bet is fair, or at least not unfair, whatever this distribution is. (We are assuming, of course, that fair bets are those which define a zero expectation, that the bets are made voluntarily, that no one cheats, and so on.) Any distribution summing to the initial stock of cash held by everyone could result from a series of fair bets; hence all of these distributions are, in this sense, equally fair. The distribution which results is fair simply because it is the outcome. Now when there is pure procedural justice, the procedure for determining the just result must actually be carried out; for in this case there is no independent criterion by reference to which an outcome can be known to be just. Obviously we cannot say that a particular state of affairs is just because it could have been reached by following a just procedure. This would permit far too much and lead to absurdly unjust consequences. In the case of gambling, for example, it would entail that any distribution whatever could be imposed. What makes the final outcome of the betting fair, or not unfair, is that it is the one which has arisen after a series of fair gambles.

In order, therefore, to establish just distributive shares a just total system of institutions must be set up and impartially administered. Given a just constitution and the smooth working of the four branches of government, and so on, there exists a procedure such that the actual distribution of wealth, whatever it turns out to be, is just. It will have come about as a consequence of a just system of institutions satisfying the principles to which everyone would agree and against which no one can complain. The situation is one of pure procedural justice, since there is no independent criterion by which the outcome can be judged. Nor can we say that a particular distribution of wealth is just because it is one which could have resulted from just institutions although it has not, as this would be to allow too much. Clearly there are many distributions which may be reached by just institutions, and this is true whether we count patterns of distributions among social classes or whether we count distributions of particular goods and services among particular individuals. There are indefinitely many outcomes and what makes one of these just is that it has been achieved by actually carrying out a just scheme of cooperation as it is publicly understood. It is the result which has arisen when everyone receives that to which he is entitled given his and others' actions guided by their legitimate expectations and their obligations to one another. We can no more arrive at a just distribution of wealth except by working together within the framework of a just system of institutions than we can win or lose fairly without actually betting.

This account of distributive shares is simply an elaboration of the familiar idea that economic rewards will be just once a perfectly competitive price system is organized as a fair game. But in order to do this we have to begin with the choice of a social system as a whole, for the basic structure of the entire arrangement must be just. The economy must be surrounded with the appropriate framework of institutions, since even a perfectly efficient price system has no tendency to determine just distributive shares when left to itself.

Not only must economic activity be regulated by a just constitution and controlled by the four branches of government, but a just saving-function must be adopted to estimate the provision to be made for future generations. Thus, we cannot, in general, consider only piecewise reforms, for unless all of these fundamental questions are properly handled, there is no assurance that the resulting distributive shares will be just; while if the correct initial choices of institutions are made, the matter of distributive justice may be left to take care of itself. Within the framework of a just system citizens may be permitted to form associations and groupings as they please so long as they respect the like liberty of others. With social ingenuity it should be possible to invent many different kinds of economic and social activities appealing to a wide variety of tastes and talents; and as long as the justice of the basic structure of the whole is not affected, individuals may be allowed, in accordance with the principle of free association, to enter into and to take part in whatever activities they wish. The resulting distribution will be just whatever it happens to be. The system of institutions which we have described is, let's suppose, the basic structure of a well-ordered society. This system exhibits the content of the two principles of justice by showing how they may be perfectly satisfied; and it defines a social ideal by reference to which political judgement among second-bests, and the long range direction of reform, may be guided.

14

We may conclude by considering the third question: whether this conception of distributive shares is compatible with common-sense notions of justice. In elaborating the contract doctrine we have been led to what seems to be a rather special, even eccentric, conception the peculiarities of which centre in the difference principle. Clear statements of it seem to be rare, and it differs rather widely from traditional utilitarian and intuitionist notions. But this question is not an easy one to answer, for philosophical conceptions of justice, including the one we have been discussing, and our common-sense convictions, are not very precise. Moreover, a comparison is made difficult by our tendency in practice to adopt combinations of principles and precepts the consequences of which depend essentially upon how they are weighted; but the weighting may be undefined and allowed to vary with circumstances, and thus relies on the intuitive judgements which we are trying to systematize.

Consider the following conception of right: social justice depends positively on two things, on the equality of distribution (understood as equality in levels of well-being) and total welfare (understood as the sum of utilities taken over all individuals). On this view one social system is better than another without ambiguity if it is better on both counts, that is, if the expectations it defines are both less unequal and sum to a larger total. Another conception of right can be obtained by substituting the principle of a social minimum for the principle of equality; and thus an arrangement of institutions is preferable to another without ambiguity if the expectations sum to a larger total and it provides for a higher minimum. The idea here is to maximize the sum of expectations subject to the constraint that no one be allowed to fall below some recognized standard of life. In these conceptions the principles of equality and of a social minimum represent the demands of justice, and the principle of total welfare that of efficiency. The principle of utility assumes the role of the principle of efficiency the force of which is limited by a principle of justice.

Now in practice combinations of principles of this kind are not without value. There is no question but that they identify plausible standards by reference to which policies may be appraised, and given the appropriate background of institutions, they may give correct conclusions. Consider the first conception: a person guided by it may frequently decide rightly. For example, he would be in favour of equality of opportunity, for it seems evident that having more equal chances for all both improves efficiency and decreases inequality. The real question arises, however, when an institution is approved by one principle but not by the other. In this case everything depends on how the principles are weighted, but how is this to be done? The combination of principles yields no answer to this question, and the judgement must be left to intuition. For every arrangement combining a particular total welfare with a particular degree of inequality one simply has to decide, without the guidance from principle, how much of an increase (or decrease) in total welfare, say, compensates for a given decrease (or increase) in equality.

Anyone using the two principles of justice, however, would also appear to be striking a balance between equality and total welfare. How do we know, then, that a person who claims to adopt a combination of principles does not, in fact, rely on the two principles of justice in weighing them, not consciously certainly, but in the sense that the weights he gives to equality and total welfare are those which he would give to them if he applied the two principles of justice? We need not say, of course, that those who in practice refer to a combination of principles, or whatever, rely on the contract doctrine, but only that until their conception of right is completely specified the question is still open. The leeway provided by the determination of weights leaves the matter unsettled.

Moreover, the same sort of situation arises with other practical standards. It is widely agreed for example, that the distribution of income should depend upon the claims of entitlement, such as training and experience, responsibility and contribution, and so on, weighed against the claims of need and security. But how are these common-sense precepts to be balanced? Again, it is generally accepted that important ends of economic policy are competitive efficiency, full employment, an appropriate rate of growth, a decent social minimum, and a more equal distribution of income. In a modern democratic state these aims are to be advanced in ways consistent with equal liberty and equality of opportunity. There is no argument with these objectives; they would be recognized by anyone who accepted the two principles of justice. But different political views balance these ends differently, and how are we to choose between them? The fact is that we agree to little when we acknowledge precepts and ends of this kind; it must be recognized that a fairly detailed weighting is implicit in any complete conception of justice. Often we content ourselves with enumerating common-sense precepts and objectives of policy, adding that on particular questions we must strike a balance between them having studied the relevant facts. While this is sound practical advice, it does not express a conception of justice. Whereas on the contract doctrine all combinations of principle, precepts, and objectives of policy are given a weight in maximizing the expectations of the least advantaged consistent with making the required saving and maintaining the system of equal liberty and equality of opportunity.

Thus despite the fact that the contract doctrine seems at first to be a somewhat special conception, particularly in its treatment of inequalities, it may still express the principles of justice which stand in the background and control the weights expressed in our everyday judgements. Whether this is indeed the case can be decided only by developing the consequences of the two principles in more detail and noting if any discrepancies turn up. Possibly there will be no conflicts; certainly we hope there are none with the fixed points of our considered judgements. The main question perhaps is whether one is prepared to accept the further definition of one's conception of right which the two principles represent. For, as we have seen, common sense presumably leaves the matter of weights undecided. The two principles may not so much oppose ordinary ideas as provide a relatively precise principle where common sense has little to say.

Finally, it is a political convention in a democratic society to appeal to the common good. No political party would admit to pressing for legislation to the disadvantage of any recognized social interest. But how, from a philosophical point of view, is this convention to be understood? Surely it is something more than the principle of efficiency (in its Paretian form) and we cannot assume that government always affects everyone's interests equally. Yet since we cannot maximize with respect to more than one point of view, it is natural, given the ethos of a democratic society, to single out that of the least advantaged and maximize their long-term prospects consistent with the liberties of equal citizenship. Moreover, it does seem that the policies which we most confidently think to be just do at least contribute positively to the well-being of this class, and hence that these policies are just throughout. Thus the difference principle seems to be a reasonable extension of the political convention of a democracy once we face up to the necessity of choosing a complete conception of justice.

References

GAUTHIER, D. (1963), *Practical Reasoning*, no. 126.

HARE, R. M. (1963), *Freedom and Reason*, Clarendon Press.

HARSANYI, J. C. (1953), 'Cardinal utility in welfare economics and in the theory of risk-taking', *J. polit. Econ.*, vol. 61, no. 434.

HARSANYI, J. C. (1955), 'Cardinal welfare, individualistic ethics and interpersonal comparisons of utility', *J. polit. Econ.*, vol. 63, no. 309.

HUME, D. (1779), *A Treatise of Human Nature*, book 3, part 3, section 1.

KALDOR, N. (1955), *An Expenditure Tax*, Allen & Unwin.

KANT, I. (1786), *The Foundation of the Metaphysics of Morals*, Bobbs–Merrill, 1959.

MILL, J. S. (1867), *Utilitarianism*, Doubleday, 1965.

NELSON, L. (1956), *System of Ethics*, trans. N. Guterman, Yale University Press.

PARETO, V. (1909), *Manuel d'Économie Politique*, Kelley.

PENNOCK, J. R. (1950), *Liberal Democracy: Its Merits and Prospects*, Holt, Rinehart & Winston.

PERRY, R. B. (1944), *Puritanism and Democracy*, Vanguard.

RAPHAEL, D. D. (1950–51), 'Justice and liberty', *Proceedings of the Aristotelian Society*, new series, vol. 51, pp. 187ff.

RAWLS, J. (1958), 'Justice as fairness', *philos. Rev.*, vol. 67, no. 164.

RAWLS, J. (1963), 'Constitutional liberty and the concept of justice', *Nomos*, vol. 6.

RAWLS, J. (1967), 'Distributive justice', in P. Laslett and W. G. Runciman (eds.), *Philosophy, Politics, and Society*, 3rd series, Blackwell.

RAWLS, J. (1968), 'Distributive justice: some addenda', *natural Law Forum*, vol. 13.

RAWLS, J. (1971), *A Theory of Justice*, Harvard University Press.

SANTAYANA, G. (1906), *Reason and Society*, Scribner.

SIDGWICK, H. (1907), *The Methods of Ethics*, 7th edn, Macmillan.

SPIEGELBERG, H. (1944), 'A defense of human equality', *philosoph. Rev.*, vol. 53, no. 101, pp. 113–23.

TAWNEY, R. H. (1952), *Equality*, 4th edn, Allen & Unwin.

VON HAYEK, F. (1960), *The Constitution of Liberty*, University of Chicago Press.

14 A. Rand

Government Financing in a Free Society

A. Rand, 'Government financing in a free society', *The Objectivist Newsletter*, 1964, February, reprinted in A. Rand, *The Virtue of Selfishness*, The New American Library, 1964, pp. 116–20.

'What would be the proper method of financing the government in a fully free society?'

This question is usually asked in connection with the objectivist principle that the government of a free society may not initiate the use of physical force and may use force only in retaliation against those who initiate its use. Since the imposition of taxes does represent an initiation of force, how, it is asked, would the government of a free country raise the money needed to finance its proper services?

In a fully free society, taxation – or, to be exact, payment for governmental services – would be *voluntary*. Since the proper services of a government – the police, the armed forces, the law courts – are demonstrably needed by individual citizens and affect their interests directly, the citizens would (and should) be willing to pay for such services, as they pay for insurance.

The question of how to implement the principle of voluntary government financing – how to determine the best means of applying it in practice – is a very complex one and belongs to the field of the philosophy of law. The task of political philosophy is only to establish the nature of the principle and to demonstrate that it is practicable. The choice of a specific method of implementation is more than premature today – since the principle will be practicable only in a *fully* free society, a society whose government has been constitutionally reduced to its proper, basic functions.

There are many possible methods of voluntary government financing. A government lottery, which has been used in some European countries, is one such method. There are others.

As an illustration (and *only* as an illustration), consider the following possibility. One of the most vitally needed services, which only a government can render, is the protection of contractual agreements among citizens. Suppose that the government were to protect – i.e. to recognize as legally valid and enforceable – only those contracts which had been insured by the payment, to the government, of a premium in the amount of a legally fixed percentage of the sums involved in the contractual transaction. Such an insurance would not be compulsory; there would be no legal penalty imposed on those who did not choose to take it – they would be free to make verbal agreements or to sign uninsured contracts, if they so wished. The only consequence would be that such agreements or contracts would not be legally enforceable; if they were broken, the injured party would not be able to seek redress in a court of law.

All credit transactions are *contractual agreements*. A credit transaction is any exchange which involves a passage of time between the payment and the receipt of goods or services. This includes the vast majority of economic transactions in a complex industrial society. Only a very small part of the gigantic network of credit transactions ever ends up in court, but the entire network is made possible by the existence of the courts, and would collapse overnight without that protection. *This* is a government service which people need, use, rely upon and should pay for. Yet, today, this service is provided gratuitously and amounts, in effect, to a subsidy.

When one considers the magnitude of the wealth involved in credit transactions, one can see that the percentage required to pay for such governmental insurance would be infinitesimal – much smaller than that paid for other types of insurance – yet it would be sufficient to finance all the other functions of a proper government. (If necessary, that percentage could be legally increased in time of war; or other, but similar, methods of raising money could be established for *clearly defined* wartime needs.)

This particular 'plan' is mentioned here only as an illustration of a possible method of approach to the problem – *not* as a definitive answer nor as a programme to advocate at present. The legal and technical difficulties involved are enormous: they include such questions as the need of an ironclad constitutional provision to prevent the government from dictating the *content* of private contracts (an issue which exists today and needs much more objective definitions) – the need of objective standards (or safeguards) for establishing the amount of the premiums, which cannot be left to the arbitrary discretion of the government, etc.

Any programme of voluntary government financing is the last, *not* the first, step on the road to a free society – the last, *not* the first, reform to advocate. It would work only when the basic principles and institutions of a free society have been established. It would not work today.

Men would pay voluntarily for insurance protecting their contracts. But they would not pay voluntarily for insurance against the danger of aggression by Cambodia. Nor would the plywood manufacturers of Wisconsin and their workers pay voluntarily for insurance to assist the development of the plywood industry of Japan which would put them out of business.

A programme of voluntary government financing would be amply sufficient to pay for the legitimate functions of a proper government. It would not be sufficient to provide unearned support for the entire globe. But no type of taxation is sufficient for that – only the suicide of a great country might be and then only temporarily.

Just as the growth of controls, taxes and 'government obligations' in this country was not accomplished overnight – so the process of liberation cannot be accomplished overnight. A process of liberation would be much more rapid than the process of enslavement had been, since the facts of reality would be its ally. But still, a gradual process is required – and any programme of voluntary government financing has to be regarded as a goal for a distant future.

What the advocates of a fully free society have to know, at present, is only the principle by which that goal can be achieved.

The principle of voluntary government financing rests on the following premises: that the government is *not* the owner of the citizens' income and, therefore, cannot hold a blank cheque on that income – that the nature of the proper governmental services must be constitutionally defined and delimited, leaving the government no power to enlarge the scope of its services at its own arbitrary discretion. Consequently, the principle of voluntary government financing regards the government as the servant, not the ruler, of the citizens – as an *agent* who must be paid for his services, not as a benefactor whose services are gratuitous, who dispenses something for nothing.

This last, along with the notion of compulsory taxation, is a remnant of the time when the government was regarded as the omnipotent ruler of the citizens. An absolute monarch, who owned the work, income, property and lives of his subjects, had to be an unpaid 'benefactor', protector and dispenser of favours. Such a monarch would have considered it demeaning to be paid for his services – just as the atavistic mentalities of his descendants-in-spirit (the remnants of Europe's ancient feudal aristocracy, and the modern welfare statists) still consider an earned, *commercial* income as demeaning and as morally inferior to an unearned one which is acquired by mooching or looting, by charitable donations or government force.

When a government, be it a monarch or a 'democratic' parliament, is regarded as a provider of gratuitous services, it is only a question of time before it begins to enlarge its services and the sphere of the gratuitous (today, this process is called the growth of 'the public sector of the economy') until it becomes, and has to become, the instrument of pressure-group warfare – of economic groups looting one another.

The premise to check (and to challenge) in this context is the primordial notion that any government services (even the legitimate ones) should be given to the citizens gratuitously. In order fully to translate into practice the American concept of the government as a *servant* of the citizens, one has to regard the government as a *paid servant*. Then, on that basis, one can proceed to devise the appropriate means of tying government revenues directly to the government services rendered.

It may be observed, in the example given above, that the cost of such voluntary government financing would be automatically proportionate to the scale of an individual's economic activity; those on the lowest economic levels (who seldom, if ever, engage in credit transactions) would be virtually exempt – though they would still enjoy the benefits of legal protection, such as that offered by the armed forces, by the police and by the courts dealing with criminal offences. These benefits may be regarded as a bonus to the men of lesser economic ability, made possible by the men of greater economic ability – *without any sacrifice of the latter to the former*.

It is in their own interests that the men of greater ability have to pay for the maintenance of armed forces, for the protection of their country against invasion; their expenses are not increased by the fact that a marginal part of the population is unable to contribute to these costs. Economically, that marginal group is nonexistent as far as the costs of war are concerned. The same is true of the costs of maintaining a police force: it is in their own interests that the abler men have to pay for the apprehension of criminals, regardless of whether the specific victim of a given crime is rich or poor.

It is important to note that this type of free protection for the noncontributors represents an *indirect benefit* and is merely a marginal consequence of the contributors' own interests and expenses. This type of bonus cannot be stretched to cover *direct* benefits, or to claim – as the welfare statists are claiming – that direct handouts to the nonproducers are in the producers' own interests.

The difference, briefly, is as follows: if a railroad were running a train and allowed the poor to ride without payment in the seats left empty, it would not be the same thing (nor the same principle) as providing the poor with first-class carriages and special trains.

Any type of *non-sacrificial* assistance, of social bonus, gratuitous benefit or gift value possible among men, is possible only in a free society, and is proper so long as it is non-sacrificial. But, in a free society, under a system of voluntary government financing, there would be no legal loophole, no legal possibility, for any 'redistribution of wealth' – for the unearned support of some men by the forced labour and extorted income of others – for the draining, exploitation and destruction of those who are able to pay the costs of maintaining a civilized society, in favour of those who are unable or unwilling to pay the cost of maintaining their own existence.

Part Five
Justice, Economics and Government Policy

This concluding section studies, within the context of very simple economic models, the implications for public policy of the utilitarian-type and Rawls-type criteria of distributive justice. Taxation and public expenditure are the two areas of policy considered. The first paper is by poor Edgeworth who had a very hard time getting Professor Seligmann and others to see that their criteria of equal sacrifice and equal proportionate sacrifice made no ethical sense. Edgeworth takes up the cause of equi-marginal sacrifice which he deduces from utilitarianism. It was not until the pioneering work of James Mirrlees, however, that economists began to examine the character of optimal tax functions when taxation is necessarily of the distortionary non-lump-sum kind. Much of Mirrlees' and others' work is surveyed in the paper by Atkinson. Sheshinski and Phelps examine the optimality of the 'negative income tax', linear and non-linear, a redistributive device that Edgeworth did not envisage. The paper by Arrow examines the question of the progressivity of public expenditures under the utilitarian criterion. In the final selection, Tobin muses over the variety of subsidy programmes and stamp plans that legislatures seem to favour over the use of money as the means of limiting poverty.

15 F. Y. Edgeworth

The Pure Theory of Progressive Taxation

F. Y. Edgeworth, 'The pure theory of taxation', third paper, *Economic Journal*, 1897, reprinted in F. Y. Edgeworth, *Papers Relating to Political Economy*, Macmillan, 1925, pp. 100–116.

The purest, as being the most deductive, form of utilitarianism is that from which Bentham reasoned down to equality (1859a; 1859b; 1859c).[1] There are those who regard this form as also purest, in that its first principle is the most apt to be universally accepted. That principle proposes as the end of action, or criterion of conduct, the greatest sum-total of happiness; the intensification of pleasure, its prolongation and distribution among increased numbers being approved only when they conduct to that end. The conception has been formulated mathematically by the present writer (1881).[2] In extending the summation of pleasure, according to the formula, over all time and all sentence, it is to be considered that, just as egoism is never so perfect but that distance in time renders pleasure less attractive, so utilitarianism is never so perfect but that persons whose interests are widely separate will not each 'count for one' to the other.

This remark may seem particularly appropriate to the adoption of utilitarianism as the rule of political action. The average citizen cannot be expected to care much for the interests of the foreigner, perhaps not very much for the interests of fellow-citizens outside his own class, nor at all for a remote posterity.

The proof of utilitarianism as the principle of political action has been variously conceived. The same speculative height is reached by different paths.[3] There is an approach on the economic side which it may be allowable to point out here. Let it be granted that there is a

1. J. S. Mill's doctrine of equality is not so clear (1867a, p. 93).

2. On the pleonastic words 'of the greatest number' commonly suffixed to 'greatest-happiness', see Edgeworth, (1881, p. 117).

3. There are some valuable reflections on Bentham's proof, or want of proof, in Professor Sidgwick's article on Bentham (1877, p. 647).

certain analogy between political and industrial cooperation or con-certed action – an analogy admitted by many high authorities with respect to the fiscal action of the State.[4] We must not regard as an essential feature of the analogy the circumstance that in economic bargains there generally prevails a rate of exchange corresponding to final utility. That circumstance is brought about by competition, which does not exist in the case of the political contract. It is there-fore improper, with Lord Auckland, to call income-tax 'a fair price for protection', to ask with Thiers, 'What is society if not a stock company in which every one has more or fewer shares?'. This is the fundamental fallacy of the 'quid pro quo principle' or 'benefit theory,' which is justly rejected by J. S. Mill, Seligman, and other high authorities. The 'economic' theory of taxation propounded by Sax, his 'conception of tax as a value-phenomenon', appears open to a similar objection. The truer analogy is with those economic bargains which are not governed by competition; for instance, an agreement between an employer or an association of employers and a trade union, or, as in the case of a 'boundary' dispute, two trade unions. Is there any general principle governing such agreements?

The present writer has suggested, as the principle apt to be adopted by two (or, *mutatis mutandis*, a few) self-interested parties contracting in the absence of competition, the greatest-happiness principle, slightly modified: that arrangement to be made which conduces to the greatest sum-total welfare of both parties, subject to the con-dition that neither should lose by the contract (1881, p. 53). Of course each party would rather have his own way completely. But the action of self-interest being suspended by mutual opposition, the more delicate force of amity which even in economic men is not entirely wanting,[5] may become felt. Moreover, each party may reflect that, in the long run of various cases, the maximum sum-total utility corresponds to the maximum individual utility. He cannot expect in the long run to obtain the larger share of the total welfare. But of all principles of distribution which would afford him now a greater, now a smaller proportion of the sum-total utility obtainable

4. E.g. the well-conceived analogy between the State in its fiscal capacity and a cooperative institution in Professor De Viti (1893, p. 103).

5. Much evidence was given before the Labour Commission as to the beneficial effects of 'closer acquaintanceship between the parties' (Group A, Q.607; see also Q2.019, 15,072–3, etc.).

on each occasion, the principle that the collective utility should be on each occasion a maximum is most likely to afford the greatest utility in the long run to him individually.[6] Thus the recommendation of utilitarianism to self-interested parties would not be – as Bentham's teaching has been said to be – like making ropes out of sand (see Sidgwick, 1877). *A fortiori*, the higher the degree of public spirit which is ascribed to the parties.

On these or other grounds assuming the greatest-happiness principle to be the test of governmental action, at least with respect to taxation, let us proceed to apply the principle. The primary problem is to determine the distribution of those taxes which are applied to common purposes, the benefits whereof cannot be allocated to particular classes of citizens. The condition that the total net utility procured by taxation should be a maximum then reduces to the condition that the total disutility should be a minimum.[7] From the condition that the total disutility should be a minimum, it follows in general that the marginal disutility incurred by each taxpayer should be the same. But if the inequality of fortunes is considerable with respect to the specified amount of taxation, there may not be taxation enough to go round, so to speak. The solution of the problem is that the higher incomes should be cut down to a certain level. At the same time the fact that the general marginal condition is not perfectly satisfied, suggests the solution of a wider, a *secondary* problem, namely, to determine the distribution of taxation, not being limited to that amount of which the benefit is indiscriminate. The solution

6. Thus it would appear reasonable that a foreman who is insolent to the workpeople, and not particularly serviceable to the employer, should be dismissed, if thereby the employer's profits are not sensibly diminished, while the workpeople gain considerably in freedom from annoyance; or, again, that workmen should consent, on terms not extravagant, to do a little extra work on an emergency, if thereby the employer is saved from considerable loss. But to illustrate fully the applicability of the principle would be out of place in this article.

7. The authority of Bentham may be cited in favour of this theory of taxation: 'It is therefore necessary that those who create wealth by their labour should give up a portion of it to supply the wants of the guardians of the State. . . . All government is only a tissue of sacrifices. The best government is that in which the value of those sacrifices is reduced to the smallest amount' (1859a, part 1, chapter 13).

'To take care that this pain of constraint and privation be reduced to the lowest term' (1859b).

of this problem in the abstract is that the richer should be taxed for the benefit of the poorer up to the point at which complete equality of fortunes is attained. The *acme* of socialism is thus for a moment sighted; but it is immediately clouded over by doubts and reservations.

In this misty and precipitous region let us take Sidgwick as our chief guide. He best has contemplated the crowning height of the utilitarian first principle, from which the steps of a sublime deduction lead to the high tableland of equality (1883, book 3, chapter 7, section 1); but he also discerns the enormous interposing chasms which deter practical wisdom from moving directly towards that ideal.

In the first place it is conceivable that a greater equality in the distribution of produce would lead ultimately to a reduction in the total amount to be distributed in consequence of a general preference of leisure to the results of labour on the part of the classes whose snares of produce had increased (section 2).

There is also the danger

That the increase through equalization of the incomes of the poorer classes will cause the population to increase at a more rapid rate than at present; so that ultimately the increment of an average worker's share will be partly spent in supporting a larger number of children, and partly reduced through the decrease in the efficiency of the more crowded labour.

It is remarkable that Mill should have apprehended the dangers of deficient production and excessive population less than the danger to liberty. The weighty sentence into which he condenses the substance of his teaching on liberty deserves to be repeated.

It is yet to be ascertained whether the Communistic scheme would be consistent with that multiform development of human nature, those manifold unlikenesses, that diversity of tastes and talents, and variety of intellectual points of view which not only form a great part of the interest of human life, but in bringing intellects into stimulating collision and by presenting to each innumerable notions that he would not have conceived of himself, are the mainspring of mental and moral progression (1848, book 2, section 3).

Liberty is not the only one of the higher goods which is threatened by a dull equality: there is also the 'function of maintaining and developing knowledge and culture', the performance of which function, as pointed out by Sidgwick, has hitherto been largely due to 'rich and leisured persons' (1883).

The transition is easy to another reservation, which is in some sense more intrinsic than the preceding. The Benthamic argument that equality of means tends to maximum of happiness, presupposes a certain equality of natures: but if the capacity for happiness[8] of different classes is different, the argument leads not to equal, but to unequal distribution. The testimony of Sidgwick that Bentham would probably have recognized this reservation[9] carries a double weight of authority. The possibility corroborated by so high evidence is calculated to temper the more drastic applications of utilitarianism.

The preceding reservations relate to the pursuit of socialistic equality by any methods; the following relate more particularly to the pursuit of that end by means of taxation. A progressive tax rising to such a rate that it would not be in the interest of the taxpayer to increase his fortune by saving or enterprise above a certain amount, while improving the distribution, would check the augmentation of the community's wealth. There is, however, to be set off the probable increase of saving among the poorer classes. Especially the investment of capital in persons by way of education might be increased. There would be an increase of production also so far as the proceeds of socialistic taxation are applied to render the poorer classes more efficient. But against this increase in the efficiency of the poor might have to be set some decrease in the efficiency of the not very rich.

Again, there is the general presumption against governmental

8. This terminology has been employed by the present writer (1881, p. 57; see also pp. 64, 125) to designate differences both in the amount of means which different individuals may require in order to attain the threshold or zero-point of happiness, and in the amounts of utility which they may derive from the same additions of means above that point. Compare Carver's weighty observations (1895, p. 82) upon difference in *wants* – a term which may also refer to differences in the amount of means needed for efficiency.

9. Sidgwick says: 'I do not however think that Bentham intended to deny (1) that one person may be more capable of happiness than another, or (2) that, if so, the former's happiness is more important than the latter's, as an element of general happiness.' (1883, p. 583, note 2. See also note 3 for a fuller statement of Sidgwick's own view.)

action, the special danger that taxation extended beyond its proper objects will be abused. The warning comes with less weight from those who are ready to employ taxation for a collateral purpose of which they themselves approve – the correction of intemperance.

In fine, the increase of taxation is limited by evasion.

These extensive, though briefly indicated, reservations reduce the prima facie revolutionary dictates of pure utilitarianism to the limits of common sense. The position thus defined is much the same as Mill's. 'That the State should use the instrument of taxation as a means of mitigating the inequality of wealth' is not to be demanded when a 'tax on industry and economy,' a check to the growth of wealth, is thereby imposed (Mill, 1867b, book 5, chapter 2, section3). But the utilitarian will be as 'desirous as any one that means should be taken to diminish those inequalities': such means as the limitation of inheritances and the taxation of unearned increments, so far as these means are free from the dangers above enumerated. A similar reconcilement between equality and security is taught in an article replete with utilitarian wisdom on 'The ethical basis of distribution', by Carver (1895, p. 97).

The minimum amount of repression (or check to the growth of wealth) is secured by imposing an equal sacrifice on all members of the community, but the minimum amount of sacrifice is secured by collecting the whole tax from those few incomes which have the lowest final utility. No rational writer advocates the latter plan exclusively, but many rational writers do advocate the former plan. Yet it is not beyond dispute that the former plan ought to be followed exclusively.

This passage, read with the context, almost exactly expresses the thesis here maintained; except that the last sentence is asserted rather too diffidently, and the first clause much too confidently. *Minimum sacrifice*, the direct emanation of pure utilitarianism, is the sovereign principle of taxation; it requires no doubt to be limited in practice; but query whether the requisite limitation is to be obtained from *equal sacrifice*, or any of the cognate subsidiary forms of the hedonic principle which are presently to be considered?

Before leaving the principle of minimum sacrifice, let it be observed that, under the limitations which have been described, this principle may also be applied to justify differential taxation on the ground of differences in other respects besides size of income: for instance, difference in the permanence of the income, differences in civil state, number of children, age, and other attributes.

Besides the principle of minimum sacrifice, which has been considered, there are other species of the hedonic theory of taxation. The most familiar are the principles of equal and of proportional sacrifice: that each taxpayer should sacrifice an equal amount of utility, or an equal proportion of the total utility which he derives from material resources. The former species is the commonest in England; the latter flourishes in Holland. The two species might be included in a genus termed 'like sacrifice.'

It will be convenient to consider first the practical consequences, next the theoretical proof of these two principles.

In order to deduce conclusions from either premise, there is required another premise relating to the law of diminishing utility. There are some reasons for assuming – it is at least the simplest hypothesis – that utility diminishes in inverse ratio to means, after the law of Bernoulli. Upon this assumption the principle of equal sacrifice gives proportional taxation; the principle of proportional sacrifice gives progressive taxation.

But there seem to be better reasons for assuming that the utility diminishes with the increase of income at a faster rate. There is the testimony of high authorities, Montesquieu, Paley, Say and many others cited in the learned pages of Seligman. True, Mill regards the doctrine as 'too disputable altogether' with regard to the higher incomes. But neither Mill nor any other considerable authority has held that the diminution is *less* than in the inverse ratio of the income. Mill's estimate being the lowest, we may take as the most probable estimate one intermediate between his and others, and assume that the utility diminishes at a rate exceeding the increase of income, if not for the highest incomes, at any rate for incomes considerably above the usually exempted minimum.

This presumption is confirmed by the observation that the property in question, the diminution of utility out of proportion to the inverse income, almost certainly holds for large differences as distinguished from differential variations; As Meyer has well argued. But, if such is the character of the utility-curve as to finite differences, it is probably also its character as to differential variations. The observed circumstances would not be consistent with the prevalence of Bernoulli's law throughout. It must be assumed that for a considerable tract of the curve – supposed not violently discontinuous – the property in question prevails.

Some doubt may remain as to the extremity of the curve which corresponds to very high incomes. It has been supposed by several high and independent authorities, that ultimately the law of Bernoulli holds good. Some of the reasons assigned are to be found in the passages cited below from eminent authors. It is here submitted that the character ascribed to the extremity of the utility-curve is not sufficiently evidenced. First, as to capitalization, regarding it as an application of income to future gratifications (whether personal or vicarious), one does not see why it should not approach satiety with a rapidity greater than that which is assigned by the Bernoullian law. It may be suspected, too, that an improper inference is drawn from the circumstance that as the income is increased by equal increments the differences between the successive increments of utility become less. But it is not with these differences that we are concerned, but with the *ratio* between successive increments of utility. And there is nothing to show that this ratio does not increase more rapidly than according to the Bernoullian law. The pleasure derived from a certain income may well increase with the income somewhat as, according to the theory of errors of observation, the probability that an error will occur within a certain distance increases with the distance.[10] Ultimately the additions become imperceptible, but not the less do they obey the law that a disproportionately large increment of the inde-

10. The marginal utility of money – the measure of the increment of welfare which corresponds to an increment of income – might quite well have some such form as the probability-curve, viz.

$$y\left(= \frac{du}{dx} \right) = Ae^{-(x-a)^2}$$

where x, the independent variable, is the amount of income, y, the dependent variable, is the marginal utility of income (the differential of u, the total utility of income); a is the minimum of existence, and A another constant. In order that the sacrifices (first supposed small) made by two individuals having incomes x_1 and x_2 should be equal, the respective contributions should be, not as $x_1:x_2$, but as $e^{+(x_1-a)^2}:e^{+(x_2-a)^2}$. And this disproportion of contribution to income would not only be maintained, but increased, as the income is indefinitely increased. *A fortiori*, if proportional, not equal, sacrifice is aimed at. *A fortiori*, too, if the sacrifices are not small.

pendent variable is required to produce the same increment of the dependent one. In fine the view here combated has no doubt derived some adventitious aid from the supposed practical necessity of adopting a proportional income-tax for very high incomes; which could only be justified by the principle of equal sacrifice upon the assumption of the Bernoullian law.

It is to be admitted, however, that the property in question has been accepted by Cohen-Stuart, who cannot be suspected of mathematical confusion, and who has expressly distinguished the theoretical and practical points of view (1889, p. 134).

Here are his reasons:

For the millionaire – or rather . . . the *milliardaire* – the possession of his income signifies no more than a cipher, the increase of which has no longer any influence on his consumption. To see the cipher increased by 4 per cent for instance, if it is a pleasure to a man with 10 million [francs per annum] or one with 100 or 500 millions, would be, I should say, about the same pleasure to each. . . . As soon as all personal wants are pretty well satisfied, and, *a fortiori*, after the income has passed this limit, its increase proportionately, that is by an equal percentage, must, as it seems to me, tend to afford an equal pleasure. That the addition of the same *amount* should be as strongly desired, should produce equal pleasure, however great the income, seems to me absurd; that the same *proportion* of the income should have this effect strikes me as rational (p. 155).

The mathematical reader who is not convinced by Cohen-Stuart on this point will hardly defer to others.

Upon the assumption that the diminution of marginal utility with income is (throughout) in excess of Bernoulli's law, the principle of equal sacrifice and that of proportional sacrifice both give progressive taxation, the latter in a higher degree than the former.[11] Either principle, but more probably the latter, may (upon the assumption above made) lead to a subtraction of income so great as to leave the possessor little interest in increasing his income beyond a certain limit. The two varieties of like sacrifice may in this respect resemble the principle of minimum sacrifice in requiring to be limited by a regard

11. i.e. higher for any assigned form of the utility-curve, and amount of taxation.

F. Y. Edgeworth 379

for other disutilities beside the constraint and privation occasioned to the taxpayer.[12]

The method of applying the limitation might well be, for all the forms of the sacrifice theory, the use of such a scale of progression as would be given by the principle of proportional taxation *upon the supposition* that the extreme tract of the utility-curve was such as it has been conceived by Cohen-Stuart and others. Practical reasons, not deductions from any form of the first principle, would thus lead to a 'degressive progression' culminating in a simply proportionate tax of the higher incomes, such as in fact seems to be coming into vogue. Then those who hold the principle of proportional sacrifice might avail themselves of the curious theorem given by Cohen-Stuart, that an approximately proportional tax being imposed on the higher incomes, the law of progression for the tax on the lower incomes, as deduced from the principle of proportional sacrifice, would be much the same, however the law of utility might vary, between wide limits.

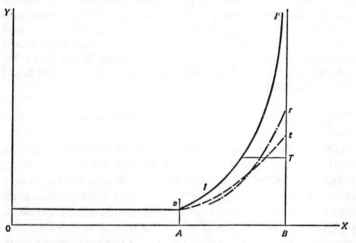

Figure 1 Income tax schedule

12. The relation between the different modes of the sacrifice theory might thus be exhibited diagrammatically. Let Y measured along the axis OY represent size of income; and construct the curve II' such that the co-ordinate to any assigned Y represents the number of incomes smaller than Y. Thus the strip of area $Y\Delta X$ represents the portion of the national income which consists of incomes of the size Y. The curve II' is probably shaped as in the figure; in conformity to Pareto's

The distinction between like sacrifice and minimum sacrifice is not more serious when the principles are applied to differences in other respects besides amount of income (see source of this Reading, p. 556). For example, whether it is easier to say that incomes which are not equally permanent should not be taxed equally, because the sacrifices would not be equal to each other, as Mill has it (1867b, book 5, chapter 2, section 4, note), or because their total would not be a minimum, as here proposed? So the doctrine of minimum sacrifice, as well as that of proportional sacrifice, may use the proposition affirmed by Cohen-Stuart, that for the purposes of taxation the married differ from the unmarried chiefly in having a higher minimum of exemption.

To have deduced the precepts will aid us in estimating the authority of *like sacrifice*. This may best be effected, from the utilitarian point of view adopted in this article, by determining the relation of the principle under consideration to the supreme principle. That relation is one of complete autonomy, if like sacrifice is prescribed by

---

beautiful theory of income-curves (1890). II' may be regarded as asymptotic to – or at least terminating on – a perpendicular through B, where OB is the total number of incomes; Aa may be taken as a minimum exempted from taxation.

Then to apply the principle of minimum sacrifice, find a point, T, on the ordinate through B, such that the area intercepted by that ordinate, the horizontal through T and the curve II' should represent a portion of the national income equal to the required amount of taxation. To apply the principle of proportional taxation, find t on the same ordinate such that the required amount of taxation may be equal to the amount represented by the area intercepted between that ordinate, the curve II', and a curve at which the ordinate η at every point fulfils the condition

$$(y-\eta) \times \left(\frac{du}{dy}\right) \div u = \text{constant};$$

where u is the total amount of utility derived (on an average) from the income y. This curve is represented by the continuously dotted curve line in the figure (upon a certain supposition as to the minimum of exemption, see Cohen-Stuart (1889), on the 'Bestaans-minimum'). To apply the principle of equal sacrifice, find τ, on the same ordinate, such that the required amount of taxation may be represented by the area contained between the ordinate, the curve II', and the curve of which the ordinate η fulfils the condition

$$(y-\eta)(du/dy) = \text{constant}$$

A part of this curve is represented by the discontinuously dotted (broken) line in the figure. If completed this curve may be expected to meet II' asymptotically intuitive justice. But the utilitarian will not accept this *imperium in imperio*. He will object to like *sacrifice* thus supported, what several acute dialecticians have objected to proportional sacrifice, that its propriety is not self-evident.

A position more neutral with regard to utilitarianism is taken by Cohen-Stuart when he maintains that proportional sacrifice, leaving the relation between all the parties in respect of welfare unchanged, is *the* principle for the Manchester man. Somewhat similar appears to be the position of Sidgwick, except that he has explicitly recognized the supremacy of the greatest-happiness principle, and admits the possibility of its being employed to promote equality by taxation. But he regards this direct interposition of the supreme principle as liable to a dangerous excess. The principle of equal sacrifice is therefore deputed to act, a deputy not liable, like the principal, to be betrayed into imprudent concessions. This paraphrase is based on the following passages and their context:

The obviously equitable principle – assuming that the existing distribution of wealth is accepted as just, or not unjust – is that equal sacrifices should be imposed on all; and this [is] also obviously the most economic[13] adjustment of the burden except so far as it is thought to make taxation a means of redressing the inequalities of income that would exist apart from governmental interference.

The introduction, however, of this latter principle to any marked extent involves the danger [described in the preceding chapter]. And the danger is much greater here . . . because if the principle is applied at all, any limit to its application seems quite arbitrary.

---

below A. But, doubtless, regard to efficiency and other practical considerations may lead to the deformation of the curve, so as to join on at an earlier point to II'.

It will be apparent from this illustration that equal sacrifice is less socialistic than proportional sacrifice, and proportional sacrifice less so than minimum. But in what degree either mode of like sacrifice is less socialistic than minimum sacrifice, we have no data, it is submitted, for determining. It is quite possible that the curve through τ, and, *a fortiori*, the curve through t, should prescribe a taxation of the higher incomes, which in the interests of production it would be fatal to carry out. Like sacrifice can no more, or not much more, than minimum sacrifice be trusted to act without checks. What, then, is the ground for preferring like sacrifice?

13. 'Economic' is, of course, used here in the same sense as in the preceding chapter; that is, nearly equivalent to utilitarian in our first sense. (See source of this Reading, book 3, chapter 7, section 1, paragraph 1.)

The position of Cohen-Stuart with respect to proportional sacrifice and that of Sidgwick with respect to equal sacrifice are tenable, so long as we hold with Cohen-Stuart that the utility-curve is ultimately of the Bernoullian form. But if, as above contended, this premise is not tenable, then a rapidly progressive taxation following from the principle of proportional sacrifice, the Manchester man could hardly be expected to acquiesce in that principle. Nor could the principle of equal sacrifice be safely deputed to act on behalf of the supreme principle. Of the deputy as well as of the sovereign, we might then say: 'if the principle is applied at all, any limit to its application seems quite arbitrary. At any rate, the only certain limit to the application of equal sacrifice – viz. that more than the necessary minimum of taxation should not be raised and more should not be required from the higher incomes than would bring down all above a certain level to that level[14] – is greatly in excess of practical limitations. Is it not simpler to dismiss the deputed principle of equal sacrifice, and to adopt as the true norm of taxation minimum sacrifice tempered by a regard for the growth of wealth and other advantages above enumerated?

The capacity of like sacrifice to act independently is even less upon another view of its authority. What if, as compared with the utilitarian code, it is not a sort of by-law, as just now in effect supposed, but simply a clause, a badly-transcribed clause, of the code itself? What if *equal sacrifice* is but a corrupt reading for *equi-marginal sacrifice*, the condition of minimum disutility? (See above, p. 398). Thus Mill, in that classical passage which has influenced the most influential of his successors, in the same breath proclaims the principles of equal and of least sacrifice:

Whatever sacrifices it [a government] requires from them [persons or classes] should be made to bear as nearly as possible with the same pressure upon all, which, it must be observed, is the mode by which least sacrifice is occasioned on the whole.[15]

It is remarkable that in support of one of the principal reforms

14. As appears from the position of the curve through *t* in note 12.

15. Mill (1867b, book 5, chapter 2, section 2, paragraph 1). The divergence between the principle of equal sacrifice presented by Mill and that of minimum sacrifice is indicated by the present writer (1881, p. 118). Carver calls attention to the fact that Mill affirmed the two divergent principles in the same passage (1895, p. 95).

with respect to taxation which he advocated, Mill should have employed the genuine utilitarian reasoning in favour of equality rather than the questionable principle of equal sacrifice.[16] Thus when he first introduces the proposal to limit inheritances:

It must be apparent to every one that the difference to the happiness of the possessor between a moderate independence and five times as much is insignificant when weighed against the enjoyment that might be given, and the permanent benefit diffused by some other disposal of the four-fifths (1848, book 2, chapter 2, section 4).

And in a later chapter on inheritance, he refers to 'the deeper consideration that the diffusion of wealth, not its concentration, is desirable' (1848, book 5, chapter 9, seven 2).

So McCulloch can see no halting-place, such as the principle of equal sacrifice is supposed to supply, between a proportional income-tax and that levelling of the higher incomes which, as above shown, is the inference from the principle of minimum sacrifice (1833, p. 164).

So Meyer describes as 'the commonest argument' in favour of progressive taxation one which rests upon an interpretation of equal sacrifice which makes it virtually identical with equi-marginal sacrifice.

So some of the high authorities who have advocated progressive taxation on the ground of equal sacrifice may be credited with an 'unconsciously implicit'[17] utilitarianism of the pure type. Cohen-Stuart indeed has argued that several of these high authorities hold the principle of proportional sacrifice. For whereas they have deduced progressive taxation from the principle of equal sacrifice, *simpliciter* and without any *datum* as to the law according to which utility diminishes, this fallacious reasoning is explicable, he thinks, on the former supposition, but on the latter inexplicable. But what if there was in the confused minds of these distinguished publicists not *equal* sacrifice nor yet *proportional* sacrifice, but *equi-marginal* sacrifice (leading to *minimum* sacrifice)? It is true that this premise is less consonant to their statements than the other. But then their con-

16. Bentham is always clearer than Mill in the deduction of equality from greatest-happiness, because he virtually employs the differential calculus: adding and subtracting 'particles of wealth', as in (1859c, vol. 3, p. 231).

17. The happy term applied by Sidgwick to the utilitarianism which is latent in current ethical opinion.

clusion really does follow from this premise. Obliged as we are to make a compromise between obscure premises and fallacious reasoning, may not the line of least confusion, so to speak, be – not the assumption that the premise was somewhat obscure and the reasoning somewhat erroneous, but – that the premise was quite confused and the reasoning quite exact?

Altogether, whatever view we take of the relation of the principle of like sacrifice to pure utilitarianism, the sphere of its action independently of that supreme principle appears to be insignificant.

References

BENTHAM, J. (1859a), 'Propositions of pathology upon which the advantage of equality is founded', in 'Principals of the Civil Code', *Works*, vol. 1, p. 304.
BENTHAM, J. (1859b), 'Constitutional code', *Works*, vol. 9.
BENTHAM, J. (1859c), 'Pannomiai fragments', *Works*, vol. 3.
BENTHAM, J. (1859d), 'View of a complete code of laws', *Works*, vol. 3, p. 204.
CARVER, T. N. (1895), *American Academy of Political Science*.
CARVER, T. N. (1895), 'The ethical basis of distribution', *Annals of the American Academy*.
COHEN-STUART, A. J. (1889), '*Bijdrage tot de Theorie der Progressieve Inkomstenbelastung*', Martins Nijhoff, The Hague.
EDGEWORTH, F. Y. (1881), *Mathematical Psychics*, Kegan Paul.
McCULLOCH, J. R. (1833), *Edinburgh Rev.*, vol. 57.
MILL, J. S. (1867a), *Utilitarianism*, Longman.
MILL, J. S. (1867b), *Principles of Political Economy*, Longman.
PARETO, V. (1890), 'Cours d'économie politique pure: courbe des revenus', Paris.
SELIGMAN, E. R. A. (1902), *Progressive Taxation*, Princeton University Press.
SIDGWICK, H. (1883), *Principles of Political Economy*, Macmillan.
SIDGWICK, H. (1877), Article on Bentham, *Fortnightly Rev.*, vol. 21.
VITI, A. DE (1893), *Carattere Teoricetico dell'Economia Finanzieria*, Torino.

16 A. B. Atkinson

How Progressive Should Income-Tax Be?

A. B. Atkinson, 'How progressive should income-tax be?', in M. Parkin (ed.), Essays on Modern Economics, Longman, 1973.

The moment you abandon . . . the cardinal principle of exacting from all individuals the same proportion of their income or their property, you are at sea without rudder or compass, and there is no amount of injustice or folly you may not commit. . . . Graduation is not an evil to be paltered with. Adopt it and you will effectively paralyse industry. . . . The savages described by Montesquieu, who to get at the fruit cut down the tree, are about as good financiers as the advocates of this sort of taxes. (McCulloch, 1845).

1 Introduction

In Britain the marginal rate of income tax on earned income is zero initially, rises to 30 per cent for a very wide range of incomes and then increases quite sharply to a maximum rate of 75 per cent for sur-tax payers. Is this structure too progressive or insufficiently so? The aim of this paper is to explore some of the arguments that could be applied in the unlikely event of the Chancellor of the Exchequer asking economists for guidance on this question, and to see just what can be said about how progressive the income-tax should be. The first half of the paper surveys the current state of knowledge: the traditional sacrifice theories and the more recent extensions of these by Mirrlees and others. The second half of the paper introduces a simple model designed to throw light on the way in which the aims of the government influence the optimal degree of progression and to bring out considerations which have been obscured in the earlier literature.

It should be made clear at the outset that the paper makes no attempt to provide a definite answer to the question posed in the title. Indeed one of the main conclusions is that such an answer cannot be given without further clarification of social objectives. Instead the paper attempts to illuminate the basic structure of the problem and to provide insight into the kind of argument required to justify positions which are commonly taken on this question. Two other qualifications should also be entered. The paper is concerned only with the taxation of earned income and not with the taxation of investment income, which introduces quite different considerations. Second, the paper deals only with income-taxes and does not consider the possibility that other forms of taxation (such as a wage tax) might be employed.

2 The minimum-sacrifice theory

Those textbooks which discuss the question of the optimal degree of progression usually begin by referring to the theories of equal sacrifice. The statements by Adam Smith that subjects should 'contribute in proportion to their respective abilities' and by John Stuart Mill that 'whatever sacrifices [the government] requires . . . should be made to bear as nearly as possible with the same pressure upon all' were translated by later writers into more precise principles of equal sacrifice. These took a number of different forms, but the principle of equal marginal sacrifice put forward by Edgeworth, Pigou and others had the clearest rationale, being derived from the utilitarian objective of the maximization of the sum of individual utilities.

Let us suppose that individuals differ in their earning ability and that this is denoted by n. The before tax earnings of a person of type n are denoted by $z(n)$ and the tax paid by $T(n)$. The utility derived from the after tax income is given by $U_n[z(n)-T(n)]$, so that if $f(n)$ is the frequency distribution of people of type n the sum of individual utilities is denoted by

$$W = \int_0^\infty U_n[z(n)-T(n)]f(n)\,dn. \qquad 1$$

The government is assumed to choose the tax rates to maximize W subject to the revenue constraint

$$\int_0^\infty T(n)f(n)\,dn = \bar{R}, \qquad 2$$

(where $\bar{R}$ denotes the net revenue to be raised and $T(n)$ may be negative)[1]. The solution is straightforward (on the assumption that U is concave):

$$U_n'[z(n)-T(n)] \text{ equal all } n, \qquad\qquad 3$$

and if an identical marginal utility of income schedule is assumed, the tax structure is such that after-tax incomes are equalized:[2] 'A system of equimarginal sacrifice fully carried out would involve lopping off the tops of all incomes above the minimum income and leaving everybody, after taxation, with equal incomes' (Pigou, 1947, pp. 57–8).

The minimum-sacrifice theory has come under a great deal of attack and is dismissed by most authors. Two main lines of criticism may be distinguished:

1. That the minimum-sacrifice theory takes no account of the possible disincentive effect of taxation ($z(n)$ may be influenced by the tax structure).

2. That the underlying utilitarian framework is inadequate.

The next section of this paper examines the contribution made by the recent work of Mirrlees and others to overcoming the first of these objections. The second line of criticism is taken up later in the paper.

3 Income-tax progression and work incentives

The importance of the possible disincentive effect of taxation was clearly recognized in the discussion by Sidgwick: 'It is conceivable that a greater equality in the distribution of produce would lead ulti- mately to a reduction in the total amount to be distributed in conse- quence of a general preference of leisure to the results of labour' (quoted in Edgeworth, 1925, p. 104). The proponents of the minimum- sacrifice approach did not, however, make any attempt to arrive at a tax formula incorporating these considerations. One of the main contributions of the recent papers in this area has been to fill this gap and to derive optimal tax schedules taking account of the effects of

1. If $T(n)$ were constrained to be non-negative, we would have the solution described by Dalton: 'taxing only the largest incomes, cutting down all above a certain level to that level, and exempting all below that level' (1954, p. 59).

2. This will only, of course, ensure an equal level of utility where the origins of the utility functions are identical (they are fully comparable, see Sen, 1970).

taxation on work effort. This section describes the formulation of the problem and the principal results obtained.

The recent revival of interest in this area is largely attributable to the important paper by Mirrlees (1971), where he considers the influence of taxation on the work/leisure choice. A person of type n determines the proportion of the day he spends at work $(y(n))$ so as to maximize his utility $U[x(n), y(n)]$ where $x(n)$ denotes his after-tax income and is given by

$$x(n) = z(n) - T[z(n)] \qquad \qquad 4$$

and $\quad z(n) = ny(n),$ 5

(i.e. the parameter of earning ability, n, represents the wage per unit of time for a man of type n). Otherwise, the formulation is identical to that described in section 2. The government chooses the income-tax function $T(z)$ to maximize the sum of individual utilities (where it is assumed that all individuals have identical utility functions):[3]

$$W = \int\limits_{0}^{\infty} U[x(n), y(n)]f(n)\, dn \qquad \qquad 6$$

subject to the revenue constraint 2.

With the introduction of the work/leisure choice, the problem becomes a considerably more difficult one than the simple minimum sacrifice theory. The first part of Mirrlees's paper is concerned with the derivation of general properties of the optimal tax function $T(z)$, but the results he obtains are limited to establishing that:

(a) the optimal marginal tax rate lies between zero and one,

(b) it will be optimal (in most interesting cases) for some of the population to remain idle (i.e. $y(n) = 0$).

More than this cannot be said: 'The optimum tax schedule depends upon the distribution of skills within the population, in such a complicated way that it is not possible to say in general whether marginal tax rates should be higher for high-income, low-income, or intermediate income groups' (1971, p. 186).

3. No account is taken in this paper of differing needs and this problem clearly requires further analysis. For discussion of the variation of taxation with family size, see Mirrlees (1972).

In the later part of his paper, Mirrlees goes on, therefore, to consider the special case where

$$U = \log_e [x^a (1-y)]$$

and $f(n)$ is either the lognormal or the Pareto distribution. This special case is considered analytically in section 8 of his paper, and for a range of numerical calculations (with $a = 1$ and $f(n)$) lognormal in section 9.

On the basis of his analysis, and in particular of the numerical calculations, Mirrlees draws a number of (qualified) conclusions. Two of the most important for policy purposes are that: (a) the optimal tax structure is appoximately linear: i.e. a constant marginal tax rate, with an exemption level below which negative tax supplements are payable; (b) the marginal tax rates are rather low and tend to fall rather than rise with the level of income – see Table 1 for two illustrative cases. The second conclusion is an unexpected one. Mirrlees comments that 'I had expected the rigorous analysis of income taxation in the utilitarian manner to provide an argument for high tax rates', and expresses surprise that it has not done so.

Table 1 *Optimal tax rates–Mirrlees cases 1 and 2*

| | Case 1 | | Case 2 | |
	Average tax rate %	Marginal tax rate %	Average tax rate %	Marginal tax rate %
Bottom decile	−5	24	−50	20
Median	5	22	−12	19
Top decile	13	19	2	17
Top percentile	14	17	7	16

Source: Interpolated from Mirrlees (1971, tables 1–4). In Case 1 the revenue requirement is positive, in Case 2 it is negative (the government is disposing of the profits of public sector production).

It is clear that the conclusions drawn by Mirrlees rest heavily on the particular assumptions made. In his concluding section he draws attention to the fact that 'the shape of the optimum earned-income tax schedule is rather sensitive to the distribution of skills within the population and to the income–leisure preferences postulated'. The latter assumption is, as he says 'heroic' and may well overstate the sensitivity of labour supply to changes in the marginal rate of income-tax. There is, however, an aspect of the special cases taken by Mirrlees to which he does not draw adequate attention – the effect of the choice of a particular functional form to represent given income/leisure preferences.

In the minimum sacrifice theory, the particular cardinalization selected did not affect the tax structure (providing it was the same for all). If we replace U by $G[U]$ where $G' > 0$, $G'' < 0$ the first-order condition is

$$G'\{U'[z(n)-T(n)]\} \text{ equal all } n$$

giving the same solution. In the present case, however, this is no longer true. In order to clarify this point, let us consider the particular transformations of the utility function

$$V^{(1-\rho)}/1-\rho, \quad \rho \geqslant 0, \qquad\qquad 7$$

where V is normalized, so that for $\rho = 0$ it just satisfies the concavity requirement, which in the present case means that

$$V = x^A(1-y)^{1-A}. \qquad\qquad 8$$

The case taken in Table 1 corresponds to $\log_e V$ or to $\rho = 1$.[4] If, however, we were to take a higher value of ρ, this would lead to the optimal tax structure being more progressive. As ρ rises, the marginal utility of income diminishes more rapidly and the 'cost' of inequality (in terms of the loss of aggregate utility) increases.

The effect of changes in ρ may be illustrated by the numerical examples given by Mirrlees where

$$G = -e^{-U} \qquad\qquad 9$$

which corresponds to the case $\rho = 2$. His results are not presented in such a way as to facilitate the comparison, since the amount of revenue to be raised is not held constant in the different cases. However, the optimal marginal tax rate tends to fall as the revenue to be collected falls, so that the comparisons shown in Table 2 will tend to understate the rise in the optimal tax rate as ρ increases. It is clear in fact that the increase in ρ leads to definitely higher marginal tax rates.

4. $\log_e V$ is the limit of $V^{1-\rho}/1-\rho$ as $\rho \to 1$ – see Hardy, Littlewood and Polya (1952, chapter 2).

Table 2 *Effect of increase in ρ on optimal marginal tax rates*

	$\rho = 1$	$\rho = 2$
	Revenue 7% of income *Marginal tax rate %*	*Revenue 2% of income* *Marginal tax rate %*
Bottom decile	24	33
Median	22	30
Top decile	19	26
Top percentile	17	21
	Revenue 10% of income *Marginal tax rate %*	*Revenue 20% of income* *Marginal tax rate %*
Bottom decile	20	28
Median	19	26
Top decile	17	24
Top percentile	16	21

Source: Interpolated from Mirrlees (1971, tables 1–8).

This conclusion leads one to ask how Mirrlees's results would be affected by taking still larger values of ρ. Is it possible that he would have found optimal tax rates of the order of 50 per cent or more if he had chosen higher values of ρ? One way in which we can test this is by taking the limit as $\rho \to \infty$, and hence

$$W = \frac{\min}{n} V(n), \qquad\qquad 10$$

i.e. we can obtain an upper bound on the effect of increasing ρ by examining the tax structure which maximizes the utility of the worst-off person.

A second important recent contribution is that by Fair (1971). The model considered by him differs from that of Mirrlees in two important respects:

(a) Hourly earnings are assumed to be a function not only of ability but also of the level of education. If we denote the proportion of working hours spent in education by E, earnings are

$$z(n) = y(1-E)g(n, E), \qquad\qquad 11$$

where $g(n, E)$ is the wage rate per working hour.

The individual utility function is the same as (2.4) – education is purely an investment and does not provide consumption benefits – and E is chosen to maximize $z(n)$.

(b) the range of tax schedules under consideration is restricted to

$$T'(z) = a_0 \log_e(1+z),$$

or $T(z) = a_0[(z+1)\log_e(1+z)] - a,$ **12**

where a represents a guaranteed minimum income (if $z = 0$).

The results obtained by Fair are numerical ones only, and are based on a normal distribution of abilities and an approximated relationship $g(n, E)$. The conclusions are primarily summarized in terms of the Gini coefficient of concentration, but it is possible to calculate the average and marginal tax rates for two of his nine earnings functions for people at different points on the ability range.

Table 3 *Optimal tax rates: results of Fair*

	Earnings function 5		Earnings function 8	
	Average tax rate %	Marginal tax rate %	Average tax rate %	Marginal tax rate %
Individual's position in ability range				
2% from bottom	17	29	<0	29
Median	23	32	19	41
2% from top	32	38	40	43

Source: Calculated from Fair (1971, table 6) (case where $a = 2.3$).

The optimal rates of tax are rather higher than in the case of the results reached by Mirrlees. At the same time, the top rates (those on the man 2 per cent from the top of the ability range) are still a long way below those indicated by the Edgeworth–Pigou analysis. Again, the form of the utility function adopted is important. The results given all relate to a case where $\rho = 1$, and it may be expected that higher values of ρ would have led to a more progressive tax structure.[5]

4 Recent work: conclusions

The recent contributions by Mirrlees and Fair suggest that the introduction of efficiency considerations may lead to a considerably less

5. Fair does report briefly on the results obtained when $\rho = 0$ (p. 574) and comments that 'the results did not change much'. However, the results are given in terms of the after-tax Gini coefficient and it is hard to see what is implied for the marginal rates of taxation.

progressive tax structure than that indicated by the minimum sacrifice theory. At the same time they do not adequately consider the sensitivity of their results to the specification of the government objectives. In particular, the precise cardinalization adopted, which was not important in the Edgeworth–Pigou analysis, may significantly affect the optimal tax structure.

The work of these authors has demonstrated that the introduction of the work/leisure choice adds considerably to the complexity of the solution and that analytic results are very difficult to obtain. This means that we have to choose between strongly simplified models for which analytic solutions can be obtained and more realistic models solved numerically. While the latter will undoubtedly be necessary for the formulation of actual policy prescriptions, at the present time it seems more useful to concentrate on identifying the considerations which are likely to have a significant influence on the solution. In the remainder of this paper a model is developed which, while highly stylized, does serve this purpose.

5 A simple model

The model developed in this section is considerably simpler than that considered by Mirrlees and Fair, and in particular assumes:

(a) that attention is restricted to the case of linear tax schedules:

$$T(z) = (1-\beta)z - a, \tag{13}$$

i.e. a guaranteed minimum income a combined with a proportional tax on all income at rate $(1-\beta)$ (see Figure 1). This is the simplest

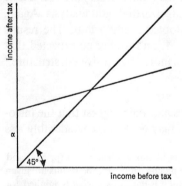

Figure 1 Income tax Schedule

form of progressive tax to consider; and corresponds quite closely to the kind of tax schedule actually in force.[6]

(b) that the distribution of abilities is assumed to be Pareto in form:

$$f(n) = \mu n^{\mu} \text{n}^{-\mu-1} \qquad \qquad 14$$

where n represents the lowest value of n (see Figure 2). The exponent

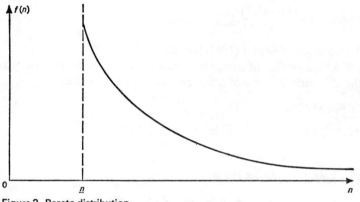

Figure 2   Pareto distribution

μ is assumed to be greater than or equal to 2. This assumption is made primarily for its analytical convenience, and is one of the least satisfactory aspects of the model.[7]

(c) that the individual's earnings are assumed to depend only on ability (n) and on the number of years of education received (S): i.e. hours of work (effort) are assumed to be fixed. While undergoing education the individual has zero earnings and is not eligible for the guaranteed minimum. He earns $z(n, S)$ when at work and

6. The linear tax case is examined by Sheshinski (1972), Wesson (1972) and Atkinson (1972). It should be noted that Blum and Kalven (1963) regard such a tax as being basically different from a general progressive tax with increasing marginal rates of tax, and that it does not allow us to consider the desirability of a 'surtax' or of a negative income tax rate different from that for the positive tax schedule.

7. Lydall (1968, chapter 3) produces evidence that the upper tail of the earnings distribution approximately follows the Pareto law. It is also well known that the distribution of the number of scientific papers published per author is approximately Pareto in form (Simon, 1955)!

retires after R years of work. He maximizes the present value (at interest rate i) of his lifetime income:

$$I = \int_{S}^{R+S} [z - T(z)] e^{-it} dt$$
$$= A[z - T(z)] e^{-iS}, \qquad\qquad 15$$

where $A = \dfrac{(1 - e^{-iR})}{i}$.

A suggestion of Becker (1964) is that $z(n, S) = nS$.[8]

Combining the different elements of the model, we can see that the individual's choice of S will be determined by maximizing

$$(a + \beta nS) e^{-iS},$$

which gives $\quad S = 1/i - a/\beta n \quad$ for $n \geqslant ia/\beta \equiv n_0$,

and $\qquad\qquad S = 0 \quad$ for $n \leqslant n_0$. $\qquad\qquad 16$

The resulting level of I is given by

$$I = A(\beta n/i) e^{(ai/\beta n - 1)} \quad \text{for } n \geqslant n_0. \qquad 17$$

and for $n \leqslant n_0$, $\quad I = Aa$.

It may be noted that in the absence of taxation everyone would choose the same level of S; the effect of taxation is to widen pre-tax income differentials while narrowing after-tax differentials.

From the individual supply functions we can derive the possibilities open to the government, as determined by the revenue constraint:

$$\int_{0}^{\infty} T(z) f(n) \, dn = 0 \qquad\qquad 18$$

where it is assumed that the population is constant in size (so that there are the same number of tax payers for each n) and that no net

8. This model owes a great deal to that of Sheshinski (forthcoming). His formulation is, however, different:

$$I = z - T(z) - g(S)$$

and is rather more difficult to interpret.

revenue is required ($\overline{R} = 0$). With the particular distribution chosen, the constraint may take one of two forms:

Case A $n_0 \leqslant n$,
Case B $n_0 > n$.

Attention is focused here on case A where the revenue constraint is,

since $\displaystyle\int_n^\infty f(n) \, dn = 1$,

$$a = (1-\beta)\int_n^\infty (n/i - a/\beta) f(n) \, dn.$$

Using the fact that $n_0 = ia/\beta$, this can be written

$$n_0 \beta/(1-\beta) = \bar{n} - n_0,$$

where $\bar{n}$ denotes the mean value, and this gives

$$\beta = 1 - n_0/\bar{n}. \qquad\qquad \textbf{19}$$

Equation **19** gives the combinations of β and n_0 (which together determine the optimal tax structure) satisfying the revenue constraint (subject to $n_0 \leqslant n$)[9]

As a background to the problem faced by the government, it is interesting to examine the choice that would be made by an individual aiming to maximize $I(n)$, where we denote by $n_0^*(n)$ the value of n_0 satisfying **19** chosen by a man of type n. Given that $n_0^*(n) \leqslant n$, the person maximizes $\beta e^{n_0*/n}$, or (from **19**),

$$n_0^*/n + \log_e(1 - n_0/\bar{n}).$$

9. In case B, the revenue constraint is

$$a = (1-\beta)\int_{n_0}^\infty (n/i - a/\beta) f(n) \, dn.$$

Using the fact that $n_0 = ia/\beta$,

$$n_0 \beta/(1-\beta) = \mu\int_{n_0}^\infty (n/n)^{-\mu} \, dn - n_0 (n_0/n)^{-\mu},$$

or $\beta/(1-\beta) = [1/(\mu-1)](n^0/n)^{-\mu}.$

The first-order condition is given by

$$\bar{n}/n = 1/(1 - n_0/\bar{n})$$

reducing to $\quad 1 - \beta = n_0/\bar{n} = 1 - m/\bar{n}.$

Since

$$\bar{n} = [\mu/(\mu - 1)]n,$$

the tax rate chosen falls from $1/\mu$ to zero at $n = \bar{n}$. Those with above average n would choose a lump sum tax and subsidy on earnings ($a < 0$, $\beta > 1$) if that were possible (see Figure 3).[10]

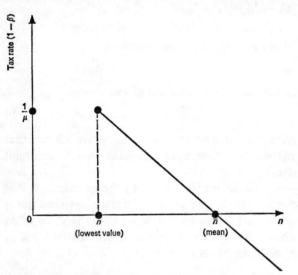

Figure 3 Tax rate chosen by person of type n

The presentation in terms of individual choice about taxation allows us to consider the possibility of majority voting. Although it is unlikely that the precise details of the tax structure would be the subject of voting, issues of broad policy regarding the degree of progression may well be settled by appeal to the electorate. This question

10. The solution for $n^*(n)$ is given by $n/\mu - 1$, which is less than or equal to n for $\mu \geqslant 2$, so that there revenue constraint is of type A.

has been discussed by Foley (1967), who considers the stability of different tax structures against majority rule (i.e. whether there is a tax schedule for which there will always be a majority in favour against any alternative). As he points out, where the class of tax schedules under consideration is unrestricted, no element is stable against majority rule, but if attention is restricted to the class of linear tax schedules (for example), this will contain a stable element. Foley does not allow for the effect of taxation on the earnings of the individual, but his results can readily be extended to that case. In terms of the model set out above, an increase in n_0 ($= ia/\beta$) will always be preferred by those for whom $n_0^* > n_0$ and opposed by those for whom $n_0^* < n_0$. It follows that the tax rate reached as a result of majority voting will be that given by $n_0^*(n_m)$ where n_m is the median, which can be calculated to be

$$1-\beta = 1-2^{1/\mu}(1-1/\mu),$$

so that for $\mu = 2$ we obtain 29 per cent and for $\mu = 3$ we obtain 16 per cent (since the distribution is skew, $n_m < n$, so this would always give a positive tax rate.)

6 Utilitarian and other objectives

Let us examine first the optimal tax structure where the government pursues the utilitarian objective of maximizing the sum of individual utilities:[11]

$$W = \int\limits_{n}^{\infty} U[I(n)]f(n)\, dn. \qquad\qquad 20$$

As we have seen in section 3, the solution depends on the precise form of the function $U(I)$. In order to explore this further, let us suppose that U can be written in the iso-elastic form

$$U = \frac{I^{1-\rho}}{1-\rho}.$$

The case $\rho = 1$ corresponds to that taken by Mirrlees in the first of his examples and means that the maximand becomes

11. It is assumed here, as earlier, that an individual's utility depends only on his own income.

$$W = \int_n^\infty \log[I(n)]f(n)\,dn$$

$$= \log\beta + \int_n^\infty \log(An/i)f(n)\,dn + \int_n^\infty (n_0/n - 1)f(n)\,dn. \qquad \textbf{21}$$

Substituting from the revenue constraint and differentiating, we obtain the first-order condition

$$\int_n^\infty n^{-1}f(n)\,dn = 1/\beta\bar{n}. \qquad \textbf{22}$$

From this it follows that

$$\beta = \frac{1+\mu}{\mu}\left(\frac{n}{\bar{n}}\right) = 1 - \frac{1}{\mu^2},$$

i.e. the optimal tax rate is $1/\mu^2$. If $\mu = 2$, this indicates a tax rate of 25 per cent; if $\mu = 4$, the tax rate is as low as 6·25 per cent.[12]

As ρ increases, the optimal rate of tax rises. This can be seen as follows. In the case where $\rho \neq 1$, we have

$$W = \left(\frac{\beta^{1-\rho}}{1-\rho}\right)\left(\frac{Ae^{-1}}{i}\right)^{1-\rho}\int_n^\infty n^{(1-\rho)}e^{n}o^{(1-\rho)/n}f(n)\,dn. \qquad \textbf{23}$$

Using the revenue constraint 3.7,

$$\frac{\partial W}{\partial n_0} = (1-\rho)W\left\{\frac{1}{\beta}\frac{\partial\beta}{\partial n_0} + \right.$$

$$\left. + \int_n^\infty n^{-\rho}e^{n_0(1-\rho)/n}f(n)\,dn \middle/ \int_n^\infty n^{1-\rho}e^{n_0(1-\rho)/n}f(n)\,dn\right\} \qquad \textbf{24}$$

giving a first-order condition

$$\beta = \int_n^\infty n^{1-\rho}e^{n_0(1-\rho)/n}f(n)\,dn \middle/ \int_n^\infty \left(\frac{\bar{n}}{n}\right)n^{1-\rho}e^{n_0(1-\rho)/n}f(n)\,dn.$$

12. The data given by Lydall (1868) for Britain, France, Germany and the United States suggest values of μ between 2·27 and 3·5.

Writing $K(\mu, \rho) = [n_0(\rho-1)]^{\rho+\mu-1} \int\limits_{n}^{\infty} n^{-(\rho+\mu)} e^{n_0^{(1-\rho)/n}} \, dn,$

this gives an equation for n_0

$$1-(n_0/\bar{n}) = n_0(\rho-1)\bar{n}\, K(\mu, \rho)/K(\mu+1, \rho).\qquad\textbf{25}$$

The solution to this equation for different values of ρ and μ is given in Table 4 .[13] As ρ increases above 1, the optimal tax rate rises quite significantly. For $\rho = 2$ (the second case considered by Mirrlees), the tax rate is 33 per cent rather than 25 per cent (where $\mu = 2$). Moreover, the limit as $\rho \to \infty$ can be derived from the earlier analysis: as $\rho \to \infty$ the social welfare function tends to the maximin form

$$\max I(n),$$

Table 4 *Optimal tax rates obtained from equation* 25

	Value of μ		
Value of ρ	2·0	3·0	4·0
	%	%	%
1·0	25	11	6
2·0	33	18	9
4·0	36	21	14
6·0	39	24	15
8·0	40	25	18
16·0	43	28	21
Limit	50	33	25

13. Substituting

$$m = n_0(\rho-1)/n$$

gives the incomplete gamma function

$$K(\mu, \rho) = \int\limits_{0}^{m} e^{-m} m^{\mu+\rho-2} \, dm$$

where $m = n_0(\rho-1)/n$. The equation to be solved may be written as

$$\frac{K(\mu, \rho)}{K(\mu+1, \rho)} = \frac{1}{m}\left(1-\frac{1}{\mu}\right) - \frac{1}{(\rho-1)}.$$

The left hand side is evaluated using the tables published by Pearson (1965).

and from an earlier analysis not included here we can see that the optimal rate is $1/\mu$. As ρ increases, the optimal tax rate moves up along the lines shown in Figure 4. At the extreme point the optimal tax is considerably larger (by a factor of μ) than at $\rho = 1$.

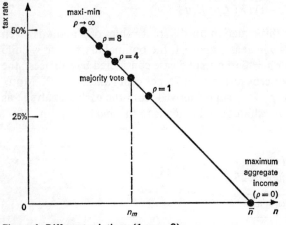

Figure 4   Different solutions ($1n\mu = 2$)

The results given in Table 4 suggest that the optimal rate of income taxation may depend quite sensitively on the particular cardinalization adopted. At the same time it is not clear that we can obtain any firm estimate from individual behaviour of the value that is likely to be taken by ρ (the elasticity of the marginal utility of income). Moreover, we have to consider the possibility that ρ may reflect social values as well as individual utility. Mirrlees's formulation, for example, allows for the possibility that the objective function is

$$\int G[U]f(n) \, dn,$$

where G is a social welfare function defined on individual utilities. In this case ρ represents the elasticity of the *social* marginal utility of income, which may be expected to be higher than the private elasticity. For these reasons there is no clear *a priori* expectation that the value of ρ would lie between 1 and 2 (the values taken by Mirrlees) and we should entertain the possibility that it may be considerably higher.

To this point the basic utilitarian framework has not been discussed. This framework does however suffer from well-known disadvantages, and these have led many authors to draw the conclusion that the equi-marginal or other sacrifice principles cannot provide a useful guide to policy. Prest, for example, writes that: 'It seems reasonable to conclude that sacrifice is not only unmeasurable and incapable of quantification for any one individual but also not comparable as between individuals. With such fundamental objections it would seem to be impossible to accept the conclusions derived from the theories of sacrifice' (1967, pp. 117–18).

In the same way, Johansen concludes that 'On the whole . . . the ability principle, in so far as attempts have been made to define and elaborate it with the aid of the theory of utility function, is mainly of abstract theoretical interest, and will not be able to play any significant role in the actual formulation of income taxation' (1965, p. 217).

If the utilitarian approach underlying the minimum sacrifice theories, and the recent extensions of these, is to be rejected, it is reasonable to ask what can be offered in its place. As Irving Fisher commented, 'philosophic doubt is right and proper, but the problems of life cannot and do not wait' (1927, p. 180). There are in fact two main alternative approaches which can be identified: (a) maximization of the welfare of the worst-off individual; (b) considerations of income inequality.

(a) Fairness and 'maximin'

The first of these lines of argument has been developed by Rawls from considerations of the nature of the social contract. The foundation of this approach are the two basic principles of justice put forward by Rawls: 'first, each person engaged in an institution . . . has an equal right to the most extensive liberty compatible with a like liberty for all; and second, inequalities . . . are arbitrary unless it is reasonable to expect that they will work out to everyone's advantage' (1967, p. 61).

The second of these principles is interpreted by Rawls to mean the maximization of the welfare of the worst-off individual (a 'maximin' criterion): 'The basic structure is just throughout when the advantages of the more fortunate promote the well-being of the least fortunate, that is, when a decrease in their advantages would make the least fortunate even worse off than they are now' (1967, p. 66).

This formulation does not, of course, avoid all the difficulties of utilitarianism; at the same time the requirements are rather different (to apply the maximin criterion, we require comparability of welfare levels, but not cardinality – see Sen (1970). Moreover, the maximin criterion does seem to capture some of the notions of 'fairness' which are current in public discussion and it is interesting to examine its implications.

If we can assume that individual utility is related to income in such a way that the worst-off individual is the man with the lowest n, the solution with this objective can be seen from the preceding analysis to be $1/\mu$. This tax rate may well seem surprisingly low. Although not much weight should be attached to the actual numerical values, it would indicate a tax rate of between 30 per cent and 45 per cent using the values of μ estimated by Lydall (1968). These rates are considerably higher than those given by Mirrlees, but nonetheless lower than one could expect from such an apparently egalitarian objective function. It is interesting to compare the maximin case with the egalitarian prescriptions of Pigou and Edgeworth, which led to 100 per cent marginal rate of tax. In the present case this does not happen because of the effects on the work decisions of the better-off groups. It is in the interests of the worst-off person to reduce the rate below 100 per cent to increase the revenue raised from those higher up the scale.[14]

(b) Income inequality

The second alternative approach is well described by Simons:

Taxation must affect the distribution of income ... and it is only sensible to face the question as to what kind of effects are desirable. To do this is to reduce the discussion frankly to the level of ethics or aesthetics. Such

14. The extent to which this is worth while depends, of course, on the elasticity of the supply of labour. In this context it should be noted that the labour supply function assumed here may well over-emphasize the effect of taxation on work incentives. The earnings function is in fact identical with that obtained from the utility function

$$U(x, y) = \log x - iy$$

where x denotes consumption and y hours of work. The fact that this corresponds to a perfectly elastic supply of effort suggests that the simple model used here may understate the optimal tax rate.

procedure, however, is certainly preferable to the traditional one of 'describing' the attributes of the good life in terms which simply are not descriptive. The case for drastic progression in taxation must be rested on the case against inequality—on the ethical or aesthetic judgement that the prevailing distribution of wealth and income reveals a degree (and/or kind) of inequality which is distinctly evil or unlovely (1938).

If, however, considerations of income inequality are to provide a guide to the rate of income taxation, they have to be more precisely formulated. A natural way in which this can be done is through one of the summary measures of inequality which are commonly employed in empirical studies of tax progression; we could, for example, choose the optimal income tax so as to minimize the Gini coefficient. This kind of procedure suffers, however, from two disadvantages:

1. As I have argued elsewhere (1970), the conventional summary measures have no inherent rationale and little interpretation can be given to them,

2. The use of such measures implicitly involves a trade-off between inequality and some measure of the average level of incomes, and this trade-off has to be specified.[15]

One way of overcoming these difficulties is to follow the approach examined in Atkinson (1970) which assumes that we rank income distributions according to a social welfare function

$$J = \int\limits_{n}^{\infty} H[I(n)]f(n)\,dn, \qquad\qquad 26$$

where $H(I)$ denotes the social valuation of income accruing to an individual. The particular functional form explored is

$$H = [I^{(1-\rho)}/1-\rho)]\ p \geqslant 0$$

It appears at first sight that this is identical to the utilitarian approach discussed earlier. It is important to emphasize, however, that H represents the *social* valuation of income,[16] and that the choice of ρ is

15. The Gini coefficient would be minimized, for example, if all incomes were zero.

16. This formulation is in effect that proposed by Musgrave: 'the concept of subjective utility is translated into one of social income utility. We may then postulate a marginal-utility schedule that seems proper as a matter of social

based on social values about inequality. The parameter ρ reflects in fact the degree of aversion to inequality in the society: $\rho = 0$ corresponds to maximizing the sum of incomes, and increasing values of ρ mean that the society is more averse to inequality. The solutions obtained using this approach can be read off from Table 4. For $\rho = 0$ (zero inequality aversion), the optimal solution is a zero tax rate, and for higher values of ρ the optimal tax rate increases until it reaches the limiting case of maximin ($\rho \to \infty$).

The fact that the maximin solution represents the limiting case, and that, as we have seen, this does not necessarily lead to very high rates of taxation, may lead us to question whether the formulation 26 adequately captures our values about inequality. In particular it is not necessarily clear that the social welfare function is increasing in all its arguments: it is quite conceivable that a gift of £1 from Mars to the richest person in Britain may be considered to lower the level of social welfare. It is possible that we may attach particular weight to the distance between the top and the bottom. Fair (1971) refers to the belief of Plato that no one in a society should be more than four times richer than the poorest member of society. If this is so, we may well choose tax rates higher than the maximin solution. Although this would reduce the lifetime income of the poorest man it would narrow the gap between him and those at the top. In the present model the after-tax income of the lowest man as a percentage of the average is (for $n_0 < n$)

$$(1 - 1/\mu)\, e^{t/(\mu - 1)}.$$

The value of this ratio for different values of t (where $\mu = 3$) is given

$t = 0$	ratio = 66 per cent,
$t = 33\frac{1}{3}$ per cent (maximin solution)	ratio = 79 per cent,
$t = 50$ per cent	ratio = 86 per cent,
$t = 66\frac{2}{3}$ per cent	ratio = 94 per cent.

It is possible, therefore, that concern for income inequality may lead to the choice of a tax rate above that indicated by the maximin criterion. This would involve the government selecting a policy

policy. . . . If we proceed along these lines, the principle of ability to pay ceases to be the subjective matter that J. S. Mill had thought it to be. It becomes a question of social value' (1959, p. 109).

which in terms of individual lifetime incomes was Pareto-inferior.[17] If the tax rate is above $1/\mu$, all individuals would favour a tax reduction. The reason the government might choose such a policy is that the loss to the highest income groups is larger than to the lowest, and hence the gap between them would be narrowed.

7 Conclusions

The value of a model such as that discussed in this paper does not lie in the precise solutions obtained. It should indeed be obvious that the specification of the model is inadequate to provide any detailed prescriptions as to what the rate of income tax should be. The labour supply assumptions, for example, are highly stylized and leave out many important factors. The analysis may however have served to provide some insight into the structure of the arguments and to bring out the significance of considerations not discussed adequately in earlier contributions. In particular, I have tried to emphasize the role played by the formulation of the objectives of the government. This has been shown to be important at two levels. First, within the utilitarian framework underlying the minimum sacrifice theories and the recent work by Mirrlees and others, the results may depend sensitively on the particular cardinalization adopted. Second, alternative approaches based on considerations of 'fairness' or 'inequality' may lead to very different results.

One point which emerges clearly as significant is the importance of the maximin solution. Not only does it have considerable intuitive appeal, but also it provides a limiting case for the utilitarian approach and an interesting watershed for those concerned about inequality. In further work in this area, with more complex models, it seems interesting therefore to consider first the maximin criterion. This will give an upper bound on the utilitarian solution, and we will only expect higher rates of tax to emerge from an inequality approach if the government attaches a negative weight to increases in income for well-off individuals.

17. It is important to emphasize at this point that no account has been taken of interdependencies (the possibility that a person's welfare may depend on the incomes of others). If such interdependencies exist, raising the tax rate above $1/\mu$ may still be Pareto-optimal in terms of individual utilities.

References

ATKINSON, A. B. (1970), 'On the measurement of inequality', *J. econ. Theory*, September, pp. 244–63.

ATKINSON, A. B. (1972), '"Maximin" and optimal income taxation', mimeo.

BECKER, G. S. (1964), *Human Capital*, Columbia University Press.

BLUM, W. J., and KALVEN, H. (1963), *The Uneasy Case for Progressive Taxation* (Phoenix edn), University of Chicago Press.

DALTON, H. (1954), *Principles of Public Finance*, Routledge & Kegan Paul.

EDGEWORTH, F. Y. (1925), *Papers Relating to Political Economy*, vol. 2, Royal Economic Society.

FAGAN, E. (1938), 'Recent and contemporary theories of progressive taxation', *J. polit. Econ.*, August, pp. 457–98.

FAIR, R. C. (1971), 'The optimal distribution of income', *Q. J. Econ.*, November, pp. 551–79.

FISHER, I. (1927), 'A statistical method for measuring "marginal utility" and testing the justice of a progressive income tax', in *Economic Essays Contributed in Honour of John Bates Clark*, New York.

FOLEY, D. (1967), 'Resource allocation and the public sector', *Yale econ. Essays*, vol. 7, Spring, pp. 45–98.

HARDY, G. H., LITTLEWOOD, J. E., and POLYA, G. (1952), *Inequalities*, 2nd edn, Cambridge University Press.

JOHANSEN, L. (1965), *Public Economics*, North-Holland.

LYDALL, H. F. (1968), *The Structure of Earnings*, Oxford University Press.

MIRRLEES, J. A. (1971), 'An exploration in the theory of optimum income taxation', *Rev. econ. Stud.*, April, pp. 175–208.

MIRRLEES, J. A. (1972), 'Population policy and the taxation of family size', *J. public Econ.*, August, pp. 169–98.

MUSGRAVE, R. A. (1959), *The Theory of Public Finance*, McGraw-Hill.

PEARSON, K. (ed.) (1965), *Tables of the Incomplete F-Function*, Cambridge University Press.

PIGOU, A. C. (1947), *A Study in Public Finance*, 3rd edn, Macmillan.

PREST, A. R. (1967), *Public Finance in Theory and Practice*, 3rd edn, Weidenfeld & Nicolson.

RAWLS, J. (1967), 'Distributive justice', in P. Laslett and W. G. Runciman (eds.), *Philosophy, Politics and Society*, third series, Blackwell.

SEN, A. K. (1970), *Collective Choice and Social Welfare*, Oliver & Boyd.

SHESHINSKI, E. (1972), 'The optimal linear income tax', *Rev. econ. Stud.*, July.

SHESHINSKI, E. (forthcoming), 'On the theory of optimal income taxation', *J. public Econ.*

SIMONS, H. (1938), *Personal Income Taxation*, University of Chicago Press.

SIMON, H. A. (1955), 'On a class of skew distribution functions', *Biometrika*, vol. 42, pp. 425–40.

WESSON, J. (1972), 'On the distribution of personal incomes', *Rev. econ. Stud.*, January.

17 E. Sheshinski

The Optimal Linear Income-Tax

E. Sheshinski, 'The optimal linear income-tax', *Review of Economic Studies*, 1972.

1 Introduction

The conflict between equity and efficiency considerations in income taxation is a familiar problem, but no rules for optimal income redistribution that take both of these considerations into account have yet been developed. Despite the advocacy of such general moral principles as the 'ability to pay' or 'equal sacrifice', it is not known, for example, under what conditions the optimal income-tax should be progressive or regressive.

An original contribution to the theory of optimal income taxation has recently been made by Mirrlees (forthcoming). He developed a model in which individuals are assumed to maximize identical utility functions that depend on consumption and labour. The return to labour is assumed to depend partly on an innate skill factor associated with each individual. Through individual decisions, the distribution of skills in the population ultimately determines the distributions of labour, consumption, and utility. Income taxation is then introduced in order to improve income distribution and social welfare, defined as the sum of individual utilities. In various examples calculated by Mirrlees, the optimal income-tax schedule appears to be approximately linear with a negative tax at low incomes. It is not known, however, in what way these results depend on the particular form of the utility and distribution functions chosen for these examples.

In this paper we prove, using Mirrlees's model, that under very general assumptions about the individual utility function, *among all linear income-tax functions, the optimal tax is always progressive, i.e. it provides a positive lump-sum at zero income and has a positive marginal tax rate. Furthermore, the optimal marginal tax rate is shown to be bounded from above by a fraction that is related to the elasticity of labour supply.*

A similar result has also been obtained for a somewhat different model (Sheshinski, 1971).

2 Individual behaviour

All individuals are assumed to have an identical utility function, u, that depends on consumption, c, and labour, l,

$$u = u(c, l).\qquad\qquad\textbf{1}$$

u is assumed to be continuously differentiable, strictly concave,[1] with a positive marginal utility for consumption and a negative marginal utility for labour

$$\begin{aligned}
&u_1 > 0, \qquad u_2 < 0, \\
&u_{11} < 0, \qquad u_{22} < 0, \\
&u_{11}u_{22} - u_{21}^2 > 0.
\end{aligned}\qquad\qquad\textbf{2}$$

Let y be before-tax income and let $t(y)$ be a linear income-tax function defined on y

$$t(y) = -a + (1-\beta)y,\qquad\qquad\textbf{3}$$

where a and β are the tax-schedule parameters. The parameter a is a lump-sum tax ($a < 0$) or subsidy ($a > 0$) given to an individual with no income. $1 - \beta$ is the marginal tax rate, i.e. $0 \leqslant \beta \leqslant 1$ implies a non-negative marginal tax rate, not exceeding unity.

After-tax income is equal to consumption:

$$c = y - t(y) = a + \beta y.\qquad\qquad\textbf{4}$$

Income is assumed to depend positively on the amount of labour and on a factor that is referred to as 'ability' and denoted by an index number n ($0 \leqslant n \leqslant \infty$). For simplicity, it is assumed that this relation is multiplicative

$$y = y(n, l) = nl.\qquad\qquad\textbf{5}$$

1. For the analysis of individual behaviour it is only required that u be quasi-concave, i.e.

$$u_{11}u_2^2 - 2u_1 u_2 u_{12} + u_{22}u_1^2 \leqslant 0,$$

but for the social welfare analysis, concavity of u is required in order to make complete equality the first-best optimum.

It is assumed that each individual decides about the optimal amount of consumption and labour so as to maximize his utility **1** subject to the budget constraint **4**. For an individual with ability n, the first order condition for this maximum is, in view of 5^2

$$-u_2/u_1 = \beta n \quad \text{or} \quad -\beta n u_1 = u_2. \qquad \qquad 6$$

This equation, together with the budget constraint **4**, defines implicitly the optimal labour supply and consumption as functions of βn and a

$$\hat{l} = \hat{l}(\beta n, a), \quad \text{and} \quad c = a + \beta n \hat{l}(\beta n, a). \qquad \qquad 7$$

We assume that leisure is a normal good; that is,

$$\partial \hat{l}/\partial a \leqslant 0. \qquad \qquad 8$$

Differentiating the first-order condition, we can obtain the derivative of the labour-supply function with respect to a in terms of the derivatives of the utility function

$$\partial \hat{l}/\partial a = (u_1 u_2 u_{11} - u_1 u_{12})/(u_{11} u_2^2 - 2u_1 u_2 u_{12} + u_{22} u_1^2). \qquad \qquad 9$$

Hence, in view of **2**, normality requires

$$u_{11} - (u_1/u_2) u_{12} \leqslant 0. \qquad \qquad 10$$

It is also assumed that the supply of labour is a non-decreasing function of its unit return; that is[3]

$$\partial \hat{l}/\partial \beta \geqslant 0. \qquad \qquad 11$$

This condition, in terms of the derivatives of the utility function, is found to be

$$\frac{\partial \hat{l}}{\partial \beta} = \frac{1}{\beta} \frac{u_2 u_1 - u_2^2 \{u_{11} - (u_1/u_2) u_{12}\} \hat{l}}{u_{11} u_2^2 - 2u_1 u_2 u_{12} + u_{22} u_1^2} \geqslant 0. \qquad \qquad 12$$

Let λ be the lowest elasticity of the labour supply function,[4] i.e.

$$(\beta/\hat{l})(\partial \hat{l}/\partial \beta) \geqslant \lambda \qquad \qquad 13$$

2. Assuming the optimal solutions are positive. In view of **2** the second order condition is also satisfied.

3. It is possible, of course, that $l = 0$ for small β (when the more general first-order condition $u_2/u_1 \leqslant \beta n$ yields a corner solution). With a 'backward-bending' supply function of labour, income could be decreasing as n increases. It would then be impossible to redistribute income by means of a progressive income-tax!

4. More precisely, $\lambda = \lim_n \inf(\beta/\hat{l})(\partial \hat{l}/\partial \beta)$.

for all n. Given the tax parameters a and β, the amounts of labour, income and utility can be regarded as functions of n. Since l depends on the product $\beta \cdot n$, clearly the signs of $\partial l/\partial \beta$ and $\partial l/\partial n$ are the same. Hence, in view of **11**, l is a non-decreasing function of n. It follows that y is strictly increasing in n

$$\partial y/\partial n = \partial(n \cdot l)/\partial n = l + n(\partial l/\partial n) > 0. \tag{14}$$

Utility is also seen to be strictly increasing in n

$$\partial u/\partial n = u_1(\partial c/\partial n) + u_2(\partial l/\partial n) = u_1[(\partial c/\partial n) - \beta n(\partial l/\partial n)] \tag{15}$$

$$= u_1 \beta l > 0,$$

making use of **4** and **6**.

3 The optimal linear income-tax

Let $f(n)$ be the density function of ability, i.e. the ratio of the number of individuals with ability n to the total number of individuals,

$$\int_0^\infty f(n) \, dn = 1.$$

The social welfare function, V, is assumed to be the sum of individual utilities. Normalizing for size,

$$V = \int_0^\infty u(c, l) f(n) \, dn. \tag{16}$$

The optimal linear income-tax problem is to find parameters a and β that maximize **16**, subject to the constraint that total tax proceeds be equal to zero, i.e.

$$\int_0^\infty t(y) f(n) \, dn = \int_0^\infty (y - a - \beta y) f(n) \, dn = 0,$$

or $\quad a = (1 - \beta) \int_0^\infty y f(n) \, dn. \tag{17}$

To solve the problem, we form the function

$$W = \int_0^\infty [u(c,l) - q\{a - (1-\beta)y\}]f(n)\, dn, \qquad\qquad 18$$

where q is the shadow-price of constraint **16**. The first-order conditions for a maximum of W with respect to a and β, using **4–6**, are

$$\partial W/\partial a = \int_0^\infty (u_1 - q)f(n)\, dn + q(1-\beta) \int_0^\infty n(\partial l/\partial a)f(n)\, dn = 0, \qquad 19$$

$$\partial W/\partial \beta = \int_0^\infty (u_1 - q)n\hat{l}f(n)\, dn + q(1-\beta) \int_0^\infty n(\partial l/\partial \beta)f(n)\, dn = 0. \qquad 20$$

Denote the optimal parameters by a^* and β^*. We now prove the following:

Theorem. Under assumptions **2**, **8** *and* **11**, $\lambda/(1+\lambda) < \beta^* < 1$ *and* $a^* > 0$.

Proof. Obviously $\beta^* > 0$ (or else $c = l = 0$ for all n). Suppose that $\beta^* \geqslant 1$. Then, in view of **8** and **19**

$$\int_0^\infty (u_1 - q)f(n)\, dn \leqslant 0. \qquad\qquad 21$$

We now wish to prove that **21** implies that

$$\int_0^\infty (u_1 - q)n\hat{l}f(n)\, dn < 0. \qquad\qquad 22$$

From **2**, **4–6**, **10** and **11**, u_1 is seen to be strictly decreasing in n

$$\begin{aligned}
\partial u_1/\partial n &= u_{11}(\partial c/\partial n) + u_{12}(\partial l/\partial n) \qquad\qquad 23\\
&= u_{11}\beta\hat{l} + [u_{12} - (u_2/u_1)u_{11}](\partial \hat{l}/\partial n)\\
&< 0.
\end{aligned}$$

$y = nl$ has been shown to be strictly increasing in n. Thus, **22** is obvious when $u_1 - q \leqslant 0$ for all n. More generally, there exists a number $n_0 \geqslant 0$ such that $(u_1 - q) > 0$ for $n < n_0$ and $(u_1 - q) < 0$ for $n > n_0$. Let $\hat{l}(n_0) = l_0$. In view of **14** and **23**

$$(u_1 - q)nl < n_0 l_0 (u_1 - q)$$

for all n. Multiplying both sides of this inequality by $f(n)$ and integrating, we find, in view of **21**,

$$\int_0^\infty (u_1 - q)n\hat{l}f(n)\,dn < n_0 l_0 \int_0^\infty (u_1 - q)f(n)\,dn \leqslant 0.$$

This establishes **22**. From **20**, however, it is seen that **22** is impossible when $\partial \hat{l}/\partial \beta = 0$, and when $\partial \hat{l}/\partial \beta > 0$, **22** implies that $\beta^* < 1$ contrary to assumption. Thus, $\beta^* < 1$. From **17** we then find that $a^* > 0$.

Now, let us rewrite **20**

$$\int_0^\infty u_1 n\hat{l}f(n)\,dn + q \int_0^\infty [\{(1-\beta^*)/\beta^*\}(\beta/l\,\partial l/\partial \beta) - 1]n\hat{l}f(n)\,dn = 0. \qquad \textbf{24}$$

Since the first term in **24** positive, clearly

$$\int_0^\infty [1 - \{(1-\beta^*)/\beta^*\}(\beta/l)(\partial l/\partial \beta)]n\hat{l}f(n)\,dn > 0.$$

From **13**, then

$$\{1 - (1-\beta^*\lambda)/\beta^*\} \int_0^\infty n\hat{l}f(n)\,dn \geqslant \int_0^\infty [1 - \{(1-\beta^*/\beta^*\}(\beta/l)(\partial l/\partial \beta)]n\hat{l}f(n)\,dn$$

$$> 0$$

for which it is necessary that

$$\{(1-\beta^*)/\beta^*\}\lambda < 1,$$

i.e. $\quad \beta^* > \lambda/(1+\lambda)$. $\hfill$ QED

Notice that in the above proof, λ can be taken as the lowest elasticity over open intervals in which the density $f(n)$ is positive. One has, therefore, to evaluate this elasticity only for the range of actual incomes.

The above theorem implies, by definition, that the optimal marginal tax rate $1-\beta^*$ is less than $1/(1+\lambda)$.

4 Two examples

Consider the following examples:

(a) $u(c,l) = c(\hat{l}-l)$ $\hat{l} > 0$ is the maximum feasible labour supply, i.e. $0 \leqslant l \leqslant \hat{l}$. From the first-order condition 6 and the budget constraint 4 one can derive the optimal labour supply

$$\hat{l}(\beta n, a) = \begin{cases} 0 & n \leqslant n_0, \\ \tfrac{1}{2}(\hat{l}-a/\beta n) & n > n_0, \end{cases} \qquad\qquad 25$$

where $n_0 = a/\beta\hat{l}$. For $l > 0$, $\partial l/\partial a < 0$ and $\partial l/\partial\beta > 0$, satisfying assumptions 8 and 11.

The elasticity of labour supply is found to be

$$(\beta/l)(\partial l/\partial\beta) = a/(\beta n l - a), \qquad\qquad 26$$

a monotonically decreasing function of n. Let $\bar{n}$ be the highest n for which $f(n) > 0$. In this range

$$(\beta/l)(\partial l/\partial\beta) \geqslant a/(\beta\bar{n}\hat{l}-a) = \lambda.$$

Thus, the condition $\beta^* > \lambda/(1+\lambda)$ is in this case given by

$$\beta^* > a^*/\beta^*\bar{n}\hat{l} \quad \text{or} \quad \beta^* > \sqrt{(a^*/\bar{n}\hat{l})}. \qquad\qquad 27$$

Now, a^* is the lowest after-tax income, while $\bar{n}\hat{l}$ is approximately the highest before-tax income.[5] For example, if $a^*/\bar{n}\hat{l} = 1/4$ then $\beta^* > \tfrac{1}{2}$; i.e. the marginal tax rate should not exceed 50 per cent. If $a^*/\bar{n}\hat{l} = \tfrac{1}{9}$ then $\beta^* > \tfrac{1}{3}$, i.e. the marginal rate should not exceed two-thirds. Even the latter number seems to be rather low.

(b) $u(c,l) = c + \{1/(1-\delta)\}(\hat{l}-l)^{1-\delta}$ $\quad(0 < \delta < 1)$.

From the first-order condition 6 and the budget constraint 4 one can show that the optimal labour supply function is given by

$$l(\beta n, a) = \begin{cases} 0 & n \leqslant n_0, \\ \hat{l}-(\beta n)^{-1/\delta} & n > n_0, \end{cases} \qquad\qquad 28$$

5. Since $n \leqslant \bar{n}$ (in the relevant range) and $l \leqslant \hat{l}$, it follows that $y = nl \leqslant \bar{n}\hat{l}$.

where $n_0 = (1/\beta)^{\bar{l}-\delta}$. Notice that in this case labour is a neutral good (i.e. a zero income effect). The parameter δ is related to the elasticity of the marginal utility of labour.[6] One can calculate from **28** the

6. $(l/u_2)(\partial u_2/\partial l) = l(l/\bar{l}-l)$. When $l/l = 2$, then the elasticity is exactly equal to δ.

elasticity

$$(\beta/l)(\partial l/\partial \beta) = (1/\delta)\{(\bar{l}-l)/l\}, \qquad\qquad 29$$

which is seen to be an increasing function of n. Let $\bar{l}$ be the largest amount of labour supplied, and define $\lambda = (1/\delta)\{(\bar{l}-\tilde{l})/\tilde{l}\}$. Clearly $(\beta/l)(\partial l/\partial \beta) \geqslant \lambda$ in the relevant range. Suppose, for example, that $\bar{l}/\tilde{l} = 2$, then $\lambda = 1/\delta$, and the condition $\beta^* > \lambda/(1+\lambda)$ is given by $\beta^* > 1/(1+\delta)$.

References

MIRRLEES, J. A. (forthcoming), 'An exploration in the theory of optimum income taxation', *Rev. econ. Stud.*

SHESHINSKI, E. (1971), 'On the theory of optimal income taxation', Discussion paper no. 172, Harvard Institute for Economic Research, January.

18 E. S. Phelps

Wage Taxation for Economic Justice

E. S. Phelps, 'Taxation of wage income for economic justice', Quarterly Journal of Economics, 1973.

Sidgwick's principle of equity requires that 'whatever action any of us judges to be right for himself, he implicitly judges to be right for all similar persons in similar circumstances'.[1] With regard to tax systems, if an individual whose situation and attributes are x ought to pay tax t, then, on the principle of equity, every other individual having the identical x ought to pay the same tax, $t(x)$. It is clear that (horizontal) tax equity is incomplete as a criterion of just taxation, being only a necessary condition for fair taxation that many tax systems could satisfy, not all of which would otherwise be satisfactory.[2] Moreover the requirement of equity becomes empty if the vector x is so lengthy or personal as to allow tailoring the tax to each person within wide limits. This suggests that the applicability of equity depends upon some deeper notion of impartiality or fairness.

Much of the economics of taxation is concerned with the principle of Paretian efficiency. If the purchases of some commodity (or commodities) were to be added to the tax base (to individuals' xs) and all tax rates re-set as desired, would the resulting utility feasibility frontier lie outside the old one *somewhere*? In such regions of the utility space, would some activities then become inefficient to tax at positive rates (and hence freely eliminable from the tax base)? It is interesting here that a range of natural candidates for an expanded tax base, such as school achievements and various child test scores, are tacitly excluded from consideration in the usual analysis. It is true that individuals would have an incentive to disguise their earning poten-

---

1. Sidgwick (1907, p. 379); see also the rule of universalizability in Hare (1963, pp. 89–90).

2. Thus Anatole France's remark that the laws of France are perfectly just, the rich and the poor having equal rights to sleep under the bridges of Paris.

tials by underachieving if their grades and scores were a basis for their future tax; but the analogous objective to the disincentive effects of graduated taxation of realized earnings has never been held to be fatal. The exclusion of such quasi-lump-sum taxes would seem to be based in part on the view that, in a world of imperfect information where people's potential to earn income cannot be perfectly forecast, it would risk unfairness in some sense (or a loss of expected social welfare) to tax an individual according to the forecast of his earning power in the future as a substitute, in whole or part, for taxation of his actual earnings by that time.[3] This exemplifies the familiar point that efficiency is only a necessary condition and desirable only relative to some criterion of social welfare or distributive justice. A tax system efficient in securing the wrong distributive results may be 'worse' than some (improvably) inefficient tax systems. Neither equity nor efficiency then has any necessary merit apart from a satisfactory principle of distributive justice, at least in formal policy analysis.

The conception of distributive justice advocated by John Rawls, most comprehensively in *A Theory of Justice* (1971) appears to be the first complete principle of social choice to command wide and serious interest since the time of sum-of-satisfactions utilitarianism.[4] My purpose in this paper is to derive the implications of the Rawls criterion for the graduated taxation of wage incomes within the context of two simple models of household earning decisions. The next section describes the criterion and briefly addresses his defence of that principle.

1 'Maximin' justice

Rawls refers to the general concept of justice as the notion of a standard by which the distribution of the burdens and benefits from cooperation by the individuals in society is to be determined. The particular conception of justice, the specific distribution criterion, argued for in *Justice* is what he calls the 'difference principle': in the just economy, the welfare of the worst-off is as large as feasible. The

3. This is at any rate plausible if individuals' observable earnings in the future are believed to show perfect, or at any rate much higher, rank-correlation with their actual earning power in the future. .

4. By complete principle I mean an exact specification as distinct from a set of ethical postulates that narrow down the social ordering of social states or utility distributions to some restricted class.

principle does not imply the obliteration of all inequalities in well-being. Differences in liberty and opportunity, income and other primary social goods are justifiable in so far as they benefit the least well-off.[5] It is the modern-day analogue of Aquinas: Everything for the greater utility of the poor.

The criterion is more aptly labelled 'maximin' than 'favour the least advantaged'. The latter can be ambiguous when the individuals having least utility vary from state to state. We are to identify the smallest individual utility in each social state – the utility of the least well-off *in that state* – and choose the social state where this minimum utility is maximized. It is possible that this chosen state is not one which the least well-off like best: if so, it is chosen nevertheless because their preferred state would make some others even less well-off than are those who are least well-off in the chosen state.[6] Thus the criterion does not necessarily make any individual a 'dictator', even a post-determined one, let alone one pre-designated without regard to the eventual distribution of utilities. Yet the structure of social opportunities may very well be such that the maximin criterion will select the social state preferred by the individuals who are the least disadvantaged in that state. In such cases, Arrow's 'non-dictatorship' axiom is apparently not met. However, the 'dictator' is not someone pre-ordained according to proper names but rather some individual determined impartially from ordinal comparisons of individual well-being.[7]

The Rawls criterion is lexicographic (or lexical, as he calls it). Of two or more social states tied for largest minimum utility, choose the one (or ones) giving the largest next-to-minimum utility and so on. (In the same spirit, Rawls would have us treat the primary goods serially: liberty has the first priority, then the other social values.)

5. Rawls typically refers to two principles, of which the first is that 'each person is to have an equal right to the most extensive basic liberty compatible with a similar liberty for others', and the second (difference) principle applies to social and economic inequalities (1971, p. 60). But he acknowledges (p. 83) that the difference principle really is to be applied to 'all primary goods including liberty'.

6. See Rawls's discussion of chain-connection (1971, p. 80).

7. Arrow (1964, p. 30). Of course, something in Arrow's system must go if we are to obtain the social ordering Rawls wants. Arrow excludes interpersonal utility comparisons in the definition of the Arrow social welfare function (p. 23). Only the individual orderings are 'fed in'.

Such an ordering of social states is not representable by a Bergson social welfare function, $W(u_1, u_2, ..., u_n)$. In the absence of ties, the sense of the Rawls ordering is expressed by $W = \min(u_1, ..., u_n)$.

The working of the Rawls criterion is illustrated in Figure 1, virtually an ideogram of Rawls's proposal.[8] It pictures a two-class economy in which, by assumption, the incentive effects of redistributive measures (say, graduated income taxation and transfers) cause the representative persons' utility feasibility frontier, *FF*, to slope upwards sufficiently near the egalitarian 45-degree line. The Rawls criterion, with its right-angled 'contours' like *JJ*, picks out *R* on this frontier. The Benthamian sum-of-satisfactions criterion chooses *B* and the Bernoulli–Nash product-of-utilities function selects *N*.

It is Rawls's conviction that this maximin criterion will emerge from a proper construction of social contract doctrine. To think about what is just, free from the known facts of his special interests, a per-

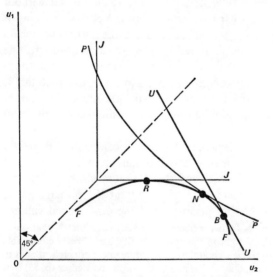

Figure 1   The Rawlsian maximin criterion selects *R* on the per capita utility feasibility frontier, *FF*. The product-of-per-capita-utilities criterion selects *N* and the sum of utilities criterion selects *B*.

8. Rawls (1971, p. 76). As Rawls notes, the Bentham contours in the diagram have a slope that depends upon the relative numbers of persons in the two classes.

son may at any time figuratively 'ascend' to the 'original position' – a hypothetical situation of initial fairness in which the members of society are imagined to deliberate on the social and economic structure to be chosen without knowledge of the respective natural endowments, social advantages and psychological propensities that they will possess, though with a general understanding of human behaviour and an awareness that having more of the various primary goods would help anyone to realize whatever style or plan of life he may find he desires. '. . . On the contract view, the theory of justice [as a general concept] is part of the theory of rational choice' (1971, p. 47).

The most prominent rival to the maximin rule is undoubtedly utilitarianism, modern or classical. Rawls gives three grounds for his contention that, in the original position, the maximin rule would be chosen over any utilitarian or neo-utilitarian rule (1971, especially pp. 150–83).

The first ground is that, because the agreement on a distributive principle is to be final and binding, any individual would want to protect against the worst imaginable eventualities. Now Rawls's original position is reminiscent of the neo-utilitarian approach of Harsanyi and Vickrey in which an individual's 'ethical preference' is for that social structure, with its redistributive policies, which maximizes the mathematical expectation of utility when he believes it is equi-probable that he will be in each person's shoes and, knowing the technology and people's preferences, he can calculate the payoff (under each social structure) attaching to every pair of shoes.[9] A risk-neutral Harsanyi–Vickrey calculator would choose B on FF while a risk-averse individual would select a point left of B though, unless he is completely risk-phobic, *right* of R. In Rawls's construction of the original position, individuals do not have the numerical data for such calculations of expected utility. They do not, for example, know the relative numbers who are top-dogs and bottom-dogs. Why not? One reason Rawls gives is that the original position is needed to resolve questions of justice among generations into the future, so that technologies and preferences cannot generally be

9. Harsanyi (1955) and Vickrey (1960). Neither author resolves the problem of a conflict among individuals' ethical preferences owing to differing attitudes toward risk.

known anyway. But were such data obtainable they would not be wanted, for we seek an agreement on principle that treats all equally as moral persons, not an agreement biased by arbitrary contingencies of nature and social advantage (1971, pp. 137–42). Might, I believe Rawls means, does not make right, including might that is the result of sheer relative numerical superiority. Under such informational constraints, selection of the maximin rule does indeed seem natural.

The second ground is that, by their adoption of the maximin rule to outlaw policies and institutions that injure those with poor life prospects as the means to improve the life prospects of those more advantaged, people would be expressing their respect for one another in the very constitution of society. In contrast, recognition of the principle of utilitarianism (simple or generalized) may well entail some loss of self-esteem. For in allowing higher life prospects for some to counterbalance lower life prospects for others already less fortunate in natural and social advantages, it would have us exploit to a degree, rather than neutralizing, the contingencies of nature and social circumstance on behalf of the more fortunate – 'as though we belonged to a lower order, as though we were a creature whose first principles are decided by natural contingencies' instead of as 'free and equal rational beings with a liberty to choose' (1971, p. 256). Since a person's self-respect normally depends on the respect of others, and the more self-respect one has the likelier it is that he will respect others, public acceptance of the maximin rule is likely to give greater support to people's self-respect all round. Thus, in choosing the maximin principle, people would be insuring their self-esteem as it is rational for them to do.

Third, the utilitarian principle would ask the less advantaged to view the greater advantages of others as a sufficient reason for accepting still lower life prospects than they could be allowed. This is an extreme demand that individuals in the original position would not feel it wise to commit themselves to. The difference principle, Rawls writes, seems to be one 'on the basis of which those better endowed or more fortunate in their social position, neither of which we (*sic*) can be said to deserve, could expect the willing cooperation of others when some workable scheme is a necessary condition of the welfare of all' (1971, p. 15; see also pp. 496–504 on 'relative stability'). This suggestion here is apparently that points to the right of R, on the top-most utility frontier at any rate, are not Nash equilibria if the poor can do better by concerted violations of such social contracts. Of course, no such Nash equilibria need occur anywhere on that frontier. Rawls argues only that R has the merit of being stable enough.

The maximin rule has also to be defended against neo-egalitarian proposals from the direction opposite to neo-utilitarianism. It has been argued that some point on the utility frontier to the left of R – even though below R – would be morally preferable in view of the 'relative deprivation' of the poor at R (Runciman, 1966). On this view, the maximin criterion is too conservative – as conservative as the British Tory justification of a small reduction of tax burdens on the prosperous on the ground it would so release incentives as to cause an upward movement toward R that would benefit all. Rawls resists the idea that any envy by the poor for the rich at R would induce the deliberators in the original position to prefer a leftward point that would put a crimp in the life prospects of all.[10] Resentment is a response to unjust treatment, while envy is one of Kant's 'vices of hating mankind'.

We shall hardly be able to decide these matters here and now. As Rawls remarks, the idea of the original position and of an agreement on principles there can serve only as the beginning (1971, p. 47). Yet in a two-way contest between neo-utilitarianism and neo-egalitarianism, the Schellingesque salience of the Rawls point, R, recommends it as a point of obvious compromise. I find it highly appealing, especially when compared to utilitarianism, and believe that it merits the exploration of its applications that follows. To this Rawls would himself add that such exercises serve as checks on the acceptability of the distributive criterion itself, for the resolution of ethical principles comes about through a process of *tatonnement* in which postulates are revised when their implications are found unsatisfactory.[11]

10. Rawls makes some qualifications in regard to 'excusable envy' which I cannot explicate here (see 1971, pp. 534, 546).

11. See (1971, pp. 19–21). In a letter of comments on the present paper, Rawls writes: '. . . We should not accept a standard, it seems to me, *whatever* the implications of it. Therefore how [the maximin criterion] applies to economic questions like taxation is not a matter of *mere* application. One is testing the viability of the conception of distributive justice itself, perhaps not as decisively in this sort of

2 Just taxation in two earnings models

We analyse here the implications of maximin justice for wage-income taxation in two market models of individual earnings. These models highlight different effects upon incentives to earn wages, and hence to accrue tax liability, of the graduated (i.e. non-lump-sum) taxation of wages. In the first model, which Sheshinski (1971) developed to study the implications for taxation of maximizing average utility, the disincentives from positive marginal tax rates fall on private education. In the second model, used by Mirrlees (1971) to study the maximization of an additive social welfare function, the corresponding disincentives fall on effort (say, hours worked). Throughout this section we shall suppose, with those authors, that income other than wages is non-existent or at least completely independent of wage earnings. Intertemporal and international aspects are ignored. Some questions concerning just taxation in a larger model – one in which the present ones can be imbedded – are discussed in the concluding section.

Some features common to both models can be indicated here. Individuals have identical preferences. They differ in opportunity or ability to earn income according to differences in a parameter, n, that ranges from 0 to $N < \infty$. Let $F(n)$ denote the proportion of individuals whose ability is less than or equal to n. It will be supposed that $F(n)$ is continuous, monotone increasing and right-differentiable:

$$F(n) = F(0) + \int_0^n f(s)\, ds \quad 0 \leqslant n \leqslant N,$$
$$F'(n) = f(n) > 0, \qquad\qquad\qquad\qquad\qquad\qquad \textbf{1}$$
$$F(0) \geqslant 0,$$
$$F(N) = 1.$$

There are not, therefore, any no-man's stretches between 0 and N over which persons having such ability levels are nil. While we do not generally require it, differentiability of the destiny function, f, is needed for some propositions.

A person of type n exploits his opportunity by selecting a variable

---

question as some others, but still one is testing it. The kind of exploration you present is necessary if we are to determine whether the criterion is really reasonable.'

within his control, $x(n)$, which determines his before-tax wage earnings, $y(n)$. In Mirrlees, x is manhours worked per day in a competitive labour market and so, omitting the index where it is understood,

$$y = nx. \qquad\qquad 2$$

In Sheshinski, x is an index of time spent in private education which is supposed to augment individual earning power in the same multiplicative manner. A person's n is thus measurable by the wage he would receive when his $x = 1$. Every person's private marginal product is a constant, n, independent of his x and others'. There are no externalities, so that we may interpret a person's n as his marginal social product as well.

The problem studied here is essentially finding the *net* tax function, $k(y)$, or corresponding disposable-income function, $Z(y) = y - k(y)$ such that minimum utility is maximized. This maximization is constrained by the budgetary arithmetic that aggregate (gross) tax revenue net of transfers covers any fixed government expenditure, γ, and fixed desired budgetary surplus, σ:

$$\int_0^N k[y(n)]\, dF(n) = \gamma + \sigma = \text{constant}.$$

Without loss of generality, we may view k as equal to a gross tax, $t(y)$ with $t(0) = 0$, *less* a 'minimum-disposable-income' transfer or lump-sum grant paid to all individuals, g:

$$Z(y) = y + g - t(y), \qquad t(0) = 0. \qquad\qquad 3$$

Our problem then is to find the function $t(y)$ that maximizes minimum utility, subject to the relation

$$g = \int_0^N t[y(n)]\, dF(n) - \gamma - \sigma. \qquad\qquad 4$$

An individual of ability $n_2 > 0$ can and will earn more utility than persons of type n_1, $0 < n_1 \leqslant n_2$, for *every* g and t function. This is because an n_1-type individual can assure himself at least

$$Z(n_1) = y(n_1) + g - t\{y(n_1)\},$$

namely by choosing

$$x = y(n_1)/n_2 < x(n_1) = y(n_1)/n_1,$$

and this smaller x leaves him with more utility than the n_1-type – either from less disutility of effort (Mirrlees) or less outlay for education and thus less consumption foregone. It follows from such reasoning that the minimum utility for *every t* function is that received by persons with $n = 0$. Their utility is an increasing function of g and a function of nothing else, given γ and σ. Thus the maximization of minimum utility entails finding the tax function that maximizes g in **4**. The problem of taxation for maximin justice in the present models, therefore, is the problem of maximizing aggregate (gross) tax revenue – of achieving *taxable capacity*.

The questions concerning the 'maximin' tax function of greatest interest would appear to be these: Is the tax an *everywhere* increasing function of earnings? Is the tax uniformly progressive? That is, does the average tax rate, net or gross, rise with earnings throughout? Does the marginal tax rate, $t'(y)$ vary with earnings and, if so, is there a tendency for it to rise or fall with income?[12]

(a) The training incentive model

Each individual acts to maximize utility which depends, given the configuration of government expenditure, γ, only upon his private consumption:

$$u = u(c), \qquad u'(c) > 0, \qquad c \geqslant 0. \qquad\qquad\qquad 5$$

Hours worked may accordingly be imagined to be fixed.

12. Before proceeding, I should acknowledge that income taxation *might*, from a formal point of view, be regardable as sub-optimal. If the government could measure people's y/x at little or no cost – the model does not stipulate this one way or the other – then it could lump-sum-tax individuals according to their n values so calculated, thus to enlarge taxable capacity and to increase the maximum grant, g. In a richer model where there is a variety of occupations of differing disutilities to choose from, individuals could disguise their abilities by opting for less well-paid jobs having more non-pecuniary compensations (at the cost to themselves of bidding down further the pay in these jobs). In view of these difficulties in ability measurement, and possibly other obstacles and objections to lump-sum taxation, the exploration of wage-income taxation seems amply justified at the present time.

While there is no disutility of education, there is a resource cost. The private (equals social) cost in terms of consumption foregone of an amount of education x for any individual is denoted $j(x)$ and is the same for all n.

$$c+j(x) = y-t(y)+g. \qquad\qquad 6$$

This cost function is postulated to exhibit positive and rising marginal costs. More fully,

$$
\begin{aligned}
&j(0) = 0, \qquad j'(0) = 0, \qquad j'(\infty) = \infty \\
&j'(x) > 0, \qquad j''(x) > 0, \qquad \text{for } x > 0.
\end{aligned}
\qquad 7
$$

The maximization of utility by a type-n individual with respect to his x yields the first-order condition

$$\partial c/\partial x = n\{1-t'(nx)\}-j'(x) = 0, \quad 0 \leqslant n \leqslant N, \qquad 8$$

for an interior maximum. Let us assume provisionally that tax revenue maximization implies $t(y)$ to be twice continuously differentiable with marginal tax rate $m(y) \equiv t'(y) < 1$ for all y.[13] Then $x > 0$ for all $n > 0$, and $x = 0$ at $n = 0$ in any case. We also make the provisional assumption that the 'maximin' tax function causes the second-order condition for a relative maximum to be satisfied:

$$\partial^2 c/\partial x^2 = -n^2 t''(nx)-j''(x) < 0. \qquad\qquad 9$$

Subject to the condition that $m < 1$ and 9 hold for *all x*, 8 gives the individual's global utility maximum. Then the individual's optimal x in 8 is free of 'income effects' from taxation, being dependent on the marginal tax rate but independent of the level of the tax paid at optimal y, $t(y)$.

Equation 8, which we may rewrite as

$$n[1-m(y)]-j'(x) = 0, \qquad\qquad 8'$$

makes x an implicit function of m and n, say $\chi(m,n)$, and makes y another function of m and n, $\psi(m,n) = n \cdot \chi(m,n)$. Differentiation of 8 yields

13. If there were some interval over which $t'(y) \geqslant 1$ is better than $t'(y) < 1$, then a discontinuous jump of t at the beginning of the interval would be as good or better. Hence the question reduces to the continuity of t.

$$\partial x/\partial m \equiv \chi_m(m,n) = -n/j'' < 0,$$

$$\partial x/\partial n \equiv \chi_n(m,n) = (1-m)/j'' > 0,$$

$$dx/dn = \{\chi_n(m,n) + xm'\chi_m(m,n)\}/\{1 - nm'\chi_m(m,n)\} \qquad \textbf{10}$$

$$= (l-m-ym')/(j''+n^2m') \gtreqless 0 \quad \text{as} \quad ym' \lesseqgtr 1-m,$$

and

$$\partial y/\partial m \equiv \psi_m(m,n) = n(\partial x/\partial m) = (-n^2/j'') < 0,$$

$$\partial y/\partial n \equiv \psi_n(m,n) = x + n(\partial x/\partial n) = x + (j'/j'') > 0, \qquad \textbf{11}$$

$$dy/dn = \psi_n(m,n)/\{l - m'\psi_m(m,n)\} = (j' + xj'')/(j'' + n^2m') > 0.$$

Thus education would decrease with n if m rose with income sufficiently steeply, but income must rise with n in any case, provided $1-m = j'/n > 0$ as we are assuming.[14] As for consumption, we have from **5** and **7'**

$$dc/dn = (1-m)x + [(1-m)n - j'](dx/dn) = (1-m)x > 0. \qquad \textbf{12}$$

Our problem now is to find that distribution of tax burdens that maximizes aggregate tax revenue, and thus also the lump-sum grant, so as to make minimum consumption (and hence utility) as large as is feasible. Here the taxes paid by individuals are to be a direct function of earnings, equal to $t(y)$; tax payments are only a derivable function of ability, n, deducible from **11**. It is natural, therefore, to express aggregate tax revenue as the integral over *income* of individuals' tax payments, rather than the integral over ability. In these terms, our problem is

$$\underset{\{t(y)\}}{\text{maximize}} \int_0^\infty t(y)dB(y) \quad \text{subject to } t(0) = 0. \qquad \textbf{13}$$

where $B(y)$ is the proportion of individuals with earnings below or equal to y. Of course the distribution of income depends both upon the distribution of ability, $F(n)$, and the tax function itself. To make

14. It was already established that n-types could do better than n_1 types, for all $n > n_1 > 0$ and any admissible tax structure, $t(y) < y+g$. Equation **12** *measures* that advantage and it states that the advantage from higher n is continuous in n on the assumption that t is continuous and $1-m > 0$ everywhere.

this transformation of variables from n to y we invert $y = \psi(m, n)$ to obtain a function $n = \theta(m, y)$ which gives the ability level that any individual has if he chooses to earn y and faces the corresponding marginal tax rate $m(y)$. That is, using

$$dy = \psi_m \, dm + \psi_n \, dn, \quad \psi_n > 0$$

we obtain

$$\partial n/\partial m \equiv \theta_m(m, y) = -\psi_m(m, n)/\psi_n(m, n) = n^2/(xj'' + j') > 0,$$

$$\partial n/\partial y \equiv \theta_y(m, y) = 1/\psi_n(m, n) = j''/(xj'' + j') > 0, \qquad \textbf{14}$$

$$\theta(m, 0) = 0 \quad \text{(if } m < 1\text{);} \qquad \theta(m, Y) = N.$$

Hence

$$B(y) = F[\theta(m(y), y)],$$

$$B(0) = F(0) \geqslant 0, \quad B(Y) = F(N) = 1,$$

$$\begin{aligned} b(y) \equiv B'(y) &= F'(\theta)[\theta_m \, m'(y) + \theta_y] \\ &= f(\theta)(n^2 m' + j'')/(xj'' + j') > 0, \end{aligned} \qquad \textbf{15}$$

where $b(y)$ is the density of persons with income $y > 0$, and where Y is the largest earnings attained.

So armed, one's instinct is proceed in the spirit of **13** with the problem:

$$\underset{\{m'(y)\}}{\text{maximize }} R = \int_0^\infty t(y)f\{\theta(m(y), y)\}[\theta_m \, m'(y) + \theta_y] \, dy, \qquad \textbf{16}$$

given $t'(y) = m(y), \quad t(0) = 0$.

Here the *rate of change* of the marginal tax rate is the control variable, and there are two state variables, t and m. While the linearity of the integral in $m'(y)$ excludes a classical analysis in terms of an Euler equation in $m''(y)$, the methods of control theory yield the solution.

Shying at first from the complexities of this maximization, the author fortunately stumbled on to a much more expedient formulation of the tax revenue maximand. Clearly aggregate revenue equals the marginal tax rate on the first 'dollar' of earnings times the number of persons earning a dollar or more, *plus* the marginal rate on the second dollar times the number earning two dollars or more, and so on to the last dollar of the highest earners. Hence[15]

$$\int\limits_0^\infty t(y)\, b(y)\, dy = \int\limits_0^\infty m(y)[1-B(y)]\, dy. \qquad \textbf{17}$$

Therefore our problem can be cast in the simpler form

$$\text{maximize } R(m) = \int\limits_0^\infty m\,(1-F[\theta(m,y)])\, dy. \qquad \textbf{18}$$
$$\{m(y)\}$$

The first-order condition for revenue maximization is simply that at each y the corresponding m satisfy

$$\partial R/\partial m = 1-F[\theta(m,y)]-m\partial F[\theta(m,y)]/\partial m = 0, \quad 0 \leqslant y \leqslant \infty; \qquad \textbf{19}$$

that is $\quad 1-B(y) = m\theta_m(m,y)f[\theta(m,y)], \quad 0 \leqslant y \leqslant \infty. \qquad \textbf{19}'$

The lefthand side is the increment to aggregate revenue ('marginal revenue') from a small increase of m at given y owing to the presence of $1-B$ persons who would have their taxes increased by that amount given the m for each higher y. The righthand side is the loss of revenue ('marginal cost') from the same small increase of m owing to the reduction of earnings it would cause which is to be multiplied by the marginal tax rate. These quantities are equal at the maximizing m for each y. The second-order condition is

$$\partial^2 R/\partial m^2 = -2f\theta_m - m[f\theta_{mm} + \theta_m^2 f'] < 0, \quad 0 \leqslant y \leqslant Y. \qquad \textbf{20}$$

15. The result in **17** is derivable from integration by parts:

$$\int uv'\, dy + \int vu'\, dy = (uv)\infty - (uv), \qquad \textbf{a}$$

Let $\quad u \equiv t, v \equiv B \quad$ where $t(0) = 0, B(Y) = 1.$
Then the right hand side of **17** is

$$\int (1-v)u'\, dy = \int u'\, dy - \int u'v\, dy \qquad \textbf{b}$$
$$= u_Y - u_0 - \int u'v\, dy$$
$$= u_Y\, v_Y - u_0 v_0 - \int u'v\, dy \quad [\text{using } v_Y = 1, u_0 = 0]$$
$$= \int uv'\, dy \quad [\text{from a}].$$

It is clear from continuity considerations that for each y in the interval $0 < y < Y$ there exists at least one finite m satisfying **19**. If we restrict f' to satisfy the inequality in **20** for every m, then optimal m is unique for each such y. In particular, it is clear from **19'** that for all $y < Y$, where we have $1 - B(y) > 0$, the maximizing m is *positive*. Hence $t(y)$ rises monotonically with y.

It is also implied by **19'** that at $y = Y$, where $1 - B = 0$, the optimal m equals zero. This is because there is no additional revenue from raising m above zero at Y – there is no higher-earning individual whose tax will thereby be raised – while for every $m > 0$ there is a certain loss in revenue equal to $t'(Y)(dy/dm) > 0$ (per largest earner) per unit of any rise of m on the last dollar earned, Y. The whole rationale of positive $m(y_1)$ rests on the presence of persons with $y > y_1$ whose tax is thus made higher (given intervening m between y_1 and y) than it otherwise would be. When y_1 is so large that no such persons would be left even though m were to decline as sharply as desired, the case for $m > 0$ vanishes.[16] Of course, because $m(y) > 0$ for all $y < Y$, $t(Y) > t(y)$ for all $y < Y$; hence there is no inequity in the resulting tax function.

Now as we consider smaller and smaller y away from Y, does $m(y)$ increase throughout? Differentiation of **19** yields the Euler-like equation for the rate of change of m with respect to y:

$$m'(y) = \frac{f\theta_y + m(f\theta_{my} + \theta f'\theta_y)}{-[2f\theta_m + m(f\theta_{mm} + \theta_m^2 f')]}. \qquad \textbf{21}$$

The denominator is negative according to **20**. The numerator is positive for m sufficiently close to zero and hence, because m is continuous in y, for y sufficiently close to Y. For larger m we need the sign of θ_{my} which depends upon the unsigned j'''. If, by way of example, we suppose that $xj''/j' = \lambda = \text{constant} > 0$, then

$$\theta_{my} = \lambda[x(\lambda+1)(1-m)n]^{-1} > 0$$

16. Equation **19** leaves no doubt that $m(Y) = 0$ when $f\{\theta(m, Y)\} > 0$, as in **1**. If f vanishes at Y, use l'Hôpital's rule to obtain
$$m(Y) = \lim_{y \to Y} \frac{(d/dy)[1 - B(y)]}{(d/dy)(\theta_m f)}$$
$$= \frac{-f(dn/dy)}{f(d\theta_m/dy) + \theta_m(dn/dy)f'}$$
$$= 0 \text{ if } f'\{\theta(m, Y)\} < 0.$$

In that case, there is a presumption that $m'(y) < 0$. Only where f' is sufficiently negative is the numerator possibly negative; but $f' < 0$ is likeliest, in fact, where n and y are large, and there m is small which tends to make the numerator positive.[17] It should not be surprising that, in the absence of restrictions on f', we cannot show m to be *everywhere* decreasing in y.

Before turning to a concrete example of $f(n)$, let us consider the behaviour of m as y goes to zero. Equation 19 admits the possibility that m approaches some $m(0) > 1$. There there will exist some initial interval, $0 < y < y^o$, over which $m(y) > 1$ with $m(y^o) = 1$, and a larger interval, $0 < y \leqslant y_0$, over which $t(y) \geqslant y$, with $t(y_0) = y_0$. If such is the case, then $B(y_0) = B(O)$; no household will fall in this interval. Consequently there would seem at first to be an unnecessary loss of earning incentives, and of tax revenue, in so reaching the corresponding $t(y_0)$. It would at first seem that there must be a better way to reach $t(y_0)$, say through still higher m at y near zero and lower

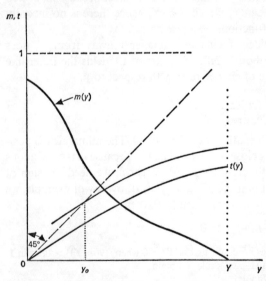

Figure 2 In the well-behaved case, $m < 1$ so $t < y$. If $m > 1$ at small y, the tax schedule will cross the 45° line at some earnings level, y_0.

17. Of course, 20 places a lower found on f' in relation to optimal m, but this leaves room for negative numerator and hence $m'(y) > 0$.

m near y^0. If such could be argued, then by taking smaller and smaller y^0, we could thus show $m(y)$ to be always less than one for every $y > 0$. But such an argument collapses when we realize that by reason of the conditions for the individual's global utility maximum, if $t(y_0) = y_0$ there will exist no $m(y_0)$ sufficiently small to induce n_0-types to earn $\psi(m, n_0) = y_0$ when $t(y_0) = y_0$. It does not seem possible to exclude the presence of a 'shut-down' earnings zone, $0 < y \leqslant y_0$, such that $t(y) \geqslant y$ (with $m(y) < 1$ typically for $y \geqslant y_0$). In this region, $m(y)$ is indeterminate though larger than one 'on average'. The usefulness of this zone is in providing a 'running start' in the taxation of people whose abilities will induce them to earn incomes above y_0 when faced with low marginal rates.[18] Accordingly, we have to interpret 19 as valid only for the region, $y_0 \leqslant y \leqslant Y$. Note that y_0 is not trivial to determine since $m(y_0)$ is unknown until y_0 is known.[19] For each y_0 candidate, given $t(0) = 0$, $t(y_0) = y_0$, and $m(y)$ from 19 for all $y \geqslant y_0$, one has to calculate maximized revenue, $g(y_0) = \max_m R(m; Y_0)$, and then optimize y_0. Whether or not optimal $y_0 > 0$, equation 19 remains valid as a description of marginal tax rates at $y \geqslant y_0$.

Example. Consider the cost function

$$j(x) = \{a/(\lambda+1)\}x^{(\lambda+1)}, \quad \lambda = \text{constant} > 0,$$

where λ is the constant elasticity, xj''/j', of marginal cost, $j' = ax^\lambda$. Using 8 we have

$$\theta(m, y) = (a/1-m)^{1/(\lambda+1)}y^{\lambda/(\lambda+1)},$$

$$\theta_m(m, y) = \theta(m, y)/(1-m)(\lambda+1).$$

In this example, formula 19 may be written

$$1 - F(\theta) = (m/1-m)\theta F'(\theta)\{1/(\lambda+1)\}.$$

18. In principle there could be a further zone, (y_2, y_3), over which 'ineffective' marginal rates would exceed one, for the same kind of purpose, if a discontinuous jump in $t(y)$ at y_2 were desirable but not allowed. No such jump in t is desired in the present model in view of 19 and our continuity assumptions.

19. With m continuous in 19, and assuming $m'(y) < 0$, $t(y_0) = y_0$ implies $y_0 > y^0$, the latter uniquely determined by

$$1 - F[\theta(1, y^0)] = \theta_m(1, y^0)_m f[\theta(1, y^0)].$$

We see again that $F' > 0$ implies $m = 0$ at $F(\theta) = 1$; that is, $m(Y) = 0$. For $\theta < N$, we may divide by both m and $1-F$ to obtain

$$1-m/m = \{F/(1-F)\}\{\theta F'(\theta)/F\}\{1/(\lambda+1)\}$$

Hence $0 < m < 1$ wherever $\theta > 0$ and $0 < F < 1$, remembering that $F'(\theta) > 0$. In the limit, as θ approaches zero, $(1-m)$ goes to zero. Hence $m(0) = 1$. There is no $y_0 > 0$, such that $t(y_0) = y_0$.

In the extraordinary event that the elasticity of F is constant – this rules out $F(0) > 0$ – and equal to $\lambda+1$, we have $m = 1-F$. One's marginal income-retention rate, $Z'(y) = 1-m(y)$ is equal to the percentile score of one's income. In the case of the rectangular or uniform distribution, it is easily checked from the derivative, dm/dF, that m falls more slowly at first, beginning with slope $(\lambda+1)^{-1}$, and faster at the end, with final slope $\lambda+1$.

Generally, for any constant-elasticity function F, m declines *monotonically* with increasing $F(\theta)$, that is, $m'(y) < 0$ for all $y, 0 \leqslant y \leqslant Y$. This follows from

$$1-m = \beta F/\{1-(1-\beta)F\}, \quad 0 \leqslant F \leqslant 1,$$

where β denotes the ratio of the distribution elasticity to $\lambda+1$. There is no closed-form expression for m as a function of y, even in the rectangular case, and the differential equation in $m'(y)$ adds little to what has already been said. However, the cost-function example is seen to be very powerful *computationally*. By considering β a function of F all manner of distributions yield to computation of $m(\theta)$, whence ultimately $m(y)$.

(a) The effort incentive model

This model is more complex than the previous one for its admission of income effects upon effort, x, of changes in the net tax, $t(y)-g$. In place of 5 we write the ordinal utility function

$$u = u(c, x), \quad u_1(c, x) > 0, \quad u_2(c, x) < 0 \quad (x > 0). \qquad \textbf{5b}$$

Each individual maximizes his utility subject to

$$c = nx - t(nx) + g \geqslant 0, \quad 0 \leqslant n \leqslant N. \qquad \textbf{6b}$$

We can deduce the implications

$$\{u_{11}u_2^2 - 2u_1u_2u_{12} + u_{22}u_1^2\}u_1^{-2} \equiv D < 0, \qquad \text{(i)} \qquad\qquad \textbf{7b}$$

$$u_{11}(-u_2/u_1) + u_{21} < 0, \qquad \text{(ii)}$$

$$u_{22} + u_{21}(-u_2/u_1) < 0, \qquad \text{(iii)}$$

from the postulates that each individual achieves an interior utility maximum for which the first-order condition is

$$du/dx = (1-m)n\, u_1(c, x) + u_2(c, x) = 0, \qquad\qquad \textbf{8b}$$

and the second-order condition

$$d^2u/dx^2 = -n^2m'(y)u_1 + D < 0, \qquad\qquad \textbf{9b}$$

with stipulated properties that $\psi(t, m, n; g) = n\chi(t, m, n; g)$ satisfy

$$0 < \psi_t \equiv \partial y/\partial t = n[u_{11}(-u_2/u_1) + u_{21}]D^{-1}, \qquad\qquad \textbf{10b}$$

$$0 > \psi_m \equiv \partial y/\partial m = n^2u_1\, D^{-1},$$

$$0 < \psi_n \equiv \partial y/\partial n = \{-u_1(-u_2/u_1) + x[u_{22} + u_{21}(-u_2/u_1)]\}D^{-1}.$$

The first of these postulates states that leisure is a normal good and the last that leisure decreases with n assuredly, no matter how strong the income effect on consumption (so that consumption must also be normal).

Then one can calculate

$$\begin{aligned}
dy/dn &= \psi_n/(1 - m'\psi_m - m\psi_t) \\
&= [-(1-m)nu_1 + x\{u_{22} + u_{12}(-u_2/u_1)\}]/(-n^2m'u_1 + D) \\
&> 0
\end{aligned} \qquad\qquad \textbf{11b}$$

and, using **6b** and **8b**,

$$du/dn = u_1(dc/dn) + u_2(dx/dn) = u_1(1-m)x > 0. \qquad\qquad \textbf{12b}$$

Our problem again is to maximize aggregate tax revenue so as to achieve the largest feasible minimum utility, $u(g, 0)$. For this purpose we again invert $\psi(t, m, n; g)$ to obtain $n = \theta(t, m, y; g)$ with the properties:

$$\partial n/\partial t \equiv \theta_t(t, m, y; g) = -\psi_t(t, m, y; g)/\psi_n(t, m, y; g) < 0,$$

$$\partial n/\partial m \equiv \theta_m(t, m, y; g) = -\psi_m(t, m, y; g)/\psi_n(t, m, y; g) > 0, \qquad \textbf{14b}$$

$$\partial n/\partial y \equiv \theta_y(t, m, y; g) = \qquad\qquad 1/\psi_n(t, m, y; g) > 0.$$

Hence

$$B(y) = F[\theta(t, m, y; g)],$$ **15b**

$$B(0) = F(0) \geqslant 0, \quad B(Y) = F(N) = 1,$$

$$b(y) \equiv B'(y) = F'(\theta)[\theta_t \, m + \theta_m \, m' + \theta_y] = f(\theta) dn/dy > 0.$$

Once again one could maximize

$$R = \int\limits_0^\infty t(y) \, b(y) dy, \quad \text{such that} \quad t'(y) = m(y), \, t(0) = 0,$$ **16b**

where $m'(y)$ is the control variable. But, as in the Sheshinski model, it is more expedient to cast the problem thus:

$$\underset{\{m(y)\}}{\text{maximize}} \; R(m; t_0) = \int\limits_0^\infty m \, (1 - F[\theta(t, m, y; g)]) \, dy,$$ **18b**

subject to (a) $t'(y) = m(y)$, (b) $t(0) = t_0 = 0$,

where it is understood that $g = \max R(m; 0) - \gamma - \sigma > 0$.

This is a 'dynamic' programming problem, unlike **18**, since $t(y)$ at any $y_1 > 0$ affects $B(y_1)$ and it depends on $m(y)$ at 'earlier' y, $y < y_1$.

The first-order condition for maximizing m is the Euler differential equation

$$\frac{d}{dy}\Big\{1 - F(\theta) - m\theta_m \, f(\theta)\Big\} = -mf(\theta)\theta_t, \quad 0 \leqslant y \leqslant Y.$$ **19b**

The second-order requirement is the Legendre condition,

$$\partial^2 R/\partial m^2 = -2f\theta_m - m[f\theta_{mm} + \theta_m^2 f'] < 0, \quad 0 \leqslant y \leqslant Y.$$ **20b**

Carrying out the differentiation in (**19b**) leads to the analogue of **21**:

$$m'(y) = \frac{f\theta y + m(f\theta_{my} + \theta_m f'\theta y + mf\theta_{mt} + mf'\theta_m \theta_t)}{-[2f\theta_m + m(f\theta_{mm} + \theta_m^2 f')]}$$ **21b**

It can be argued that the first integral of **19b** is

$$[1 - \int\limits_0^Y m(s) f\{\theta(s)\}\theta_t(s) \, ds] - F - m\theta_m f = -\int\limits_0^Y m(s) f\{\theta(s)\}\theta_t(s) \, ds$$ **19'b**

or, equivalently,

$$m\theta_m f(\theta) = 1 - F(\theta) - \int_y^Y m(s)f'\{\theta(s)\}\theta_t(s)\,ds. \qquad \textbf{19''b}$$

It follows at once that $m(Y) = 0$ along the same reasoning as in the previous model. For all $y < Y$, $m(y) > 0$. Also if θ_m goes to infinity fast enough as m approaches one (as in the example), then $m(0) \leqslant 1$, thus precluding complications of t(y) $\geqslant$ y near y $= 0$.

In Model A, where $\theta_t \equiv 0$, $1 - F$ is interpretable as the 'shadow price' of higher $t(y)$ at y, to which quantity the 'marginal cost' of higher m is to be equated. Here, $1 - F$ understates the shadow price because an increase of $t(y)$ at any $y < Y$ would reduce $\theta(s)$ for all $y \leqslant s \leqslant Y$ (recalling $\theta_t < 0$), hence would increase $1 - B(s)$ so as to bring in the extra revenue yield indicated by the integral expression. Thus if θ_m is comparatively insensitive to $t(y)$ at $y = \psi(t, m, \theta)$ at each θ, $\textbf{19''b}$ affords the presumption that m tends to be higher for every θ when $\theta_t < 0$ than in Model A where $\theta_t \equiv 0$. If this presumption is correct, it accords with intuition: the income effect of higher taxation inducing greater effort, expressed by $\psi_t > 0$, presents an extra incentive for higher m – in the sense of m tending to decline with rising y more slowly. In this case, because the aggregate net tax collected is constrained to equal $\lambda + \sigma \geqslant 0$ in both models, g is higher in model B and $t(y)$ is higher for every $y > 0$.

3 Concluding remarks

The principal finding here is that the maximin rule calls for the marginal tax rate on wage income to decrease toward zero, though not necessarily to decrease monotonically, this subject to the qualification concerning the initial tax at some small income level. The extent to which this proposition will hold good in more general models remains to be investigated. Merely lifting the assumption that different persons' (n-augmented) labour inputs are perfect technical substitutes may pose difficulties. There is also the broader question of the optimal importance of wage income taxation, the degree to which the least-advantaged individuals in society would gain (or lose) from a shift in the mix of taxes on wages, profits and rents and the possibilities for increased revenue through novel taxes according to wage rates and other individual data. In all cases, however, if the least-advantaged are unable to earn income, the maximin rule would appear to call for the realization of taxable capacity.

References

ARROW, K. J. (1964), *Social Choice and Individual Values*, 2nd edn, Wiley.

HARE, R. M. (1963), *Freedom and Reason*, Clarendon Press.

HARSANYI, J. C. (1955), 'Cardinal welfare, individualistic ethics and interpersonal comparisons of utility', *J. polit. Econ.*, August.

MIRRLEES, J. A. (1971), 'An exploration in the theory of optimal income taxation', *Rev. econ. Stud.*, April.

RAWLS, J. (1971), *A Theory of Justice*, Harvard University Press.

RUNCIMAN, W. G. (1966), *Relative Deprivation and Social Justice*, Routledge & Kegan Paul.

SHESKINSKI, E. (1971), 'On the theory of optimal income taxation', Harvard Discussion Paper, February.

SIDGWICK, H. (1907), *The Method of Ethics*, Macmillan.

VICKREY, W. S. (1960), 'Utility, strategy and social decision rules', *Q. J. Econ.*, November.

19 K. J. Arrow

The Utilitarian Approach to the Concept of Equality in Public Expenditure

K. J. Arrow, 'The utilitarian approach to the concept of equality in public expenditure', *Quarterly Journal of Economics*, 1971.

Coleman and doubtless many others have stressed the distinction between equality of output and equality of input in evaluating public expenditures, particularly those devoted to individual benefit, as in the case of education or health (1968). The point is that the benefit derived by an individual from a given volume of government expenditures depends upon other characteristics of that individual. Hence, the dictum that the government ought to treat its citizens equally becomes ambiguous; equality of expenditures on different individuals does not produce equality of benefit to them.

I suggest here a reconsideration of the whole concept of equality in this domain by reverting to the utilitarian concepts of Bentham, as applied more precisely to the economic realm by Edgeworth (1881, pp. 56–82; and 1925, pp. 100–22). That is, instead of discussing equality *per se*, we seek to derive the concept from a maximization of the sum of individual utilities.[1] In the utilitarian discussion of income distribution, equality of income is derived from the maximization conditions if it is further assumed that individuals have the same utility functions, each with diminishing marginal utility. The utilitarian approach is not currently fashionable, partly for the very good reason that interpersonally comparable utilities are hard to define; nevertheless, no simple substitute has yet appeared, and I think it will be useful to pursue this line of study for whatever clarification it will bring.

1. This analysis corresponds to the interpretation of tax equity as equal marginal sacrifice, thereby permitting the same condition to meet both efficiency and equity criteria. Other views of tax equity in terms of equal or proportional sacrifice (Pigou, 1951, part 2) or maximization of minimum ability (Rawls, 1967, pp. 58–82) may also be considered with regard to expenditure analysis.

I assume that when we speak of seeking to equalize government expenditures, or, more especially, expenditures in some particular field, we want to study that problem in some isolation from the general problem of income distribution. In other words, we seek to equalize, e.g. educational expenditures, or, in utilitarian terms, to maximize the benefit from a given volume of such expenditures, but we do not consider these expenditures as a compensation for other income qualities. Therefore, it is assumed that there is for each individual a function relating the volume of expenditures to the utility derived from them. These utilities are taken to be interpersonally comparable, and the total volume of expenditures is to be allocated among individuals so as to maximize the sum of these utilities. The utility function for any given individual, however, depends not only on the expenditures on him but also on some personal characteristics. For simplicity, we term the latter, 'ability'. Since individuals of identical ability are identical from the government's point of view, an allocation policy consists of determining expenditures as a function of ability.

1 The formal statement of the model and the analysis of input equality

Let x = ability of a given individual, y = expenditures on a given individual, $U(x,y)$ = utility derived by the individual.

In this context, we understand ability to mean capacity to benefit from the expenditures in question, so that necessarily

$$U_x > 0;$$ 1

we also assume that expenditures are always productive of some benefit, i.e.

$$U_y > 0.$$ 2

Then an optimal policy (from the utilitarian viewpoint) satisfies the condition

$$U_y = \text{constant over individuals.}$$ 3

We will assume that suitable concavity conditions are satisfied.

$$U_{yy} < 0.$$ 4

Relation **3** determines y as a function of x, and this is the optimal allocation policy. The constant is determined by the budget level. The expenditures y are the inputs into the individuals' production of benefits; therefore we define

D.1 The policy $y(x)$ is *input-equal* if $dy/dx = 0$.

More generally, we may want to define

D.2 The policy $y(x)$ is *input-progressive* if $dy/dx < 0$ and *input-regressive* if $dy/dx > 0$.

These terms correspond to usual usage with regard to taxation, except that we are dealing with 'ability to receive' rather than 'ability to pay'. If we start from an initial situation of input equality, then by **1** higher utility is associated with higher ability. Hence, a shift toward an input-regressive policy is a reallocation of resources in favour of the better off.

From **3**, at the optimal policy, U_y is constant over individuals and therefore independent of x. If we differentiate **3** totally with respect to x, we find,

$$U_{xy} + U_{yy}(dy/dx) = 0. \qquad\qquad 5$$

In view of **4** and **D.1–2**, we can state

Proposition 1. The optimal policy is input-progressive, -equal, or -regressive according as $U_{xy} < 0$, $= 0$, or > 0.

Thus, the optimal policy is input-progressive if the utility increase attributable to a given volume of government expenditures is less for individuals of higher ability.

The conditions for input equality will be analysed more closely. Suppose we have a policy which is input-equal throughout, and further suppose that the optimal policy would remain input-equal even if the budget level were to change. Then it must be that U_{xy} is identically equal to zero, at least in some region of (x, y)-space. As is well known, this is equivalent to the assertion that the utility function can be written as the sum of a function of x and a function of y.

D.3 A function $f(x, y)$ is *additively separable* if it can be written $f(x, y) = g(x) + h(y)$.

An additively separable function is one that can be calculated on a suitably constructed slide rule.

Proposition 2. The optimal policy is input-equal for all budgets if and only if the utility function, $U(x, y)$ is additively separable.

2 Output equality

In this model, the output of the system is the utility itself, $U(x, y)$, with $y = y(x)$, or, $U[x, y(x)]$.

D.4 The policy $y(x)$ is *output-equal* if $dU[x, y(x)]/dx = 0$, *output-progressive* if $dU/dx < 0$, and *output-regressive* if $dU/dx > 0$.

By straightforward differentiation,

$$dU/dx = U_x + U_y(dy/dx).\qquad\qquad 6$$

Suppose $dy/dx \geqslant 0$. Then, since $U_x > 0$, $U_y > 0$, by **1–2**, it must be that $dU/dx > 0$.

Proposition 3. If a policy is input-equal or input-regressive, it is necessarily output-regressive. If a policy is output-equal or output-progressive, it is necessarily input-progressive.

(The two sentences of this proposition make the same assertion in different words.)

Multiply both sides of **6** by U_{yy} and substitute from **5**.

$$U_{yy}(dU/dx) = U_x U_{yy} - U_y U_{xy}.\qquad\qquad 7$$

For analysis of output equality, it turns out to be useful to express expenditures as a function of ability and of the utility achieved. That is, we define $V(x, u)$ as the value of y for which $U(x, y) = u$, so that the relation,

$$U[x, V(x, u)] = u,\qquad\qquad 8$$

is an identity. Differentiate **8** partially, first with respect to x and then with respect to u.

$$U_x + U_y V_x = 0,\qquad\qquad 9$$

$$U_y V_u = 1.\qquad\qquad 10$$

Now differentiate **10** partially with respect to x, holding u constant. Notice that U_y is a function of x both directly and through $y = V(x, u)$, so that

$\partial U_y / \partial x = U_{xy} + U_{yy} V_x$,

and therefore,

$(U_{xy} + U_{yy} V_x)V_u + U_y V_{ux} = 0$.

Multiply through by U_y^2. Note that $U_y V_u = 1$, by **10**, so that $U_y^2 V_u = U_y$, and $U_y^2 V_u V_x = U_y V_x = -U_x$, by **9**.

$U_y U_{xy} - U_{yy} U_x + U_y^3 V_{ux} = 0$,

or, from **7**,

$U_y^3 V_{ux} = U_{yy}(dU/dx)$.

Since $U_y > 0, U_{yy} < 0$, it follows that dU/dx has a sign opposite to that of V_{ux}.

Proposition 4. The optimal policy is output-progressive if and only if the following condition holds: when initially expenditures have been so adjusted to ability that all individuals have the same utility, then the cost of achieving a given increment of utility is higher for individuals of higher ability. The conditions for output equality and output regressivity are obtained by substituting the words 'equal' and 'less', respectively, for 'greater' in the preceding sentence.

The condition for output equality for all budgets is that V_{ux} be identically zero and therefore that V be additively separable. From **1, 2, 9**, and **10**,

$V_x < 0, V_u > 0$,   **11**

so that $V(x, u)$ can be written as the difference between an increasing function of utility and an increasing function of ability.

Proposition 5. The optimal policy is output-equal for all budgets if and only if the expenditures needed to achieve a given utility level for a given ability can be expressed as the difference between a function of utility and a function of ability, both functions being increasing in their respective arguments.

3 The case of objectively measurable outputs

In many situations, the benefits derived from government expenditures are measured in some objective way, not merely in terms of utility. Thus, educational accomplishments may be measured in terms of various test scores, manpower training in terms of increased wages and employment opportunities, or health benefits in terms of longevity and decreased morbidity. It is natural in those circumstances to consider the utility as a function of the measured output, and the output in turn as a function of the two 'inputs', ability and expenditures. Let z = measured output, $U(z)$ = utility, $z = f(x, y)$; the last may be thought of as a production function.

The utility derived from a given ability, x, and expenditures, y, is then given by $U[f(x, y)]$, which plays the role taken by $U(x, y)$ in the preceding sections. All the earlier propositions remain valid, of course; indeed, the model of this section is simply a special case. However, some further conclusions can be drawn if special assumptions are made about the production relation.

D.5 The production *relation*, $z = f(x, y)$, will be termed *additively separable* if there exist monotonic functions, $H(z), F(x)$, and $G(y)$, such that $H(z) = F(x)+G(y)$ whenever $z = f(x, y)$.

The statement that the production *relation* is additively separable is considerably weaker than the statement that the production *function* is additively separable; the latter would require that $z = F(x)+G(y)$. Additive separability is a frequently made hypothesis in the study of production functions; C E S production functions, including in particular Cobb-Douglas functions, imply additively separable production relations.

In the special case where $H(z)$ happens to be the same as $U(z)$, the derived utility function $U[f(x, y)]$ is additively separable and, by proposition 2, the optimal policy exhibits input equality. In general, we have, by differentiation of the production relation in additively separated form,

$$H'f_x = F'(x), \qquad H'f_y = G'(y). \hspace{2cm} \textbf{12}$$

Let U_x and U_y be the partial derivatives of $U[f(x, y)]$. Then, with the aid of **12**,

$$U_x = U'(z)f_x = [U'(z)/H'(z)]F'(x).$$

Differentiate this with respect to y, holding x constant.

$$U_{xy} = F'(x) \frac{d(U/H)}{dz} f_y = \frac{F'G'}{H'} \frac{d(U'/H')}{zd}.$$

We may obviously suppose that F, G, and H are all increasing functions, and therefore F', G', and H' are all positive. Then the sign of U_{xy} is the same as that of $\dfrac{d(U'/H')}{dz}$. In view of proposition 1, we have

Proposition 6. If the production relation is additively separable, the optimal policy is input-progressive, -equal, or -regressive according as U'/H' is a decreasing, constant, or increasing function of z.

We can give a similar characterization of output equality for the case of additively separable production. Define $z(u)$ as the solution of the equation $U(z) = u$. Then the function $V(x,u)$, defined in the preceding section, satisfies the following relation identically in x and u:

$$H[z(u)] = F(x)+G[V(x,u)].$$

Differentiate partially with respect to x, and then differentiate the resulting equation partially with respect to u.

$$0 = F'(x) + G'(y)V_x,$$
$$G''(y)V_xV_u+G'(y)V_{ux} = 0.$$

From **11** and the fact that $G' > 0$, it follows directly that V_{ux} has the same sign as G''. Proposition 4 then implies

Proposition 7. If the production relation is additively separable, then the optimal policy is output-progressive, -equal, or -regressive according as $G''(y)$ is positive, zero, or negative.

In propositions 6 and 7, the special cases of input or output equality reduce to those already noted in propositions 2 and 5.

4 Comments

Obviously not much in the way of policy implications should be drawn from such a simplified model. However, some tentative observations may be ventured.

1. In the case of education and many other contexts, we ordinarily assume that ability is correlated with the securing of benefits from government expenditures at the margin as well as in total; hence, proposition 4 seems to suggest that the utilitarian criterion leads to output regressivity, which is certainly the policy currently in use, at least in the field of education. In the field of health, however, ability

means essentially 'state of health'; expenditures will be less productive of increased utility for a healthier individual, so we would expect output progressivity and *a fortiori* input progressivity to be the norm.

On the other hand, proposition 6 makes it somewhat plausible that there should be input progressivity, particularly if U' is decreasing at all rapidly.

2. The relevance of the analysis of section 3 depends on the possibility of appropriate econometric investigations into the relevant production functions. It does suggest caution in using functional forms, e.g. linearity, which imply the nature of the optimal policy even before knowing the results of empirical study.

3. The case for equality may be made on other than utilitarian grounds; thus Rawls (1967) has argued for maximizing the minimum utility, rather than the sum of utilities, as an ethical criterion, and this criterion would tend toward output equality and therefore strong input progressivity.

References

COLEMAN, J. S. (1968), 'The concept of equality of educational opportunity', *Harvard Educ. Rev.*, vol. 38, pp. 14–22.

EDGEWORTH, F. Y. (1881), *Mathematical Physics*, Routledge & Kegan Paul.

EDGEWORTH, F. Y. (1925), 'The pure theory of taxation', in *Papers Relating to Political Economy*, vol. 2, Macmillan; originally published in *econ. J.*, 1897, vol. 7, pp. 46–70, 226–38, 550–71.

PIGOU, A. C. (1951), *A Study in Public Finance*, Macmillan.

RAWLS, J. (1967), 'Distributive justice', in P. Laslett and W. G. Runciman (eds.), *Philosophy, Politics, and Society*, third series, Blackwell.

20 J. Tobin

On Limiting the Domain of Inequality

J. Tobin, 'On limiting the domain of inequality', *Journal of Law and Economics*, vol. 13, 1970, October.

The most difficult issues of political economy are those where goals of efficiency, freedom of choice, and equality conflict. It is hard enough to propose an intellectually defensible compromise among them, even harder to find a politically viable compromise. These are ancient issues. The agenda of economics and politics have always featured policies whose effects on economic inequality and on efficiency in resource allocation are hopelessly intertwined. But it is only in the last five years that they have regained the centre of attention of American economists, with whom stabilization, full employment, and growth took the highest priority for the preceding three decades.

When a distinguished colleague in political science asked me about ten years ago why economists did not talk about the distribution of income any more, I followed my *pro forma* denial of his factual premise by replying that the potential gains to the poor from full employment and growth were much larger, and much less socially and politically divisive, than those from redistribution. One reason that distribution has returned to the forefront of professional and public attention is that great progress was made in the postwar period, and especially in the 1960s, toward solving the problems of full employment and growth.

It is natural that debate should now focus on intrinsically harder issues of the composition and distribution of the national product, and it is also natural, though disappointing, to find people with short memories questioning whether full employment and growth ever were problems worth worrying about. There are of course other reasons for the recent shift of emphasis, notably the belated commitment of the society to racial equality and the diffuse concern for social justice that is one feature of the cultural revolution of the young.

American attitudes toward economic inequality are complex. The egalitarian sentiments of contemporary college campuses are not necessarily shared by the not-so-silent majority. Our society, I believe, accepts and approves a large measure of inequality, even of inherited inequality. Americans commonly perceive differences of wealth and income as earned and regard the differential earnings of effort, skill, foresight, and enterprise as deserved. Even the prizes of sheer luck cause very little resentment. People are much more contented with the legitimacy, legality, and fairness of large gains than with their sheer size.

But willingness to accept inequality in general is, I detect, tempered by a persistent and durable strain of what I shall call *specific egalitarianism*. This is the view that certain specific scarce commodities should be distributed less unequally than the ability to pay for them. Candidates for such sentiments include basic necessities of life, health, and citizenship. Our institutions and policies already modify market distributions in many cases, and the issues raised by specific egalitarianism are central to many proposals now before the country.

The trained instincts of most economists set them against these policies and proposals. To the extent that economists are egalitarians at all, they are general egalitarians. The reason is their belief that specific interventions, whether in the name of equality or not, introduce inefficiencies, and the more specific the intervention the more serious the inefficiency. Henry Simons eloquently articulated these instincts and proposed a clear-cut practical resolution of the conflict between efficiency and equality (1948).

Simons' design is a very attractive one, deceptively so. He splits economic policy into two departments, one for equity and one for efficiency. Problems of equity and social justice are resolved at the most general level, in legislation for taxation of income and wealth. As for efficiency, the objective of government policy is to make markets work competitively. The government does not intervene in particular labour or product markets on behalf of distributive justice. Reformers interested in reducing, or increasing, economic inequality are referred to the Ways and Means Committee. They cannot seek these ends by fixing milk prices or minimum wages or oil imports or apartment rents or wheat acreage or subway fares – or, for that matter, by rent subsidies or food stamps. Simons says, 'It is urgently necessary for us to quit confusing measures for regulating relative prices and wages with devices for diminishing inequality. One difference between competent economists and charlatans is that, at this point, the former sometimes discipline their sentimentality with a little reflection on the mechanics of an exchange economy' (1948, p. 83).

While concerned laymen who observe people with shabby housing or too little to eat instinctively want to provide them with decent housing and adequate food, economists instinctively want to provide them with more cash income. Then they can buy the housing and food if they want to, and if they choose not to, the presumption is that they have a better use for the money. To those who complain about the unequal distribution of shelter or of food, our first response – and Simons' – is that they should look at the distribution of wealth and income. If the social critics approve that distribution, then they should accept its implications, including the unequal distribution of specific commodities. If they don't like it, then they should attack the generalized inequality rather than the specific inequality. Economists, especially some trained at the University of Chicago, think they can prove that, given the distribution of generalized purchasing power, competitive production and distribution of specific commodities will be optimal.

This answer rarely satisfies the intelligent egalitarian layman. He knows, partly because he has learned it from economists, that there are pragmatic limits on the redistributive use of taxation and cash transfers. These instruments are not as neutral in their allocative effects as Simons appeared to believe; they may seriously distort choices between work and leisure, selections of occupations and jobs, allocations of savings among competing investments, etc. We have yet to conjure into reality the economist's dream tax – the lump sum tax that no one can avoid or diminish by altering his own behaviour.

Simons knew, no doubt, that progressive taxation was not neutral in its allocative effect, but he was writing in the days of small government and was not contemplating very heavy taxes. Nor does he seem to have contemplated what we now call negative taxes, although such transfers would have been a logical extension of his programme.

Serious redistribution by tax and transfer will involve high tax rates, as the following simple calculation illustrates. Suppose the government gives every citizen a certain amount $m (a guaranteed minimum income) and collects by income tax enough to pay these grants and to finance government activities which cost c per capita. Tax rates must be high enough to collect the fraction $(m+c)/\bar{y}$ of total income, where $\bar{y}$ is average income per capita. If the guarantee level m is a quarter or a third of mean income, and especially if the government is purchasing for substantive use any significant fraction of national output, the necessary tax rates will be so high that incentive and allocational effects cannot be ignored.

The layman therefore wonders why we cannot arrange things so that certain crucial commodities are distributed less unequally than is general income – or, more precisely, less unequally than the market would distribute them given an unequal income distribution. The idea has great social appeal. The social conscience is more offended by severe inequality in nutrition and basic shelter, or in access to medical care or to legal assistance, than by inequality in automobiles, books, clothes, furniture, boats. Can we somehow remove the necessities of life and health from the prizes that serve as incentives for economic activity, and instead let people strive and compete for non-essential luxuries and amenities?

This is essentially what the United States and other countries did in the Second World War when the supplies of normal consumption goods were drastically limited by the drafts of resources for the war effort. The public was not taxed enough to accomplish the transfer of resources in the market, in large part because of fear of the disincentive effects of the high tax rates that would have been necessary. Prices and wages were controlled to repress, and postpone, the latent inflation. At the controlled prices there was chronic excess demand for consumption goods, and market distribution of these goods was supplanted by a more egalitarian distribution via official and unofficial rationing. Incentives to work, beyond sheer patriotism, were maintained by the prospect that incomes, though inconvertible into consumption at the time, would become convertible later, after the end of the war.

Specific egalitarianism takes a number of different forms, with a number of different motivations and rationalizations. There are some commodities where strict equality of distribution is deemed a crucially important objective, so important that society cannot permit an individual even voluntarily to transfer his share to someone else.

These 'commodities' include civil rights and privileges – and their converse, civil obligations – where equality among citizens is basic to the political constitution. The vote is a prime example, the military draft possibly another. The category includes also biological or social necessities which are scarce in aggregate supply, so scarce that if they are unequally distributed, some citizens must be consuming below a tolerable minimum. Examples include essential foods in wartime, and probably medical care here and now. In these cases there is a strong paternalistic element in the state's insistence that the individual may not, even voluntarily, transfer his ration to some-one else.

At the other end of the spectrum there are commodities of ample supply, or at least of potentially ample supply, where the egalitarian objective is, so to speak, one-sided, not a strictly equal distribution but an assured universal minimum. Ample aggregate supply means that if everyone received only the tolerable minimum, there would be a surplus. Food and possibly housing are examples in the United States today.

In every case a crucial issue is the elasticity of supply, in the short run and the long run, of the commodity in question. When the scarce commodity is in fixed supply, then arrangements for distributing it equally, or on any other non-market criterion, can be made without worrying about efficiency. This is also the case in which social concern about specific inequality makes the most sense.

In wartime Britain tea was in short and inelastic supply; there was no way by which selling it to the highest bidder could increase the imports; and it made sense to worry specifically about the fairness of the distribution of tea. In peacetime United States there is social concern about inequality of access to medical care: luxury medical care for the rich uses resources that could be saving the lives or life chances of the poor. Specific redistribution makes sense if medical care, like tea in wartime Britain, is in inelastic supply. It makes less sense if additional medical care can be obtained by drawing resources from other uses. To that degree the medical deprivations of the poor can be laid to rich consumers of automobiles, boats, and higher education as fairly as to rich over-consumers of the services of physicians and hospitals.

The state has at its disposal a number of instruments for modifying or supplanting the market distribution of a commodity. By market distribution, I mean the distribution among consumers that would result from the expenditure of their money incomes after taxes and cash transfer payments, in the absence of any interventions to set prices or allocations. The concept is clear for privately produced goods and services. But some 'commodities' of interest are produced and dispensed by the state; indeed some are rights or privileges rather than goods and services in the usual sense. In the case of state-controlled commodities, I shall use the term market distribution to refer to the result of auctioning the supply to the highest bidders.

One instrument is to forbid the delivery of the commodity to consumers without the surrender of *ration tickets*, of which the government controls the allocation. Ration tickets may be either *personal* or *transferable*. A second instrument is the *commodity voucher* or *stamp*, of which the government likewise controls the allocation. The consumer can use the voucher or stamp only for a specific commodity or class of commodities. The government redeems in cash the vouchers presented by a supplier. Like ration tickets, vouchers can be either personal or transferable. Finally, although ration tickets are usually necessary but not sufficient to purchase a rationed good, it is possible for ration tickets to serve also as vouchers. I shall find it convenient to use these terms in a figurative sense, that is, to apply them to a number of situations which can be described as if there are ration coupons and vouchers even though such pieces of paper do not or need not literally exist.

I propose now to discuss a number of illustrative cases of specific egalitarianism, actual or proposed.

Wartime rationing

The rationing of scarce necessities of life in time of war or its aftermath is, as noted above, a common example of specific egalitarianism. It is worth further brief discussion, because it illustrates some of the issues and problems that arise in contemporary manifestations of specific egalitarianism.

One common system was specific rationing. Ration tickets for a single commodity, sugar or orange juice or tea or meat or gasoline, were distributed equally or in relation to some criteria of need. They were not transferable, either for money or for other ration coupons. The rationale was a combination of egalitarianism and paternalism. Rich children should not have all the orange juice, and no family should bargain away its children's vitamins even if the parents want to do so. Of course, even though ration tickets themselves are not transferable, it is difficult to prevent informal or black market exchanges and sales of the commodities themselves, except when the commodities are highly perishable or personal.

Once delivery of a commodity is effectively forbidden except in exchange for ration tickets, the government has at least indirect control of the money price. Left to the market, the price will be set so that the available supply will be equal to ration-limited demand. This could be as low as zero if the ration coupons cover no more than the available supply. If the government sets a positive price, then it will induce some consumers to leave coupons unused; the real value of remaining coupons will correspondingly increase. Conversely, if coupon values are set too high then a positive money price will arise in order to squeeze out excess consumers.

If equality is really the aim, if consumption is to be strictly independent of unequal money income, then a positive money price must not be allowed to squeeze anyone out. Indeed, ration tickets must double as vouchers, with the government paying the suppliers by redeeming the ration-vouchers with money.

If the supply is inelastic, as was typically the case in wartime, the terms of redemption are purely a distributive matter, as between the general taxpayers and the suppliers of the scarce commodity. But if the supply is responsive, then the government's payment will be one of the determinants of the future supply.

Another model is the negotiable ration ticket. Ration coupons are equally distributed, and the scarce commodity cannot be purchased without one. But coupons can be transferred. The rich and eager can consume an above average share of the commodity, but only by transferring purchasing power over other goods to the poor and indifferent. Equality of specific consumption is not maintained, but those who wish more than their share must find and compensate someone willing to get along with less. The same effect could be achieved by giving everyone a lump sum dollar grant and levying a tax on the consumption of the commodity, just enough to pay for the grant. The advantage of the ration mechanism is that the market makes what would be a difficult calculation for the tax collector. The equity of the system is that high consumers of the scarce commodity, rather than general taxpayers, are made to subsidize the poor and other low consumers.

The transferable ration system does not give the right signals when supply is elastic. It does not make sense to levy an excise tax on an essential commodity in short supply. The way out is for the government, in effect, to buy the supply at its supply price and to distribute it by ration-vouchers at a lower money price or free.

Voting

There are some rights and privileges, and some duties, which the society desires to distribute precisely equally among its members, or among a sub-group of its members. The distribution is supposed to be wholly independent of income and wealth. Furthermore the distribution is supposed to be independent of individual preferences; society would not approve an individual's voluntary assignment of his share to someone else even if the assignee were of equal or lower income.

Perhaps the clearest example is the vote in a democratic polity. The modern democratic ethic excludes property qualifications, obvious or disguised, for the suffrage. Votes are not transferable; buying or selling them is illegal, and the secret ballot makes such contracts unenforceable. In some countries, indeed, citizens are penalized simply for not voting. Any good second year graduate student in economics could write a short examination paper proving that voluntary transactions in votes would increase the welfare of the sellers as well as the buyers. But the legitimacy of the political process rests on the prohibition of such transactions. A vote market would concentrate political power in the rich, and especially in those who owe their wealth to government privilege.

The instrument used for equal distribution of the vote could be described, in the terms previously introduced, as a non-transferable combined ration ticket and voucher. Obviously an egalitarian distribution can be enforced without any loss of efficiency. The aggregate supply of votes is intrinsically inelastic. Allowing a free market in votes could not augment the power of the electorate as a whole; it would serve only to redistribute it differently.

The draft

Military service is a duty rather than a right, but the same issues arise with respect to its distribution. In some nations it is regarded as a non-negotiable obligation of citizenship, just as the vote is a non-negotiable right. This conception applies in some countries even in peacetime. But the notion that the obligation should not be distributed among citizens on the basis of income and wealth is of course strongest in wartime, when it becomes a matter of distributing risks of death and injury. The national conscience was scandalized, at the time and in retrospect, by the civil war spectacle of rich fathers' purchasing substitutes for their drafted sons. The power of the purse saved the life of one boy in exchange for the death of another. Subsequent draft laws in this country have excluded this kind of transaction.

Nevertheless many of the criteria of selective service are highly correlated with economic status. The correlation is difficult to avoid so long as selections must be made, so long as the number of persons needed in the armed services is smaller than the physically eligible population. That is one reason why the draft today is so much more difficult and socially divisive a problem than it was in the Second World War. Although equality of exposure could be achieved in current circumstances by short enlistments, too rapid a turnover would make it impossible for the armed services to accomplish their missions.

In these circumstances a lottery, with no deferments, is the only egalitarian device available. Forbidding the exchange of a vulnerable draft number for a safe number is conceptually equivalent to prohibiting the sale of votes or of ration tickets – once again a paternalistic insistence on an egalitarian distribution takes precedence over the standard economist's presumption that a voluntary exchange increases the welfare of both parties.

A further condition of a strictly egalitarian solution is hardly ever squarely faced. The possibility that poor young men may risk their lives for money can be wholly avoided only by prohibiting volunteering or by setting soldiers' pay well below effective civilian alternatives.

A volunteer army is subject to the same objections on egalitarian grounds as a free market in negotiable military obligations. It is just a more civilized and less obvious way of doing the same thing, that is, allocating military service to those eligible young men who place the least monetary value on their safety and on alternative uses of their time. There is one important difference, however. With a volunteer army, the general taxpayer must provide the funds necessary to draw into military service the number of soldiers needed. With a free market in draft obligations, much of this burden is picked up by the draftees who are buying substitutes, or by their families. The general taxpayer bears only the costs of the official soldiers' pay, which in a draft system is of course below the market supply price. Young men who escape the obligation are, in effect, taxed to pay the young men who take it on. It is certainly not obvious that the volunteer army solution, whatever its other merits, is the more equitable of these two arrangements.

As for efficiency on the supply side, it is not clear whether the size of the armed forces should be regarded as a fixed demand for manpower independent of its cost. If so, then there is no problem of resource allocation, only a problem of equitable distribution, and nothing is lost by an egalitarian draft. It may be argued, on the other hand, that voters, the Congress, the President, and the Pentagon would and should attune their foreign policies and military technologies to the costs of military manpower, and that the draft biases their decisions toward using more military personnel than they would if defence budgets reflected the true marginal costs. The volunteer army solution would correct this distortion. In principle it could also be corrected within the framework of the opposite solution, a stochastic draft with volunteering prohibited, but with military pay set at the conjectural supply price of the size army the government wants.

Rights to bear children

Contemporary worries about the prospects of overpopulation have led to spreading conviction that society will eventually have to control population growth by rationing births. The Zero Population Growth movement, popular on campuses, wants every mother to be limited to two children. We can imagine that medical technology will some day permit social control of periods of fertility.

I am not interested in discussing here whether worries about overpopulation are justified or whether, even if they are, society should in fact regulate births. What is relevant to my subject is how such regulation would be carried out. Should each and every mother be limited to two children or less? Or should each woman be issued two – or two and a fraction tickets, whatever is consistent with zero population growth – and be allowed to transfer whole or fractional tickets to other women? Or should the government fix an annual quota of births and auction the tickets to the highest bidders?

The first system is the most egalitarian, but excludes many voluntary transfers of 'birth rights' that would in principle increase the utility of all parties concerned. The second system allows such transfers, but also opens up the possibility that rights to have children will be concentrated in the rich. At least the poor and others who give up their rights will be well compensated. This is not the case under the third system, the auction, where the rich can still buy up the rights but to the benefit of the general taxpayer rather than of would-be mothers who lose out in the auction.

Education

The American system of elementary and secondary education is one of non-transferable ration vouchers along with a paternalistically motivated compulsory requirement for minimum consumption. Every child is entitled to free schooling. His 'ticket' cannot be transferred to anyone else; there is no direct way in which one parent, by accepting less schooling for his child, can provide more for another. A child may use his 'voucher' only in the public schools. If he does not use it, he must buy an approved substitute version of the same commodity. His voucher is no good for that purpose, but neither is he limited by his ration. His parent may purchase for him as much education, beyond the minimum requirement, as he chooses.

In recent years support has been growing for what I shall call an extended voucher system, under which the education voucher is usable in any approved school of the parent's choice, not just in public schools. I note in passing that the advocates of the extended voucher system find it possible to reconcile some paternalism with their libertarian principles. They do not propose to abandon compulsory education and to compensate non-consumers of public education in money.

One of the effects of the present arrangement is to require high income parents who wish their children to have more or better education than the public schools provide to pay not only the extra costs but also part of the expenses of educating the children of the less affluent. In this respect the present system is a measure of specific egalitarianism. The proposed reform would shift the burden now borne by those who opt out of the public system to the society at large in higher taxes, or to the lower-income consumers of public education in lower quality.

Reducing the cost of luxury education would no doubt increase the demand for it, and draw teachers and others resources into it, partly from the public schools, partly but more slowly from the rest of the economy. Whatever its other merits, principally in encouraging greater competition and innovation in the supply of education, the extended voucher proposal would increase the inequality of education. This effect could be largely avoided by restricting the use of the vouchers to those private schools that hold other charges on the parents to zero or within prescribed limits.

Another difficulty with the extended voucher proposal arises from the externalities of the education process – that is, the contributions to the education of students made by other students. The relationships here are complex and uncertain, and excessive heterogeneity in schools and classrooms may be as unproductive as excessive homogeneity. But the evidence seems to be that some racial, social, and intellectual heterogeneity is productive. A major problem of American education today is that public schools, reflecting and in turn influencing residential patterns, are becoming increasingly homogenous. The proposed extension of the voucher system might well accentuate this trend, by making it cheaper for parents to group their children homogeneously in private schools.

This possibility raises the question of how much selectivity in admission and retention private schools eligible for parentally disposed funds would be allowed to practice. So long as schooling is compulsory, there must be some schools that cannot be selective. Are public schools to become the residual depository for all students that publicly financed private schools cannot or will not cope with? To some degree, this is already true, and private and parochial schools gain reputations for intellectual achievement, discipline, and good behaviour, simply by pushing difficult and risky cases back to the public schools. Perhaps beneficiary schools should be required to admit all applicants – or in case of oversubscription to select among them in an unbiased way – and to dismiss or suspend students only by the same rules as apply to the public schools.

Medical care

There are not many commodities in prosperous peacetime America that are scarce in the sense in which some necessities of life were scarce in wartime, but this could be said of medical care. The available supplies of physicians, hospitals, and other personnel and facilities are still low relative to the needs of the population. Even if the supplies were equally distributed, the medical needs unmet at the margin would evidently be far from trivial. This fact is, of course, the basic reason for social concern about the inequality of access to medical care. If people differed only in the attention they received with respect to cosmetic or orthodontic problems, or the number of psychoanalyses they enjoyed, or the hotel-like amenities provided to new mothers, inequality of medical care would not be a big issue. What is disturbing to many observers is the suspicion that chances of death and disability are unequally distributed, that some people consume for trivial purposes resources that could be crucial to the health of others.

In the case of medical care, equality would mean that the treatment of an individual depends only on his medical condition and symptoms, not on his ability or willingness to pay. Everyone would be compelled to have the same medical insurance policy, and no one could obtain medical care except on the terms prescribed in the common policy. This would be, in principle, a non-transferable ration-voucher system, as defined above in other illustrations. But ration-vouchers for medical care would be complicated contingent claims, and stating their value in services so as to balance demand and supply would be extremely difficult.

If medical care were delivered through a ration-voucher system, the government would in effect be purchasing *all* the services of physicians, hospitals, and other suppliers. The prices paid would have to be set so as to draw new resources into the medical industry. Past experience suggests, however, that the mechanism of supply response to price is slow and imperfect, and there may well be more effective ways to get new doctors, medical schools, hospitals, and clinics than simply to add to the rents of the present practitioners.

The system just sketched is compatible with a great deal of decentralization and free choice, but there is no getting around the fact that it is socialized medicine. It is hard to see how there can be equality of medical care otherwise. Although this prospect may shock many people today, including many at the University of Chicago, it would not have shocked Henry Simons. In 1934 he wrote, in connection with his proposal for a rigorously thorough and progressive income-tax, as follows: 'On the expenditure side, we may look forward confidently to continued augmenting of the 'free income' of the masses, in the form of commodities and services made available by government, either without charge or with considerable modification of prevailing price controls. There are remarkable opportunities for extending the range of socialized consumption (medical services, recreation, education, music, drama, etc.). . .(1948, p. 68).

The system toward which the country is moving is quite different. More and more medical vouchers are being provided, through Medicare, Medicaid, and perhaps in the not too distant future, universal health insurance. But no formal rationing is being imposed. Inequality is reduced as the medical care of the poor is brought up to a minimum standard, but the rich can buy medical care in higher quantity and quality. The addition of voucher demands to the unrestricted private market drives prices up. If the government fixes the money value of its vouchers too low, doctors shift their attention to other patients. If the government tries to regulate all fees, not just those charged voucher patients, the result is informal rationing and queueing, with considerable inefficiency, inequity, and annoyance. There will be no good solution short of the day when resources for medical care are so abundant that a hypochrondiac can consume them for low priority purposes, if that way of spending money suits his taste, without depriving someone else of vital care.

Food stamps

The society's propensity to give assistance to the poor in kind rather than in cash is most clearly evidenced by the political popularity of food stamps and housing subsidies. These are what I earlier called one-sided egalitarian measures. The intent is to increase the consumption of these necessities of life by the poorly nourished and poorly housed, not to reduce the luxury amounts going to heavy consumers. Indeed these commodities are not, in aggregate, scarce in the sense that medical care is in short supply. Food supplies can easily and quickly be expanded in response to new demand, and present supplies are ample, if equally distributed, for meeting socially accepted standards of nutrition. There is no reason that gourmets and gourmands in particular, rather than high-income people in general, should pay for raising the food consumption of the poor.

Paternalism is presumably the motive for assisting poor people with food vouchers rather than generalized purchasing power. But the actual and proposed systems do not live up to the rationale, which would imply compulsory nutrition in the manner of compulsory education. Given the fungibility of stamps and foods, the plans do not even insure adequate diets for their beneficiaries. And, although based on the premise that adequate income is no guarantee of adequate nutrition, income-conditioned food vouchers do nothing to insure adequate nutrition for those whose incomes make them ineligible. In short, food vouchers are just an inferior currency, and taxpayers' funds would be better spent in general income assistance. It is quite true that society has an obligation to protect children whose parents cannot be trusted to nourish them. But this obligation is independent of the size and source of the parents' income.

Subsidized housing

Paternalism once again is a major reason for society's willingness to subsidize the housing rather than the incomes of the poor. No doubt the neighbourhood effects of poor housing, help to explain the appeal of subsidized housing. A paternalistic policy of housing vouchers is far more likely to be successful than food vouchers, because housing services are much less transferable and fungible.

Engineering a less unequal distribution of housing services is, however, particularly difficult because the services are generated by a specific housing stock inherited from the past. No doubt the resources invested in the current stock are more than enough to meet minimal standards for the whole population. But the high degree of inequality of density and quality built into the present stock limits the possibilities of equalizing its use in the short run. Likewise, expansion of the supply of housing services can occur only as fast as the stock can be augmented. It would take a long time for the market by itself to adapt the supply of housing to a significantly less unequal distribution of general income and wealth.

Present policies are neither fair nor effective. The income tests for housing subsidies are not very severe compared to the tests imposed for current and proposed cash assistance programmes. Housing subsidies would be very expensive if everyone who could meet the income tests actually received them. But the subsidies are available only for an accidentally or arbitrarily selected few. The result is that some low income taxpapers are subsidizing the rents of families with equal or higher incomes. One reason that the spread of subsidized low-rent housing is slow is that, with minor exceptions, subsidies are connected only with designated new construction. Perhaps the concentration on new construction reflects the ambivalence of motivation for the programmes, which are designed to make cities look better as well as to help low-income families. If the latter purpose is to be sought with housing vouchers, it would make sense to use them to improve the allocation of existing as well as new structures. A disadvantage of the present approach is that it publicly tags the residents of subsidized projects as recipients of public assistance.

I personally see little convincing justification in the long run for specific egalitarianism in housing. There are numerous reasons for preferring a system in which everyone can and does buy decent housing to his taste in the same market. But it does not follow that the supply of housing can be left to the market as now organized and regulated. There are too many cases of racial discrimination, too many ways in which zoning ordinances, building codes, and land taxes favour low-density housing, too many restrictive practices in the home-building industry, too many government subsidies to affluent home-owners, etc. Poor people ought to be given dollars – or housing vouchers if that is preferred – that they can spend for housing anywhere. But at the same time governments do have an obligation to see that these dollars and vouchers have some value.

In conclusion, I believe that Simons and the mainstream of the economics tradition have been right to insist that general taxation, positive and negative, is the best way to moderate the inequalities of income and wealth generated by a competitive market economy. I have no doubt that a cash negative income tax would be, dollar for dollar, the most effective anti-poverty and pro-equality programme that could be adopted at this time. At the other end of the economic spectrum, the urgency of reform of income and estate taxation was scarcely diminished by the tax legislation of 1969. The interests opposed to egalitarian reform of the tax-and-transfer system are formidable. The cause could use some enthusiastic and intelligent support, and it deserves more energy and attention than most youthful egalitarians in our midst have been giving it. Still more fundamental, and certainly more difficult, are policies to diminish the distribution of income before taxes and transfers. These include removal of those barriers to competition, whether private or governmental in origin, which protect some positions of high wealth and income. They include efforts to diminish inequalities of endowment of human capital and of opportunity to accumulate it.

These approaches to the problem of economic inequality deserve priority, but they do not entitle us to dismiss out of hand every proposal for specific egalitarianism or to acquiesce in a market distribution of every scarce commodity. It does make sense in some cases to adopt non-market egalitarian distributions of commodities essential to life and citizenship. It makes sense when the scarcity of the commodity cannot be overcome by drawing resources from the general economy. Difficult practical cases arise when, as in the case of medical care and housing, supply is inelastic in the short run but responsive to increased demand in the long run. In some instances, notably education and medical care, a specific egalitarian distribution today may be essential for improving the distribution of human capital and earning capacity tomorrow.

Reference

SIMONS, H. (1948), *Economic Policy for a Free Society*, University of Chicago Press.

Further Reading

The bibliography below is classified according to the topics
in the five sections in this volume, though in many cases these allocations
are somewhat arbitrary.[1] To students using this volume I would
recommend that it be read alongside Rawls, *A Theory of Justice* (1971)
and Sen, *Collective Choice and Social Welfare* (1970a).

General

K. J. Arrow, *Social Choice and Individual Values*, Wiley, 1963,
1st edn 1951.

A. B. Atkinson (ed.), *Inequality*, Penguin, 1973.

H. A. Bedau (ed.), *Justice and Equality*, Prentice-Hall, 1971.

E. C. Budd (ed.), *Inequality and Poverty*, Norton, 1969.

R. M. Hare, *The Language of Morals*, Oxford University Press,
1961, 1st edn 1953.

S. Hook (ed.), *Human Values and Economic Policy*, New York
University Press, 1967.

F. H. Knight, *The Ethics of Competition*, Augustus Kelley, 1935.

P. Laslett and W. G. Runciman (eds.), *Philosophy, Politics and
Society*, Blackwell, 1958, 1962, 1967.

J. Rawls, *A Theory of Justice*, Harvard, 1971.

L. Robbins, *An Essay on the Nature and Significance of Economic
Science*, Macmillan, 1935.

D. H. Robertson, *Utility and All That*, Macmillan (1952).

A. K. Sen, *Collective Choice and Social Welfare*, Holden-Day, 1970a.

W. S. Vickrey, 'Goals of economic life: an exchange of questions
between economics and philosophy', in A. D. Ward (ed.),

1. It should be noted that two additional topics, mathematical politics and
private voluntary redistributions (of unilateral or cooperative type), while ger-
mane to economic justice, had to be excluded from this volume for reasons of
space and energy.

Goals of Economic Life, Harper, 1953; reprinted in this volume, Reading 1.

A. D. Ward, (ed.), *Goals of Economic Life*, Harper, 1953.

Theoretical Pareto–Bergson Welfare Economics

K. J. Arrow and T. Scitovsky, (eds.), *Readings in Welfare Economics*, Richard D. Irwin, 1971.

R. F. Harrod, 'Another fundamental objection to laissez-faire', *Economic Journal*, March, 1936.

J. R. Hicks, 'The foundations of welfare economics', *Economic Journal*, December, 1939.

J. de V. Graff, *Theoretical Welfare Economics*, Cambridge University Press, 1957.

N. Kaldor, 'Welfare propositions and interpersonal comparisons of utility', *Economic Journal*, September, 1939.

O. Lange, 'Foundations of Welfare Economics', *Econometrica*, July–October, 1942.

I. M. D. Little, *A Critique of Welfare Economics*, Oxford University Press, 1950.

E. J. Mishan, 'A Survey of Welfare Economics, 1939–59', in *Surveys of Economic Theory*, Royal Economic Society, Macmillan, 1965.

A. C. Pigou, *The Economics of Welfare*, Macmillan, 1932.

P. A. Samuelson, *Foundations of Welfare Economics*, Harvard University Press, 1948.

P. A. Samuelson, 'Evaluation of real national income', *Oxford Economic Papers*, January, 1950; reprinted in this volume, Reading 2.

T. Scitovsky, 'A note on welfare propositions in economics', *Review of Economic Studies*, November, 1941.

A. K. Sen, 'The impossible Paretian liberal', *Journal of Political Economy*, June, 1970b.

V. J. Tarascio, 'Paretian welfare theory: some neglected aspects', *Journal of Political Economy*, February, 1969.

D. M. Winch, *Analytical Welfare Economics*, Penguin, 1972.

Social Welfare Functions and Arrow's Theorem

K. J. Arrow, 'Values and collective decision-making, in
P. Laslett and W. G. Runciman (eds.), *Philosophy, Politics and
Society*, Blackwell, 1967; reprinted in this volume, Reading 4.

K. J. Arrow, 'A difficulty in the concept of social welfare',
Journal of Political Economy, 1950.

A. Bergson, 'A reformulation of certain aspects of welfare
Economics', *Quarterly Journal of Economics*, vol. 52, 1938,
pp. 310–34, reprinted in A. Bergson, *Essays in Normative Economics*,
Harvard University Press, 1966.

A. Bergson, 'On the concept of social welfare', *Quarterly Journal of
Economics*, May, 1954.

J. H. Blau, 'A direct proof of arrow's theorem', *Econometrica*,
January, 1972.

J. de V. Graaff, *Theoretical Welfare Economics*, Cambridge
University Press, 1957.

I. M. D. Little, 'Social choice and individual values', *Journal of
Political Economy*, October 1952; reprinted in this volume,
Reading 5.

P. K. Pattanaik, *Voting and Collective Choice*, Cambridge
University Press, 1971.

P. A. Samuelson, 'Arrow's Mathematical Politics', in S. Hook (ed.),
Human Values and Economic Policy, New York University Press.

Ethical Conceptions of Social Welfare

T. K. Abbot, *Fundamental Principles of the Metaphysics of Ethics*,
1795, Longmans, 3rd edn., 1907.

J. Bentham, *Principles of Morals and Legislation:*, 1789,
Doubleday, 1961.

P. A. Diamond, 'Cardinal welfare, individualistic ethics, and
interpersonal comparisons of utility: a comment', *Journal of
Political Economy*, October 1967.

M. Fleming, 'A cardinal concept of welfare', *Quarterly Journal of Economics*, vol. 66, 1952; reprinted in this volume, Reading 9.

W. K. Guthrie, *History of Greek Philosophy*, Cambridge University Press, 1970.

J. C. Harsanyi, 'Cardinal welfare, individualistic ethics and interpersonal comparisons of utility', *Journal of Political Economy*, 1955; reprinted in this volume, Reading 10.

I. Kant (1795), *Grundlegung zur Metaphysik der Sitten*, trans. T. K. Abbott, *Fundamental Principles of the Metaphysics of Ethics*, Longman, 1907.

I. Kant, H. Reiss (ed.), *Kant's Political Writings*, Cambridge University Press, 1970; reprinted in this volume, Reading 6.

K. Marx, *Critique of the Gotha Program*, in R. C. Tucker (ed.), *The Marx–Engels Reader*, W. W. Norton, 1972.

P. K. Pattanaik, 'Risk, impersonality, and the social welfare function', *Journal of Political Economy*, December 1968; reprinted in this volume; Reading 12.

A. Rand, 'Government financing in a free society', in A. Rand, *The Virtue of Selfishness*, New American Library, 1964; reprinted in this volume, Reading 14.

J. Rawls, 'Distributive justice'; reprinted in P. Laslett and W. G. Runciman (eds.), *Philosophy*, *Politics and Society*, Blackwell; 1967, reprinted in this volume, Reading 13.

J. J. Rousseau, *The Social Contract*, 1763, trans., M. Cranston, Penguin, 1968.

W. G. Runciman, *Relative Deprivation and Social Justice*, Routledge & Kegan Paul, 1966.

A. K. Sen, 'Interpersonal aggregation and partial comparability', *Econometrica*, 1970b.

H. Sidgwick, *The Method of Ethics*, Macmillan 1893, New York, 1966; reprinted in this volume, Reading 8.

P. Suppes, 'Some formal models of grading principles', *Synthese*; reprinted in P. Suppes, *Studies in the Methodology and Foundations of Science*, D. Reidel, 1966.

W. S. Vickrey, 'Utility, strategy and social decision rules', *Quarterly Journal of Economics*, November, 1960.

W. S. Vickrey, 'Risk, utility, and social policy', *Social Research*, Summer, 1961; reprinted in this volume, Reading 11.

J. Viner, 'Bentham and J. S. Mill', *American Economic Review*, March, 1949; reprinted in this volume, Reading 1.

A. W. Wood, 'The Marxian critique of justice', *Philosophy and Public Affairs*, Spring, 1972.

Ethics, Economics and Government Policy

K. J. Arrow, 'The utilitarian approach to equality in public expenditure', *Quarterly Journal of Economics*, August, 1971; reprinted in this volume, Reading 19.

A. B. Atkinson, 'How Progressive Should Income Tax Be?' in J. M. Parkin (ed.), *Essays in Modern Economics*, Longman, 1973; 1972; reprinted in this volume, Reading 16.

P. A. Diamond and J. A. Mirrlees, 'Optimal taxation and public production', *American Economic Review*, March–June, 1971.

L. E. Dubins and E. H. Spanier, 'How to cut a cake fairly,' *American Mathematical Monthly*, January, 1961; reprinted in P. Newman (ed.), *Readings in Mathematical Economics*, vol. 1, John Hopkins Press, 1968.

F. Y. Edgeworth, 'The pure theory of taxation', *Economic Journal*, December, 1897; reprinted in F. Y. Edgeworth, *Papers Relating to Political Economy*, vol. 2, Macmillan, 1925; reprinted in this volume, Reading 15.

R. C. Fair, 'The optimal distribution of income', *Quarterly Journal of Economics*, November, 1971.

M. S. Feldstein, 'Equity and efficiency in public pricing', *Quarterly Journal of Economics*, May, 1972.

J. Green and E. Sheshinski forthcoming, 'On the progressivity of optimal capital expenditure', *Quarterly Journal of Economics*.

R. W. Houghton (ed.), *Public Finance*, Penguin, 1970.

A. P. Lerner, *The Economics of Control*, Macmillan, 1944.

J. A. Mirrlees, 'An exploration in the theory of optimal income taxation', *Review of Economic Studies*, April, 1971.

R. A. Musgrave and C. S. Shoup (eds.), *Readings in the Economics of Taxation*, Richard D. Irwin, 1959.

E. S. Phelps, 'Taxation of wage income for economic justice', *Quarterly Journal of Economics*, 1973; reprinted in this volume, Reading 18.

A. C. Pigou, *A Study in Public Finance*, Macmillan, 1928, 1947, 3rd edn.

E. Sheshinski, 'The optimal linear income tax', *Review of Economic Studies*, October, 1972; reprinted in this volume, Reading 17.

H. Steinhaus, 'Sur la division pragmatique', *Econometrica*, October, 1949.

J. Tobin, 'On limiting the domain of inequality', *Journal of Law and Economics*, October, 1970; reprinted in this volume, Reading 20.

Acknowledgements

For permission to reproduce the Readings in this volume,
acknowledgement is made to the following:

1 Harper & Row Inc.
2 The Clarendon Press
3 Cambridge University Press
4 Basil Blackwell Publishers
5 University of Chicago Press
6a Cambridge University Press
6b Bobbs-Merrill Co. Inc.
7 American Economic Association
9 *Quarterly Journal of Economics*
10 University of Chicago Press
11 *Social Research*
12 University of Chicago Press
13 Basil Blackwell Publishers
14 New American Library Inc.
15 Royal Economic Society
16 Longman Group Ltd
17 *Review of Economic Studies*
18 *Quarterly Journal of Economics*
19 *Quarterly Journal of Economics*
20 *Journal of Law and Economics*

Author Index

Subject Index

Value order
distinguished from decision order, 150
Voluntary government financing
methods, 363–5
premises, 365
subsidization of low income levels, 366
Von Neumann–Morgenstern index, 23, 260, 287

limitations, 312–16
Voting, 454

Welfare frontier, 13
properties, 93–5
relationship with efficiency locus, 99–100
shifts, 96–8
twists, 97
see also Utility-possibility function

Some other books published by Penguin
are described on the following pages.

Economic Systems and Society

George Dalton

The aim in this survey of nineteenth- and twentieth-century capitalism, communism, socialism, and Third World development is to introduce the reader to the salient features of today's economic systems, to the meanings of mercantilism and the Industrial Revolution, and to the ideas of David Ricardo, Karl Marx, and John Maynard Keynes. Reviewing his subject in historical sequence, George Dalton considers how nineteenth-century capitalism was transformed into the twentieth-century welfare state, how and why the Soviet economy of the Stalinist period is being reformed, and how the ideas of utopian, Marxian, and democratic socialism have influenced economic policy. Throughout, the social consequences of modern economic systems are stressed. George Dalton holds a joint appointment as Professor in the Departments of Economics and Anthropology at Northwestern University.

A Critique of Economic Theory

Edited by E. K. Hunt and Jesse G. Schwartz

This trenchant set of articles brings radical criticism of mainstream economics into coherent form. It stringently attacks the underlying assumptions of academic economists — the ideas of constraints, the premise of social harmony, consumer sovereignty, the state as an impartial arbitrator, and the superiority of capitalism over other systems. The twenty individual essays include Ronald Meek's "The Marginal Revolution and Its Aftermath," Karl Marx's "Estranged Labor and Capital," Howard J. Sherman's "Value and Market Allocation," and Bob Fitch's "A Galbraith Reappraisal: The Ideologue as Gadfly." E. K. Hunt is Professor of Economics at the University of California at Riverside. Jesse G. Schwartz is Professor of Economics and Politics at Cambridge University.

Job Power:
Blue and White Collar Democracy
David Jenkins

Here is a look at industrial democracy, or the abolition of
autocratic management in favor of decision-making power for
employees. David Jenkins has examined such innovations in
Israel, Sweden, Norway, Germany, and Yugoslavia, as well as in
U.S. corporations like General Foods and Procter & Gamble.
Concluding that industrial democracy is "a revolution that works,"
he calls on industrialists to give workers power and involvement
through job rotations, work teams, "job enrichment," and "total
awareness" of the factory. Indeed, *Job Power* shows that industrial
democracy may be the answer to the most stressing problems now
faced by industrial capitalism.

Chile's Road to Socialism

Salvador Allende
Edited by Joan E. Garces

This is a selection from the late Salvador Allende's speeches and statements during the first six months of his presidency. Included are his inaugural address and his first annual message to Congress. When Allende was in power, his election was called "the most positive event in the continent since the victory of the Cuban guerrillas a decade earlier." Allende himself wrote: "I have always said that I am not a caudillo or a man sent by providence. I am a militant socialist who realized that only in unity lay a hope of victory for the people." *Chile's Road to Socialism* joins other volumes in the Pelican Latin American Library — a series that attacks the current ignorance of an area where hundreds thrive and thousands starve.